"King of Critics"

"King of Critics"

George Saintsbury, 1845–1933,
Critic, Journalist, Historian, Professor

Dorothy Richardson Jones

Ann Arbor
THE UNIVERSITY OF MICHIGAN PRESS

Library of Congress Cataloging-in-Publication Data

Jones, Dorothy Richardson, 1932–
    "King of critics" : George Saintsbury, 1845–1933, critic,
journalist, historian, professor / Dorothy Richardson Jones.
       p.   cm.
    Includes bibliographical references and index.
    ISBN 0-472-10316-4 (alk. paper)
    1. Saintsbury, George, 1845–1933. 2. English literature—History
and criticism—Theory, etc. 3. French literature—History and
criticism—Theory, etc. 4. Literary historians—Great Britain—
Biography. 5. English teachers—Great Britain—Biography.
6. Journalists—Great Britain—Biography. 7. Critics—Great
Britain—Biography. 8. Criticism—Great Britain—History.
I. Title.
PR5295.J6   1992
809—dc20   91-45198
[B]   CIP

King of Critics in our time . . . the
Magnificent Saintsbury.
        —*Christopher Morley*

Preface

"King of Critics in our time...the magnificent Saintsbury." Thus Christopher Morley hailed George Saintsbury in an introduction to *Bartlett's Quotations* in 1937. Critics of 1895 would have agreed, but not many would have done so in Morley's time, the era of the New Criticism, because close reading of the text rather than literary appreciation and historical placing had become the chief method of criticism and teaching. But what do we know of George Saintsbury half a century later?

Biography, a major form of literary art in our century, encompasses a wide variety of fine "lives" and it is widely read. George Saintsbury, the biographer of four men, did not wish to be the subject of a biography. Matthew Arnold, one of those four men, shared his feeling. Their reasons were a mixture of modesty and personal reticence in otherwise proud men, a reaction against the huge tomes of Victorian hagiography that embalmed their major contemporaries and, in Saintsbury, a feeling that the position of literary critic and historian as a service role does not justify such attention. From an early age he was convinced that he was born not to create but to interpret literature. He said that his life had in it no great event and described his three small *Scrap Books* (1923–25) as all the autobiography he wished to leave. As for any other reasons for his attitude, one can only speculate.

But Saintsbury's performance for over a half-century as literary critic, journalist, editor, literary historian, and professor warrants a full study of his extensive and varied writings and the life of which they are the main substance. No one has attempted the task heretofore. After the brief memoirs done by Oliver Elton for the British Academy and by Adam Blyth Webster for the University of Edinburgh, there was nothing until the slight volume, *George Saintsbury*, by Walter Leuba (1967). It is hardly a biography or even an adequate critical study. The present volume attempts both of these goals, with the main focus on Saintsbury's published writings.

I grew up in the late 1920s when emphasis was placed on students' knowing all the facts of English literary history. Subjected to *Twelve Centuries of English Literature* as a senior in high school, I again met it as a college student in *Beowulf to Hardy,* the text of the survey required of all students. As an English major for the B.A. I was again examined on all the names, dates, titles, schools, forms, and genres. How we struggled after reading only two or three lyrics of each to remember who was a Metaphysical and who was a Cavalier poet! All this in the years just after I. A. Richards, in *Practical Criticism,* had raised the question of whether Oxford students knew how to read poetry and answered with damning negative evidence. We began to suspect Richards's conclusions might apply to us. Meanwhile, in a small college library, I was always being sent to Saintsbury for period history, prosody, the history of criticism, and so forth, or met him often in the pages of that old standby, the *Cambridge History of English Literature.* Little did I realize how he would have approved the "mindmap" I struggled to make and master.

Moving to Columbia University and then to the University of Michigan, I still had to qualify on the details of the whole scope of English and American literature, first in seven hours for the M.A., then in eighteen hours of written preliminary examinations for the Ph.D. Saintsbury was still a familiar source, though now he was but one in a host of more modern, specialized sources one had to know. And the New Critics were challenging us to question all past methods and all attitudes toward literature. With my memory of how large a part Saintsbury had played in my earlier education, I asked myself just what was his status in the history of criticism? How influential had he been? What was his reputation today? And what would a final evaluation be? A 1938 Ph.D. dissertation was the result, an effort too close to his career to yield adequate answers.

More recently I have thought more about the man behind the books and have tried to answer questions about his personality and his personal life that have been so overshadowed by the bulk and range of his written works. In 1947, Edmund Wilson, in one of his typical flashes of insight, faced the question: Why did Saintsbury not want his biography written? He guessed at the significance of that wish. Seeing a parallel to Thackeray, he suggested that some domestic tragedy had "shadowed Saintsbury's life" and led to "the voracity with which he fed himself on books . . . as both a gourmet and something of a glutton, transferring to literature his whole emotional and moral life."

This guess of Wilson's about the reasons for Saintsbury's "bookishness" was never followed up by Wilson or anyone else. Yet, like a stone dropped into calm but opaque waters, it creates widening circles of speculation if considered with a knowledge of the intimate details of Saintsbury's life, domestic and professional, that were not available to Wilson.

Over a number of years, I have gradually pieced together many of these details, though the full picture will probably never emerge. These include the story of Saintsbury's epistolary love affair with Helen Waddell, two versions of which have recently become public in the slim, not wholly reliable memoir by Mona Blackett, *The Mark of the Maker: A Portrait of Helen Waddell* (1973), and the excellent biography, *Helen Waddell* (1986), by Dame Felicitas Corrigan. I have consulted both authors and had their gracious cooperation and have myself examined the correspondence between George Saintsbury and Helen Waddell. In the light of this and other biographical details, I have looked at his writing as a reflection of personal character.

When Saintsbury and Helen met in 1914 she was twenty-five and forty-four years his junior. He called her "My Lady of Dreams" and "La Princesse Lointaine." And he wrote her, "dreams are the best thing in the world." This tale, significant as it may be, is but one clue to a pervasive element in Saintsbury's complex personality: his life-long habit of evasion and escape from reality into literary fantasy and dreams, where the real and the imagined shift and exchange places and at times merge, giving him the greatest happiness of his life—in books and in bookish fantasy.

Over the many decades of his literary life, an occasional critic saw Saintsbury as living in a "booklined universe" or as substituting literature for life, but no one except Edmund Wilson seriously asked why. They have cast him as a Victorian romantic without exploring the role that escapism played in both his personal life and his literary work. *A Last Vintage* (1950) contained essays by Helen Waddell and Dorothy Margaret Stuart, each telling just so much as she wanted to tell of their friendships with Saintsbury in his last years. Their stories have their place here: Miss Stuart's belongs to the last chapter since they first met only in 1926. Miss Waddell has a larger part in the last quarter of Saintsbury's life. Her side of the story is well told by Dame Felicitas Corrigan, whose sharing with me of her materials, her knowledge, and her time were most generous. I am much in her debt as I recount Saintsbury's part in the relationship of eighteen years. During these years he wrote her at least 322 letters that are now filed in the Library of Queen's University, Belfast. He received many in reply. These too survive since, contrary to their agreement, Miss Waddell preserved all of them.

But this evasive pattern extends into many aspects of Saintsbury's life—his virtual denial of affectionate family relationships; his Toryism and devout High Church faith and practice; his devotion to wine and the virtues of alcohol, celebrated in *Notes on a Cellar Book* (1920); his enjoying "time-deodorized" Rabelais while damning Zola for grime and nastiness, a kind of alienation from all the realistic and psychologically revealing literature of his adult years; and his primary attention to form rather than matter, and to the auditory more than to the visual in poetry. Why all this evasion is the question to which I have sought some answers.

When, within ten days in January, 1933, death claimed John Galsworthy, George Moore, and Saintsbury, Helen Waddell commented, "What a reaping!" To Enid Starkie she wrote, "There'll never be another Saintsbury." T.S. Eliot paid him respectful tribute in *Homage to John Dryden* (1924) and elsewhere. In 1912, Irving Babbitt had lamented that he was "almost the official English critic." Saintsbury, more realistic himself, in 1899 spoke of criticism as the most precarious of literary forms, the most likely to date, and more facetiously suggested that old critics are "to all but experts (and apparently to some of them) as useless as old moons" (*Matthew Arnold*, 225).

The belletrists of the later nineteenth century were treated rather derogatorily by John Gross in *The Rise and Fall of the English Man of Letters* (1969). Since the 1960s, most of them have been the subjects of modern biographies (e.g. John Addington Symonds, Arthur Symons, George Henry Lewes, Andrew Lang, Leslie Stephen, and, most recently, Edmund Gosse). In 1984, Walter Orel chose seven of them (Walter Bagehot, Richard Hutton, Lewes, Stephen, Lang, Saintsbury, and Gosse) as subjects of his brief but ambitious study, *Victorian Literary Critics*. Orel focused upon their criticism of their contemporaries and their value for the later twentieth-century reader. Rightly, he defined their audience as a literate and cultivated one whom they addressed with respect, and he discussed the many attitudes they shared. For men of such vast output as these the treatment is too slight and casual. For Saintsbury, the effect is that of once over lightly, and there are numerous errors of fact in the text. Yet Orel observes that scarcely an essay or chapter in all Saintsbury's tens of thousands of pages lacks a characteristic observation worth attending to. Gross also concluded that, unlike many of his contemporaries, Saintsbury was always worth returning to. In his *History of Modern Criticism* (vol. 4, 1965) René Wellek considered him worth a chapter.

These judgments suggest that a fresh examination and assessment of Saintsbury and his reputation may be due in the 1990s. Any such study must begin by acknowledging defects as well as virtues in the subject. He was unreliable on dates and cared little about such details, and he often made other errors, though he did not share Gosse's "genius for inaccuracy." He minimized the importance of ideas and social movements and neglected theory. His complex, often crabbed style packed with allusions may annoy. All of this has been frequently pointed out since the first surveys appeared. But the positive virtues prevail. Since my first experience with the *History of Nineteenth Century Literature* in the 1920s, I have always enjoyed reading him, as have countless others. He led me back to poetry, the novels, and the essays he treated and made me seek out the minor writers he never neglected. I have enjoyed the allusions I could recognize and have reveled in the eloquent passages of praise he lavished on the writers he valued most—Rabelais, Donne, Swift, Horace Walpole—and even on those he quarreled with, notably Arnold. And I have read all of the signed and a fair share of the unsigned work (by his own estimate more than a hundred volumes), something no one will do in the 1990s.

Criticism has suffered many sea changes since I first knew Saintsbury. In the era of structuralism, deconstruction, semiotics, feminist, ethnic, and political criticism I have asked myself what does Saintsbury, once almost the laureate of criticism, have to offer in leading us back to the pleasures of reading? Students no longer have to know all the historical facts or sample all of the writers at any level of their literary education. They have seen texts subjected to close reading and given linguistic and semiotic analysis, and they have seen them devalued as every kind of written text has been equated with the greatest by some postmodernists. They have heard the feminist, the ethnic, and the Marxist views and have been exposed to literature from the whole world. Saintsbury may not tell them how to read for all the values one might wish, but he may help them cultivate appreciation, develop an ear and a sensitivity to feeling and mood. He will give them access to and encourage them to sample the vast range of European literature and its pleasures, especially French.

In her biography of Gosse, Ann Thwaite (1984) did a thorough and soundly critical job of interpreting this Victorian whose top priorities were literary friendships and contact with the literary giants of his time. He was a man who kept a record of everything. His story differs from that of Saintsbury, tempting as parallels and contrasts may be, but Mrs. Thwaite puts in her debt anyone concerned with Gosse's friends and literary contemporaries. The focus of Saintsbury's public image is that of the literary historian and critic, the journalist and editor. But his personal life, which unlike Gosse he guarded as essentially private, must play a minor but important part in any account of the real man. The record is small and the very absence of information about his family life in his letters and autobiographical "scraps" has meaning in any effort to interpret his personality. Yet this man of wide knowledge and vast energies and enthusiasms speaks in every line of his writings. Some of his idiosyncrasies are easily portrayed, as witnessed in a BBC radio program of May 1, 1986, entitled "St. George and the Pussyfoots." Others require more analysis and informed speculation.

I have had the advantage of contact with some of those who saw Saintsbury plain: his grandson George and granddaughter Elizabeth; his niece Sylvia Austin; Oliver Elton in 1939; David Nichol Smith in 1961; Dr. George Kitchin, one of his two Edinburgh assistants; Miss Mary Thomas, a daughter of the family who were Saintsbury's landlords in Bath (1916–33); and Dorothy Margaret Stuart the year before her death in 1963. In addition, a sizable number of his University of Edinburgh Honors students kindly entertained me in their homes in 1962; others shared their memories in letters. I was also helped by Professor John Butt and the librarians of the University of Edinburgh during a month's stay in Edinburgh. To all of these people who helped bring the man alive for me, I am grateful.

I have had encouragement and help from many individuals.

Among them are friends and colleagues and others who shared their information about Saintsbury. To them I express my gratitude. They include: Oliver Elton, David Nichol Smith, George Kitchin, George Fraser, Arthur Humphreys, Roger Lancelyn Green, Mona Blackett, Lord Bridges, Brenda Green Insley, Harold Rubinstein, Janet Adam Smith, Geoffrey Tillotson, Alban Dobson, Monica Dickens, Beatrice White, Dr. Louis Rose, Clarence D. Thorpe, Charles Molesworth, Leslie Moore (curator of the Rosenbach Museum and Library), Geroge B. Parks, and my late husband, Ernest van B. Jones.

I also wish to thank Colin Day, director of the University of Michigan Press, Joyce Harrison, my editor, an anonymous reader, and Robert H. Super for their encouragement and welcome assistance.

For their friendly services as typists, I am indebted to Jeannette Fleisher, Alison Mabry, and Maryanne Muscato. For valuable help in checking the bibliography and notes, I wish to thank Eleanor Withington, a generous friend and Queens College colleague. For information provided, I wish to thank Macmillan and Company, the Clarendon Press, Oxford; the secretary of King's College School; the officers of Elizabeth College, Guernsey; and the Education Authority, Elgin, Scotland. I also thank the *New Statesman* and *Nation* for access to the signed files of the *Athenaeum*.

The London Library provided me with a pleasant year's membership; Blackwood and Sons permitted me to use the correspondence of Saintsbury with the firm. I thank them both.

For a 1962 grant for research in Edinburgh, I am grateful to the American Council of Learned Societies.

I acknowledge with appreciation the permission granted me for the use of Saintsbury correspondence and other materials by the following: the Right Reverend George L. Saintsbury, V.G.; the Warden and Fellows of Merton College, Oxford University (for the Saintsbury-Hunt correspondence); Dame Felicitas Corrigan, Miss Mary M. Martin, Stanbrook Abbey, and Queen's University Library of Belfast (for the Saintsbury-Waddell correspondence); the Brotherton Library, University of Leeds (for materials from the Gosse Collection); and the University of Edinburgh Library. I appreciate the kind help I received from the librarians of these institutions.

For photographs and prints I am indebted to George Kitchin, James Thin, Ltd. (Edinburgh booksellers), and Stanbrook Abbey.

Finally, my warmest gratitude to my friend, Wyatt Claiborne Jones, professor emeritus of Brandeis University, for his confidence in the book, his support and knowledge, and patient editing; all of these made completion of my work possible over the last several years.

Contents

CHAPTER 1

A Mid-Victorian Boy

A London schoolboy of the early 1860s leaves the King's College School in the Strand in late afternoon, lingering here and there over bookstalls, lighting at one of them upon the Creech edition of Lucretius, or—pulling from his bookpack—the school library's *Pendennis,* he plunges into its pages as he walks through Hyde Park and Kensington Gardens. Oblivious of the people he bumps and nudges or barely misses, his nearsighted eyes devour the pages as he makes his way slowly home to Notting Hill, reading, reading, reading, as he was to do for three-score years and ten to come. The omnilegent George Saintsbury is foreshadowed in this, his own description of the schoolboy he was.

So he appears again in a small scrap of blue paper that has survived from those days of adolescent literary enthusiasms. Headed "Things and Persons to be Adored," it reads:

Tennyson's Poems entire
La Morte d'Arthaure [sic]
Kingsley's Westward Ho and Yeast (whole)
Avillion by the Author of J[ohn] Halifax [Gentleman]
Guido's Beatrice Cenci
"The Land of the Leal"
King Charles the Martyr
Shelley (passages)
   Personages
Sir Launcelot
King Arthur
Sir Bors
Queen Guinevere
Guy Morville [the hero of Charlotte Yonge's *The Heir of Redcliffe*]
Argemone in "Yeast"

Ida in "The Princess"
Byron's "Parisina"

G. E. B. S.[1]

This list, compiled before Thackeray or his *Pendennis* had captured Saintsbury's permanent devotion, speaks for the lifelong lover of romance and the Middle Ages. It indicates an ear for verbal music that made the liquid rhythms of Tennyson and Shelley his favorites first and last. "King Charles the Martyr" suggests the High Church "Tory of Tories" he early became. The boy, always reading, even on foot in the park, is forerunner of the man who later confessed that, for him, reading was "mental breathing" and that books made better, safer friends than men.

His lifelong ties with Hyde Park and Kensington Gardens began even before his birth: the Saintsburys were living, in the 1830s and 1840s, in Kensington Square, where they later always had many friends. At least one of the two sisters, Elizabeth Sophia and Josephine, older than George by six and eight years, had been born there. So far as is known, they were a London family transplanted to Southhampton only just before the boy, George Edward Bateman, was born on October 23, 1845, at Lottery Hall, St. Mary's.[2]

Saintsbury says little of Southampton, but he does recall, "I was born in a port, and have as a small boy lunched under the star of cutlasses in the gunroom (or whatever it was) of the *Victory*."[3] He claimed he always loved the sea, though as an adult he seems not to have ventured upon it. He returned to Southampton to live briefly in 1916; he had married a Southampton girl and they are buried there. But it is Kensington he remembers most fondly: "that singular place which, like Oxford and the West Country, contrives somehow or other to make those who were once free of it its slaves in a manner forever."[4]

Of his mother, born Elizabeth Wright, he tells us almost nothing. She died in 1877 and we learn only that the sale of the London house then allowed him to pay off the last of his Oxford debts. Her grandchildren remembered nothing about her. There are references to London cousins in Brompton, to an aunt in Cannonbury, to his father's brother John,[5] but none at all to grandparents or to family origins. Surviving members of the family are equally ignorant about origins, though some of them cherish variants of a vague, legendary quarrel between two branches of the family during which, as the story goes, one branch having gone into trade, dropped the *t* from the name because of the disgust of the other branch. Geneological records indicate Sainsbury as the older and more common form of the name, and the legend has no foundation, but, as such legends do, it has had strong survival value, especially in academic circles. People have said that Professor Saintsbury himself snobbishly requested that the *t* be dropped from the grocers' name. It matched their image of him and amused them to repeat the myth as Sainsbury's has grown in size and become a household word. The archivist of the firm provides an amusing footnote.[6] The Sainsbury family, who had been in trade as picture framers and coal merchants, opened a dairy store in Drury Lane in 1869. This was the year after young George Saintsbury, fresh from Oxford, became a schoolmaster and long before he could have had any influence.

The Saintsburys had another cherished theory that traces their origins to the Gloucestershire village of Saintbury that, however, appears as "Swinesberie" in Domesday. It is odd that a man so conservative and traditional in religion and politics and so concerned with "the gentleman" as the Victorians conceived of him should have shown no interest in his own ancestry, but this may be of a piece with other forms of secrecy and silence, reticence or evasion that characterized Saintsbury's later life. It is of his father, whom he lost when he was fourteen, that he tells us most.

The elder George Saintsbury, a London businessman, served during the years in Southampton as secretary to the Southhampton Dock Company and, on his return to London in 1850, was, for a good part at least of the nine years before his death, secretary of the East India and China Association, with offices in Cornhill. Though the more famous son liked to boast that no one ever influenced his views, one could wish to know more about his father. The son recalls a letter received when he was six, instructing him "how not to fall off a pony"; he also remembered his father's giving him small guns on successive birthdays: "a tiny swivel gun on a telescope stand" with which he shot a grasshopper in a Notting Hill garden, "a miniature Pièce de Quatre brought from the Paris exhibition of 1856(?)" that was "too pretty to fire" and a "Holborn battery . . . that consumed plenty of powder" and later passed to his grandson.[7]

Saintsbury recalls visits to his father's office, luncheons and outings in and about the city, and trips to Blackwall and Greenwich—one of these made by "rowing in the good old style" to see the *Great Eastern* launched. In 1852, they saw the great Duke's funeral, "lying in state and procession both"—a sight that engraved itself on the memory of the seven-year-old boy who later could recall nothing of the Great Exhibition of the year before. He did recall, from 1862, his first ride on the new Underground and the night of illuminations celebrating the wedding of Prince Edward and Princess Alexandra, when he wandered alone for many hours in the huge, good-natured crowds— the length of Oxford Street to Holborn, then back Piccadilly, Pall Mall, and the Strand.

Saintsbury described a portrait of his father clad in a long cape of the sort worn by Spanish refugees in the 1830s. His father had heard Irving preach, he recalled, and he had many West Indian friends who brought them gifts of limes and papaws and served good Madeira wine with apologies. A Tory by conviction, the older Saintsbury never talked politics in his son's presence, but gave him "some knowledge of good wines and horror of bad" and he inspired some boyhood chemistry experiments. One of these produced brandy, the savor of which survives in the *Notes on a Cellar Book* (1920).

Though not a university man, the father had a decent library and seemed, to his son, in retrospect "strangely knowledgeable in persons and things...." He dedicated his *First Book of English Literature* (1914) to his father with the inscription *Ego a patri ita eram deductus.*[8] His father was a friend of French literary critic Philarète Chasles, when he was a refugee in England, a fact that suggests that he spoke French.[9] Saintsbury believed that he inherited a sturdy often-asserted independence and quick temper from his father. These qualities color his account of a clash while at Oxford with Mark Pattison by "George, the son of George" when "the blood of his father" bade him "stand no browbeating." Neither of them could keep his temper at chess, and the son confesses that his own temper was "none too steady in serious matters."

His father's death in 1859 left Saintsbury under the influence of his mother and his two older sisters, who seem to have shared and fostered his literary leanings. Good students of languages whatever their schooling, at their father's death the girls took on the responsibility of assuring the young brother a proper education. Going about London by omnibus in their stiff, unwieldy crinolines, they gave language lessons and served as governesses to supplement the family income. He suggests their interests and education in an aside in his *History of the French Novel:* "Every girl from Scott's heroines to my own sisters seem to have been taught Dante and Petrarch and Tasso and even Ariosto, as a matter of course."[10] Josephine translated some French sermons, and their interest in French may well have helped to develop his own: he recalls being amused by Eugene Foa's *Petit Robinson de Paris* (1848) when he was ten. His Oxford account book testifies to their generous sharing in the form of loans from Sophie, "Phrene," and Mama. Counterbalancing entries indicate gifts to one or another of the three: an umbrella, a pocketbook, "sweetmeats for Sophie," and "a chain and cross for Mama." They shard a strong religious concern and his observances at Oxford indicate habits formed in a devout family. Josephine always, in his words, "good and foolish," converted to Roman Catholicism after the death of Pusey (1882), whose personal influence had long "kept her straight." Saintsbury, who was temporarily angered and alienated by her break, himself never felt the lure of Rome.[11]

All Saintsbury's boyhood days were spent in Pembridge Villas, a new "patch of houses" midway between Notting Hill Gate and Westbourne Grove. Following the move from Southhampton to London when George was five (1850), the family spent a brief time in nearby Chepstow Place and in a house on the east side of Pembridge Villas. His father then purchased the newly built number 31 on the western or Notting Hill side, a good, detached three-story stucco house. The house still stands in a row of similar substantial dignified "villas" appropriate to the family of a prosperous City businessman of the 1850s—now crowded behind the bustling commercial center of Notting Hill. It remained the family home until his mother's death in 1877. The area was still somewhat rural; dismal fields extended from Portobello Lane to the Canal and the Great Western Railway, with "dust-heaps" at their end that he compared to those in *Our Mutual Friend*. On the south, the proximity to Kensington Gardens and Hyde Park was more pleasant. Westbourne Grove, like the High Street of Notting Hill, resembled the High Street of a small, lively country town. At its opposite ends were two preparatory schools Saintsbury was to attend. The first, a dame school in Norfolk Terrace, held a dozen small boys from eight to eleven and "one very small girl of the same age, the younger sister of the Dame who kept it." After two or three years here, young George moved to the far end of the Grove to one of the half-dozen "proprietary and preparatory schools of King's College, London," for another five years.

On the large playing field behind the old converted farmhouse buildings of this school, between the Grove and the Railway, George joined in "not very rigid Rugby football" although, with his near-sighted eyes and a malformed hand, he was "too blind and too clumsy" for cricket. His right hand, he told Helen Waddell, was weakened by an early bout of scarlet fever that left his thumb without feeling and accounted not only for his avoiding sports but for his infamously illegible handwriting and his left-handed typing.

More appealing than sports to one with Saintsbury's literary and imaginative tastes and more cherished in memory were the solitary charms of Kensington Gardens with the great Orangerie and its broad lawns and, behind them, a great, open gravel pit surrounded with "yew wood black as night." To the young Saintsbury it seemed a fit scene for Tennyson's "Oriana," while the tiny ranger's cottage near the Serpentine would serve "to hide a heroine or engineer a murder if necessary." In wilder parts of the park one could "lounge and dream and wander for hours," undisturbed by the park keepers or other people even if one indulged in "a mild picnic."[12] Here he first developed his taste for solitary walking and escaped into romantic fantasy.

This not untypical, middle-class, Victorian family was in comfortable prosperity at least until the father's death. They shared homely common tastes and interests, but he was rarely at home after 1868. One family "byword" preserved the standard reply of their charwoman to any advice or suggestion, "I was just a-going to say, Mum."[13] The boy was called "Ted" by his family though he never thought of himself that way. He says, "I believe in myself as George though never called it by the human voice."[14] Later friends called him "Saint." That he tells so little about homelife is significant.

Of his early reading Saintsbury had more to say. "I was brought up on Dickens," he records, " and was devoted to *Pickwick* at the age of ten or eleven." He was reading *Sartor Resartus* at an age when "a great part of it must have been abracadabra," and all of Carlyle was to follow. He grew fond of Macaulay's essays and verse, and he read *Jane Eyre* so early that he never seemed to have read it for the first time.[15]

Having known Poe and Longfellow in childhood, he was enthusiastically reading Blake's "Mad Song" at ten. Soon came his passionate reading of Tennyson, including the *Idylls* fresh from the press inspiring worship of Tennyson's heroes and heroines to which his list of "Things and Persons to be Adored" attests as it does to his love of Malory and Kingsley. In his father's library there was a small early edition of Shelley; no Keats or Browning, but he read and loved *Endymion* at fifteen. These and other English poets, as well as some bad Greek and Latin, he first met in "that godsend to youth of the late 'fifties' and early 'sixties', Dr. Holden's 'Foliorum Silvula' and his 'Foliorum Centuriae.'" Sunday reading, restricted as it was in many Victorian homes, focused upon a few books read and reread so as to become lifelong companions; among them, Bunyan, Scott's poems, *Lalla Rookh*, the *Essays of Elia,* and Southey's *The Doctor.* As Saintsbury saw it in 1923: "If a boy does not rejoice, however imperfectly, in *The Knights, The True History, The Canterbury Tales, Gargantua and Pantagruel, L'Avare, Gulliver* or *Pickwick* the first time he reads them in the original, there is no help or hope for him. The milk of fun should attract him: the meat of life—criticism, and the wine of art can wait."[16]

Given this record of early reading, one should look more closely at Saintsbury's list of "Things and Persons to be Adored." These are the choice of a highly romantic teenage boy. He loved the adventure of *Westward Ho* like any boy, but Arthur and Guinevere, Launcelot, Sir Bors, and *Le Morte d'Arthur* dominate the list. He knew them in Malory and Tennyson and relished the escape into medieval romance, as he continued to do all his life. In Shelley's Beatrice Cenci, he could find drama and passion; in Princess Ida and Argemone, in *Yeast,* and in the hero of the *Heir of Redcliffe* (by the strongly High Church Charlotte Yonge) he would have found a Victorian kind of moral idealism. In Byron's melodramatic *Parasina* he must have "adored" the lyrically passionate woodland tryst between the Prince's bastard son and his queen Parasina who then betrays their guilty secret by murmuring his name in her sleep. Did he thrill also to the scene of the son's death as he accuses his father of having stolen his "destined bride" and refuses to have his eyes bound before he is beheaded while Parasina, forced to watch the horror, swoons and goes mad? Later in life he valued Byron less than he did Tennyson and Shelley, whose lyric rhythms his ear was early attuned to. He had read Dickens, Scott, Keats, Browning, and *Jane Eyre* but they are not in his list of the most adored. This ranking Saintsbury would always maintain, though he valued them highly. This is a private list, made on spontaneous impulse and scarcely final or exhaustive, but it expressed strong feeling. Other Victorian boys were reading the *Idylls of the King* as they appeared but to few could they have continued to mean so much. Fifty years later Saintsbury, writing to Helen Waddell, often described their epistolary romance as a journey to Camelot, to Joyous Gard and Samarkand.

This early reading and his formal Westbourne Grove schooling stood Saintsbury in good stead when, at just under thirteen, he entered the Upper Fourth at King's College School in September, 1858. Among his fellow students were Charles J. Lyall, W. G. Duggan, Charles Taylor (later Master of St. John's, Cambridge), Ingram Bywater, Leopold de Rothschild, and William Thistleton Dyer (later Director of Kew). The last two remained his close friends through life. Bywater he joined at the University of Edinburgh in 1895. The headmaster, the Reverend John Richardson Major, M.A., had been a close friend of his father.[17]

No one has paid higher tribute to his school training than George Saintsbury: whatever he may have contributed to literary study, he tells us, is due to that training, which was thoroughly classical and mathematical though also thoroughly literary. Among the masters were Thomas Oswald Cockayne of the fourth, "ill-fated and ill-treated Anglo-Saxon Scholar but a person of exceptional brains" and "one of the least pedantic and most original schoolmasters that anyone ever had the luck to be taught by";[18] Dasent of the fifth, "a really elegant humanist," and Heywood of the lower sixth, "an all round man of culture with one of the sharpest tongues I've come across."

But it was the elderly, mild-mannered "Doctor" Major, the headmaster and a humanist of the old school, who, taking the upper sixth entirely himself, molded Saintsbury in significant ways for three of his five years at the school. Dr. Major taught Latin, Greek, even Hebrew thoroughly and well while soaking the students in the literary spirit. He gave no regular hours to English instruction but demanded "copious learning by heart of Greek and Latin poetry." Saintsbury recalls having learned in three or four years, "the first three books of the *Aeneid*, the Odes of Horace, some Homer, and most of the iambic part, with some of the choruses, of two or three Greek plays," gaining thus, as a permanent possession, "large patterns and examples of the most perfect literary form that the world has produced."[19] Dr. Major allowed the translating of classical verse into English verse on examination and gave weekly exercises in translating English passages into Latin and Greek, passages chosen by the head boys of the Form. Saintsbury learned to write better in Greek than in Latin, and he thought it all "diffused a sense of literature" among these boys. Discussions of the translations gave him his "earliest memories of practical literary criticism," while all the memorized verse shaped his sense of prosody as a foundation for his later works on prosody and prose rhythm.

A good sixth form library fed the boy's appetite for English poems and novels and belles lettres. Later he rejoiced that he had escaped formal discussion of modern literature. He reports that his masters oddly found him a "dab" at mathematics and urged him to go in for double honors, an ambition wisely discouraged by the Merton College mathematics tutor, Esson. At fifteen, Saintsbury was reading much and rummaging the bookshops, buying from Hotten not only Lucretius but "a Catullus with the usual adjuncts of Tibullus and Propertius," and a six-volume Homer. At seventeen, in his last year at school, he began a subscription to Rolandi's Foreign Circulating Library. His range and a typical discursive tendency show up in one of the few diary entries he preserved: "Read four hours—Heine, *Les Trois Mousquetaires,* Hebrew and Thucydides."

Housed in basement rooms and devoid of such amenities as playing fields, King's College School offered its boys a thorough grounding in the classics, "plenty of history, geography, etc., as well as French and German." Saintsbury stood well in competition: in January, 1862, he was fourth in competition for the First Class Scholarship; in February, 1863, he shared the First with one Clinton; in 1862, he won the English verse prize with his poem "Sicilia" and, in 1863, he was awarded the English Essay prize. On April 20, 1863, he got his Postmastership at Merton—a triumph tempered by an accidental upset in a canvas boat on the Thames while he waited for the results of the examination. He later comments (with Horatian echoes), "Fors Fortuna doubtless laughed and said: 'I have given you this day two commodities—a scholarship and a spill: learn as much as thou wilt and profit as much as thou canst from *both.*'"[20]

Competition for Oxford scholarships was becoming keener once the university reforms of 1854 had abolished tests of orthodoxy for non-conformists and tightened standards for entrance. Prior to his success at Merton, Saintsbury, in the spring of 1862, had sat unsuccessfully for a Christ Church scholarship. Being told that his failure was due to some "weakness...of technical 'scholarship,'" he settled to some strenuous weeks' work with a Jelf-Kuhner Greek lexicon, an experience he recalled as more powerfully "whetting" his mind than almost any other—however little it may have done for his scholarship.

The prize poem "Sicilia" runs true to form for such contests with their set subjects. It ticks off the stages of Sicilian history in seventy-five conventional eighteenth-century couplets, but it gave the author occasion to voice his amused judgment upon it in his old age.

Gladstone, who presented the prizes, praised the poem's form "with the usual amiable excess." This was the only meeting ever of these two. But to this young Tory who, twenty years later, in the *Saturday Review,* played anonymous gadfly on the subject of his Home Rule battles, the Liberal statesman intimated "with a mixture of kindness and indignation—handclasp and eyeflash"—that he "couldn't at all agree with the sentiments."[21]

From its opening Tennysonian flourish

> As gleams the pavement of a Gothic hall
> When through the tracery-lights the splendours fall

("not inferior to Mr. Pendennis's own," the author later termed them), it moves through Sicily's fate as the "strayest spoiler's prey, prize of the field in many a bloody day," touching upon Persephone, the Athenian expedition, the struggles of Rome and Carthage, Byzantine and Turk, till "came the Norman lance and drove away / The swart invaders from their hard-earned prey." Of line thirty, "Till the cross sank before the Crescent's sweep," the author says, in retrospect, "I think I must have stolen [it] I don't know from whom." A description of the countryside "and a lot of flowers," and praise of Theocritus are followed by a passage expressing antiteetotaling sentiments that anticipate those of the wine connoisseur of *Notes on a Cellar Book* (1920) mixed with echoes of Horace and Pope:

> And last but not least the vine, the Bacchic vine
> Yields to the grateful swain its fruit divine.

What wonder Paracelsus vainly thought
To have found in wine the elixir which he sought?
O dulcet juice, Magician that thou art,
Gladdening and mellowing man's unwearied heart.
And though like all God's gifts thou are abused
No reason that, why thou shouldst be refused.
In thee the tired wretch forgets his cares
With thee the sick man his lost strength repairs
Through and beyond all time thou still shalt stream
The oppressed's succour and the poet's theme.

There follows what Saintsbury later calls "a miniature gazeteer of Agrigentum and Syracuse, Messina and Palermo," and a romantic lament for the death of chivalry with lame echoes of Tennyson:

... the "old order" of all things is gone
And out of date is that which brightly shone.
Loosed is the mystic bond of Chivalry
That half poetic half religious tie
And our sham loyalty can stand no test;
Once it sat throned on every knightly crest
And hurtling through the reeling melee bore
The brunt of battle and the tug of war.

The young Tory concludes with a self-righteous denunciation of Garibaldian "treason" and of Sicily's "crime—so foul, so damning—black of hue . . . "

By thine own hand the fatal blow is given
Thus are thy banners torn, thy scutcheons riven.

The elderly Saintsbury summed up his reaction, "Sometimes when I am very melancholy I read it, to make me laugh a little." But the political view was, for him, still correct.

The poem should be weighed no more seriously than other such prize pieces. Imitative, immature, trite, often stiff, unwieldy, and naively romantic, it was cramped by a set topic that could only be handled at second hand. Written by the future historian of prosody and a critic who held the music and rhythm of poetic form to be of paramount importance, the couplets are correct but no better and no worse than many such schoolboy efforts. They do not suggest that the boy, whose ear was already alive to the music of Blake, Shelley, Byron, and DeQuincey, and to the cadence of the Psalms, would be a poet. Rather "Sicilia" supports the modest but realistic judgment of its author: "At a very early time of my life, it was borne in upon me that I was not destined to create great literature, but that I might have some faculty of appreciating it, and might even to some extent assist that appreciation in others."[22]

The early recognition that he was not basically creative must have been more a blow to Saintsbury than he admits. The very fact that he records the experience several times and the consequent decision to become a critic implies that he had dreamed of becoming a poet. He came to terms with the decision and began his critical reviewing before he was thirty, but the sense of shortcoming may well have contributed to his seeking escape in the world of fantasy and dream he had already discovered as a boy.

Saintsbury's London school friends called him the "Dictionary of Useless Knowledge," a label suggesting a mind widely ranging, insatiably curious, but not primarily creative. As compensation, even then, he craved to read everything, often without direction or method, while his retentive memory was building that store of knowledge at which later generations marveled.[23]

Thus equipped, the young man, five days short of his eighteenth birthday, went up to Merton College to spend the next four years taking on that mold and tempering he recorded and praised as Oxford's peculiar gift.

CHAPTER 2

Oxford "Tempering"

For there can be, or should be, few passages in life with
greater capabilities than that when a man is for the first
time almost his own master, for the first time wholly arbiter
of whatsoever sports and whatsoever studies he shall pursue, and when he is subjected to local, historical, sensual
and other influences, suprasensual, such as might not only
"draw three souls out of one weaver," but infuse something
like *one* soul even into the stupidest and most graceless of
boys.

—Preface, *Second Scrap Book*

No man can wholly judge his own university career, either its total
shape and color or its influence upon his character. None can measure how large a role that period played in making him the man he
is. On some the influence is slight, indeed temporary. Others find
their own bent and settle permanently in those impressionable years
into attitudes and ideas from which they depart little thereafter. The
more one knows of George Saintsbury, the more one recognizes that
he fell early into ways of thinking and feeling that were never to
change—a fact that led someone to comment at his death that his
mind scarcely seemed to have a history.

Oxford has always laid something of her characteristic imprint
upon her sons in all their variety. In the young Saintsbury she found
an eager, receptive, somewhat malleable subject but one who brought
Tory and High Church views that would not alter, and a habit of
romantic fantasy and literary enthusiasms already shaping. It helps
one understand him and his work if one looks at the man he became
in those Oxford days and at the life that filled them. The autobiographical "Oxford Sixty Years Ago,"[1] the one hundred pages he wrote
in 1923 at the urging of friends, preserves those formative days and
recreates an era in the history of the University from his special angle.

13

Few have paid her more gracious tribute or praised her training more highly; few have captured more vividly the day-to-day life in what he terms this "witches' cauldron." It differs from the Oxford of Arnold, Wilde, or Waugh and other rebels but has its value.

He could tell the story because he had a retentive memory and had preserved his diaries, his cash account book, and other memorabilia. The diaries are gone, destroyed as he wished all personal records to be, but to support his telling of the tale, there is a well-worn cashbook[2] ($6^{1}/_{2}''$ × $4^{1}/_{2}''$, in maroon leather and marbelized boards) that, in a neatly legible script, records all receipts and expenditures of those Oxford years—meticulous to the last pence for a beggar, for offertory, for a tollgate fee—from October 17, 1863, to August 1, 1868. The conscientious detail is one clue to character in this tale told in figures, reflecting the young man who wrote it and recording one sort of Oxford undergraduate life in the 1860s.

In the years midway between the two University Commissions (1851 and 1874), Oxford had its distinctive qualities amid the "traditional ferment." The University Reform Act of 1854 removed the religous tests for matriculation and the B.A., though not for the M.A. or for fellowships or a vote in convocation. The Church's hold on the colleges had been weakened, but clerical power was still real. Closed fellowships and scholarships had been thrown open and the level of scholarship was gradually rising. Professorships had multiplied, and intercollege lectures supplemented college tutorials and lectures—an invasion of college independence long resented by conservatives. Like Pusey, Merton's warden, R. Bullock Marsham, declared "for law and ancient usage," and many of his fellows and undergraduates were strong opponents of reform. Some reforms had to wait for the Commission of 1874; others came gradually through revision of college statutes, changes that were resisted or delayed in most colleges.

Entrance standards were higher and undergraduates worked harder than their counterparts of the first half-century, though, in the 1860s, only about thirty percent were honors candidates. Men were free to plan their own reading and to decide when to sit examinations. By 1868, Mark Pattison was complaining, with some justice, that the university had become a mere training ground for undergraduates, that too few fellows wrote books or became the scholars they should be.[3]

Socially, the snobbishness of earlier times had grown less, though it had scarcely disappeared as Saintsbury liked to believe. The young nobleman no longer held exclusive privileges, but distinctions between college men and those in the halls, between scholars and commoners, counted socially and intellectually. Some shift had taken place; the scholar and honors man stood above the pass-men, and to be a member of one of the older, more famous and distinguished foundations was important. "There was no prejudice against reading," Saintsbury says, or against the unconventional. The ideal was the "all round man," and "most men were learning the rules of the game," but "if you were a gentleman and a good fellow," the out-of-the-way or eccentric was allowed.

> He should not *merely* read,... if he were not great at sports he should at any rate take an interest in them;... he should not wholly eschew wines and suppers and such more forbidden but harmless things as college steeplechases;... he might fill his rooms with "triptychs and Madonnas" or keep strange beasts in them, or compose... waltzes... or do anything else in reason or sometimes a little out of it.[4]

Undergraduates now came in large and steadily growing proportions from middle-class homes where the degree was beginning to be valued not only for status or prestige but as a financial asset, a change that sparked Pattison's protest that some scholars "have come here as a commercial speculation."[5] Dress was more formal than anything seen in the "High" today. Wine parties and gambling—at cards and in other forms—were traditionally common diversions of the Fellows and a Common Room "betting book" was maintained. Similar diversions were popular among their juniors; and mild sorts of rowdyism—window smashing, even bread throwing, bear fighting at the wine club, bonfires, fireworks, and other schoolboy tricks—held their place.

The November bonfire in Merton's "Mob Squad" in 1865, for which the entire college was "gated" for a week, had its splendors celebrated in a "ballad epic" and was followed for a week by "solemn" processions round the Fellows' Quad, to protest the "injustice" of their having been gated—all to the accompaniment of penny whistles, crackers, and tea trays as drums. Saintsbury's November 2d entry in his account book is "fireworks, gunpowder, mask, 13s."[6]

These young Victorians, eager to break class bonds, aped the ways of their aristocratic predecessors—with an inevitable difference. Arnold's dandyism of the 1840s had its parallels in the 1860s, but new elements of a changing world were shaping it—elements social, political, scientific, moral, and religious. Arnold is now Professor of Poetry and author of *Essays in Criticism* (1865); Ruskin's preoccupations with art have given way to economic and social concerns, while the influence of his "moral aesthetic" continues in art and letters and Pater is being heard on the pure aesthetic in "Aesthetic Poetry." Tennyson and Browning are still the reigning poets, but pre-Raphaelite voices are growing stronger.[7] Darwinism and the heresy-hunting conflict over *Essays and Reviews* are having their unsettling effects. Pressures for change in Church and university go along with political pressures that bring parliamentary reform in the "Shooting of Niagara" of 1867. Which of these affected Saintsbury?

Some of the forces at work in the Oxford microcosm originated there. The Oxford Movement, now "out of Egypt and the Wilderness," possessed many of the best brains in the Church. Its influence was strong, indeed dominant, in some Common Rooms, but it was challenged by the Liberals, Jowett and Pattison among them. Its appeal to the undergraduates was a potent mixture of the devotional and the aesthetic. The Brotherhood of the Holy Trinity, which Saintsbury promptly joined, offered in its rules for personal discipline a focus for men who, though not in much danger of turning to Rome, wanted the forms and traditions emphasized and felt the need of group identity. It helped form their ideals of the Christian gentleman, and its somewhat naive rules (i.e., "not to take more than three glasses of wine *after* dinner") provided what Saintsbury later termed "a good disciplinary institution . . . absolutely loyal to the church." Of soul searching, doubt, or conflict one hears nothing in Saintsbury's group. Did they read Darwin or Huxley?

The High Church and Tory beliefs Saintsbury brought with him to Merton in 1863 only deepened and grew more fixed for life. In an Oxford Tory society of which Dean Henry Mansel and Dr. Richard Mitchell were the leaders, Saintsbury soon gained a reputation for the "deep-dyed creed with which he confronted their laxer faith"; it amused his intimates to hear "'old George' growl at an England daily going more persistently to the dogs and with no hope of a return till the first reform bill was repealed." He rejoiced over Gladstone's loss of his University seat (1865) and Disraeli's "enlistment of the side of the Angels." As the *Apologia* appeared in pamphlet form (1864–

65), he read it with a strong desire to meet Newman's arguments more effectively than he thought Kingsley had done. Mandell Creighton suggested Saintsbury's religious devotion when he pictured him as always carrying a picture of the Virgin in his prayer book. A faithful attendant at chapel, morning and evening—with a never tiring joy in the Bidding Prayer[8]—he took keen pleasure in other university services and in university sermons. Fortunately Oxford then offered as fine examples of preaching as any since the seventeenth century: Pusey, whose charm of voice added to a fine devotional intensity; Dean Mansel, who with his severer rhetoric and fine, cadenced rhythms "heard long after in memory's ear" gave one a "logical education as well";[9] and Bishop Wilberforce, whose art was admired regardless of "floating doubts as to sincerity."

Merton College, founded in 1264, was approaching its 600th anniversary. It had a lay head and forty undergraduates in 1863, increased in 1864 to fifty-six with the opening of the new building. These undergraduates were almost equally divided between Postmasters, Exhibitioners, and Bible Clerks on the one hand and Commoners on the other. "The majority were Eton men, brought there through the influence of the Warden, . . . men who loved hunting and other sports, had plenty of money to spend, and no particular intention of doing any work. . . . The scholars . . . formed a nucleus of reading men."[10] These last Saintsbury knew best. Though not expensive for the undergraduate and reputed to have the best dinners in Oxford, Merton required undergraduates to dine in hall except when dining out of college and required three years of "living in." A new college spirit was growing, and at Merton, "the most sociable of colleges," the small group was one social unit, making up one wine club. It met regularly after six o'clock dinner in various men's rooms for talk. Among the more exclusive groups were the Whist Club formed by a dozen men in Saintsbury's second year, a "Contra Club" soon formed by the excluded, and the "Merton Popes" or "Saints." These last made themselves somewhat unpopular by absenting themselves from dinner in hall on Lenten Wednesdays and other fast days—to hold "eggy teas" in their rooms while reading St. Augustine's *Confessions* aloud. Saintsbury was a member of both the Whist Club and the "Saints."

Such social and religious snobberies had their importance for the King's College School boy who, in his own terms, was in 1863 "shy, rather poor,...only *day*-schooled..., ungregarious." He had no family tradition of university behind him and found security in the Tory High Church views he could share with friends, who, like him, had no real impulse to rebel, but this description implies that he felt the lack of the Public School connection. In his first year, despite the sociableness of Merton and the friendliness of Senior Postmaster Mandell Creighton, he made few new friends and "lived rather a recluse" in tiny rooms opposite the Porter's Lodge. Here he was "ragged" or "drawn" once "with salutary effect"; here, through his window looking onto Merton Street, he "could gratify thirsty outside friends with drinks through the bars which made no cage for hospitality." Here also he did a great deal of reading as he began preparation for "Mods" with John King as his tutor for scholarship and William Sidgewick for logic while he attended Professor Wall's university lectures. His account book includes subscriptions for boat club and "Grinds" (private college horse races), outings by boat and pony cart, and much walking;[11] a dinner at Wallingford (October 28th), lunch at Faringdon (November 30th), lunch at Witney (February 15th), and "boat, lock and beer" at Stow Wood (February 15th).

That first year Saintsbury kept up contact with school friends in other colleges: most important and intimate was the old friendship with Thistleton Dyer now at Christ Church, but W. B. Duggan was at Lincoln and others were at Balliol, Brasenose, Exeter, Worcester, New College, Queens, and other colleges. These gave him an early chance to feel at home among the colleges. Later he did less external visiting. In the summer term, Creighton (later Bishop of London), who had come up in 1862, undertook to "draw him out," then quickly became Saintsbury's closest friend.[12] Only then did "Saint," as he came to be known, begin to become "the thorough Mertonian" that he still proclaimed himself at seventy-eight.

For his second and third year Saintsbury had his choice of rooms, fine ones in the new building with a view over the meadow and the Broadwalk and his circle widened until he was friendly with everyone in the college.[13] Creighton, Foster Alleyne, Alberic Bertie, "one Harding," and Reginald Copleston (later Bishop Metropolitan of India) made up his special set. Others were R. T. Raikes; "Jenkins, a mighty hunter who sold horses to Napoleon III"; Mowbray Morris, later editor of *Macmillans Magazine* and a lifetime friend of Saintsbury; Bakmeteff, later a Russian diplomat; H. W. Challis, later of the Bar, and for Saintsbury, a man "of more pure brains" than anyone he ever knew; and Sir Stafford Northcote.

Among friends in other colleges were H. J. Hood; William Hunt, the later church historian, at Magdalen; Walter Phillemore and Robert Bridges at Christ Church, with all of whom Saintsbury maintained friendship throughout life, and Bridges' close friend, Gerard Manley Hopkins, whom Saintsbury knew only casually, Bridges, writing in the year of his own death, recalled affectionately Saintsbury's "old bolstering matches" with Thistleton Dyer.[14]

Outings with these friends were frequent. Creighton had "an amiable knack of organizing expeditions," and Saintsbury describes one of these: "One Trinity Sunday 1865, . . . he and I and two men drove to Witney, went to church there, then walked for twenty miles or so through Wychwood, dined late at the Marlborough Arms, and drove back to Oxford just in time for twelve o'clock, on one of the most glorious summer nights I ever remember."[15] Creighton recreates another such Sunday when five of them walked to Wolvercot and Wytham and lunched at Godstow: "We had old Saintsbury on the fuss about things in general. . . . He said that when he was a parson he would strictly adhere to the Canon, and report to the Bishop all his parishoners who did not fast on Fridays, and would prosecute his village butcher in the Court of Arches for selling meat on that day. . . ."[16] The flavor of their talk is also in a diary entry Saintsbury preserved: "Desperate argument with C . . . till 2:45 (A.M.)"; also in Copleston's recollection: "Creighton and Saintsbury talked about the 'immensities' and the 'everlasting no,' and divided us all into those who were 'in contact' and those who were not 'in contact' with the great Heart of the Universe."[17] They were "full of Carlyle" and were strongly opposed to the growing influence of John Stuart Mill. Contrary to Mill's ideal of the "open mind," "you were to take which side you liked on as large a number of questions as possible and fight like a 'Swiss of Heaven' for that."[18]

Saintsbury describes a lively evening "symposium court" arranged by William Sidgewick to discuss changes made in chapel services, with Sidgewick arguing on one side, Saintsbury and another Postmaster on the other (against change probably). Like most clever undergraduates, Saintsbury enjoyed "breaking eggs" intellectually, and, in old age, he boasted of the three or four times he thought he had scored against the dons. Once, as a guest in the Common Room, in reply to

George Broderick's assertion that "all persons of sense and decency" took the Liberal side in the Governor Eyre case, he queried, "Then nearly all Tories, besides Tennyson and Carlyle and Kingsley, are *not* persons of sense and decency?" And in his first term, he had discomfited his tutor, "the shy . . . extremely pudibund . . . Johnny King," by translating one of Catullus's more obscene pieces complete and entire "not merely in metre but in paraphrase and drapery," then reading it to the increasingly embarrassed tutor, who finally burst out, "but . . . not quite the passage I meant." It was probably King who had Saintsbury translate Emily Brontë's "Remembrance" into Latin elegiacs.

Of an encounter with Jowett, both Saintsbury's version and that of the "excellent raconteur" Creighton survive. At a tutorial on Plato's *Laws* (these two were reading for Greats) Saintsbury read an essay that deliberately presented, as its climax, the Platonic sentence of death on dissenters. When asked whether he agreed with Plato, the writer replied tongue-in-cheek, "I shouldn't dare disagree with Plato." This brought the sharp retort from Jowett, "Then I *don't* agree with him."[19] Undergraduate leg pulling all this, but along with a youthful arrogance it reflects Saintsbury's lifelong love of verbal play, his frequent facetious parentheses, his love of argument, his somewhat controversial temperament, and his rigidly conservative convictions that deprived him of more profitable contact with Jowett.

Saintsbury apologizes several times in his Oxford narrative for disproportionate emphasis upon the nonacademic side, but one recognizes the traditional Oxbridge pattern. He claims that the games and walks, talk and debate, and the "fun and fooling" play a valuable part in that "indefinite, various, rather mystical tempering" that is Oxford's best gift. Not everyone would acquire that tempering, Saintsbury knew, since it required certain gifts in the student.

> . . . the eye to see . . . some love for the past and some knowledge of it; some sense of historic continuity . . . some sympathy with or at least some conception of the great movements (some of them not so distant) of which [Oxford] has been the home; some remembrance of the men who have lived, and died, and read, and felt, and sometimes fought within or around its walls; some touch of imaginative compassion for all the fantastic and fallacious hopes, all the dreams sent from the ivory gate, that have flitted thicker than any motes in its thousand chambers.[20]

Thus he saw it in 1896—romantically, with emphasis on the past and its dreams, wholly omitting the receptivity to the new and radical need to respond to the revolutionary ideas of science, religion, and politics that were in the Oxford ferment of the 1860s.

The terms' days passed then much as they do now: mornings devoted to chapel, tutorials, lectures (one or two), and reading; afternoons to recreation; evenings to reading interspersed with talk, whist, perhaps some essay writing, even a tutorial (Sidgewick's preference for late appointments was not popular though he was well liked). Creighton and Saintsbury enjoyed reading in each other's rooms. "Night-wanderings" Saintsbury calls the long, profitable evenings. With dinner at six and a "wine" to follow, five or six hours lay ahead for drifting in and out of each other's rooms, for reading, cards, billiards, "forty winks" to put off sleep, the brewing of punch and drinking it, waltzing, and discoursing on every possible subject, ending sometimes in what they termed a "seance"—a heated discussion lasting into the morning hours. Sunday nights came to include a "verboten" walk round "the Southern edge of the parks . . . and home by St. Clements and Magdalen Bridge" with a somewhat perilous climb round the spiked arch of the Cherwell bridge gate, made more perilous by the gowns still commonly worn.

The long vacations of 1864 and 1865 saw Saintsbury on walking tours of the west country with a friend, usually Thistleton Dyer, reading and exploring the landscape and literary scenes such as the Claverings of *Pendennis* and Nether Stowey, Avebury and Brent Tor; Yeovil, Exeter, Wells and Bristol; Minehead and Taunton; Clovelly and Ilfracombe—the southwestern countryside he came to prefer to all others. Another holiday saw him in Tennyson's Lincolnshire, and, in 1866, he and Dyer spent two months (July 11th to September 12th) walking in Brittany while making some forays into French literature, and no doubt exploring botany, Dyer's specialty. They had lodging with board somewhere near or in St. Malo, had dinners and an evening of theatre there, and made excursions to Mont St. Michel, Rennes, Cancale, Dinard, Saint Sulfac, and elsewhere—details that have special point because strangely, considering all his work on French literature, Saintsbury was never in France after 1870.

In his first two years at Oxford, Saintsbury grew in confidence and life grew steadily more pleasant; the peak came with his First in "Mods" in June, 1865, for which John King's tutoring deserves the share of credit his pupil accords him. An expert in his subject, he offered some discipline to a "rather unconcentrated reader" who, amid "a welter of interests," felt that the best lifebelt was "an intelligent but not merely intellectual enjoyment of them *all* or as many of them as your nature makes it possible for you to enjoy."[21] This ideal, a kind of aesthetic omniscience that Saintsbury later too loosely identified with Walter Pater's creed, he found strong in the climate of Oxford, which had sheltered Pater since 1858. It was an attitude also embraced by Oscar Wilde when he came up to Oxford in 1872, but both Pater and Wilde later came to distrust the emphasis on the unlimited quantity of experience rather than the quality to be embraced. Saintsbury, as we shall see, never seemed really to have questioned the limits of his or other people's capacity to absorb literary experience.

This range and "universality of taste" reminds one of Pendennis, home from Oxbridge, reading Paul de Kock and other light French literature, drinking up the family bin of claret, interesting himself in French fashions, whist, and écarté, and of Major Pendennis's view: "Let him make his first *entrée* into the world as a gentleman."[22] Pen had gone up "liberally allowanced," only to find himself "plucked" and £700 in debt after two years. Saintsbury later recognized Pen's pattern as not unlike his own.

Its effects on Saintsbury's Oxford career were real and immediate. With his First in "Mods" and his tutors' recommendations for "Greats" in hand, Saintsbury was full of ambition and overconfidence. He began his third year determined to sit the *Literae Humaniores* examinations early in order to leave time for Second Schools in law and history. At Merton, only he and Creighton were then reading for "Greats"; they attended lectures by W. W. Shirley in ecclesiastical history, Jowett in Greek, the newly arrived Edmund Caird in philosophy and Roman history and William Sidgewick in logic. Saintsbury had individual tutorials with the last three. He praises Caird as a popular and polished lecturer, "not the very best kind" but "unsurpassable" in his discussion of essays. He cherished Caird's surprising verdict that he had more "philosophical ethos" than any other pupil he had ever had, later judges notwithstanding; yet he reports Caird's complaint that he "would get into logical coaches and let himself be carried away"—a judgment immediately provoked by a foolish essay on "The Value and Interest of Falsehood."[23] Saintsbury's recalling these judgments fifty years later suggests that he suspected the latter was valid and hoped the first was true.

Sidgewick, Saintsbury's official tutor, who advised him to do Aristotle's *Ethics* rather than the *Politics* (the decision to do so brought bad results), offered amusing and stimulating lectures that, with only two or three listeners, were really conversations; these for Saintsbury had a "bush-harrowing" or "fermentative" effect on the mind and "took one out of a rut." Saintsbury recalls his pleasure in lectures by Edward Mansel, given in the Hall at Magdalen, those of Canon Shirley, which made ecclesiastical history "so very much alive," and a single one by Pusey given to an unexpected "full house," in his own canonical "vast and rather ghostly drawing room."

Creighton shared rooms in "the High" with Saintsbury in the first term of 1866–67, the year that ended in failures for Saintsbury. For whatever reasons—overconfidence, haste, arguing foolishly over the *Ethics* with one of the oral examiners (as he claims to have done), his "irregular fashion of reading and habit of indulging in alarums and excursions," his tendency to superficiality, or the diversion of too much energy to the social life of Oxford—nemesis came in June of 1866 with a Second in "Greats."

The failure left its lasting impression, and Saintsbury records his bitter disappointment:

> I wonder if there is anything, not involving severe bodily pain, utter financial ruin, real disgrace, or the death of a dear friend, which *hurts* so abominably and lasts so long as getting a Second. . . . The sting of a Second is almost incurable.[24]

The reading he had done was ample and not bad in quality, and it sank into a retentive and capacious memory. Diary entries show its diversity and range, but they also reveal a lack of focus or system and an admitted "contrariness—a besetting sin." He tells of taking a fancy to Scholasticism and "reading Haureau and Prantl which couldn't possibly pay," of an attempt to trace the journey of Io in *Prometheus* and his request to a startled librarian for "a copy of Gassendi to compare with Lucretius," and his buying Stallbaum's large *Plato* and reading it through when supposedly preparing for second schools in modern history. Selected diary entries record typical mornings and evenings.

Refused four wines. Read Logic and Lucretius 4 hours. . . . Read the *Choephorae* and *Pickwick* all morning. . . . Finished the *Eumenides,* wrote Greek prose, and read *Pickwick* and Spenser . . . two books of Homer in five hours . . . Logic, Browning, Cosin and Dr. Syntax, 2 3/4 hours . . . the *Ethics, Peter Wilkins,* and the *Cornhill* . . .

These diary entries and his comments on his habits and on what he imagines would be the reactions of conventional pedagogues emphasize his lack of concentration: what would they have thought of his "not being able to read Virgil without going off to Appollonius Rhodius," or his "equal enjoyment of the first appearance of *Rhoda Fleming* and a lecture of Mansel's on Heraclitus?" He smiles over the memory of the Greek Romances, which could not possibly have "paid off" in the examinations or in the soon-to-come schoolmastering but did join the credit side of the ledger fifty-five years later in an introduction for a new edition of Longus's *Daphnis and Chloë.* In 1920, he was still wishing for time to write a history of Scholasticism out of the interest begun at Oxford. The range of reading relates to his claim, made at the age of seventy-eight, that he had used something learned at Oxford "every year, if indeed not every day" of the intervening years. The learning stuck and some of it was deep, but the direction was always to range, not depth.

Among his diary entries appear early favorites, *Pickwick* and Spenser, and Lucretius, which he chose as a book for "Mods." He had begun his habit of rereading. Here also is the *Saturday Review,* to which he subscribed in his first week in Oxford. It probably had been in his home from its beginning in 1855; it was later to become the center of his professional life (1879–94). The many entries from English literature remind us that Oxford did not examine on these for many years after he left but that Saintsbury kept up his earlier habits. This vast, unconcentrated pattern was some preparation for the life of a journalist, and it reflects other qualities familiar in his later writing—that capacity for equal enjoyment of major and minor works in every genre and period, the catholicity that was to make his criticism of minor writers often most valuable, and that lively enthusiasm that sends his reader to Croker or Wilson, Murger or the *Anti-Jacobin,* to Susan Ferrier or some minor seventeenth-century versifier with expectations that are occasionally disappointed by the original.[25]

How much of a library Saintsbury acquired in these Oxford years it is impossible to say since the titles of books bought are often concealed in booksellers' bills and not itemized in the account book. Sophocles's *Ajax* was the first (on October 19, 1863) followed two days later by Virgil and his schooldays favorite, *La Morte d'Arthur,* then Thucydides, the Lachmann Lucretius, Cicero's *Philippics,* Demosthenes, and a Batterman's *Lexilogus.* More surprising is the purchase of a second Virgil, Gossran's *Aeneid,* during the first long vacation. Despite early exposure, he admits he never was a devotee.[26]

Personal taste speaks in the *Enoch Arden* bought on a July, 1864, visit to King's College School and first read during a walk through Hyde Park and Kensington Gardens, where he had earlier come to "adore" Tennyson. The new poems disappointed the "fanatical Tennysonian," who asked "Where is 'The Lotus Eaters'?" But in July, 1866, he was buying *Maud,* and in the next two years he reread Morris's *Defense of Guinevere, Jason,* and *The Earthly Paradise* with enthusiasm. Browning, who had not been an early favorite, he was "reading night and day" after the appearance of *Dramatis Personae* (1864).

One group of purchases made in late 1866 and 1867 had immediate significance: Swinburne's "Vindication" on November 3d, three copies of *Poems and Ballads* on November 6th, *Les Fleurs du mal,* December 28th, 1866; Gautier's *Poems,* January 8th, 1867; and, during the spring of 1867, Swinburne's *Queen Mother* and *Songs of Italy* and Whitman's *Leaves of Grass.* The fashion—and the passion—of the hour were the Pre-Raphaelites, whose paintings were fading on the Oxford Union walls, Swinburne, and the French art-for-art's-sake writers to whom he had sent his devotees several years before Pater proclaimed the creed of art-for-art's-sake in English in 1873.

Saintsbury lovingly recalls the impact of Swinburne's "bombshell" upon Oxford undergraduates: how they waited patiently for the promised *Poems and Ballads* (some of them circulated in manuscript early in 1866 while rumors of their sensational quality multiplied). Announced in May, the volume was held up, supposedly for correction of errors and a need for rebinding, until August 4th, when John Morley's anonymous attack in the *Saturday Review* accused the poet of moral depravity and scared the publisher, Moxon, into withdrawing the volume before it reached the bookshops. Then came Swinburne's "Vindication." Saintsbury and his Merton friends had read *Atalanta* and "been swept off their feet with rapture" by its choruses; they had not been disappointed by *Chastelard* and were eager for more when, in October, Hotten finally brought out the new volume. Saintsbury went to London on November 3d to eat his first dinner at the Inner Temple and came back on the 5th with one copy of *Notes on Poems and Reviews* (the "Vindication"), three copies "of the precious volume with Moxon on the cover and John Camden Hotten on the title page,"—and fireworks for Guy Fawkes. Creighton and Alleyne were the recipients of the extra two copies of *Poems and Ballads,* which had set off its own fireworks in the literary world of the 1860s, an era rightly described by Edmund Gosse as "the most quiescent, the most sedate ... perhaps ... the least effective and efficient in our national poetry."[27]

The effect of the rich music and sensuality of these first *Poems and Ballads* was powerful on that autumn Sunday.

> We sat next afternoon ... from luncheon till chapel bell rang, reading aloud by turns in a select company "Dolores" and "The Triumph of Time," "Laus Veneris" and "Faustine" and all the other wonders of the volume ... surely never did old things become so new and new things so old as when one turned the page and came on

> > Out of the golden remote wild west,
> >   where the sea with shore is,

> and all the wonders from

> > I found in dreams a place of wind
> >   and flowers

> to

> > Night sinks on the sea

Along with these poetic glories, these young devotees absorbed Swinburne's challenge:

> Whether or not the first and last requisite of art is to give no offense; whether or not all that cannot be lisped in the nursery or

fingered in the schoolroom is therefore to be cast out of the library; whether or not the domestic circle is to be for all men and writers the outer limit and extreme horizon of their world at work. For to this we have come; and all students of art must face the matter . . . .[28]

This issue had come to English attention four years earlier with the publication of Baudelaire's *Les Fleurs du mal* and Swinburne's review praising Baudelaire's attitudes in the *Spectator* (September 6, 1862). Saintsbury's next book purchase was *Les Fleurs du mal*, a second edition brought from Paris by a friend during the Christmas holiday of 1866. He next bought Swinburne's *William Blake* (1868), with its strong attack on "l'hérésie de l'enseignement," and himself soon took up the challenge to become a champion of art-for-art's-sake as Swinburne, Baudelaire, Gautier, and Pater represented it to him. My next chapter will deal with this advocacy that pervades his early reviewing, but the role that the new aestheticism at Oxford played in shaping his outlook must not be underestimated, High Church devoutness notwithstanding. In his last two years at Merton, Saintsbury's first signed literary essay—that on Baudelaire, which would appear in 1875—was taking shape in partially written form. And attitudes he retained throughout life were being set in an Oxford where Pater and Arnold were exercising their direct but conflicting influences.[29]

These shared enthusiasms must have have helped ease the immediate pain of Saintsbury's entry into "the Purgatory of Seconds," an experience he shared with many other promising candidates before and after him (Arnold, Clough, Newman, Pater, Mark Pattison, Creighton and W. P. Ker, among near contemporaries). The scar, traditionally a sore and deep one for those whose hearts are set upon the scholar's life, is sometimes offset by the receipt of a fellowship. Here too nemesis was at work. Simultaneous with the "smash in 'Greats'" came Saintsbury's unsuccessful try for a Merton fellowship; then, in three successive, heart-breaking weeks of the summer term of 1867, the failure repeated itself at Wadham, Lincoln, and Corpus, and a second time at Merton. He believed he lost one of them for advocating art-for-art's-sake in an essay, but there had to be other reasons. Did they weigh his preference for range over depth, his undiscriminating enthusiasms and strong prejudices?

The die was cast: he knew he must relinquish his desire for the life of an Oxford don—"one of the most perfectly conditioned of lives,"[30] as he thought it to the end of his life. For the scholar and literary historian he was to become, the loss was substantial. The continuing discipline, coupled with freedom and leisure for reading and research or even "to lie fallow awhile," might have supplied to the young man who was still just twenty-two some of the habits of accuracy and precise scholarship he lacked and to which he always later expressed indifference. The price would have been the loss of other strengths he gained amid the pressures of the journalistic life to which he turned after eight years of schoolmastering. But the dream persisted—that of the protected celibate life of a Fellow as it was until the 1870s when, by special action, his friend Creighton was allowed to marry, a life focused on literary study, leisurely and congenial, apart from the world's conflicts.

Saintsbury once protested Arnold's account of Oxford in his *Schools and Universities on the Continent* (1868) as inaccurate because it failed to treat either the honors system that had raised standards far above those of the *haut lycée* or the scholarship system that, Saintsbury believed, "provided an entrance standard actually higher—far higher in some ways—than the *concluding* examination of the French *baccalaureat*." In his own Oxford years, he maintained, at least four hundred men obtained scholarships on this standard and the pass-men were "a pretty bare majority." He went on to claim that the Oxford *Literae Humaniores* is "the best intellectual training in the world."[31] Much later he spoke of the good fortune of his generation in having a classical education: "nothing startled us or puzzled us merely because it was not of today in time and of our own milieu in condition."[32] Having idealized this education, he failed to recognize that it did not prevent his rejecting the new as he increasingly did.

Not least among the many elements Saintsbury valued in the Oxford "tempering" was the "complicated and mysterious but infinitely powerful and specific influences of the 'College proper,' its traditions and ceremonies as well as those other ancient ones belonging to the whole University, and the sense of continuity with a hundred generations who have . . . read and thought and eaten and drunk, and even danced (*manca volupta*) in these rooms." The long-remembered disappointments—"my days of Merton mourning"—like much else reflect a person who needed the security of belonging. In his *Matthew Arnold* he speaks of "a certain republicanism and a certain tyranny about Oxford's idea" that were not congenial to Arnold's "aspiring and restless spirit." The tyranny was not a problem for his own temperament because, for all his sturdy independence, it made him a lifelong Tory and a conservative churchman; it made him identify with the traditional Oxford life he came to love, and it made him, like many other bright and ambitious undergraduates, proud of his status as a Merton scholar and hopeful of becoming an Oxford Fellow.

As he gained his First in "Mods" and his Second in "Greats," he became a more confident, somewhat contentious third-year man; his interests became more sophisticated and his tastes more those of the young gentleman with which Oxford tempted her sons. The simpler college pleasures—walking, boating, talk—go on as does serious reading, but both his account book and the *Scrap Book* memoir show a growing emphasis on wine and whist, gambling at various card games and on "grinds," the giving of lavish suppers, and the courting of young London "Angels." There are holiday stalls at the opera, theatre and dinners at London hotels, and ample provision of wines, cigars, pipes, and tobacco. He confesses to the purchase of a pair of dueling pistols for five guineas (never used and sold later for thirty shillings) and to ordering handmade embroidered white kid gloves as a gift, then matching them in black for himself with a "quincunx of blue silk crosses" on the white, of red ones on the black.

His account book lists the waltzes he bought: "Marie," "Hilda," "Mabel," "The Borderers," "The Water Babies Waltz," and "Airs from *L'Africaine*," and he recalls dancing all night in London, then walking to Oxford.[33] He paid a £40 fee for privileges at the Inner Temple, and after eating a half-dozen dinners, he paid the annual fee for a decade, partly out of habit and sentiment, partly for "a certain sense of dignity and association."[34] His account book tells of betting losses on the Derby and Oaks races and at whist, écarté, piquet, and billiards. The betting was modest, the dinners seem not so many or so lavish, and the debts that he labeled unjustifiable were paid, though not entirely for a decade, a not uncommon story for Oxbridge and much less serious than that of Wilde a few years later. But these "gentlemanly expenses" were a problem for a young man with a very small income whose reliance was increasingly upon loans from a widowed mother and two generous sisters, one of whom married while he was at Oxford.

In the 1860s, £200 was supposed to keep a "tolerably economical youngster at Oxford for a year," according to Saintsbury. His own income from scholarships and allowance was £100 or less, eked out by loans, by £25 earned by coaching in 1866–67, and a £250 mortgage raised July 2, 1867, presumably on their London house. A sharp rise in expenditures confirms the growing taste for somewhat "high living": the £249, £258, and £221 for his first three years becomes £512 for 1866–67 and £105 for the fall term, 1867.[35] As he saw it, the pleasures and rewards were real, but the "nemesis" was not uninvited.[36]

Those Oxford men of the 1860s shared that vague ideal of the gentleman so much spoken of in Victorian life and literature. The taste in wine and foods and the gambling suggest the Regency dandy; the taste for embroidered gloves reminds one of Beau Brummel, Count D'Orsay, and the later aesthetes.[37] Manners are important. Late in life Saintsbury says, "Brains, beauty, strength, riches, birth, etc. are gifts; morals are subject to temptation; but manners everyone can have by choosing to have them." Taking manners to mean "taste," as he seems to do, Saintsbury chose to pursue this ideal throughout life as far as means, health, and a demanding career would allow. A 1924 note headed "Taste," though not original, embodies that conception of a discriminating, refined sensibility he found in Pater and made his own:

Taste is . . . a habit of not merely speaking, but acting, behaving, liking, disliking—*living,* you may almost say . . . you cannot be said to fully live unless you exercise this Taste in almost every waking moment—on the things you drink and eat, "on the faces you meet," on the books you read and the scripts you write, on public and private affairs of almost every—perhaps of every—kind . . . to provide avoidance, as far as possible, of the evil and enjoyment as far as possible, of the good in things of the body and things of the soul, in things of the sense and things of the intellect. . . .[38]

The young gentleman of the 1860s at Oxford was the Regency gentleman as he had been refined, intellectualized, moralized, and aestheticized under the influence of Carlyle, Arnold, Newman, Ruskin, Swinburne, Pater, and French aestheticism during the three decades since Carlyle and *Fraser's Magazine* had attacked dandification. Add to these the moralistic influence of *John Halifax,*

Gentleman (1859), a novel much read by Saintsbury's generation, for whom education was one means of achieving the status of a gentleman.

The contradictions were many. Saintsbury's group (two later bishops, Copleston and Creighton, among them) could mingle enthusiasm for Carlyle and Arnold with devout High Church religious practices, Tory politics, and enthusiasm for Swinburne and Baudelaire, Gautier and Flaubert, "triptychs and madonnas," wine, whist, college steeplechase, fasting, and fine dining. At Merton (Caird in 1865 called it "a tyranny of epigrams"), cultivation of the arts was in vogue, and Saintsbury sampled them all. He included concert hall and opera in his London jaunts and recalls having seen all the leading actors and actresses of the decade. Of a liking for the visual arts he offers less evidence, but his bequest to Merton College included a Rosetti drawing.[39] Pursuing "as many interests as possible," he developed and later persisted in this connoisseurship in literature alone. The gambling quickly declined. He claims never to have placed a bet after the 1870s, though his pleasures in whist, like his interest in the Derby and other races, continued. The debts had their immediate chastening effects. The theatre he later avoided, preferring like Lamb to read plays.

The closest parallel to these young men sowing their wild oats in the shadow of the Second Reform Bill is the dandified young Arnold of the 1840s who had since become "a Jeremiah in kid gloves" or the young Thackeray of the 1830s dissipating his inheritance and his energies at Cambridge. There was "high seriousness" of a sort, like Arnold's own, with ironic overtones. It had little of the pose or ennui of the younger generation, Wilde and his contemporaries, who diverted aestheticism into less innocent channels and vulgarized, even "satanized" it, thus giving art-for-art's-sake the more perverse direction that fulfilled the fears that made Pater withdraw the Conclusion from the second edition of his *Studies* in 1877.

"To burn with a pure gemlike flame" was the ideal of the earlier generation, with the emphasis on *pure,* as Pater was later to emphasize it in *Marius, the Epicurean.* When Saintsbury defined their goal as "apostles" in 1906, he praised, as "the true Paterism,"

...the perfecting, refining, illuminating of interest in things...a highly respectable creed: and I would undertake to reconcile it with the extremest orthodoxies of the best kinds. The more your interests are, the better; the higher, the nobler, the purer the subjects of them are, of course, the better; but the main thing is to get *themselves* intensified, purified, ennobled; to make sure that they are your interests. . . .[40]

The emphasis here on purifying and on orthodoxies indicates the difference between these "apostles" and Wilde and his followers. Their joy in Swinburne's *Poems and Ballads* is in their sound and rhythms, not in the substance or the decadent import of "Dolores." They seem not to have sensed where the aesthetic gesture was to lead with Huysmans and *Dorian Gray*.

Saintsbury's sympathetic understanding of Pater's philosophy, however superficial, he rightly attributes to their common Oxford background. There they both found their lifetime direction; and there Saintsbury became convinced of the rewards of a life devoted to literary study as he later described them: "You will always have, with regret, to leave some things untasted; but . . . you can go on tasting; and if you have prepared yourself properly, your taste will refine and strengthen. . . . The whole world of speech and thought is your province. . . ."[41] He did not meet Pater until 1878.

Saintsbury called 1867–68 "a Mahomet's Coffin existence . . . half Oxford and half nothing." Still reading for second schools, chiefly in economics, he was in residence only the first term. He felt heavy upon him the "ill luck and doubtful doing" of the previous spring and, somewhat at loose ends, could not shake off the sense of being a burden both to his family and to the college. He spent the spring holiday of 1867 in the Isle of Wight. The summer before he had consoled himself with a second three-week trip to the Channel Islands with Dyer again as companion. They combined walking with much reading of modern light French literature—Dumas, Feydeau, Bernard, Achard, and others. Some of these became subjects of essays Saintsbury wrote a decade later for the *Fortnightly Review*.[42] Having landed in Jersey, they gave a day to Sark, two to Alderney, and three to Guernsey, used three days for a return visit to St. Malo, Avranches, and Granville, then had a final two days in Jersey. On September 10th he was off to Devon and Cornwall and then to the Scilly Isles (September 24 to October 4), then again in Devon and Somerset until October

31st. He spent another month sometime in that year at the Southampton home of his sister, Sophie Green. Ostensibly at work on an essay in Spanish history for the Stanhope prize, he read with delight through Weber's Beaumont and Fletcher in his brother-in-law's library, thus adding to an "already considerable" knowledge of Elizabethan drama.

There was less reading during this year—and some distraction. He became engaged to Emily Fenn King, a daughter of Dr. Henry King, a Southampton surgeon, and a friend of his sisters. Being eager to marry, he sought a job and, in March 1868, accepted a teaching place at the Manchester Grammar School on a salary of £180 a year, which, he says later, "in those benighted times gentlemen of some breeding and more than some education were glad to accept."

Gentlemen is the key term in this description indicating Saintsbury's image of himself as he left Oxford in 1868. He had come up feeling poor and "day-schooled." He was Tory High Church with a habit of romantic escapism already fixed. Not in revolt against his world or his home, he came through his Oxford years insulated by his immersion in the early, more innocent phase of aesthetic revolt and in the Tory and High Church concerns he shared with his Merton friends. They were a small sector of Oxford students rooted in tradition and the past, largely escaping the impact of Darwin and the social changes of their times. They were ready to lead in the maintenance of the status quo. As Creighton depicts them, Saintsbury was the most reactionary of them all. His own account of the Oxford years is selective, slanted, and distanced by over fifty years, but within those limits it is reliable. He found a security in his ideal of the gentleman as he turned somewhat reluctantly to schoolmastering. Still poor and in debt, he had some sense of falling short. His Second in "Greats" and his not having achieved a fellowship would continue to rankle. He was in love, but the engagement comes as a surprise at the end of his account of his Oxford years because he has told us nothing of the courtship and nothing about Emily as a person. The Oxford diaries he destroyed might have revealed more, but otherwise one finds nothing except a reference to remembered curls and a letter to Helen Waddell written just after his wife's death in 1924. In it he says his violent passion through fifty-six years made him want her in her coffin as much as he did at the start—an odd, somewhat pathological confession that belongs to a later chapter. The lack of anything more is in line with the fact he recorded so little about his childhood and family while he wrote, both early and late, so much of other, less personal things.

CHAPTER 3

Schoolmaster: Manchester, Guernsey, and Elgin

Saintsbury spent March 2, 1868, visiting his fiancee, Emily King, at Southampton. He came back to Oxford to find the offer of a teaching appointment in the upper forms of the Manchester Grammar School, then headed by Frederick William Walker. He left Oxford the next day for this his first six months' experience of teaching and his first acquaintance with Manchester, a history of which he was to write two decades later. He found lodgings somewhat out of the city and a few days later joined the Manchester Athenaeum where, as the ticket (made out erroneously to a "Mr. Santzburg") promised, one could "'advance and instruct in knowledge' . . . read the papers, smoke, play billiards, and . . . lunch lightly." At this time, the school's quarters were so severely crammed as to make some such refuge necessary. There were no Common Rooms and "the very classes were held in soon-to-be-pulled-down tenement houses."

The spring saw Saintsbury settled into teaching while planning and preparing for his marriage, which took place on June 2d—presumably at Southampton. By the summer solstice, the couple had set up housekeeping in the rooms "somewhat out of the centre" where he had already settled. His account book tells of moving and household expenses and of a silk dress and a chain and cross for Emily. With characteristic reticence, Saintsbury tells us nothing more of the wedding or about his bride or those early days of marriage.

In Manchester, the young scholar was trying his hand at schoolmastering where he was soon to feel a glimmer of the distaste that made him later confess, "I never *liked* schoolmastering."[1] Yet he must have felt the challenge of the new situation, in a good school where English and the classical languages were his lot. He had begun in debt and on a low salary with "neither time nor means to invest in the gifts of Bacchus." But he and Emily were in love and eager for marriage. There was leisure for each other and for reading, and for Saintsbury's favorite physical pastime--solitary walking and exploring the countryside. A map of Lancashire was one of the first of his purchases. Here, he first saw some of Rossetti's writing while he continued his interest in French literature.

A cryptic credit entry in Saintsbury's accounts for July 26, 1868—"Cub (M.G.) 12.12"—suggests that he made his first contact with the *Manchester Guardian* in his early months in Manchester. Though C. P. Scott was not editor until 1872, Saintsbury mentions only that, in 1877, Scott gave him his "valuable apprenticeship to journalism" and "much hospitality to boot."[2] Scott, who had been a contemporary of his at Oxford, was a good friend of the Creightons and was frequently their guest in the 1870s. The *Guardian* obituary of Saintsbury assumed the earlier date, but since *Guardian* records for those years have vanished, the mystery remains.

Of the city itself as he knew it at firsthand, Saintsbury says little except in the brief popular history of it he wrote in 1887. Written for the series Historic Towns, edited by E. A. Freeman and William Hunt, it was published independently.[3] Saintsbury tried to view the city's history from a less provincial vantage point than earlier writers had done. It is no local glorification, but the *Academy* reviewer thought it vindicated the City from the "gross caricature" it suffered in Dickens's *Hard Times*.[4] Its origins and its four centuries of "barren history" are given with a touch of irony, but the rise of the cotton trade gets a straightforward account. Saintsbury warns the reader against the "element of the fantastic" in Disrael's *Sybil*, but finds "the reality and power of his drawing" superior to that of Mrs. Gaskell in *Mary Barton*. He recalls walks in the city's "sober streets" but inexplicably omits mention of the Grammar School and the *Guardian*, the two institutions he worked for and of which the city could be most rightly proud. Members of the Manchester School of Economics he saw as "totally cramped by education and inherited sympathies."[5] He later recalled the city as "the foggiest and rainiest of all our industrial hells, except Sheffield . . . a half Rembrandt, half Caillot picture."[6] He had found it sociable, and he enjoyed the Rossettis, Turners, and Coxes in the museum.[7] The book was the honest, competent product of the discipline journalism gave its author, and no more.

Guernsey (1868–74)

Whatever those few crowded months in Manchester offered the newlyweds, by September, 1868, the Saintsburys were settled in Guernsey where he was to serve as senior classical master at Elizabeth College for six years. This "Charmed Isle," one of the "Isles Fortunées," he knew from his 1867 tour. The islanders, he tells us, "included an unusually large proportion of persons of fair income, ancestral houses, and gentle blood; hospitality was abundant and the means of exercising it excellent.[8] Liquor was cheap and " . . . for a miniature and manageable assemblage of amenities I do not think you can easily beat Guernsey."[9] So he saw his life:

> . . . teaching the classics and other things to decently bred youth for hours at which even a trade union leader could hardly grumble; enjoying the bounties of King Bacchus and my Lady Venus . . . walking, whisting, waltzing; reading immense quantities of French and other literature; writing my first reviews for the *Academy* . . . "regarding the ocean" like my august neighbor and fellow *incola* M. Victor Hugo—in short, possessing almost all desirable possessions save one—to wit, money. And it was rather a comfort not to have that lest one should be in hopeless danger of Nemesis again.[10]

Given this happy capsule memoir, the picture can be filled out. Paul Stapfer, the French master at Elizabeth College during Saintsbury's first years (1866–68), in his *Victor Hugo à Guernsey*[11] defines the society—from a French vantage point—as four very distinct classes, "les *sixty,* les *forty,* les *twenty,* et les . . . rien du tout." The first of these, the nobility and the gentry, the officers of Fort George, and the "hauts fonctionnaires," admitted to their number the college masters who were Oxford or Cambridge men and foreigners of distinction. No class, Stapfer notes with amusement, acknowledged acquaintance with those below it, though even the lowest found someone to look down upon. For the college masters, acceptance afforded a pleasant social life at the top level, including that of the barracks, which Saintsbury recalled as "distinctly good"—perhaps because, to him, it seemed "college life over again" with some gambling (shilling whist and shilling loo), "plenty of fun and good fellowship."[12] Guernsey, somewhat a world apart during the period of great social and political changes in England following on the Second Reform Bill, gave a detachment that Saintsbury, in later years, regarded as both good and bad: "The looker-on sees the drift of the game more clearly, but he appreciates the motives and aims of those who take part in it less fully than the players."[13]

Saintsbury did not have the good luck to know Guernsey's most distinguished resident of this period, Victor Hugo, though on one occasion he "saw him plain" at a shop in French-speaking Saint Pierre when that eminent self-exile ejaculated to a shopkeeper who spoke French as well as he did, "Ah, Monsieur, je vien chercher des *books*, des vieux *books*."[14] Saintsbury's great admiration for the poet Hugo, which had come earlier and was permanent, he shared with Stapfer for whom Hugo was always first among French writers. Stapfer took many walks with Hugo. During the few months that his career on Guernsey overlapped that of Saintsbury, this strong bond and their talk about things French must have given fresh impetus to the young Englishman's already developed French literary interest. He was reading "more French than any other literature and more novels than anything else in French." By the end of the 1860s he was accustomed to read for style in French as in other languages, though he never spoke French to his own satisfaction.[15]

Stapfer, a good French scholar who was also interested in English literature, had taken his post to learn English, to be near Hugo, and to devote most of his time to his own writing. He was later professor at Grenoble and Bordeaux. At Guernsey, he relieved the boredom of teaching French grammar by producing *Hernani* with his older students in January, 1868, and by offering a series of outside literary lectures for young ladies. Although these met with minimal success, Saintsbury followed Stapfer's lead and the recommendation of John Oates, the headmaster, and in succeeding years at Guernsey was kept very busy (he notes eleven hours' work in one day) "with outside lectures and private coaching, not to mention reviewing."[16] Saintsbury's lectures to a Young Ladies' Educational Association were on history and logic. Some time also had to be given by a confessed nonathlete to assisting with the college sports program.

Elizabeth College, founded in 1563, had been rechartered and reopened in 1824. Its course of study stipulated "Latin and Greek in all classes ... and English Classics in all classes ... to include history (general and scriptural), rhetoric, elocution and the belles lettres. All other subjects optional...."[17] The absence of science is shocking to a modern reader.

The Reverend John Oates, who had been vice principal for eight years, became principal in 1868. A scholar of Lincoln College and an intimate friend of Mark Pattison, Oates was genial and very hospitable. Saintsbury noted his "unscholarly indolence of temper, Pattisonian flour made up into dough with milk instead of gall, its yeast unsoured by any religious conversion and soft instead of hard baked."[18] Oates presided over a relaxed and casual world, "une anarchie aimable, celle de l'age d'or ... un beau désordre et une confusion pleine de vie," according to Stapfer.[19] Some of the confusion was due to thin walls through which the noises of all classes mingled as one, a confusion enhanced by the boys' trick of releasing live crabs into the classrooms, thus producing a merry chase and a resultant caning. Despite such disorder, the school's work was of a quality that won it three scholarships in 1870, one of these at Oxford. The student group then numbered more than a hundred.

Stapfer remarks in some surprise that these boys, unlike French boys, made a "progres en sagesse"; their growth in wisdom and "la raison" corresponded to their development from children into responsible young men. He deplores the use of the cane as peculiarly English—acceptable to parents and largely a matter of indifference to the victims.[20] Saintsbury, less responsive to growing boys and more inured to the practice, says of his local military exemption (for which he paid 12*s.* 6*d.*): "One could not serve that State by caning small boys and loading and firing guns with blank cartridges at the same time."[21]

Appointed on the recommendation of a native of Guernsey, Dr. McGrath, then Fellow and later President of Magdalen College, Oxford, Saintsbury found his teaching experience there more agreeable than that later at Elgin. Always strongly in favor of the discipline of classical languages, he once offered his own scheme for that ideal "State Education in Humane Letters" which Arnold sighed for: "... the classical languages, elementary mathematics, history and geography taught in the older fashion, and modern languages within reason, but all thoroughly drummed and rubbed in from the formal point of view."[22]

As senior classical master, Saintsbury had his first opportunity to develop methods and see results. The fruit of these he presented to the Classical Association of Scotland in 1905. Giving high praise to his own Kings College School training, he specified that schoolboys should memorize large quantities of classical poetry, translate classical verse into English verse, and translate English and indeed all modern languages into Latin or Greek as well. That all such language teaching should be thoroughly "literary" was his main theme—with a placing of the authors in the history of their own literature, and with literary comparisons. Elsewhere he cites specific methods, comparison most specifically.

> You can hardly expect a boy . . . to recognize the brilliance of Meri-mée's comparison of Xenophon to Froissart. But you may lead him some way towards it by bringing out the resemblances of Xeno-phon to Scott or Kingsley, and showing him how the Retreat, if not the Advance, has all the colour, the scenery, and the dramatic arrangement, if not the character of a great historical novel.[23]

These views anticipate ideas prevalent in Saintsbury's literary histories, and they illustrate his often expressed faith in critical comparison as "the one method by which you can get at really luminous results." After such teaching, he reported, students—with no reason to ingratiate—told him that they had learned to read and enjoy literature for its own sake. Such methods, he granted, will bear fruit only with the better students, but " . . . the opportunity may always be given" and it is worthwhile "if you have the teaching of literature really at heart."[24]

Guernsey offered leisure for reading and writing. The quantity and direction of the reading he suggests in a note from 1900 where he advises a young man from age twenty-three to thirty to read until he has mastered "the best things in literature, the general range and stretch of history, the facts of politics and philosophy," making the library his university, "his tutor, his 'subject.'"[25] He was twenty-three when he went to Guernsey. Of his writing in those days, Saintsbury burned much as not good enough. One poetic sample, "Pastiche Ro-coco (Season 1870)," he preserved with the blunt estimate, "not such bad rhythm that perhaps, but quite conclusive to anyone born a critic, that he wasn't born a poet."[26] The title is a reminder of the interest in new French verse forms begun at Oxford and soon to express itself in his first reviews.

The six years in Guernsey were happy and active. Saintsbury had no complaints and social life was satisfying. He was very busy and he had begun to write. But there is a striking omission in his account. His first son, Lewis, was born on December 27, 1870 (1872?). For most men, this experience is very meaningful and worth as much comment as other things. Saintsbury records no reaction at all. One also must wonder how much of a share his wife, now busy with a young child, had in the social life he celebrates. He speaks of dancing and the "the bounties of Lady Venus" without explaining. Social life at the barracks would have been all male.

They did, however, travel together in the summer of 1869 across France and Belgium. This was the last trip he made abroad. Characteristically, he recalls an inn at Mons that offered "the most deliciously cooked mussels" he had ever eaten and an excellent Chablis; the Hotel de Musée at Waterloo, two days in Antwerp, a week at the Hotel de l'Europe in Brussels, rooms for two francs a night at Caen and at Cherbourg, and "the wilder extravagance of six francs" at Rouen. He first saw the Avon Gorge in 1870, and in 1873 made his first visit to Oxford since 1868, visiting the Creightons and taking his M. A.

The Oxford visit gave Saintsbury his first meeting with Pater who, with his sisters, was a frequent guest of the Creightons. Saintsbury does not record his reaction to Pater, but he did recall that there he first heard talk of Andrew Lang, a favorite of theirs, who was absent in the South of France fighting off a threat of tuberculosis. Creighton, whose marriage had necessitated a revision of Merton statutes (1872) for him to be retained as a clerical fellow, took orders in December of that year and, at Easter, 1875, accepted the Merton College living at Embleton on the Northumbrian coast. Having shared the excitement over *Poems and Ballads* in 1866, he continued his interest in aestheticism. He had decorated his bachelor rooms in the new style and, while on holiday, had introduced people at Falmouth to Morris wallpaper.[27] Since he was already writing for the *Guardian*, the *Academy*, and *Macmillan's Magazine*, as Saintsbury's closest friend, he became the chief means of establishing the younger man's connection with them. Saintsbury's first *Academy* review appeared on July 1, 1873; Pater's *Studies in the History of the Renaissance* had appeared in March.

Talk during the visit must have run upon aesthetic matters and upon the revival of old French verse forms and the experiments of the Parnassian poets. The tenor of the conversation Saintsbury suggests in a 1919 footnote describing an incident that took place "at the dawn of the aesthetic movement," just after Gautier's death (October 23, 1872).[28]

A visited a friend, say B, who was doing his utmost to be in the mode. A had for some time been away from the centre, and B showed him, with hopes to impress, the blue china, the Japanese mats and fans, the rush-bottomed chairs, the Morris paper and curtains, the peacock feathers, etc. But A looked coldly on them and said, "Where is your brass tray?" And B was saddened and could only plead "It is coming directly: but you know too much."

How much time Saintsbury spent in London in those years is uncertain, but visits to his mother are likely. His election to the Savile Club in June, 1874, indicates his expectation of more frequent visits. Lunching there soon after his election, he met his old Oxford friend, Henry J. Hood, who was to be the Savile's auditor for twenty years. A glance at the membership of this club,[29] where so large a share of Saintsbury's social life was to center for two decades, indicates that some of his chief contacts probably began there. Already among its five hundred members were Creighton, Lang, C. E. Appleton of the *Academy*, Leslie Stephen, T. H. Ward, John Morley, Walter H. Pollock (soon to be Saintsbury's chief on the *Saturday Review*), Frederick Greenwood, A. J. Balfour, Walter Besant, and Henry Craik. Austin Dobson, Robert Louis Stevenson, Coventry Patmore, Henry Irving, Thistleton Dyer, and Minto came in in 1874; Gosse in 1877; Henley in 1883; Kipling in 1890; and W. P. Ker in 1891. Located from 1868 to 1881 at 15 Savile Row, then at 107 Picadilly, now in Brook Street, the club had as its aim "the mixture of men of different professions and opinions" with "a thorough simplicity of arrangements."

For nineteen years, Saintsbury was to lunch here three times a week; indeed, he "scarcely passed a single weekday without crossing its threshold ... before luncheon to write letters and do odd jobs of work; after it to smoke and talk 'in the best and most orgulous manner' till one had to go to work again."[30] Walter Besant, who agrees that talk there was good, sometimes clever and amusing, characterizes

Saintsbury, one of the Saturday luncheon group, as "solid and full of knowledge, a critic to the fingertips, whether of a bottle of port, or a mutton chop, or a poet."[31]

This glimpse of club life anticipates Saintsbury's London years, but he had begun this and other important associations before settling among "the blameless and amiable Hyperboreans" at Elgin, in Morayshire, for two years.

Elgin (1874–76)

Saintsbury became headmaster of the Elgin Educational Institute, Ltd., with its inception in September, 1874, as one of several ill-fated efforts of Scotsmen to provide public schools for their sons while keeping them under home influence. "Instruction in Literature, especially English literature, receives special attention," the prospectus states. Latin and French were also compulsory, and full training for university, East Indian Civil Service Examinations, the learned professions, and "Commercial Life" were promised.[32] The founding board had taken the large, stone-built Station Hotel (in use today as the Laich Moray Hotel) for the boarding school and quarters for the headmaster and had added a series of schoolrooms along the east side.

Though perhaps doomed from the start, the experiment struggled along until 1879, when the directors, unwilling to continue at a loss, liquidated the operation. But Saintsbury was already gone. His dislike of schoolmastering had been intensified by having to supervise the boarding students in his own household, which also held two babies. He also undertook the senior English classes and all the details of administration. It proved a bad investment and cost him a good deal of his small patrimony. So, at the end of the 1875–76 school year, he resigned, thus ending "this wild goose chase," and "fled to the Press," which had already given him considerable encouragement. Since the school faced the railway station, daily trains leaving for London must have intensified this desire for flight.

This first Scottish experience had not been all bad though; on leaving he had to abandon his first library and his first "real" cellar. Grierson reports the recollection of someone who knew Saintsbury in Elgin: "If he was a success as a headmaster, he was equally a success as a guest at the dinner table, and a conversationalist."[33] His second son was born there in 1875. He remembered local people and the local countryside kindly, and he continued in his favorite avocation, solitary walking, in 1875 going "up the Findhorn and across Loch Ness and Glen Urquhart."[34] But of family life he records nothing.

Despite school tasks and some external examining done for the Bernie School near Elgin, he had leisure to continue his *Academy* reviewing and for the first of his *Fortnightly* essays. He began writing for the *Encyclopedia Britannica* (ninth edition) with an article on Samuel Butler and one on Corneille. And there was always time for reading. Here he began a "more than sporadic" study of Elizabethan literature and of a single English poet, Dryden. Both were to bear fruit shortly in book publication, though his first experience of rejection slips involved Dryden—a series of articles on that subject being refused by George Grove of *Macmillan's Magazine*. An essay on Poe, asserting him to be "of the first order of poets," met a similar fate with Leslie Stephen at the *Cornhill*.[35]

Saintsbury, continuing his interest in French literature of all periods, now began negotiations with Clarendon Press for a *Primer of French Literature*. He sent the delegates a sample chapter in November, 1876, from Elgin. The tone struck in the correspondence by this thirty-one-year-old critic who had just "thrown [himself] on the literary world for a living" is rather sarcastic and surprisingly self-confident. The first sample having proved unsatisfactory, he writes, "...if they [the delegates] are averse to the matter being rendered interesting...I could at no great trouble to myself write in a style of any degree of dryness" (Elgin, November 14th). Having sent them his *Britannica* piece on Corneille "as perhaps more to their liking," he proposes (in a December 7th letter from London) to do another sample chapter, one on the *Chansons de Gestes*. He acknowledges their asserted right of refusal and "prior right of acceptance," but claims the freedom "to consider, if occasion should offer, any propositions which other publishers may make to me for the book which I am now fully prepared and disposed to write."[36] This brash claim apparently did not antagonize the delegates, and the new offering must have proved satisfactory, because the work proceeded to the publication of this, Saintsbury's first book, in 1879.

Between these two letters, Saintsbury had spent a week or more at Embleton Vicarage on the Northumberland coast visiting the new rector, Mandell Creighton, and his wife, and no doubt gained their help and advice on his starting a journalistic career. After a brief return to Elgin, he settled his family in West Kensington, at Arundel House in Lillies Road, where they resided for a couple of years. During the autumn, his newspaper apprenticeship had begun with the *Manchester Guardian:* October 13th to 18th he had covered a Social Science Congress held at St. George's Hall, Liverpool. C. P. Scott, the twenty-five-year-old editor of the *Guardian,* had begun to shape those policies that were to give that journal its distinguished position during the next four decades. Mrs. Scott, a classical tripos at Cambridge, was in charge of the book reviewing. The literary emphasis and the presence on the staff of such men as W. T. Arnold (from 1879 on) with his special interest in French literature, R. A. M. Stevenson, novelist Comyns Carr, Richard Whiting, Frederick York Powell (another person interested in French literature), Goldwin Smith, and Creighton must have attracted Saintsbury as he settled down to write regularly for the *Guardian.*[37]

During his last year in Elgin, Saintsbury wrote a letter to Edmund Gosse, whom he had not yet met. Describing himself as "an unwilling exile" from London, he rather overpraised Gosse's *King Eric* (1876), expressed gratitude for Gosse's interest in his own critical works, then added that literary criticism was about the only occupation he cared for. "It is as much a passion with me as creative work is or ought to be with those whose vocation it is." He added his hope that, on his return to London, he would make Gosse's acquaintance.[38]

With this avowed passion came the confidence to give up the life of a schoolmaster (insecure as it had proved) and to begin twenty years of life on the London press. A gamble, by any measure, for one who had never yet earned £250 a year, who was still in debt, and now had a family of four to support. The financial details of these early years of what Saintsbury thought of as a "rather unusually hardworking life"[39] with the few human "between-the-lines" insights they afford are preserved in Saintsbury's account book. It covers his receipts for 1874 to 1932. Accounts for the first three years are summary and sketchy; those from 1877 on, precisely detailed on receipts (not expenditures), afford identification of *all* his writing, signed and anonymous, even that for which he was never paid.[40]

The decision to give up teaching was not merely an economic one or one promoted entirely by Saintsbury's literary and journalistic leanings. It involved Saintsbury's growing dislike for the job. He admits to a quick temper; very late in his life he told Dorothy Margaret Stuart of having deafened an Elgin pupil by boxing his ears with a book. His distress over the accident had been great and the troubled memory of fifty years seems relevant to the decision. One secret, as his friend put it, was that "he never really liked boys," an unfortunate fact for the father of two sons, whom he failed to educate. He speaks of his lifelong desire for a daughter, a desire shared with Andrew Lang.[41]

Little reference has been made by critics to Saintsbury's marriage or domestic life. One exception is Edmund Wilson who, on learning that Saintsbury wished no biography to be written, theorized that some domestic tragedy in Saintsbury's life had led him to transfer "his whole emotional and moral life" to literature.[42] It was a shot in the dark. The available evidence of Saintsbury's domestic difficulties or his inadequacy is not that of a great tragedy such as Thackeray's with an insane wife. Emily was probably a rather average Victorian woman, a doctor's daughter who received the typically inadequate feminine education of the time and seems not to have been able to rise to the challenge of her brilliant and energetic husband. "I never read my husband's books,"[43] she is remembered as saying, a fact that suggests one reason why Saintsbury read so enormously. His sons recalled their mother's frequent admonishing, "Don't bother your father. He's reading." Heavy habitual schedules of reading until two or three o'clock in the morning, established at Oxford, continued throughout his long career except during a couple of years of night journalism. Only weakening eyesight interfered at last. He was, he insists, not a sociable man, much as he loved wine and fine food, and not a "friend-maker," though he enjoyed his clubs both in London and in Edinburgh and the social life in Guernsey and Elgin. The prodigious literary background that reveals itself in his first published volumes (1880–82) had been accumulating steadily in the first decade of married life, solid and wide as were the Oxford beginnings. He was said to have read a French novel every morning before breakfast for eighteen years, a tale that sounds much like his own boasts about prodigious consumption made in his literary histories.

Not sharing her husband's passionate and omnivorous literary concerns, Mrs. Saintsbury was a natural subject for fears and illness. Her ailments became more and more crippling in Edinburgh, and, in the years after 1915, Saintsbury's letters to William Hunt regularly reported on "my poor Emily's troubles" with apparent sympathy. In these letters and elsewhere, he also reported her dislikes and her apparent inability to adjust to circumstances. Having bought a London house in the early 1880s, they moved, in 1887, to Reading and then into Cambridgeshire because she could not bear London. She did not care for Edinburgh or Bath, which he came to prefer of all places. He claimed to love the sea but saw little of it because she disliked it. Once transferred from London to the country, she feared loneliness as he became a commuter and was resident in London four days a week; as a result, their two sons were not sent away to school but remained at home with her.

Saintsbury's grandson George testifies that his father, Lewis Saintsbury, was "practically illiterate," a fact for which his wife blamed and bitterly resented her father-in-law. Saintsbury's other son, Christopher, suffered the same disability. Though neither one seems to have been stupid, neither ever earned a full living and both always received yearly allowances from their father. But they spent much of their early years with their mother, and they shared her pattern of chronic illness and some hypochondria. In later years, Saintsbury wrote William Hunt of the ingratitude of his grandchildren. They, in turn, recall their fear of him shared by their mother, Lewis's wife, and describe him as quite "unpaternal."

Saintsbury explained to Margaret Stuart in the 1920s that he had not sent his sons away to school because their mother pled to have them at home in Reading and that he discovered too late that the local vicar who tutored them had "taught them nothing." Though he later regretted this sacrifice, one wonders why a man so deeply concerned with education had not discovered this fact earlier. He could not have known the boys well. This failure of communication tallies with his almost never talking about them in letters. We hear almost nothing of their interests or of any shared activities before 1895. He enjoyed walking alone or with friends but so far as is known never with his sons. Their mother understandably wanted their company in Reading and in Camridgeshire, where, for a brief period until he injured his back, Lewis worked on a farm owned by Hunt. Obviously she was willing to shoulder the responsibility for the boys. As for Cambridgeshire, Saintsbury records only the fact of Lewis working and of his injury, and he describes the wine cellar he maintained there though he was there only weekends. Nothing of any other shared griefs or joys.

But what of Emily's side of the story? It was a lonely life even in London. They had, perhaps, shared a social life in Manchester. In Guernsey and Elgin she was busy caring for babies, and at Elgin there were boarding school boys in their charge. In London at first he worked nights, then no doubt kept up his constant reading. He did not like reading aloud and told Hunt that his wife read much circulating library fiction that he disliked. He says that she shared in the planning of the formal dinners they gave in London and Edinburgh (menus for some of these are in the *Cellar Book*).

If one relies only on the picture Saintsbury gives in his letters and "Scraps" of "poor Emily's troubles" in later years, one feels a sympathy for him as he nursed her for a decade while ailing himself. He seems loyally devoted to his "patient" and shows pity for her increasing helplessness—the image he chose to convey and no doubt believed in. But when one looks at the facts of their first thirty years in so far as they can be discerned, Mrs. Saintsbury begins to command respect, understanding, and sympathy for the things she coped with. These include her husband's evasion of family responsibility, his self-absorption, and his lack of the warm feeling one expects in normal family life. His very long hours of work and reading closed him off from the intimacy she probably needed, and his apparent desire to be left alone precluded any real companionship.

This speculation gets ahead of the story somewhat, but the whole picture must be kept in mind as one turns to follow Saintsbury's developing career in London. The picture is important because the evidence is so slim and scattered and has been largely ignored. Other Victorian men played the domineering paterfamilias role; they were cold and stern and avoided intimacy and expressions of affection. But of those whom Saintsbury was close to as friends—Creighton, Gosse, Dobson, Hunt, and Lang—this was not true. They had warm family ties, and, for all five of them, marriage was a close, loving relationship in which their wives were equal partners. Saintsbury observed that everyone liked and admired Nellie Gosse, an intelligent artistic individual, and he seemed to share this feeling. He perhaps even envied Gosse.[44]

Helen Waddell recorded, from his own account presumably, that Saintsbury had married and had his romance early.[45] In Manchester and Guernsey, before there were children, he says there was time for "Lady Venus." He had fallen in love with Emily's curls and girlish charms and probably, like other young men, saw his first love through a romantic haze as he did the literary heroines he adored. The silk dress he bought her in 1868 was not the only one on which he lavished artistic concern. The memory of one that never materialized lingers in his *Cellar Book*.[46] But the evidence of such interest is very slight and, in later years, wholly absent.

Edmund Wilson's guess about Saintsbury's motivations only opened the question we must pursue, but it is at least closer to the facts than a simplistic one advanced more recently by John Gross to the effect that Saintsbury's passionate pursuit of literary omniscience and his retreat into a "booklined universe" were an attempt to strike back at the university that gave him only a Second and refused him a fellowship.[47] None of Saintsbury's references to those disappointments strike such a note. He blamed himself and rarely seems to have nursed vindictive feelings or resentment. As for Wilson's speculation, we have seen that Saintsbury's escapes and evasions start very early in his life and are more complex and internal than Wilson thought. As the story further unfolds we have not yet any clue about why he rejected, perhaps feared, real intimacy and family involvement, but the fact that he did is clear.

Journalistic Beginnings (1873–76)

Saintsbury began his connection with the *Academy* with a review of Théodore de Banville's *Idylles Prussiennes* on July 1, 1873.[48] He left no room for doubt about his formalistic attitude: "the form is incomparably superior to the matter, and this fact . . . must always give it a special interest in the eyes of the instructed and critical lover of poetry." Examining the *Odes Funambulesques* and Banville's contributions to the 1869 *Parnasse Contemporain* as well as the *Idylles*, Saintsbury praised "the omnipotence and omnipresence" of Banville's art whether he was dealing with congenial or uncongenial subjects. One of the ten ballades done in the manner of Villon, the *Ballade de Banville aux Enfants Perdus* is quoted as proof of Banville's being "among the first [in rank] of contemporary poets."

Anyone still uncertain of the main interest of this new reviewer (*Academy* reviews were signed) found him even more clearly battling for his cause on August 1, in dealing with Lamartine's *Poésies Inédites*.[49] Provoked by M. Victor de Laprade's preface, which deplored the modern "importance exclusive donnée à la forme aux depens de la pensée," Saintsbury argues that Lamartine lacked the "beauty of form that is ... independent of ... casual influences," such as the sympathy between reader and writer that beauty of thought may create. Since he was "satisfied with ordinary and accepted vehicles for his thought," unlike that "impeccable poet" Gautier, he is not much read.

Without such provocation as Laprade offered, Saintsbury champions art-for-art's-sake in other reviews during 1874–76. Discussing William Cullen Bryant, he castigates critics who confuse appreciation of poetry with "a mere feeling of gratification at seeing thoughts and feelings" congenial to them given expression. Such critics are indignant at praise of Swinburne or Baudelaire.[50] Saintsbury offers a ready but startling cure for such prejudice in discussing Whitman in October, 1874: "Admiration for a creed is easily separable from admiration for the utterance and expression of that creed."[51] Whitman's ideas, distasteful as they are to the young Tory reviewer, afford slight inconvenience if one is capable of what he calls an "easy dichotomy." Since it is in his manner that Whitman's strength lies, forget the ideas and enjoy the form.

This review, extreme as its attitude is toward the relations of form and content, is important as an early recognition of Whitman in England because only William Rossetti had championed him up to that date. Whitman was well enough satisfied so that he sent Saintsbury his poems in 1876, but the *Nation* took issue with that praise.[52]

The "easy dichotomy" appears again as Saintsbury discusses a new edition of Blake. He finds Blake, in his later years, overcome by "the detestable heresy of instruction," a fatal obsession, since "a man ... once affected, whether the instruction ... be moral or immoral ... becomes careful of what he says, instead of ... how he says it; anxious to say something in any manner, rather than anxious to say everything (or it may be nothing) in the best manner possible."[53] Flaubert's famous aspiration to write beautifully about nothing is thus linked with Swinburne's "great moral heresy."[54]

The "pure art" plea resounds again in a Saintsbury review of *Bothwell*.[55] Swinburne is congratulated on his return "from that debatable land of poetical politics and theology which have diversified his literary course since 1866." Whatever good qualities the poems of the interim have had are there because "Mr. Swinburne can, as Stella said of Swift, 'write beautifully about a broomstick.'" But Saintsbury, unable to see Swinburne's liberal political loyalties as genuine poetic motivation, betrays his Tory prejudice by arguing that this treating of inferior or trivial subjects is done to conciliate "the cant of criticism," a task that had better be left to lesser artists. Having sounded his typical battle cry, the reviewer analyzes *Bothwell* and praises it handsomely while citing *Chastelard* as the poet's greatest work. Faced with Swinburne's *Essays and Studies* in January, 1875, Saintsbury again reveals his pained awareness that Swinburne had deserted the cause of pure art for politics—a fact not then clear to many others.[56]

Because Swinburne, in his Hugo essay, had deprecated the tendency of some critics to exaggerate the art-for-art's-sake approach, Saintsbury now defends the exaggeration. The critic's aim must be to see that good poetry is written and that it is "in the best possible manner appreciated." Strong convictions may lead the artist to give more attention to the conviction than to its expression; conversely, and more often, "practiced attention to form is able to surmount prejudice." The reader, too, may be swayed by prejudice in relation to subject more readily than in relation to form: he or she may, defensibly, prefer the matter of Mr. Tupper to that of Théodore de Banville, but only an idiot could prefer Mr. Tupper's form. So "there is certainly warrant for accentuating and insisting upon the art-for-art's-sake dogma. . . . It may not give us better art; it will assuredly give us better criticism and better appreciation."[57]

This quarrel with Swinburne's shifting interests points up the fact that, though Saintsbury was influenced by Swinburne's early crusade, the "separable substance" heresy, as A. C. Bradley later called it,[58] is Saintsbury's own peculiar extremism. It became, for him, a kind of art-for-art morality he never deserted, though he never admitted some of its implications as Pater and Wilde later did. At this time, Wilde was still at Oxford where the aesthetic pose was becoming popular.

Militantly, the young *Academy* reviewer, first in Guernsey then in Elgin, waged his lonely battle for the aesthetic cause while he was completing his longer and better known essay on Baudelaire. The essay had been in the process of formulation during the decade since *Les Fleurs du mal* had come to his hand.

The themes and their formulation that characterize the *Academy* reviews are all expressed in the Baudelaire article in the October,

1875, *Fortnightly Review*.[59] The study of form, Saintsbury insists, is a critical safeguard since "no mind of any power of accomplishment can ever come to the conclusion that one manner of saying a thing is as good as another." He is reluctant to treat "the relation of Baudelaire's poetry to morals"; he sees even raising the question as "a blunder and confusion of the stupidest kind." Saintsbury argues that Baudelaire requires defense because his peculiar originality has made him a kind of symbol and his name has been used steadily since 1866, even by those who have not read him, "to point any number of cheap morals."

This defense presents Baudelaire as one of "the most original . . . and most remarkable of modern French poets" and urges upon the English not only admiration but imitation of this *écrivain artiste* as "a model and stimulant" par excellence. Such writers, "the literary salt of the earth," have recognized that "writing is an art . . . and have applied themselves with the patient energy of sculptors, painters and musicians to the discovery of its secrets." Since England has too few such models, study of Baudelaire is enjoined. He also has merit as a critic because, as Saintsbury argues, "He judges much more by the form than by the matter" and hence achieves "absence of prejudice." Against possible abuse of such formal emphasis, Baudelaire's own words in *L'Ecole Paienne* are quoted to prove his sanity.

This 1875 Saintsbury essay has been recognized as one of the earliest appreciations of Baudelaire in England, its particular accomplishments being variously interpreted, though on the whole with favor.[60] Its methods afford parallels to all Saintsbury's early reviews. Baudelaire is placed within the romantic movement as the epitome of its second stage. Little attention is given to biography, but all his various types of work are described. *Les Fleurs du mal* and his other works are interpreted as a study of *l'ennui* and of all the various human efforts to avert it. Baudelaire, being gifted with superb control of his medium, achieved flexibility and variety beyond that of anyone else in his time, and, for Saintsbury, by his "quite extraordinary spirit and concentration," he records with amazing accuracy the moods of "the modern cultivated mind." Saintsbury thinks it superfluous to analyze the poetical merits of the pieces quoted as a modern critic would, though he waxes enthusiastic over the "almost endless variety of metrical and rhythmical effects" achieved in the verse and in the *Poèmes en prose*. These latter experiments he thinks are successful without exceeding the limits of their medium.

The essay has real weaknesses. Saintsbury is wrong in his assertion that French verse has but one foot, the iamb; he is inadequate in his attempt to explain Baudelaire's satanic attitudes and seems not to sense their deeper significance. But considering the date of the essay, these failures are less surprising than his positive accomplishments. The first of these is his familiarity with the whole range of works. Baudelaire would have been surprised to find his "Spleen" poems tagged as a kind of romantic "measles," but he would have liked the critic's recognition of the "depths and fullness of his passion" as far greater than that of those other eccentrics, De Quincey and Poe, who had so attracted him. The Frenchman would have been more uneasy, or even resentful, at finding the tone of *Les Fleurs du mal* dismissed as "simply a profound and incurable discontent with things in general . . . unchristian, but . . . not yet an indictable offense." He might have noted that only half a dozen of the two hundred poems are admitted to be such as "put legislators and moralists on the *qui vive*" and that for those the critic quotes Gautier's defense: they are so wise, so abstruse, and so thoroughly artistic as to be harmless. Here, the armor of a strict formalist approach protected Saintsbury from the errors of a moral critic and left him free to concentrate on the artistry. But his unphilosophical and somewhat superficial mind was indifferent to the subleties of Baudelaire's intellect and spiritual nature, and he could not wrestle with the profound ideas Baudelaire was exploring or his embracing of evil.

Saintsbury's judgments are not adequate or wholly just, and his interpretation of Baudelaire's insight into the nature of evil is not in line with modern views. But he did urge the reading of Baudelaire upon writer, critic, and general literary public in a way even Swinburne had not yet done. He concluded on the note familiar from his *Academy* reviews: the business of English artists, and especially prose writers, is to make people understand that one can "care for form apart from subject"—or, as he put it in an unconsciously revealing metaphor that comes strangely from the young father of two sons, one just born, one can enjoy the portrait of a child while still hating babies. The defense continues: Baudelaire will help the cause of true aesthetic appreciation because he offers "no line of careless or thoughtless execution, no paragraph where taste or principle has been sacrificed for praise or pay, for fear or favour, no page where the humanist and literary ideal is not steadily kept in view and exemplified."[61] One may wonder what sense the word *humanist* carried for Saintsbury, but one is certain that Baudelaire has become, for him, the touchstone for true critical judgment.

Given his temperament and the date, one must doubt that even the Turkish bath suggested by one critic would have brought Saintsbury any closer to the spirit of Baudelaire. The essay is remarkable for 1875. In England, not Swinburne, James, Gosse, George Moore, or Symons did him more justice before the turn of the century; that had to wait for Eliot and others.

Having given Baudelaire this recognition in the *Fortnightly,* Saintsbury went on, in his *Short History of French Literature* in 1882, to stress his "extraordinary merit in the way of delicate poetical suggestion and a lofty spiritualism" in his best pieces, and to praise him again as "a very accomplished critic." In 1892, he republished the essay with a few added notes but no change of view. In 1896, in a flash of insight, Saintsbury linked Baudelaire with Donne, thus anticipating T. S. Eliot by many years.[62] In 1907, he stated that Baudelaire was still not given due credit "as the great influence in French poetry of the last fifty years."[63] In 1923, he denied Middleton Murry's charge that Baudelaire and his followers disregarded content. Citing *Hymne* and *Les Enfants de la Lune,* Saintsbury described them as expressing "thoughts and feelings which one has thought and felt oneself in dumb and inorganic fashion." Despite satanic poses, he concludes, these men followed "life for life's sake" as well as art.[64] So the early championing lasted through fifty years—and Baudelaire remained, for Saintsbury, the *pierre de touche* of art-for-art's-sake as he had first presented him in 1875.

On the strength of this unsolicited essay on Baudelaire, John Morley requested one on English prose style. This essay, which appeared in the *Fortnightly* in February, 1876, while Saintsbury was still in Elgin, enlarges upon the suggestion that the English writer is in a bad way. He has little concern with style, which is defined narrowly as "the choice and arrangement of language with only subordinate regard to the meaning to be conveyed." Modern readers have been so influenced by growing scientific concerns, by the Philistine and vulgar trends of democracy, by the expanding of popular journalism, and by much novel reading that they now care chiefly for subject, not for style. Often there is no style at all, because few writers or readers recognize prose as an art "with strict rules and requirements." The novel too easily substitutes "picturesqueness" for "purely literary effect," or worse, is concerned with subject alone.[65] A few months later, Saintsbury—with some justice in relation to sections of *Daniel Deronda*—condemned George Eliot for proving that "no perfect novel can ever be written in designed illustration of a theory."[66]

In the *Fortnightly* essay, Saintsbury turns quickly from the novel to nonfictional prose. He charges that Arnold suffers from mannerism; Ruskin, from too much spontaneity and rhythms that too often become poetic; Swinburne, from the use of figures allowable only in poetry. Pater alone gives hope for the development of English prose as an art: "the subordinate and yet independent beauty of the sentences" and a "perfection of modulation," *not* ornateness, distinguish him from other writers and make him a prose master.

What then is required of the true prose artist? An ear, the study of models, and care in "the separate and subordinate finish" of sentences will give the finer style that critics should be teaching readers to demand. With this militant plea for better prose, Saintsbury anticipated Pater's essay on style by thirteen years. For its date, the essay was unique and it had its influence, though its author later observed that a good many people were feeling as he did and "their thought...impressed itself" on later prose. He himself frequently returned to consider prose style, and, in 1892, he judged his essay "rather amateurish in parts."[67] But in 1876, Saintsbury, still in Elgin, had focused attention on the formal aspects of English prose and the role of the *écrivain artiste* in a leading journal with John Morley's concurrence. Early in the spring of 1877, when Saintsbury came to London to begin his eighteen years with the press, he had the advantage that his name was already known to readers of the *Academy* and the *Fortnightly Review*.

CHAPTER 4

Art for Art's Sake and French Literature: English "Parnassianism"

> Much they talked of measures and more
>   they talked of style
> Of Form and "lucid order" and of
>   "labour of the file."
> > —Austin Dobson, "Sat est Scripsisse"

What of the other warriors in the battle for form and "pure" literature in the 1870s? The story has never been traced as fully as that of the 1890s. Swinburne, earliest in the field and most knowledgable in some respects, had deserted for other interests after he had given the spark to young men like Saintsbury, Gosse, and Lang and had sent them to the French sources. Morris, though admired by the same young men, was never sympathetic to this particular battle. The neglected story of the earlier phase of aestheticism in England, as James K. Robinson pointed out, begins "with critics like Besant and Saintsbury, translators like Rossetti, Payne, and Lang: ... a Parnassian cult of fixed French forms, headed by Austin Dobson, and a vogue of Villon translation, climaxing in the work of Payne."[1] Other key figures were Bridges, Gosse, Henley, O'Shaughnessy, and Robert Louis Stevenson.

Unlike the later generation (Arthur Symons, George Moore, Wilde, etc.), these men stopped short of admiring the symbolists and followed Gautier's pursuit of *le frisson* only in a mild concern with images of sound, scent, and color. Gosse, like Saintsbury, was uncomfortable with Baudelaire's satanism and understood it no better.[2] Though he had no particular interest in contemporary French verse, Pater must stand high in any list of early figures in the aesthetic movement because his *Studies in the History of the Renaissance,* in 1873, gave this group the doctrine of cultivation of the moment for the

57

moment's sake through art. Lang found this expressed in Gosse's *On Viol and Flute* in 1874, and he found there sweet scents as delicately and subtly traced in their "'correspondences' with delicate emotions" as they were in Baudelaire.[3] The ideal of style for them all was in Gautier's "Sculpe, lime, cisèle...," in his poem "L'Art," "the labour of the file," and his edict "La forme est tout" (*Victor Hugo* [1835]).[4]

The main bridge between these early English devotees of the aesthetic and *les Parnassiens* was Théodore de Banville, whose *Petit traité de poésie française* (reprinted in 1874) served as a handbook; his poems in the old French forms were models for the English writers more than Baudelaire's were because he set them no moral problems when they praised and imitated him. Walter Besant's *Studies in Early French Poetry* (1868) had helped to introduce English readers to Villon, Clement Marot, and Charles d'Orléans, as did Lang's *Ballades and Lyrics of Old France* (1871) and his own imitations of the French forms in the same year. Saintsbury recalls seeing Lang's efforts in *Dark Blue* before he knew him. John Payne, having dedicated his *Intaglios* (1871) to Banville, translated one of his songs in 1872 (in *Songs of Life and Death*) and met Banville in France the next year. Arthur O'Shaughnessy, meanwhile, had translated Marie de France and, in his own verse, was following the Parnassian ideal of pure form. Saintsbury reviewed O'Shaughnessy's *Songs of a Worker* in the *Academy* (August 6, 1881, 100–101).

Austin Dobson, the oldest of them all, was established at the Board of Trade at sixteen (1856) after a year in France and had been contributing lyric verse, some of it in the old French forms, to *Temple Bar* and *St. Paul's Magazine* all through the late 1860s. His *Vignettes in Rhyme* appeared in 1873. His *Proverbs in Porcelain*, the more important collection of his delicate lyrics, with its examples of the triolet, rondel, rondeau, and ballade, was issued in 1877 and evoked a letter from Banville.[5] It contained "Ars Victrix," a free translation of Gautier's "L'Art." Saintsbury reviewed it with enthusiasm in the *Academy* (June 23, 1877, 548–49).

Gosse had come to London and the British Museum in 1869 and, in 1875, transferred to the Board of Trade, a "nest of singing birds" that included Dobson, Cosmo Monkhouse, Samuel Waddington, and Théophile Marzials. He and Dobson had met in 1874, at the Pen and Pencil Club, when Gosse recognized a poem being read aloud by Dobson as a rondeau. Gerard Manley Hopkins called them "The

Rondeliers." Gosse's own *On Viol and Flute* contained rondels and one rondeau, "If Love Should Faint." The friendship of Dobson and Gosse was close. Until Dobson retired in 1901, they met almost every day, and Gosse's claim (true in the main) was that, from the time of their first meeting for the rest of Dobson's life, he saw or had read to him every line that Dobson wrote. Gosse's French could not then have been much more than elementary; also, in his first years in London, he gave more attention to Ibsen and Danish literature than to French. Nevertheless, he was quickly recognized as a champion of French literature and continued throughout his life his role of popularizer.

In the 1870s, having aligned himself with these "Rondeliers," Gosse encouraged the imitation of old French forms though he preferred French classical verse. His "Some Exotic Forms of French Verse," in the *Cornhill* in 1877, joined Dobson's more celebrated "Note on Some Foreign Forms of Verse" (an appendix to the anthology *Latter Day Lyrics* [1878])[6] as the first English attempt to define the old French forms and recommend them. Gosse's essay includes examples of the forms by Swinburne, Bridges, Dobson, and himself. The Dobson "Note" follows upon various examples, some "almost unique," as Saintsbury tells us in his *Academy* review (May 25, 1878, 455). Dobson's plea for the forms seemed "almost too modest" to Saintsbury.

> The triolet, the rondeau, and the ballade need not present themselves cap in hand...there are contemporary epics which we would give with joy for Mr. Dobson's "Rose kissed me today," or for Mr. Gosse's rondeau "If Love Should Faint"... if the British public does not like these exotic blooms, we are sorry for the British public.

Saintsbury reminds his readers that he had quoted Banville's "Aux Enfants perdus" some years earlier and urges its "value for serious poetry." The previous June (1877) he had reviewed Dobson's *Proverbs in Porcelain* with hearty praise and had quoted three triolets including "Rose kissed me today" and a rondel as having "a singular charm of urbanity and grace." As work of more substance he had cited "A Case of Cameos" and "The Prayer of the Swine for Circe." He saw them as following Banville's example in "Aux Enfants perdus" with fair success. Banville, he added with delight, is "beginning to be read in England."[7] In a letter to Gosse on his *Cornhill* essay on verse forms, Saintsbury says he had found, in Banville and his models, "a Paradise to my wearied soul for ten years or more" and now welcomes "similar delights in his own tongue" though, unlike Gosse, he will not be able to contribute examples.[8] Thus, the solitary champion of Guernsey and Elgin days joined forces with the other English Parnassians in 1877. And even he who was never a serious verse writer tried his hand at that "literary bonbon," the triolet, as we learn from a Dobson letter (1878): " ... the poor little triolet is under a cloud at present, but if we get you!" To this Saintsbury replied, "My triolets were nought and Gosse ought to have known it. But as for the triolet being out of favor—perhaps it may be with old fogies."[9] In this minor critical battle no one was more confident or insistent, no one more loyal than Saintsbury. Only in 1912 did hindsight force him to admit that there had been overproduction and excess imitation of French verse forms in the "golden" years, and then abrupt disuse of the forms.[10]

London Friendships

Settled in London in the late spring of 1877 after a few months on the *Guardian,* Saintsbury was soon acquainted with this "handful" of men. Through Creighton he had met Lang, who then introduced him to Dobson and Gosse, " ... a sort of very inferior Pléiade cut down to four, with myself for the dark star," he calls this quartet who first dined together at Lang's invitation. It was Saintsbury's first personal contact with Gosse[11] who, writing to Dobson the next day, gives a revealing glimpse of Saintsbury: " ... very interesting, isn't he, but a little feverish and perfervid. Lang ... seems very nice ... but I could not resist the 'electric' Saintsbury."[12] Lang had earlier written to Dobson, "I wish we could meet and talk rhymes, etc. ... with Mr. Saintsbury. I have asked Mr. George if he will dine with me at the Oxford and Cambridge Club on Monday, July 23, and it will give me much pleasure if you would join us and permit common tastes to take the place of an introduction."[13] Lang had reviewed the verse of Gosse and Bridges in the *Academy* in 1874.

Up to this time, Saintsbury had made few acquaintances in London, but with his Savile Club and *Academy* affiliations "a more or less loosely connected literary society came into being."[14] Lang, Dobson, Gosse, and Saintsbury were all soon frequent attendants at the Savile Saturday luncheons. Six months later, on January 13, 1878, the first of the famous Gosse Sunday evenings was held at Delamere Terrace. Among the twenty-nine guests were the Langs, Saintsbury, Swinburne, Pater and his sisters, Robert Bridges, and John Churton Collins.[15] Lang and Gosse were already writing for a number of periodicals besides the *Academy,* and Lang helped Saintsbury to get work on some of them even though, as a competitor on French subjects, he had earlier been unwilling to introduce him to the *Britannica* editor. These friendships became important strands in Saintsbury's life in London.

A substantial bulk of correspondence between Dobson (1840–1922) and Saintsbury sheds light on their friendship. For Saintsbury it was the most rewarding of all the relationships, perhaps because Dobson was the least public personality, least egotistical and his kind of poet. He refused to know politics. For forty-four years, their intimacy throve on a quiet, steady sharing of literary interests. Dobson sought and welcomed Saintsbury's criticism of his verse and gained from him much encouragement, for no one ranked Dobson higher—as minor yet "perfect in his kind," devoted as he was to the "Muse of Elegance." Regular as was their contact, Saintsbury always wished for more frequent occasions when he might hear Dobson say, *"Now,* let's talk about books."[16]

Their shared pleasure is clear as is their great confidence in each other's judgment. They never quarreled, and Saintsbury felt great gratitude for the generosity with which Dobson proposed him to edit the complete Fielding for Dent and Thackerary for the Oxford Press. It was Dobson whom he most often asked to read his early books—to evaluate the general scheme and handling. A relaxed and playful side of Saintsbury emerges in their correspondence: in the early salutation "Dear Pote" or "Dear Bard"; in his quotation of an eighteenth-century "'Chanson à boire' by a young lady,"[17] and in an illustrated letter of 1892. This last reports that he had commissioned from the ghost of Roubilliac for Dobson, "a fine marble tomb not to be used for many years with on one of its bands my family in high relief opening their mouths and you . . . casting bread into the said mouths"—to express his gratitude when Dent gave him Fielding to edit.[18] Dobson's compliments in verse to Saintsbury, written in the flyleaf of the latter's *Elizabethan Literature,* are matched by Saintsbury's "Fable" and his lines ending, "I am Dobson's choice."[19]

The Gosse-Saintsbury relationship is briefer and offers some puzzles. Saintsbury's overture from Elgin blossomed quickly into friendship, though he ceased to be among Gosse's Sunday visitors after 1878. He believed that Gosse had "a genius for friendship" while he himself did not. He describes Gosse as "extraordinarily good company" and says he could not imagine him alone. He recalls one "ambrosial" supper at Gosse's with Swinburne and Leicester Warren (later Lord de Tabley) when Saintsbury and Swinburne shared the fun of recalling "shy corners of Anderson and Chalmers."[20] Gosse (1849–1928) and Saintsbury were in "almost constant communication" from 1877 until 1895, when Saintsbury left for Edinburgh. During these years, "the Pléiade cut down to four" suffered somewhat from being tagged as such. One critic, allowing some merit to Lang and Dobson, advised his readers to "shun Gosselings and bury Saints."[21] As the focus of attack upon them intensified in the mid-1880s (led by Churton Collins and W. T. Stead), a united front helped the friendship. Saintsbury recalls many London ramblings in Gosse's company, though he remembered little shoptalk. In a letter and a postcard to Gosse (undated but probably 1878–80), Saintsbury breaks into limping verse. The postcard speaks of a slander upon himself and "a respectable newpaper whose only fault was that it happened to be full a'most to bursting," and concludes:

> Very decidedly it appears to me
> That your conduct is not nearly so much worthy of
> E.W.G. As it would be of W.E.G. [Gladstone]

The letter reflects London walks and recent press attacks:

> Oh where is the pote who indited "King Eric"?
> Where can the ghost of that good bard be?
> . . . .
> There once was a time when together a-gadding
> All parts of the town we successively sought.
> . . . .
> He helped me to lunch and he helped me to giggle
> Digestion: diversion. They came at his call.

Now unsmiling, dyspeptical I writhe and wiggle
And the little dogs bark at me, *Fraser* and all.[22]

Gosse wrote Dobson in 1880, tantalizingly, "Saintsbury is odd: such a funny experience I have to confide to you . . . ."[23] Saintsbury criticizes Gosse for saying "inconsiderate things," a not surprising charge against someone well known for his sharp tongue and one whose reputation as a gossip and tuft hunter was not unfounded. Unlike Saintsbury, who was a loner, Gosse was a collector of acquaintances, a famous host and one who had strangely intimate friendships with James, Hardy, Stevenson, and other major writers.

With Lang (1844–1912), the contact was steady during the 1880s. Together Saintsbury and Lang toiled on daily and weekly journals. Three nights a week for seven years and less frequently thereafter, they walked from the Strand to Kensington together, talking all the way. As a result, Saintsbury probably knew Lang better than anyone outside Lang's own family, and knew well "that remarkable chain . . . of 'crazes'" for which Lang was famous—Homer, Molière, folklore, Scottish history, to name but a few.[24] Delightful as talk or brief essay and more learned and less amateur than many people thought, strung out to book length, they were boring.[25]

Lang's legendary facility in composition, his versatility and range, as well as his originality, his wit, and his magnetic, languorous personal charm could and did communicate themselves to the two hundred or more volumes of writing (largely anonymous) that he poured forth so effortlessly. The inevitable charges of dilettante and amateur became harder and harder to meet as the years passed and were a growing embarrassment to his friends. Lang, the poet, always interested Saintsbury most, but by 1900 Lang had given up poetry despite Saintsbury's protests. He sensed that Lang could not or would not make "the necessary sacrifice."[26]

William Ernest Henley (1849–1903),[27] having met Robert Louis Stevenson while in the hospital in Edinburgh in 1875, followed him to London to become a journalist. Owing to Stevenson's influence, he was already a contributor to the *Britannica*, on French biography; like his friend, he was deeply interested in Italian, Spanish, and German literature. By 1877, Henley was making the acquaintance of the other four. He plunged with his typical intensity, even ferocity, into the London literary world. Wilde said he "killed by editing" the various journals he tackled. He moved rapidly from one to another with difficulties but with a gift for attracting brilliant writers to his staff (*London, Magazine of Art*, the *Scots Observer* that later became the *National Observer*, and the *New Review*). These writers were usually of his own deep-dyed Tory persuasion—Saintsbury among them. Meanwhile he free-lanced like the others for Tory journals, writing reviews that were slashing, honest, original, somewhat unpredictable—with occasional flashes of insight or foresight such as that by which he early recognized the genius of Rodin.

Henley, too, was "a balladier." He praised Banville and he tried all the French forms with technical dexterity, grace, and lightness of touch equal to that of Dobson and Lang. But he gave up verse for a decade after 1877, and by the 1890s had become one of the chief enemies of aestheticism and a jingoistic unionist in politics. A man of great energy, he was prickly but lively company and a stimulating, erudite editor who, Saintsbury testifies from his experience on *London* in his early years, did not "interfere." One could quarrel with him, as many did, but one could not dislike him.

The most original or creative among this group, and finally the most popular, much as that popularity has faded since, was Robert Louis Stevenson (1850–1894), the brilliant, gay, and intrepid young Scot, who came to London in 1875. A bit of a Bohemian, long-haired, adventurous despite ill health, he was just beginning the series of romances that Saintsbury and Lang believed would revive this form in English. It was Saintsbury who first encouraged him to publish them in book form and to go on working in that genre.[28]

Championing French Literature (1878–98)

While his fellow English Parnassians interested themselves chiefly in French verse forms, Saintsbury, once settled in London, revealed a more ambitious involvement with French literature, but one focused almost wholly on the past. He had taken to heart Matthew Arnold's 1865 injunction that English critics and English readers should know French literature, and with his proposal for a *Primer* in 1876 had begun the self-appointed task of providing the English public with all the historical facts they needed. As he did with other literary tasks later, he conceived of this one on a large scale.

While composing the *Primer* (1880) he had begun writing his many articles on French writers for the *Encyclopedia Britannica.* He was already treating French novelists in a series of eight essays for the *Fortnightly Review* (1878) and continuing his reviews for the *Academy* and other periodicals. He must soon have begun his 700-page *Short History of French Literature,*[29] because it appeared in 1882 and its companion, *Specimens of French Literature,* in 1883. Thus, in ten years, Saintsbury became the chief English interpreter of older French literature, wielding an influence, whatever its quality or direction, that has never been fully weighed.[30] He had no serious competitor, and, though only in his thirties, he brought to it a knowledge of the whole literature not matched by that of his London friends with whom he shared his enthusiasm for old French verse forms. Along with his knowledge went the conviction that no two literatures complete each other so perfectly as English and French and that they should therefore be studied together in contrast and comparison.[31] Carrying on this study and at the same time living the strenuous life of a journalist and editor, he found that it "carries one out of and corrects the merely ephemeral passages of the day" and offers "that friendship of reading . . . not the least delightful and much the safest kind of friendship."[32] He once admitted his hope that, before he died, he could read everything worth knowing in the two literatures, having begun this marathon in the 1860s with what he recognized as "a voracious acquisitiveness" and a taste "polygamous but faithful."[33] That decade of absorbing all French literature had given him the confidence to undertake the surveys; it also offered him one avenue of escape to which he turned through the rest of his life. For *Manon Lescaut,* about which he wrote eloquently in the *Primer* and *Short History,* he wrote a preface two years before his death.

In 1878, John Morley shared Saintsbury's belief that his English audience needed to know French novelists. The plan of the essays and the choice of the eight figures whom Saintsbury presented in the *Fortnightly* were proposed by Morley and Saintsbury accepted his "mild" editorial judgment as sound,[34] though he claims he would himself have included Balzac and Mérimée rather than some of the minor figures and would have preferred more analysis and criticism, less summary, and fewer chunks of translation. The intent of the essays reminds a modern reader of Edmund Wilson's *Axel's Castle* (1923), which introduced Joyce, Eliot, and Proust to a generation who found their newness strange and difficult. Morley and Saintsbury were offering Flaubert and other contemporary French novelists to an English audience largely unfamiliar with them. As Saintsbury came to realize, those readers of 1878–88 needed the summaries Morley demanded.

Saintsbury's aim becomes explicit in the Dumas essay: "Each of these writers has some special subject or style in which he is remarkable, and this is what...the critic has chiefly to look to."[35] Arthur Symons thought the essays "old-fashioned" when they were republished in 1891, but they had by then served their initial purpose for more than one generation—that of introducing their subjects. Richard Garnett reports that these essays and Saintsbury's *Primer* and *Short History of French Literature* first sent him to the French originals.[36] In breaking new ground, the going was not all smooth. Saintsbury recalls that he "'got it over the face and eyes' from proper moral men...when writing on Baudelaire in 1875 and Gautier some three years later" (*Scrap Book*, 114). The omission of Zola, the Goncourts, Maupassant, and Bourget today seems glaring, but was less so in 1878.

Of the eight novelists Saintsbury treated, five are no longer read, though perhaps Charles de Bernard and Henry Murger should be. Devoting about thirty pages to each, Saintsbury defines the special virtue of each and notes their strengths and limitations. Victor Cherbuliez, judged the least good, remains shadowy, but Charles de Bernard's invention, wit, and urbanity come through, and the many comic scenes beloved of Thackeray seem worth sampling. In one of the best of the essays, Henry Murger's sketches of Bohemian life are praised for freshness of style and humorous commonsense, and the reader is persuaded that he "deserves a place in the literature of humanity."[37] The then very popular Octave Feuillet, though given his due for dramatic quality and writing well, has his limits spelled out—"a curious sentimental compound of propriety and impropriety and an amiable weakness for excusing the sinner, and making him interesting while shaking his head very gravely over the sin."[38] Such critical insights challenged the new reader to some analysis and judgment, and Saintsbury's enthusiasm can be infectious even for a reader a century later.

The first essay, that on Jules Sandeau, makes Saintsbury's aesthetic position clear by condemning the popular English view that all

French novels deal in adultery. Sandeau, he says, presents no scandal, though he has all the artistic feelings that too often lead to the "confounding of moral distinctions, the selection of perilous and dubious subjects, the subjection of everything to the *culte féroce du beau.*" His fiction should destroy the cherished delusion that to praise the art of the writer is a cunning cloak intended to hide a taste for immorality.[39] Here *Fortnightly* readers could recognize the voice of the writer of the earlier essays on Baudelaire and English prose style. Of the three essays on more major French writers, Dumas, Gautier, and Flaubert, each has its special significance.

Despite his vast popularity and his ephemeral quality, Dumas is, for Saintsbury, one of the masters of nineteenth-century fiction and Scott's chief successor. His essay tendered Dumas the first real English appreciation since that of Thackeray.[40] Dumas offers no difficulties to a reader, and of the 250-odd works, none may survive, but previous criticism had in no adequate way defined his powers as Saintsbury saw them: his ability to engineer a novel, his great "secret of making dialogue express action," his lifelike characters and very human passion, and that skill in creating suspense that outweighs his prolixity and his lack of Gautier's "incomparable literary faculty." The essay concisely defines Dumas's claims upon any reader today as it did a century ago.

In all these essays Saintsbury declared himself "a devotee of 1830." This devotion dominates the Gautier essay: his "ardent admiration for beauty . . . saved him from all the uglier faults of immorality" and his "early and Herculean study of style" made him able to write with consistent artistry on any subject with but one negative result, that his subjects are often inferior to his treatment.[41] *Mademoiselle de Maupin* is termed one of the "sacred books" of the cult of beauty. It would be difficult to find a "Bowdler" for "our Madeleine," the critic confesses, but those who "can reject the evil and hold fast the good . . . will take her as she is and be thankful."[42] For *La Morte Amoureuse,* Saintsbury gives an extensive translation and no analysis, though he judges it the finest of Gautier's tales.[43] A long summary of *Le Capitaine Fracasse* conveys its strange magic and the irony that Saintsbury relates to that of Heine, Thackeray, and Baudelaire but finds more playful than theirs.

This essay has been assumed to be Saintsbury's first writing on Gautier, but the death of Gautier on October 23, 1872, had evoked several obituary tributes in English periodicals. Strong internal evidence indicates that Saintsbury wrote the anonymous one in the *Cornhill Magazine* in February, 1873.[44] It must therefore be taken into account though Saintsbury had had an essay on Poe rejected by the *Cornhill*.

Writing in Guernsey, in Hugo's very shadow, Saintsbury (assuming it is he) sets Gautier firmly in the Hugo circle—the young or "petit cénacle." A sketch of the romantic movement tracing its stages in literature and art is followed by a vivid paragraph depicting the hero Théo at the *Hernani* premiere of 1830, in "the fiery scarlet waistcoat" that was to become "the mystic type and legendary banner" of the second phase of the romantic movement.

Borrowing Sainte Beuve's distinction between the popular Gautier and the true artist, Saintsbury traces the pursuit of beauty and sensation, "the perpetual research" with which these "precious" young men (Gautier, Gerard de Nerval, Petrus Borel, etc.) exhausted themselves before they were twenty. "Art for art, and nothing but art, that is the instinctive law of the school." The dangers of such pursuit, Saintsbury reasons, are not an utter corruption but a descent into "vulgar voluptuousness," a retreat from the ideal that can be achieved only in great art or imagination and a descent into that reality of vulgar luxury that Gautier found in the Second Empire while he remained indifferent to social and political concerns. The writer commends to his English readers' attention Gautier's early mastery of poetic form, his command of "le mot propre" and the enrichment of the language to which he contributed, his devotion to the quest for beauty and to the revival of the intricate measures of the old lyric poets of the Pléiade, and "his lightness, precision, vivid pictorial and descriptive exactness." Thus, on many points, the memoir parallels Saintsbury's views expressed elsewhere.

Despite all this praise the writer does equivocate in a way Saintsbury rarely does in his statements of loyalty to art-for-art's-sake. He admits that the subjects of *Albertus* and *Mademoiselle de Maupin* are "according to English standards utterly intolerable." He grants that if Hugo has "a sounder vitality, higher strength and range . . . a larger atmosphere" than Gautier, this may prove that art that includes politics and humanity is greater than art without them. The editor of the *Cornhill*, Leslie Stephen, would have agreed with this qualification, and it is not unlike the view expressed in the *Academy* obituary by

G. A. Simcox.[45] In his 1878 essay, Saintsbury emphasized Gautier's wholly unpolitical temper and granted that he was "morally lax" though seldom heartless. He spoke of him as a moral tonic as compared with many later writers, then apologized for this departure from the purely literary view.[46]

The *Cornhill* eulogy represents great praise for Gautier, and Baudelaire is cited without reproach as one who carried out "with absolute completeness his maxims of 'art for art.'" Its writer is fully aware of Gautier's major initiatory role in the aesthetic revolt, a role Swinburne had also recognized. Whether he wrote this essay or not Saintsbury stands alone in English criticism in his long championing of Gautier that climaxed in his Taylorian lecture of 1904—a fact that argues strongly for his being accepted as the author of the *Cornhill* obituary.

Curiously, the famous preface to *Mademoiselle de Maupin* was not discussed in either of the 1870s essays, but, in 1904, Saintsbury gave it major attention from a new perspective. Defending Gautier against his decriers (Faguet and Planche, chiefly) and against increasing neglect, Saintsbury hails the preface as "a great literary and critical document . . . an argued defense of the principles of a very great part of modern criticism." He again cites Gautier's unique charm, "the marriage of dream and reality" and a "quiet . . . yet desperate perfection" and defends the overworked literary journalist. To the old complaint, lack of ideas, he replies, "How many people have ideas . . . the really great ideas?" Gautier, he adds, had his due share.[47]

By modern standards Saintsbury overvalued Gautier and was fighting a lost cause; his hope that Gautier's loss of popularity was merely temporary proved vain. But his loyalty reminds one of Gautier's pivotal role in the aesthetic movement, and his repeated exalting of Gautier, an attitude George Moore shared for different reasons, must have influenced some English readers.

The last of Saintsbury's 1878 essays was, no doubt by design, that on Flaubert—the longest, the best, and the only one the author retained in his *Collected Essays*.[48] The main purpose of the series is evident as he points to Flaubert's unpopularity and faces the need to initiate the reader into what he thinks is "exquisite literature . . . but not perfect fiction." He repeatedly warns that one must read and reread before the initial, often repulsive "nervous impression" gives way to pleasure in the excellence of treatment. Citing his own experience, he offers a skillful extended critical summary of each work. The results could still serve their original function for today's reluctant reader, especially the section on *Trois Contes,* the three fine examples in miniature of Flaubert's several styles.

One is not surprised that "determined and conscientious patience of workmanship" and concern for style are the chief points of Flaubert's work emphasized by Saintsbury. "He can do with a couple of epithets what Balzac takes a page of laborious analysis to do less perfectly." The essay develops the theme that Flaubert, by uniting the real and the ideal, "the material accuracy of a photograph and the artistic accuracy of a great picture," achieves true realism. By idealizing, this "most impersonal and passionless of writers" shows that the real does not have to be the unideal although he has the rare courage to depict failure objectively.

Madame Bovary is analyzed with much insight, but the discussion offers nothing new on this novel, which has been the subject of so much searching criticism since. Saintsbury compares Emma to Manon Lescaut to point up Emma's total lack of a redeeming passionate desire and sees in her only feminine snobbery. With regard to her deathbed, he suspects Flaubert may have been tempted to point a moral; if so, this is "a painful . . . lapse into the heresy of instruction on the part of a faithful servant of art." One must go elsewhere for psychological analysis.

The other Flaubert of fantasy and mystical romance Saintsbury rates highest and here he is most valuable. *La Tentation de Saint Antoine* is "the best example of dream literature" he has met and Flaubert's greatest achievement. In *Salammbô,* with all its exotic richness, "the power and the art grow on one strangely" but only after several readings. Thus, Flaubert's varied genius is interpreted with constant emphasis on his artistry and his poetic imagination. Flaubert expressed pleasure in the essay.[49]

Elton (in 1933) and Wellek (in the 1960s) both remarked that few readers would now follow Saintsbury on such obscure trails as the majority of the 1878 essays represent, but, for their time, they served well the purpose he and Morley were agreed upon, one that Saintsbury's steadily increased reviewing and his literary histories also served—broadening English readers' knowledge of all French literature and encouraging them to read it, making it accessible and attractive.

Saintsbury's eighteen years on the London press produced a great number of reviews on French subjects. For the *Manchester Guardian* he rarely handled French works, but among 235 signed reviews for the *Academy*, one to three each year were on French topics; likewise, of the 196 anonymous reviews done for the *Athenaeum*, a vast majority were on French topics—single works at first, then increasingly composite surveys of three, four, even a dozen books briefly noted. Also from 1880 on, in the *Saturday Review*, he was dealing, again in weekly or monthly surveys, with "almost everything notable (and a great deal hardly worth noting) that had appeared in France."[50] The *Athenaeum* reviews are identified in the records. *Saturday Review* records are gone, but Saintsbury's claim may be taken at face value. As editor, he occasionally assigned a French work to someone else, but it is easy to spot his hand. The importance of these many composite surveys is not in the quality of the criticism, it is too slight for that, but in the fact that one insistent English voice was regularly pointing out what in French literature was available to English readers and judging it, however briefly. The reviews are routine except for an occasional rare flash of insight.

These reviews afford a view of then current English taste. The vogue for French fiction produced a flood of translations more bad than good, and Saintsbury suffered through dozens of them, major, minor and wholly ephemeral. The reviews show skill in rapid summary and brief, decisive judgment, and they do not overpraise: for example, "not great but amusing," "could not be read twice," or "usually writes well." *Germanie Lacerteux* is "unrelieved by passion, unheightened by tragic incident." Translations of French biography, memoirs, collections of letters, and historical works became increasingly popular and were noted. The sheer bulk was immense and Saintsbury waded through most of it—damning some and praising too much in his vast tolerance. Occasionally, even his immense patience was worn out—notably by the indefatigable Catherine Charlotte, Lady Jackson and her several two-volume histories of the French court, and to one's relief he explodes, "She has no knowledge and could not write about it if she had."[51]

Readers who accepted the guidance of these surveys were spared a great deal of mediocrity and worse. And, in the longer reviews of single works, not all was pedestrian. They would have got their best guidance from Saintsbury's handling of critics—if they accepted the assumption that criticism should be "purely literary."

For example, in 1878, Saintsbury welcomed Henry James on French novelists as a "critic of life" but not of "pure literature."[52] He considered Edward Dowden thoughtful but inadequate on modern French verse.[53] He praised Bourget's treatment of Flaubert as a romantic and his giving attention to Stendhal, who is "anything but well known here as he ought to be."[54] In 1879–80 essays in the *Fortnightly* on Saint Evrémond and Renan,[55] he praised the first as an "exponent of *Gout*" but found Renan, in his concern for moral questions, too much a "critic of life" and one who lacks "absolute catholicity . . . the first requisite of a literary critic."[56] He discussed Edmond Scherer four times in the *Athenaeum* and several times in the *Saturday Review* (anonymously) before translating his *Essays on English Literature* in 1891. The translation was prompted by his belief that these essays were the most valuable in either language since Sainte-Beuve's *Causeries*. In 1878, he recommended Scherer as "the most acute and capable critic now living" despite his subject matter prejudice and an inability to appreciate what he does not like. In 1891, he recommended him to English readers as a corrective for the ill-formed "dogmatism" and "the aesthetic eccentricities of modern English criticism."[57] These judgments anticipate or parallel his treatment of these critics in his literary surveys with no serious change in judgment. He does not betray the fact that Scherer attacked him in 1887.

To sum up, through Saintsbury's reviews, mostly anonymous, the English reader of at least two major periodicals was getting an inclusive view of current French literary publication, a view informed, purely literary, guardedly moralistic, but strongly antididactic, providing some antidote to the moralizing of a Robert Buchanan or the *Spectator,* which, in 1892, found Saintsbury guilty of "indifference to the underlying unity of art and morals" with an echo of "the nearly obsolete cant of the Boulevards during the Second Empire."[58] Saintsbury's influence must, by sheer repetition, have had an impact upon English provincialism at a time when even Arnold condemned the young men of the 1880s who placed French literature on a par with ancient Greek for their "Gallomania." This influence was reinforced by his work for the *Encyclopedia Britannica*.

Saintsbury had already written three articles for the *Britannica,* those on Samuel Butler, Daniel Defoe, and Pierre Corneille, when he settled in London. Lang's fear of his rivalry was soon justified as Saintsbury came to do the major share of the articles on French authors for the ninth edition (1875–89).[59] *Britannica* policy in the ninth and eleventh editions, that of having each topic treated by an identified authority, allowed for individual opinion and feeling. The results were more diverse and more lively though less objective than those of the fourteenth edition (1929), with its "scientific" policy of impersonal schematic treatment. Twelve of Saintsbury's articles were republished in 1946 in a volume entitled *French Literature and Its Masters,* with an introduction and supplementary biographies by Huntington Cairns.[60] He thought Saintsbury was without peer as a systematic expositor of French literature to the English public, one who, though a scholar, wrote for a wider public, as he had indeed done with his eye on that body of new readers of French literature he was helping to create in the 1880s.

These articles avoid speculation; they touch briefly on scholarly interpretations and strike a balance between extreme views. Judgments show familiarity with the subject and a sureness of touch while occasionally betraying his bias (personal rather than typically English as some have characterized it): Gautier is "the most perfect poet in point of form that France has produced"; Boileau's poetry is not "in strictness, poetry at all"; Corneille is superior to Racine, who "does not attempt the highest poetry at all" and shows "defects of universality"; Baudelaire "by his choice of unpopular subjects and the terrible truth of his analysis, revolted not a few of those who . . . cannot take pleasure in the representation if they do not take pleasure in the thing represented."[61] Concern for the reputation of a writer is frequent as is comparison with English writers. Nicholas Gilbert is "the French Chatterton, or perhaps rather, the French Oldham"; Jean de Rotrou, "the French Marlowe."[62] His comment on the sources of the Reynard legend is typical of Saintsbury's dealing with controversial issues.

> It is sufficient to say that the spirit of the work seems to be more that of the borderland between France and Flanders than of any other district, and that, wherever the idea may have originally arisen, it was incomparably more fruitful in France than in any other country.[63]

Thus lighthanded is the dismissal of tomes of scholarly argument!

The bibliography accompanying the 1879 *Britannica* entry "French Literature" reveals how little secondary material was then available: no survey in English except that of Henri Van Laun, which Saintsbury had already shown to be inadequate and critically unsound,[64] and some material in Hallam, Buckle and Carlyle. There were few complete surveys in French, the most reliable being Sainte-Beuve's *Tableaux de la littérature de seizième siècle* and those of Demogeot and Geruzez.[65] Some of Demogeout had been translated into English. Many of the best editions of French writers were the product of the 1870s and 1880s, and Saintsbury acquired many of them.[66] He worked with the printed sources (never with manuscripts) and adhered to the principle he thought it necessary to state in the preface to his *Short History* and elsewhere that he would not give an opinion of any work or author unless he could speak from firsthand experience. This assertion, first made three years before Churton Collins accused Gosse of doing just that with Sidney's *Arcadia,* makes one wonder where the question had been raised and why it made him so defensive. He defended Gosse strongly and repeated his own claim in the preface to his *Elizabethan Literature.*

The tone in the *Britannica* articles is appropriate for the mature reader in search of essential detail rather than the young student. The articles on individuals offer more extended analysis and evaluation and, therefore, judgments seem less arbitrary, more qualified, and more clearly defined than in Saintsbury's historical surveys. One can still turn to them with profit for facts, for a clearly expressed, careful judgment, and for critical insights. Those on La Fontaine and Lesage are good examples; on Rabelais he is most eloquent (as always) and still useful despite a century of scholarship since. The general survey of French literature is a masterful mind map and a readable one.

The *Primer of French Literature,* with its 138 small pages, is only slightly longer than the *Britannica* survey; it was to serve as an introduction to the *Short History* as the *Specimens of French Literature* (1883) was to be its illustrative companion volume. Together they filled a national need as they gave many students their first introduction to the subject.

The tone and emphasis of the *Primer* are elementary; at times the style is awkward and oddly nationalistic, even silly, as the writer strains to explain: for example, "At the first ladies play but a small part in these *chansons* though afterwards it is different" or "assonance is what occurs when writers who do not know what they are about try to write English poetry." The style of later sections seems more mature. The frequent comparisons to English writers are often qualitative: for example, Molière is compared unfavorably to Congreve as to verbal wit.

The *Primer*'s conclusion much too hopefully predicts that students with eight hundred years of literature briefly set before them, are to see

> how far the literary utterances of a people correspond to their national character, what tendencies in the long run assert themselves . . . how far foreign influence can decide the intellectual and artistic development of peoples, how far consummate individual genius can produce perfect work against what may be called the national grain.[67]

This ambitious emphasis on the national and international aspects of French literature could barely be hinted at in the brief text. If Saintsbury believed he had demonstrated all these things, he was satisfied with very superficial generalities. In his efforts to achieve his goal, major figures are passed over lightly on the questionable assumption that they would be known to the reader. Equal space tends to suggest equal importance, as with Flaubert and his minor contemporaries, and students get little help in determining relative value or significance and little sense of quality. It is the first of many instances of Saintsbury's aims and intentions far outreaching his results, something he seems never to have realized. Despite these limitations, the volume, unique as it was, proved useful and was a commendable beginning. It ran to six editions.[68]

The *Short History* reversed the method of the *Primer* to deal more fully with the greater names. Since he was writing "for purposes of education chiefly," literary comment is subordinated to factual information. Covering French literature from its beginnings to 1880 in about seven hundred pages, this pioneer survey establishes a pattern Saintsbury followed with slight variations in the parallel *Short History of English Literature* (1898) and other surveys. Treatment of each period is by a method suitable to its character, for example, the medieval by forms, the Renaissance by authors. Interchapters give "the general lines of development" and generalization is pretty much confined to these.[69]

Saintsbury, the "first master of the short history," in Adam Blyth

Webster's phrase, had a clear conception of his work when he began. The title is derived from John R. Green's *Short History of the English People* (1869–74). Though many of Saintsbury's theoretical statements regarding literary history and critical theory were made later, his practice does not alter. The essentials are all here. Though with greater scope than the *Primer* or the *Encyclopedia* survey, this, too, was conceived of as a "literary mind map" or atlas, something Saintsbury believed essential for any informed, intelligently critical reader. The aim is accuracy, as much completeness as possible, and a "definite standpoint" to unify the whole.[70]

This "standpoint," explicit in the conclusion, expands that quoted previously from the *Primer*. The key terms in both are development, national and foreign. French literature is "the most complete example of a regularly and independently developed national literature," illustrating "spontaneous literary development with few breaks or dead seasons in its course." Resistant to foreign influence, it nevertheless showed "remarkable power of assimilation." The spirit of criticism and attention to form being more continuously present than in any other literature, it gives "the spectacle of not unreasonable difficulty skillfully overcome, in a game . . . well-played." French is "the best vehicle of expression in prose among European languages," but "the very genius of the language—the clear, sober, critical *ethos* of French" is, regrettably for the romantic Saintsbury, "*an enemy to mystery, to vagueness, to what may be called the twilight of sense—all things more or less necessary to the highest poetry.*" The italics here are mine, not Saintsbury's; the bias is his. One application of this limiting view is his denial of lyricism in La Fontaine, which Paul Bourget challenged.[71] Saintsbury did not improve matters in the second edition when he stated: "La Fontaine yet has too little of dawn or sunset, still less of twilight or moonlight, too much of the light of common day to deserve . . . the title of poet in the highest degree."

The parallel to Arnold's famous judgment that Dryden and Pope are classics not of English poetry but of its prose immediately springs to mind.[72] Saintsbury does not deny La Fontaine the title of poet, but he does deny it to Boileau-Despréaux. A general, comparative, "international" judgment follows.

No French writer is lifted by the suffrage of other nations . . . to the level of Homer, of Shakespeare, or of Dante, who reign alone. Of those of the authors of France who are indeed of the thirty [greatest] but attain not to the first three Rabelais and Molière alone unite the general suffrage.

Of such rankings Saintsbury was too fond, and critics today would dismiss them.

With such assumptions the French might well quarrel, but they would know where the author stood and where he was leading English readers. They could also expect ample fact, little speculation, little scientific or pedantic jargon, and no "parade of systematic theory." This is a literary, not a social, history, but it *is* a history, *not* a series of *causeries*. It focuses on the texts; "the thing is important in literature, not the man."[73] Biographical facts never appear for their own sake. The author's aim, the result, and the direct effect on the reader are the central facts. The question is always, in Hugo's phrase, is the work good or bad?[74] Saintsbury believed he brought to this what he demanded of any true critic: real enthusiasm for literature, catholicity, and sufficiently broad knowledge to make comparisons frequent. What he did not bring was a concern with ideas. Reputation, influence, and sources are noted as of some historical importance but are kept apart from critical evaluation. Minor figures are considered historically significant because they are often more representative than major ones and give clues as to what will follow. Form is of primary interest as one has come to expect: for example, Montaigne's style, not his sentiments or subjects, are focused upon.

Saintsbury's attitude toward development here (as later) is a practical, commonsense compromise: he accepts traditional terminology without defining; he rejects rigid causation and prefers a broad sense of "the man and the hour," the effects of the slow maturing of language, the drift of "skiey influences" by which genius satisfied the desires or needs of its time.

A good illustration of his whole method is his handling of Rabelais, on whom he is always at his best. Untroubled by the master's coarseness, Saintsbury places him among the greatest. How do the other French masters fare? Racine—so often a fatal test for English taste—has always been cited as Saintsbury's major blind spot. In the *Primer* he fails to rate him highly; he complains of endless talk in the plays and grants only that he was "one of the most industrious and careful writers."

In the *Britannica* articles and his *Short History,* he reveals why he failed to understand greatness that he nevertheless could not deny. He sees Racine as a slave to his society, one who made lovemaking the staple of his plays because it "would draw where moral grandeur would not." Saintsbury, who usually condemned reading of motives and confusion of the moral and the aesthetic, is guilty of both faults here. On the more purely literary question, he sees Racine as a great artist but one who does not attempt the highest poetry and is hampered by "the defects of stereotyped mannerisms." What he fails to appreciate is more serious. He is deaf to the sweep of passion and the bursts of literary power and fails to grasp the intricate and subtle weighing of motives and states of feeling that reveal Racine's profound grasp of life.

This critical failure should not be overemphasized since the range of sympathy in the *Primer,* the *Short History,* and the *Britannica* articles is great. As a whole, a sense of proportion is maintained, and there is clear, just weighing of merits and faults even where a man's thought or personality is unsympathetic (e.g., on Rousseau), and a real ability to define briefly the quality and rank of even very minor figures (e.g., Charles d'Orléans, Clement Marot, and Madame de la Fayette). The brief summing up of developments in forms and language (in the interchapters) shows skill, and where knowledge is limited (as on the seventeenth-century heroic romances), the reader is warned. All this until he reached the naturalists, where his bias dominates and blinds him.

The immediate reception of the *Short History* in 1882 was encouraging. The *Saturday Review,* however partial, declared Saintsbury's knowledge "unparalleled among English men of letters." The reviewers only regretted the austerity of the work, its avoidance of anecdotage, and its being unfair to Zola and Daudet.[75] More significant were the judgments of two French authorities, Paul Bourget and Gaston Paris.[76] The latter approved the author's giving the Middle Ages more attention than is usual. "*Judicieux,* intelligent, *large d'esprit*... 'clever,'" Paris calls the work that Bourget praises as a masterpiece. Bourget wished to see it translated into French for use as a student text, but he did question the lack of emphasis on intellectual history. In his view, French judgment would disagree with Saintsbury's only in rare instances. Henley mixed praise and censure. The *Encyclopedia* series, he noted, "alone represents the labor of an ordinary lifetime," but in the *Short History* the author overestimated "the gods of his idolatry"—Mérimée, Gautier, and Hugo.[77]

Thus heralded, the *Short History* went through three editions in seven years without serious competition; by 1887, when Scherer made his acrimonious attack upon it, Saintsbury had further established his authority by editing various French classics. Scherer charged that he represented a national superficiality, lack of historical method, and inadequate knowledge.[78] Just why Scherer, who had been praised by Saintsbury a number of times, waited six years to attack his work is a mystery, but it has been suggested that Churton Collins persuaded him to do it. This would not account for the unwarranted national sneer. Clearly he wanted more adequate knowledge of moral and intellectual elements and a historical method closer to his own. As for specific errors cited, Saintsbury quietly corrected them. He wanted to make French writers accessible to students and he certainly began the process. These surveys have been superceded and students today are sent to French language sources, but for several decades they served their purpose.

The first French classic Saintsbury edited was Lesage's *Gil Blas* in 1881. The introduction, one of his longest, is something of a model— not for originality but as right for its English audience at the time, who knew little of Lesage. Enlivened by anecdote, the essay, though it assumed the work to be better known than it was, emphasized the realistic, vivid character drawing and its universality. Saintsbury neglected the organic unity in construction that later critics stress but praised the style as vigorous, simple, and brisk. Seeing Lesage as "not especially French at all," he thinks that English judgment of him could be less prejudiced than French or Spanish. He credits him with wit but not with the humor of those who have more sympathy or a wider grasp of the world, such as that of Shakespeare, Fielding, Rabelais, or Montaigne. He included useful discussions of Lesage's minor works because he believed they had suffered from secondhand judgments. Faithful to art-for-art standards, he finds Lesage free from the teaching heresy and argues that, since he depicts ugliness and vice, he is more instructive and refreshing than any "rose-pink pictures" of life and offers a corrective for the naturalist school.[79]

The Clarendon Press, having issued the *Primer, Short History,* and *Specimens of French Literature,* commissioned Saintsbury to edit a number of classic texts in the early 1880s. These were *Selections,* to serve as introductions for students, from Sainte-Beuve's *Causeries du lundi* and Quinet's *Lettres à sa mère* in 1885, from Gautier's *Scenes of Travel* in 1886, also a series of French theater classics for which Saintsbury wrote essays on comedy and tragedy.[80]

Saintsbury translated the text of five French works that he edited: Scherer's *Essays* (1889), Mérimée's *Chronicle of the Reign of Charles IX* (1890), Madame de Stael's *Corinne* (1894), Balzac's *Les Chouans* (1889), and Marmontel's *Moral Tales* (1895). Like the bits of translation that appear in his essays and histories, these read idiomatically, even gracefully, and seem accurate. Arthur Symons found the Scherer translation almost flawless.[81] The *Manchester Guardian* reviewer greeted Saintsbury's translation of *Les Chouans* as a "godsend" and termed Saintsbury a "model translator" with "an exact knowledge of the language, a critical appreciation of style, and an unusual power of reproducing even its minuter shades."[82]

Saintsbury's own views on translation are expressed in scattered places. A translation, being only "a way to the original,"[83] should be faithful, but not so much so that it deceives readers into thinking they have the original. Its "vital qualities" depend less on faithfulness than upon "the spirit and the vigour of the phrase . . . the gusto and character of the version"; it should produce the effect that the original produced on its reader, as he felt Florio's Montaigne did despite inaccuracies.[84] In reviewing translations from the French, Saintsbury deplored the too faithful, the literal, or "dogged," the version "without elegance of spirit," and the translator who ignores the secret of translation—the breaking up of French sentences, essential if the result is to be "neither unfaithful nor ungainly."[85]

Perhaps the most popular of all Saintsbury's early editings was the small, attractive, parchment-bound *French Lyrics* (1882). Directed to a wider audience than the student texts, it went into many editions, and thus did its share in shaping the taste of new readers of French verse. He defined lyric poetry as verse meant to be sung. The brief introductory history of the French lyric reflects Saintsbury's prejudice that the iamb is the only foot to which French really lends itself. He praises the Parnassians for having made it "impossible for France ever to return into the Malherbe-Boileau dungeon, where the lyre was an instrument forbidden under pain of instant transformation into a Jew's harp."[86] His claim that many English critics deny the highest place to French lyric poetry reminds the reader of Arnold but also of such French critics as Sainte-Beuve and Renan who grant that French is less poetic than English. This almost traditional view was hardly to be upset in England within the nineteenth century and not by Saintsbury certainly or Gosse.[87]

The contents of *French Lyrics* are predictable from Saintsbury's earlier enthusiasms: forty-one pages of lyrics before Villon; no Racine or Corneille; two eighteenth-century drinking songs; nine lyrics by Hugo; from Gautier, four; Baudelaire, one; Banville, four including the "Ballade aux enfants perdus."

Saintsbury continued the editing of major French texts with obvious pleasure to the end of his life. The last was his preface for Helen Waddell's translation of *Manon Lescaut* in 1931. In the 1890s came one of his best, the *Heptaméron*, also Florio's Montaigne, Marmontel, and the oddest, the forty-volume Balzac (1895–98). So much of what he says is paralleled in the Histories, all do not require comment. But the *Heptaméron*, the sixteenth-century collection of tales by Margaret Angoulême, the Queen of Navarre, held a great fascination for Saintsbury,[88] and he transmits its power even to present-day readers. For a five-volume edition in 1892, he wrote a long historical essay and a brief, graceful preface presenting the work as the epitome of the Renaissance spirit and linking the writer to other key figures—Montaigne, Spenser, Raleigh, Donne, and the Pléiade. He defines the "special virtue" of the work as this unifying spirit, the peculiar paradox, " ... the fear of God, the sense of death, the voluptuous longing and voluptuous regret for the good things of life and love that pass away." He spells out some of its contradictions and vividly conveys the pervading tone and mood. He maintains that, despite internal evidence that she had professional assistance, these tales are the Queen's own and that, as modern editors agree, they are the source of the work's superiority. The preface deserved the reprinting Oliver Elton gave it in *Prefaces and Essays* (1935). To make works of such charm accessible was always one of Saintsbury's chief motives.

Marmontel is a second-rate writer without the charm or passion of the *Heptaméron*. In editing his *Moral Tales*, Saintsbury had another motive. He quoted Sainte-Beuve on the importance of minor figures and offered the tales as "the very epitome of the eighteenth century in France." He prepares his English readers for this special climate with its floods of tears, the frequent invoking of *ma mère*, and its tolerance of vice,[89] a critical job he had begun in 1882 in his essay

"A Study of Sensibility"[90] and continued in one on Alexander Hamilton in 1888. "A Study of Sensibility" is still a valuable guide to that "odd mixture of vanity, convention and sensuality" or "literary bric-a-brac" that ranges from *La Princesse de Clèves* through Marivaux to Xavier de Maistre and Constant's *Adolphe*. One need not read it all, Saintsbury maintained, but one must understand the rules of the game if one is to understand the genesis of more important related things: Jane Austen's Fanny Price, *La Nouvelle Hèloise, Manon Lescaut, Werther,* Chateaubriand, and even Byron.

By modern critical standards, Madame de la Fayette and Marivaux are not done full justice. Though Saintsbury gives Madame de la Fayette full credit for the wit and pathos that deepened, intensified, and thus transformed the dull Scudéry romance, he neglected or did not feel the unifying pessimism and sense of reality that give *La Princesse de Clèves* its importance. In his preoccupation with *marivaudage* and his reluctance even to use the word *psychology* he underrates Marivaux's concern with *la vie intérieure* though he sees *Adolphe* as "leading to Beyle and all the later analytical school." He failed to see how much the inner conflicts in character are focused upon, evident as this focus is in his quotations, a failure parallel to his neglecting the interest in inner consciousness in his English contemporaries—Dickens, Eliot, Meredith, and James. But the insights he did have and his lively and sympathetic effort to make these works more accessible even at second hand when they deserved no more than that justify his having preserved them in *Essays on French Novelists* and again in his *Collected Essays* as he did those on the minor English romantics.

He first performed the function of critic covering things the general reader need not read (thus giving what might be termed "limited access") in an article in *Fraser's Magazine* in October, 1879, "French Tragedy before Corneille, Playwrights from Jodelle to Corneille." Also in "A Frame of Miniatures," a sketch of very minor, eighteenth-century versifiers, he presented the epigrammatic Vadé and Peron; Panard, a writer of spontaneous drinking songs; and other literary "butterflies." Similarly, in 1878, he wrote on Edgar Quinet to share his reading of the twenty-six-volume works. Though he could find not one to recommend, he was intrigued by a man of first-class talent who failed because of the perpetual contradictions produced by his thinking radical and feeling conservative.

The French author most usually associated with Saintsbury is Honoré de Balzac, probably because he provided for each of the forty volumes of the English edition of the *Comédie Humaine* a brief preface and bibliographical notes. His biographical and critical memoir appeared in the volume containing *The Wild Ass's Skin*. All these essays are disappointing. Perhaps he knew too much about Balzac or did not love him enough; certainly he did not have as much time as he at first thought he would for the project. Whatever the reason, though the prefaces contain a few good things, each is so slight as to allow little significant analysis. They are uneven and far below the quality of most of his other writing on French fiction. At best they offer some technical analysis and a balanced judgment on strengths and weaknesses, and they indicate where the individual work fits into the overall scheme and how it expresses Balzac's special quality. At worst they are vague and superficial, and too many belong in this group. They also have the fault, not uncommon in Saintsbury's fiction criticism, of merely calling the roll of characters with no more than casual comment. The best are on those novels he listed as the best (but not on *Eugénie Grandet*) and on the good short stories.[91]

The preface to *Les Paysans*, which compares this late and most realistic of Balzac's novels with Zola's *La Terre*, has a unique interest. Saintsbury argues that Balzac's novel is superior to Zola's because Balzac's lifelong, first-hand contact with the country and the peasant gave him a knowledge beyond the reach of Zola, a town dweller who made brief visits to the country to work up the subject. The candor and realism of *Les Paysans*, he adds, is "as masterly as it is crushing in its indictment against the peasant."[92] The same novel is, for Marxist Georg Lukacs,[93] the best of Balzac because it is an indictment of the system.

Saintsbury's memoir is more illuminating than the prefaces. It offers insight into the interplay of the life and work of this self-destructive, egotistical, but indefatigable genius, who could never stop reworking and who carried within him (rather like Saintsbury himself) a vast burden of learning not wholly digested as well as that entire Balzacian world of over two thousand persons more imagined than observed.

Saintsbury's main contribution to Balzac criticism for his English readers was probably his defining of "The Balzacian quality," that of a *voyant* with an "apocalyptic" tone and a "gigantesque vagueness" that intoxicates, crudely illustrated in *The Wild Ass's Skin*. This anti-realist view of Balzac shared by Arthur Symons,[94] whatever his other quarrels with Saintsbury were, is later held by André Breton and other non-Marxist critics. For most modern readers, too, the chief source of Balzac's appeal is this fantastic element. That Saintsbury should emphasize this quality and clearly prefer it is not surprising to anyone who has seen him praise the marriage of dream and reality in Gautier and Flaubert. It recalls his love for the characters of Malory and the *Idylls* and his deploring the lack of mystery and vagueness, the excess of "the light of common day" in French poetry. Saintsbury argues that, because the effect of Balzac's *Human Comedy* is cumulative, it should be known as a whole. The prospect of this total knowledge becoming widespread is steadily less likely.

Saintsbury was to deal with Balzac at least three times again: in the *Britannica* eleventh edition, *The French Novel*, and the *Quarterly Review* in 1907, where he discusses ten critics whose studies of Balzac had appeared since he undertook his editing.[95] Few had appeared before that. In his *French Novel*, Saintsbury pairs Stendhal and Balzac in one chapter and he specifies the large amount of work he had done on Balzac. To add to the puzzle, he states that, in his edition, he intended "thorough prefaces" and "a very elaborate preface study." They are far from that. Did he believe he had been thorough?

When all Saintsbury's writing on French literature is considered, Arnold's range, by comparison, seems sadly restricted despite his seeing European culture as a weapon against provincialism. And since the next generation sought, in France, things foreign to Arnold's taste and were reacting against his moral and social concerns, the claim that Arnold was the major force in developing English taste for French literature seems unsound. He lacked both range and depth as regards French culture.

Like Swinburne, Saintsbury had reservations about Arnold as a guide to the understanding of French writers. Deploring Arnold's failure to appreciate French poetry in general and the power and lyric quality of the Alexandrine in particular, he questioned the kind of knowledge that would allow such high praise for Senancour or Maurice de Guérin as Arnold had given. The range and bulk of Saintsbury's work on French literature from 1877 to 1895 justifies his challenge to Arnold as it does his scoffing "amicably" when O'Shaughnessy, in 1880, claimed to have long been a lone voice speaking of modern French poetry.[96] The year before this, Saintsbury had received Guy de Maupassant's *Des Vers* for review in the *Academy,* had seen promise in it, and failed to share their Paris correspondent's moral indignation against it. His editor refused to let him review it, but in his *Short History* the next year, he hailed Maupassant as the "strongest and most accomplished versifier...in French for the last twenty years."[97]

Others concerned with modern French literature were emerging: Gosse, the Simcoxes writing for the *Academy,* W. T. Arnold, Henry James, Walter Pollock, J. A. Symonds, and later York Powell, Havelock Ellis, George Moore, and Arthur Symons. Few of these tackled the broad systematic task of increasing English knowledge of the whole corpus of French literature that Saintsbury had undertaken and would complete with *The French Novel* in 1918–19, but most of them were receptive to contemporary French literature as he was not.

CHAPTER 5

Journalist and Editor:
The *Saturday Review*

So much public interest is now taken in periodical literature, and the honourable competition in securing variety
and attractiveness is so active, that there is no risk of a
literary candle remaining long under a bushel.
—John Morley, "Memorials of a Literary Man,"
Studies in Literature

O gran bonta of those ancient times, with half-a-dozen
papers competing for one's articles.
—Saintsbury, *A Last Scrap Book*

While French literature commanded a good share of Saintsbury's
attention after 1876, he found his main living in the general London
press. As the preceding quotations suggest, opportunities had become manifold. On February 3, 1877, a somewhat mysterious new
weekly journal announced itself: "There is at present no weekly Conservative organ, and perhaps no paper, which represents Conservatism in its latest phase. Hence LONDON . . . "

With the *Daily News,* the short-lived *Daily Express,* the *Examiner,* the
Saturday Review, and the *Manchester Guardian, London* was to give
Saintsbury his first experience of the miscellaneous and political journalism he described as his "main ordinary business" from 1876 to
1895.[1] London already had its Tory papers (by 1880 there were thirteen daily papers and seven weeklies) despite the brash claim made
by the young Scot, Caldwell "Glasgow" Brown, who, with financial
backing from various Tory leaders and the blessing of Lord Bea-
consfield, launched the slightly mad and somewhat "schoolboyish"
London. It was soon to have W. E. Henley as editor (December 18,
1877) and Saintsbury, Lang, and Robert Louis Stevenson as its main
contributors—Saintsbury rather more than the others and for the

first time doing political leaders as well as "all sorts of *entre filets* to fill up corners."[2] Saintsbury mentions Stevenson and Henley "with whom also I rowed in that galley—a tight, saucy one if not exactly a *galère capitaine*."[3] He joyfully recalls from those *London* days someone's squib on a luggage shop advertisement: "Cowhide Gladstone only 30s. Very cheap at the price!"[4]

For 114 weeks, from the scantily furnished editorial office off the Strand, *London* offered a miscellany: somewhat original and varied at first, then at last almost three-fourths political. "Literature, music, the drama and other arts will not be dealt with on side issues moral or political... workmanship alone will be commended or condemned," the opening editorial promised. Included were a weekly book review, occasional translations, a series of essays on male novelists running to forty-four numbers and another of twenty-four on female novelists. Section titles had a certain flair: "St. Stephens" (on government), "Capel Court" (on business), "Feuilleton" (fiction, notably Stevenson's *Latter Day Arabian Nights* in 1878 and a good deal of Lang's and Henley's verse, including parodies of contemporary poets); also a "Whispering Gallery," "Vanity Fair," and "Bohemia" (the arts).

London's political tone is indicated by one anti-Gladstone diatribe with the Dickensian title "Stigginsism in Politics"—on praying for your opponents. This protest against "such cant" in politics may well have been written by Saintsbury in training for his later *Saturday Review* second leaders against Gladstone and Home Rule. He shared with Henley a lifelong hatred of humbug, and the term *cant* was one of his favorite pejoratives. On *London* he did his best "to see that the Whig dogs did not have the best of it." "Glasgow" Brown, in engaging Saintsbury, mentioned both Lang and Stevenson as well as an unidentified "gentleman" who had told him that Saintsbury had "a vein of humor of quite a peculiar sort."[5]

However much these friends enjoyed the vagaries of this slapdash journal[6]—as they seem to have done—*London* could scarcely give Saintsbury his main support during its brief lifetime. This came, rather, from the *Daily News* for which, under Frank Hill, he began writing immediately on his return to London in December, 1876, though still working full-time until April for the *Guardian*. Saintsbury credits Lang with introducing him both to Caldwell Brown and to

Frank Hill, also with beginning his *Saturday Review* connection in 1879 by transferring Charles Lenient's work on French satire to him for review. He did reviews, articles "when not politically impossible" for him, and obituaries for the morgue. The liberal *Daily News,* begun by Dickens in 1845, was now more narrowly political than the *Guardian,* with a powerful party hack, a Mr. Robinson, as manager, an indefatigable partisan, P. W. Clayden, as Hill's assistant, and Gladstone in the background complaining that they did not fight vigorously enough. Since the Tory Saintsbury's subjects could not be left to chance, under a "conscience clause" in his contract he wrote nonpolitical articles more or less steadily until 1883 when his *Saturday Review* work became too heavy. Soon finding night work impossible, he spent three afternoons a week in the *Daily News* offices in Bouverie Street, often writing in the same room with Frank Hill, a man of the world and a good conversationalist, who was independent enough politically to refuse compensation when, in 1886, the party and the paper went over to Home Rule and he was fired.[7]

On what kind of nonpolitical leaders Saintsbury cut his journalistic teeth under this congenial editor can only be guessed. A skimming of the 1879 volumes (the *Daily News* paid Saintsbury £350 that year) yields a fair sampling of his familiar views and phrases. Lang, who was on the *News* staff until 1896, may have done leaders "like fairy tales written by an elfish Puck," as Richard LeGallienne thought, but Saintsbury had his own lighter moments. For example, a leader writer, reporting a speech by Lord Granville, protests against Granville's faith in the progress of industrial and scientific education. The view and the choice of evidence could be Saintsbury's as Scott, Dickens, Fielding, *Emma,* and even *Hamlet* are called in to support the writer's scepticism. Two days earlier, a leader discussing a Whistler pamphlet related to the Whistler-Ruskin court case builds upon one of Saintsbury's favorite and oft-repeated quotations, Blake's assertion that anyone can be a judge of art "who has not been connoisseured out of his senses."[8] Citing Gautier, Lessing, and Diderot as proof, the writer voices another of Saintsbury's beliefs, that to have the art of appreciating, one need not possess the "art of producing." Another of his lifelong attitudes emerges in an article on a fire at the Birmingham Library. Books, the leader says, are "the only friends who never change, the only comforters who have consolation in their gift." The announcement of Zola's *Nana* described the writer, as Saintsbury would, as the realist who "seems to think nothing real that is not hideous, or malodorous, or prurient."

Saintsbury may also have made the plea for support of the Early English Text Society to protect it from "too scientific or Germanic work," citing two obscure problems—the probable color of Hotspur's kitten and the paladins of romance "who set each other's whiskers ablaze." Even more likely to be Saintsbury's is the antiteetotaling leader on a report that paupers at the Fulham workhouse had been deprived of their daily ration of a half-pint of beer. This—in line with all the recent "enforced teetotalism in poorhouses"—recalls to the writer another recently expressed "contemptible" view, that two sherries "try the strongest constitution." Could that beer hurt an old woman of seventy or "tempt her into sottish and extravagant habits" he asks. The inmates may be reconciled, but, the writer protests, the drinking of milk has increased "so much as to suggest baths and Madame Pompadour." At this the lifelong enemy of pussyfooting cries, "Extravagance! . . . there is a limit to philanthropy. There is such a thing as pampering the poor . . . Milk, like the well at which the Highland soldier was found bathing by his comrades, is for drinking; not 'for cooking.'" How this fooling struck the *Daily News* audience largely made up of dissenters one may wonder, but it sounds like the author of *Notes on a Cellar Book,* the young leader writer who, by his own report, angered Frank Hill only once. As title for a note "on the fate of some unlucky Cannibal Islands missionary named Baker he suggested, 'Tit for Tat: or the Baker baked.'"[9]

Thus, Saintsbury "got his hand in" on *London,* the *Daily News,* and elsewhere. Two other journals appear in his accounts for 1877–80: the *Examiner*[10] and the *Daily Express.*[11] The latter was a quaint, four-month-long experiment financed by High Churchmen to represent the Church of England and "the thoughtful churchman," and without party affiliation, to comment freely on current secular problems ("the Burials Bill, the Conge d'élire," etc.). One or two leaders in its somewhat solemn pages sound like Saintsbury. Commenting on a pension that had been granted to the Misses Defoe, the writer proclaims Defoe the originator of "the better sort of journalism." Another, on the choice of the Oxford Professor of Poetry, urges the winner to give a series of lectures on criticism of poetry, as guidance in a time when critics are "haphazard" and "arbitrary," and "cannot

give a reason for the faith that is in them." (This last phrase Saintsbury used over and over again throughout his life.) Also included is
a denial of the common view that "criticism of criticism" is idle, a view
that anticipates charges later made against Saintsbury's *History of Criticism.*

Meanwhile, Saintsbury had established his connection with the *Saturday Review* (1855–1933) and the *Pall Mall Gazette,* an evening newspaper and review. Under its founder-editor Frederick Greenwood,
it followed the lead of the powerful and distinguished weekly, and
together these were the center of power in Conservative journalism
in England in the latter part of the nineteenth century.[12] Their sober
pattern appealed almost wholly to cultivated, upper-middle-class
males and not to the new electorate enfranchised in 1867 or to the
generation that grew up after the 1870 Education Act. All formal,
solid, and serious, these journals contained critical leaders, verbatim
reports of political speeches that perhaps no one ever read, political
news with interpretation, and long reviews. No illustrations, no gossip
or sports or jokes, no interviews, not even cross headlines to break
up the large, solid pages. They commanded the ablest writers; they
were cheap—and influential. But all the things synonymous with
newspapers today, even as their numbers dwindle, were to become
usual only after the press revolution of the late 1880s and 1890s, a
change brought about through *TitBits* (1881), W. T. Stead's revamp-
ing of the *Pall Mall Gazette* (1883–89), *The Star* (1887) under T. P.
O'Connor, and later by Lord Northcliffe.

This "New Journalism,"[13] to borrow Arnold's phrase, expressed a
changing world but had no greater power or influence than the older
type. The older group included the *St. James's Gazette,* begun in 1880
with Greenwood as editor and a staff consisting largely of the many
Pall Mall Gazette writers who followed him there when John Morley
became editor of the *Pall Mall Gazette* (1880–83). Though Saintsbury's name is often associated with the *St. James,* the strongest of
Tory voices, his account book lists only two contributions paid for
from 1880 until 1888, when Sidney Low succeeded Greenwood.[14]
He once told Henley he could not have worked under Greenwood,
but whatever he wrote for the *St. James* and the *Pall Mall Gazette*
anonymously would not have varied in tone or temper from his *Saturday Review* and *Athenaeum* writing.

From the day of its inception (1855), the *Saturday Review,* appropriately nicknamed both the "Saturday Reviler" and "The Slashaway Review,"[15] through the best writers, a large proportion of whom it commanded, flailed away steadily at every leading figure in political, literary, and other fields. Though its brightness dimmed after the death of its superb original editor, John Douglas Cook, in 1868, it was a power to be reckoned with at least until the death of its first owner, A. J. Beresford-Hope, in 1887. It became less spontaneously independent, less able to command the best writers,[16] and duller as it settled into steady support of Toryism and Lord Salisbury, Beresford-Hope's brother-in-law. But its sceptical and critical tone, its assumption of infallibility, and its determined effort to maintain a high intellectual level persisted under the editorship of Philip Harwood (1868–83) and Walter Pollock (1883–1894). Though it carried no news, strictly speaking, it remained "a counterpart of the *Times* among the weeklies,"[17] "the most British of British periodicals,"[18] or, as a character of William Archer's put it, "Shakespeare we share with the Americans, but damn it, the *Saturday Review* is all our own."[19] Like the other weeklies and major dailies, the *Saturday Review* was a class organ, and also represented "the academic attitude towards life."[20]

As the *Edinburgh* and *Quarterly Review* had done a half-century earlier in the North, the *Saturday* made writing for periodicals respectable and practically created the profession. Undergraduates of the 1860s greeted it "with savage joy,"[21] and for many years—to the despair of some tutors—the style of its "middle" articles, "which Douglas Cook had taught a long succession of writers to produce," was a model for undergraduate essays.[22] And it attracted some of the best Oxbridge graduates to its staff.

Saintsbury, having become a subscriber during his first week at Merton, was one of those young devotees. He joined its staff in 1879 and the next year, under Harwood, began his fourteen-year career as a subeditor, though his full responsibilities began only when Pollock became editor in 1883. One can almost equate Saintsbury and the *Saturday Review* for at least a decade. Though he has long been regarded chiefly as a literary critic, historian, and professor of English literature, Saintsbury estimated his anonymous journalism at over one hundred volumes. Only half as much as Lang's, a third that of H. D. Traill, but unlike these men, he became subeditor of the most influential of weeklies, and he edited their work, reviewed them, and edited many other leading cultural figures of those years, 1880 to 1894.

Sir Frederick Pollock doubted "whether within the last forty years one could find another group of such men with such diverse talents doing the same kind of work in their own ways, and all so well."[23] Saintsbury, in letters to William Hunt, gives some insight into his relations with some of them. Blaikie was a "born complainer" to whom Walter Pollock gave work "and made him do it." Sir Frederick Pollock was "a remarkably shrewd man." Of three closer friends, he says, "I doubt whether in the history of journalism you will find a group of three illustrating in more different ways its powers and sensibilities more notably: . . . Traill for weight and punch; Lang for variety and grace; Gosse for lightness."[24]

Saintsbury says that he did more political writing than he did literary;[25] he also tells us he wrote the *Saturday's* second leaders—on Gladstone and Ireland—during the twelve years following the retirement of George Venables (1810–1888) in 1882. Venables was a distinguished barrister but, according to Sir Herbert Stephen, he made "the public work of his life . . . anonymous journalism," and "did more than any writer of his time to establish and maintain the best and strongest current style, and the highest type of political thought in journalism." He probably influenced Saintsbury, though their styles are very different.[26]

Since the *Pall Mall Gazette* became Radical-Liberal when John Morley became its editor in 1882, Saintsbury's work for it had to be largely nonpolitical, as it was for the *Daily News* and the *Guardian*. Therefore, his many political articles (with few exceptions) were written for the *Saturday Review*. Described as the "general utility man of the *Saturday Review* in the London *Times* obituary (1933), Saintsbury, by his own estimate, reviewed thousands of books including hundreds on economics regularly. Also he says, " . . . perhaps because I was a kind of abortion of a barrister . . . I had to write endless articles on crimes."[27] All this demanded constant alertness to all public matters, and it justified his telling William Blackwood in 1894 that, for fifteen years, "nothing of importance at home and abroad has escaped my attention, and there are few subjects on which I have not had to write more or less."[28] This miscellaneous writing in itself has little significance but "the literary resurrection men" (Saintsbury's term for those who dig up what rightly lies buried in newspaper graves)[29] could easily recognize his mannerisms and prejudices as well as phrases and allusions that echo through his signed writings. And anonymous though it was, it must have left some imprint on its readers. Once Saintsbury summed it all up.

> The occupations and amusements . . . never grew monotonous, and are sometimes monumental surprises. You might in my time go down to business one day and be greeted by the Phoenix Park murders. . . . Others gave you the successive episodes of the Afghan War. . . . [It was] work that began at ten and kept one up till three or four. . . ."[30]

His range was tremendous even for the age of the cultivated, omnivorous amateur. Reviewing never lost its fascination for him and he never came to dislike proofreading. Nor did all the editing ever "stale its interest."[31]

One main impression created is of how thoroughly its political slant pervades the whole of the *Saturday Review*. Any topic is excuse for a Tory argument or a dig at Mr. Gladstone, as two articles Saintsbury later identified as his own illustrate. In "A Preface to a New Book of Snobs" and "The Definition of a Snob,"[32] he purports to take up where Thackeray left off; he appeals for examples of the "snobs of this generation and this year," and more specifically of "the Snob Democratic . . . a new birth of time." "Onions," an article packed with literary allusion and wordplay on onion, union, shallot, and garlic, reminds the reader of Saintsbury's gourmet tastes.[33]

Wordplay is the secret of an amusing "middle" article, very probably his, "There let him lay." The *Western Morning News* had protested in solemn fury the *Saturday*'s supposed grammatical lapse in its use of the phrase, "There let him lay." For two columns, the *Saturday* writer lays about him, using the formula over and over to damn various things and persons political and social—the Cheap Press, the Irish and pro-Irish, and Andrew Carnegie, who had recently made an anti-British speech in Glasgow.[34] "'Let him lie' will not do," the writer explains; it would be ambiguous and "might even seem to imply a most improper toleration of vice." Then, with a sarcasm such as Saintsbury delighted in, the *Western Morning News* is relieved of its suspense:

"There let him lay" is not a creation of the wicked and ignorant *Saturday Review*, nor is it a mere adaptation of the warm and generous but incorrect diction which flows from the great heart of the people—*cor cordium et supra grammaticum*. There once was a bard of the name of Byron . . . .

The source is *Childe Harold* (4:180).

The Saintsbury tone and attitude are again evident in "Inebriety: a Study" and "A Word from Maitre Francoys."[35] A speaker at the Society for the Study and Cure of Inebriety having expressed his fear that the coming of democracy would be far from sober, the *Saturday* writer agrees, "Revolutions are not made with Apollonaris Water, and it will be a noble if appalling sight when the emancipated People rushes wildly on the cellars of the Aristocracy." The second article rejoices in a claim by the French *Revue Scientifique* that all the clamor against alcohol is "foolish false tale-bearing" since "men are born most and die least where good wine is drunk." Then comes the political twist: "even your Gladstone is a five-glass man. Would he were a five-bottle man! Shorter would have been his life, but merrier, and more for the country's good." Such were the compensatory moments of fun, however heavy-handed within the "four octave double-column volumes" that a hardworking journalist was estimated to produce yearly.

Because Saintsbury was subeditor, his hand was everywhere. He not only felt free to revise and adapt work submitted to him, but rather felt an obligation to do so—in order to bring it all into a harmonious whole. Since the marked files of the *Saturday* of 1880–94 no longer exist,[36] it can not be determined how much he wrote, but the bulk was great and his role as editor is important.

As subeditor, Saintsbury had a share in determining day-to-day policy of the *Saturday Review*. In charge of the literary department, he was responsible for keeping a good staff of reviewers. "We are doing everything we can to get everything done by the best men possible," he wrote Dobson in 1884.[37] He succeeded in keeping up the quality established when the *Saturday* first began, but the last few years saw some falling off.[38] David Hannay testified regarding Saintsbury as an editor: "A man of zest, literature and erudition (a thoroughly good fellow to boot). . . . I did not work for years with Saintsbury without finding out that he is a trump."[39] As for his relations with his chief editor, Saintsbury says, "Editor should mean 'Captain' in the good old naval sense." A good editor will offer noninterference but beneficent guidance, and Saintsbury's model was John Morley.[40] But the temperaments of Saintsbury's two successive chiefs, Harwood and Pollock, when set beside his own vibrant and independent one, suggest that he played a decisive role under both of them.

Philip Harwood, his first chief, was trained by Douglas Cook on the *Morning Chronicle* and had been with the *Saturday Review* since its inception. Walter Pollock was "born into a *Saturday Review* atmosphere and family" and was on the staff from 1875 on. T. H. Escott says both men had "the almost instinctve knowledge of the subjects possessing for the moment the public mind, of the treatment best suited to the passing taste of the hour, and of the men it would best pay the paper to employ."[41]

Harwood was a born editor by all reports and "an editor pure and simple." Nobody knew his tastes or views if he had any, and he rarely wrote for the paper. He planned ahead and began ordering articles for each issue very early in the week. Gentle and unpretentious as he seems, he was an old-fashioned editor who occupied his room "in solitary state" and sent for his aides through a stately factotum "who always knew everything." To his contributors, he seemed "a marvel of experience, patience, good sense and assiduity."[42]

One incident that illustrates Saintsbury's relation to this quiet, retiring chief was when he felt forced to warn Harwood not to buy the infamous Pigott forgeries, letters that linked Parnell to the Phoenix Park murders. The *Times* bought them and used them in the articles "Parnellism and Crime." Though disappointed and momentarily angry, Harwood had given in, thus saving Beresford-Hope a good deal of money and sparing the *Saturday* a loss of prestige such as the *Times* suffered. A person of far stronger convictions and prejudices, more articulate and broader in knowledge and interests than Harwood, Saintsbury occasionally made his views prevail.

Saintsbury's relation to Walter Pollock (1850–1926) was similar. They were contemporaries and Pollock was more sociable and had more varied interests than Harwood, including the interest in French literature he shared with Saintsbury.[43] Gosse, to whom Saintsbury seemed "electric" on first contact, saw in Pollock, "sombre airs, like a Don in disguise."[44] He suffered two handicaps: he was the son and the brother of the two distinguished Sir Frederick Pollocks, both writers for the *Saturday,* and he became its editor in its middle age. He attempted no innovations, though the public was beginning to want a new type of journalism; also he could no longer command all the brilliant writers who had earlier graced its staff.

Behind these two editors of not very forceful individuality stood the genial, cultivated, and able owner, Beresford-Hope, who never dictated or interfered but who "never let things slide."[45]

The *Saturday Review* editorial offices at Albany were quite separate from the business offices in Southampton Street, and the editors gained a reputation for being a closed corporation dwelling in Olympian aloofness. The 1855 Prospectus had announced that they would not accept free books but would provide for themselves the works they selected for criticism. This independent spirit extended to other matters. They almost never printed a correction of their errors and were generally not hospitable to outsiders; they rarely welcomed unsolicited contributions and had a reputation for snubbing correspondents to the point where few ever wrote to them. More oddly still, "contributors were supposed not to know one another."[46] The one official break in this aura of mystery was the annual staff gathering; in the 1880s and 1890s it was a fish dinner at Greenwich.[47]

Within this tight little system where anonymity ruled, the forceful, stubborn, indefatigable, and very knowledgable subeditor must have been a real power in shaping policy congenial to his own temper. Saintsbury, though not the most gifted or innovative, is a representative Tory journalist of the late nineteenth century, and he had much to say about what he labeled "Satan's Invisible World Displayed, the main thoroughfare of whose capital is Fleet Street."[48] It inspired him to other allusive flights—"Our Lady of the Press," "this later Ninon d'Enclos," a "Gypsy Queen," with a "Cleopatraesque variety," "This Island of the Sirens." Happily, he never became cynical about it, as Lang did. Despite those romantic phrases he is realistic. He refers to himself as a "mere pawn in the army of letters,"[49] and he saw himself in his early days, "serving my editors in a most contemptibly 'wageslave' manner [though] I never wrote what I didn't believe."[50]

When Saintsbury portrayed the first thirty years of the *Saturday Review* (up to 1885),[51] he labeled it "Liberal-Conservative" but "never tied . . . to party," since writers of Liberal and Radical opinions did write for it. He described its attitude as "that peculiar tone of mainly

Conservative persiflage" that has characterized a line of writers beginning with Aristophanes. Longer than any other London journal it maintained anonymity. He saw it as fearless, "on the whole fairly impartial," informed by intelligence, but, he adds, it always "hated a fool and struck at him with might and main."

Journalist, for Saintsbury, was no term of reproach though he knew that it commands a "lower talent" than literature proper and brings disadvantages. He saw it as a hard life and an uncertain one with little security. It proved for him a reasonably prosperous one, but his income from daily and weekly journalism after 1880 never supplied more than 85 percent of his total income. He says, "Perhaps only those who have tried it know what a serious tale of scattered articles at five and ten, and even twenty guineas each it takes to build up a respectable income.... "[52] He admits he was, on the whole, well paid and felt no resentment against the failed periodicals that never paid him. His experience is confirmed by a contemporary claim (1880) that the profession was tolerably profitable. In 1880, he earned £1259 yet the economic difficulties were real.[53] Twice—in 1876 and 1894— Saintsbury found himself on the street, with little in savings and a family of four to support. The painful memory made him certain of the need for "the discipline of miscellaneous journalism." The dilettante or the procrastinator could not survive. A man must be willing to do "honest journey work in default of better,"[54] in Carlyle's phrase. Since the "regular drudgery of miscellaneous article writing for the newspapers" is the only journalism that really pays,[55] one must be fit for such work, however poor a second best it may seem to anyone with literary aspirations. He must be "ready and adequate" like Gautier, "the born writer of articles," who wrote the equivalent of over three hundred volumes.[56] Elsewhere, Saintsbury weighs the advantages of the journalist's life. The gain is "the askesis—the literary practice and exercise" and the ability "to make the dash—the plunge," and the ability to adapt. He knew the temptations. The virtues may turn to slovenliness or to levity; the writer may become trivial, vulgar, diffuse, and forget principles or "conscience of workmanship."[57]

His years of daily close association with Andrew Lang kept before Saintsbury the worst effects of the "Siren voice" of the press. Lang's fabulous facility has supplied much legend: Lang dashing off an article on the train and posting it without rereading, writing leaders on his knee during editorial meetings at a pace well beyond Saintsbury's own, finishing a review between sets of tennis,[58] or "demolishing Max Müller on the corner of a club table in the interval between seeing Harwood and going down to the D.N. . . ." He wrote too much too easily until finally he was the victim of his gifts, corrupted, or, as Gosse put it not unkindly, "jaded by the toil of writing many things."[59]

No man wholly escapes the effects of this rat race. Saintsbury suffered, but he had the good fortune to leave Fleet Street after twenty years of journalism that had exacerbated his natural tendency to superficiality. He wrote too much on too many subjects and too often on the same subject; inevitably, he repeated himself despite his claims to the contrary. The age welcomed omniscience, overproduction, and the resulting superficiality—"the cultural rubble" of that period in Steven Marcus's apt phrase.[60] A review of Saintsbury's *Elizabethan Literature* gave an early warning in 1887: "Now and then the mask of the historian is thrown off . . . and the reviewer emerges."[61] But one of Saintsbury's limitations proved to be a gain. He envied Lang's "marvelous facility" though he could not match it. He confessed to Gosse in 1882:[61] "My only chance of doing anything but mere potboiling is to work all day and every day. I can do a fair lot of work; but to do it I must get at it squarely and without interruption."[62] To this degree he knew himself.

Journalistic flesh is heir to other ills than facility, as Saintsbury knew. There is the danger that "the habit of treating some subjects in the peculiar fashion most effective in journalism may spread disastrously to the treatment of other subjects which ought to be treated as literature."[63] Of this Saintsbury was sometimes guilty because he wrote so much. There is the danger of bookishness, but equally bad or more fatal is the neglect of reading.[64] Saintsbury found that Hazlitt stopped reading as he never did. H. D. Traill seemed to avoid these dangers and best measured up to Saintsbury's ideal.[65] Unfortunately, because of his almost exclusive devotion to anonymous journalism, he was little known or recognized.

Temperamental limitations also beset journalists and bedevil their editors, and Saintsbury had met them all.

. . . the contributor who is not allowed to contribute . . . the contributor who thinks himself too much edited, and the contributor who imperatively insists that his article on Chinese metaphysics shall go in at once, and the contributor who, being an excellent hand at articles on the currency, wants to be allowed to write on dancing. . . .[66]

Good editors, who must interest themselves in everything if they are to spot and avoid the dry rot, must guide and direct them all. Saintsbury's way of editing a reliable contributor, illustrated in a letter to Brander Matthews, seems flexible: "Pray do the novel you mention. Is it worth a full article? We have recently taken, as you may have noticed, to bisecting reviews . . . and to grouping novels. . . . But you will use your judgment in the matter."[67] Yet his stamp is everywhere.

Steven Marcus somewhat facetiously calls the 1880s "the world of the bookmen, the bellettrists, the clubmen of literature," where "Victorian culture was splitting up, and of the gentleman of letters little remained apart from his gentility."[68] Despite some truth, this dismissal is too glib. The 1880s were a transitional period with the giants dead or dying, the journals of the mid-century losing their youthful vigor, and a new generation of readers demanding a less snobbish, less class-oriented literature and journalism. A new generation of writers was experimenting and breaking down old barriers, and artists were finding their own new directions while protesting the restraints and the prudery of their predecessors—protest that did not truly flower until the 1890s. As the new journalists began to break the old molds, here, in between, was a generation half of the older world, half of the new.

Such an era is easy to satirize but hard to define; and it is easy to dismiss it as "cultural rubble." But the 1990s have an obligation to understand an era in which, as Marcus also more fairly and accurately pointed out, the new mass journalism began to rub elbows with the old bellettrists, and the very explosions of the new against the old were signs of continuing vigor as well as change.

John Gross contrasted Saintsbury's generation, the "bookmen," with "the Liberal Practitioners" of the previous generation—Arnold, Leslie Stephen, Hutton, Bagehot, Lewes, and Morley—men of larger vision and sterner intellect.[69] While these latter men still wrote for the journals, the "bookmen" of the Tory press were indefatigable, vastly knowing, but less original and imaginative, more heavy handed or, in the case of Gosse and Lang, often more frivolous. Lang knew he was third rate; Gosse feared he was and, in the mid-1880s, had to face the fact he was a failed scholar. Saintsbury knew he was not creative but hoped to compensate by literary omniscience and hard work. He helped preside over a journal of dwindling distinction. Too much of it was increasingly stodgy and pedestrian as it hewed to the Tory line. No one of them was going to set the world on fire. Not embracing Shaw, Wilde, Hardy, Tolstoy, Ibsen, or Zola, they retreated into the past though Gosse was ever busy cultivating the newer French poets. By 1894, Saintsbury knew that it was the end of a chapter for conservative journalism and that the new wave lay with Frank Harris's *Saturday Review*, short lived as that was to be.

CHAPTER 6

Political Writing: On Home Rule

Saintsbury terms political journalism "the most important...the most paying, but the most exhausting, and as far as results go, the most utterly thankless and evanescent division of journalism."[1] Doing so much of it for eighteen years, he brought to it not only his Tory convictions but also ideas about the qualities the good writer on politics should have and the ways one best develops these. He admits he never achieved the "wise indifference" that might be desirable. Had he done so, it might have saved him the rage that colors his *Scrap Books* (1922–24). "Bloody-minded and courageous enough at least to admit it," Orwell termed these octogenarian grumblings.[2] But shocking as they are, they do not cancel out his earlier conservative views or the discipline he imposed on himself as a political writer and about which he speaks in a number of places.

Recognizing politics as a practical science, he recommended Aristotle's *Politics* as the foundation for the armor of knowledge and "reasoned faith" political writers need. They must have passion and unselfishness, and more practically, scepticism and shrewdness, and a healthy power to laugh at rather than merely lash out at the evils and follies they attack. They need to be able to enjoy the skill and wit of the political satirists whose principles they disagree with—as Saintsbury himself did those of Peter Pindar and *The Rolliad*, though he preferred the more sympathetic *Anti-Jacobin*. Sanity, something of the gentleman and the scholar, and the vigor and confidence to make the minor as well as the major matters of the day come to life he also saw as essential.[3]

Essentially a literary man, he had great faith in literary models from Juvenal at one extreme to Blake at the other. These include: Lucian, Renaissance political verse, Dryden, the *Satire Ménippé, Epistolae Obscurorum,* and *Hudibras;* the 18th century from Pope to Peter Pindar, the *Rolliad,* and *Anti-Jacobin;* and, in prose, the more inimitable

Swift and the less great but effective journalism of Lockhart, his own friend Traill, and the vastly uneven and less knowing William Cobbett.[4] Intimidating and remote as this list might seem to a modern journalist, Saintsbury felt that these writers could teach the skills of satire and irony, "the art of making people make fools of themselves," and much more. He felt Dryden knew best how not to lose one's temper.[5] For the writer of academic taste he thought Cobbett's simplicity and his intense and furious beliefs a sound antidote.[6] Finally, he chose Lockhart as the safest model, working always from principles, "with a hatred of commonplace and cant and *populus aura*," with a conscience and thorough workmanship, with style and depth of feeling.[7]

Though he gave serious thought to all these matters, Saintsbury could scarcely achieve all these virtues in his *Saturday Review* articles. But he claimed to have imposed upon himself an ethic that required that he never be trivial, vulgar, or carelessly ignorant, that he always respect "the sanctity of private life," never be personal, "and finally that he should *always* be ready to answer in person for what he had written impersonally."[8] Saintsbury believed these things especially necessary for an honest and conscientious "man behind the mask." Though he never relinquished the view that anonymity was the best policy, he was aware of its dangers—those of abusing the mask and of irresponsibility—as well as its power.

This mask—the anonymous editorial "we"—almost universal in England and the United States until the 1880s, is still largely unchallenged in editorial writing. The "leader" is assumed to be the product of general editorial policy, specific consultation, even, at times, "virtual collaboration." The result for Saintsbury, as for H. D. Traill and others, had a "reality of meaning" beyond that of the signed article.[9] Saintsbury recognized that anonymous leaders took on "semioracular *authority*" and "mystery."[10] This authority he wielded for twelve years.

When examining the *Saturday Review* leaders on Gladstone and Ireland, Saintsbury's lifelong Tory position must be kept in mind. "Most die-hard of Tories," "simply the commonplaces of clubs and senior common rooms eighty or ninety years ago . . . merely a mass of conventional prejudice,"[11] and "Hot Tory gospeller"[12] are easy labels that have been used to judge his old-fashioned conservatism and especially the views in the *Scrap Books*. But for the man who spoke for the Tory tradition in one of its most powerful journals a century ago, this is not enough. The truth lies somewhere between these and the more favorable evaluation given in a tribute paid to his views by Conservatives in 1931, crediting him with "the larger conservatism of life and letters . . . which issues in an informed human and coherent political conservatism."[13] What were the basic elements of this creed?

H. J. C. Grierson thought Saintsbury more of a Tory than Dr. Johnson.[14] And Saintsbury cherished the friend who said in rage, "You like Carlyle because he has made you more of a Tory than the Devil had made you already."[15] Devil or not, his political views were formed so early as to seem "born alive" in the "little conservative." Already evident in his school-prize poem, they had helped shape his Oxford undergraduate reputation and made him unwilling to face the implications of the 1867 Reform Bill.[16] Later, his views had ruled out political subjects for him on the *Daily News.*

He was politically sure of himself when he came to the press, and, at the *Saturday Review,* conscience and assignment never clashed. He believed that his creed would stand the tests of "rational examination of the physical and historical facts of life": that we are born *unequal* and literally not free, and that we by nature fight and struggle for mastery. Inequality, individualism, heredity, property and the Constitution are Tory principles, he argues, and they embrace "the welfare of the whole people, not that of any class to the ill fare of any other."[17] Like Sir Walter Scott, he held strongly to "that reverence for the past, that distaste for the vulgar, that sense of continuity, of mystery, of something beyond interest and calculation," which he saw as the nobler side of Toryism.[18] Facetiously, he once pleaded for Gladstone solely on the basis of his love for Scott and his knowledge of Mumm Champagne.[19] Elsewhere Saintsbury asserts "the rights of the few against excessive (and dreary) equalitarianism" and deplores the "spoiling" of the Irish peasant, the "childifying of England, the taking from the rich. . . . "[20] Like Burke, he resorts to the analogy of the human body to justify "respect for Freedom and Property in the individual, maintenance of both, and of Privilege in so far as it hurts nothing but vanity and bad blood in other individuals." Change there will be, but reasonable resistance to change "not thoughtless reaction," he thought historically justified—especially if you disbelieve in progress as he did. The only right is "the right of possession" *not* that of "redistribution!" There must be respect for the organic state rooted in tradition, and it must exercise itself for its own safety, for fair distribution of taxation, and in public charity for the sick and the indigent. Charity seemed enough, because he was able to blind himself to the real condition of the Irish and even to that of people in the East End or the Gorbals. He turned away in disgust from the grime of Zola's naturalism and thus avoided the pain of humanitarian sympathies just as he evaded feeling in his own personal or domestic life. He was more afraid of change than he knew.

Like most political faiths, Saintsbury's had its romantic side. The Conservative or Tory puts value upon the unselfishness and dedication to service of the class "born to rule" and must exert pressure upon leaders to fulfill this ideal. He values sincerity, courage, and honesty of character and insists that it is a "fatal delusion" to believe that "a conscious charlatan can be an effective statesman."[21] His times offered examples of a high sense of public duty and responsibility in political figures of all parties—Gladstone, Disraeli, Salisbury, Balfour, Morley, in their different ways. He respected this integrity in all but Gladstone and, in later years, Morley.

Disraeli was not a favorite of Saintsbury's, but he saw the "Young England" movement as "the most striking political result of the Romantic Revival," fruitful in its mutual "interesting of one class in another," in its humanizing religious and artistic developments, and in its interest in popularizing tradition and historical continuity. These young men satisfied his idea of the English gentleman and posed no practical threat as the advocates of equality and majority rule did.[22] He feared vulgarization and the reign of mediocrity and felt that these threaten the quality of art and letters and beauty in general—a threat that troubled Victorian minds far more liberal than his.[23] These fears were made more specific in his essay, "Thoughts on Republics," in which he questioned majority rule.[24] Is this liberty or equality? "You are as false to your principles in tyrannizing as in being tyrannized over," he concluded.

The political journalism stands apart from the rest of Saintsbury's work, and those who have evaluated him have scarcely glanced at it. The long series of leaders on Home Rule written by Saintsbury expressing Tory views in a Tory organ have significance because, increasingly, their view of the Irish question became the general English view. As Arnold wrote in 1887, "The great body of quiet reasonable opinion in England wishes [the Tories] success."[25]

When Saintsbury became subeditor of the *Saturday Review*, Gladstone, at seventy-one, had just begun his second ministry (1880–85) with no specific program but with strong moral resolve "to pacify Ireland," where violence and anarchy were mounting after three years of poor crops. The peasants' misery was intense; 1880 saw 10,000 evictions and 2,500 agrarian outrages. Isaac Butt was dead and Charles Parnell, now the leader of the National Land League, was pursuing his policy of obstruction in Parliament with all his skill and energy. In John Morley's words, "... agitation and bloodshed in Ireland, violence and confusion in Parliament. The ragged Sphinx had once more come forth with deadly weapons under her tatters."[26] All this against the background of almost a decade's legislative paralysis in London was a triumph for the Parnellites. The Liberal majority of 1880–85, improvising as it went, brought in the Land Act of 1881 and introduced the Arrears Bill to relieve the Irish tenants, but at the same time it suspended habeas corpus and allowed the bungling Chief Secretary for Ireland, W. E. Forster, to order Parnell's arrest (October, 1881) and detention in Kilmainham jail for eight months.

Since Ireland was a main political preoccupation of the *Saturday Review* of these years, seldom a week passes without a leader or middle on the subject. In crises like Phoenix Park (1882), the forming of the Parnell Commission (1889), its report (February, 1890), and the O'Shea divorce (November, 1890), two, three, or four editorials appear in one issue. Saintsbury wrote weekly but did not write them all, even after Venables left in 1882. A few he acknowledges; a few have so familiar a touch as to seem unquestionably his; in all of them, the strong guiding hand was his. The views, officially those of the *Saturday Review,* were also his.

"I have never *lived* in Ireland," Saintsbury records. The same was true of Gladstone and a host of others who held strong opinions on the Irish question. As for the Parliamentary debates, we cannot know how often Saintsbury actually heard the speakers he interprets despite his occasional reference to a late return from the House of Commons. But when he describes the response of the House to Parnell's denial of the authenticity of the Pigott letters, one is persuaded he was there that night.[27] His sources were the *Times* and other daily papers and *Hansard* for so much as it then offered[28]—a practice then common to the weeklies.

As happened repeatedly, the Crimes Act, which made effective coercion possible in Ireland, lapsed in 1880 with the new ministry.

The *Saturday Review* of 1880–81, therefore, harps on the soon familiar themes. The need for force is reflected in such titles as "Irish Sedition," "Agitation and Murder" (following the murder of Lord Mountmorris), and "Irish Anarchy." Strong protest is raised against demagogues and agitators who "repeat with perfect immunity undisguised incitements to crimes" and against those Irish who "buy muskets at government sales." Scorn is heaped on the Irish MP who defends cattle maiming as a "legal right," and Gladstone's claim that the Irish need guns to shoot animals and serpents prompts the sarcasm: "Wolves have been gone from Ireland for years—and serpents since Saint Patrick!" Parnell having quoted Gladstone to support his own sneer at the murder of Lord Mountmorris, the *Saturday Review* protests "the license accorded to members of Parliament and ruffianly priests to apologize for murder." All this in 1880.

When the new Secretary for Ireland, Lord Frederick Cavendish, died by violence in Phoenix Park on May 6, 1882, along with his companion, Secretary Burke, the *Saturday Review,* reflecting the general British horror, minced no words: "The blood of Lord Frederick Cavendish lies . . . at more doors than one. But at the doors of the Land League it lies unmistakably." Since Parnell had embraced the physical force group he must share the blame, as must the government. Parnell had been released from prison, and when the letters that had been the price of his release from prison were read in Parliament, the *Saturday Review* offered an angry sweep of hyperbole that sounds like Saintsbury: "The mire in which Mr. Gladstone and his colleagues have involved themselves would make a Putrid Sea of the Atlantic." On a somewhat lighter note is the leader, "Tipperary and Tennis." Because a Tipperary priest had protested tennis being played under the walls of a convent "in foreign garb," the *Saturday* writer predicts: if now "to play Protestant tennis . . . is justly resented as a gross insult to religion and the religious," soon cricket in Phoenix Park will "be denounced as an athletic and brutal heresy. . . ." This is "a peculiar moral code . . . since priests fail to denounce murders." Thus Saintsbury, if it is he, brings the reader's attention back to the horrors and concludes, with more truth than perhaps he knew, "We shall never, never understand the Irish."

When, in 1887, the *Times* articles "Parnellism and Crime" appeared, they made use of the Pigott forgeries, letters implicating Parnell in the Phoenix Park murders. Saintsbury, who had prevented the *Saturday Review* from printing them,[29] wrote the two leaders that he later acknowledged as his own: "Yours Very Truly, Chas. S. Parnell" and "The Wood and the Holloa." In the first of these, the *Saturday Review* focused its direct and most powerful attack on Parnell's guilt. Saintsbury was not alone in knowing that Pigott had some reputation for dishonest dealings, but he moved with caution because at least one successful libel suit had recently been brought against the *Saturday Review*.[30] The title "Yours Very Truly, Chas. S. Parnell" was used to avoid even the phrase "alleged letter," and it was carefully insisted that judicial examination must settle the question of authenticity since Parnell had denied authorship in Parliament.

Saintsbury sets up every possible relation between denial, guilt, and innocence: where denial is certain beforehand, it is unimportant; denial by an innocent may strengthen the innocence; denial by the guilty does not lessen guilt. *But*—"Where the charge is of such a nature that it of itself implies . . . moral villainy, denial is simply vain breath." Saintsbury's charge is that Parnell had been guilty from the start because he encouraged violence and murder through his support of the Land League and its agitators.

The specific argument is twofold: First, if the letters prove authentic, "Mr. Parnell is quite safe from legal prosecution." Even the most damning phrase in them, "'I cannot refuse to admit that *Burke got no more than his deserts . . .*'" would not be legally prosecuted, *but* Parnell, in denying authorship, forgot to mention Burke until there were cries of "Burke" from the House. Thus, Parnell's desire, if not his share in responsibility for Burke's death, is implied. Second, his denial that he knew of the crime beforehand was unnecessary since everyone knows "he has far more wit than to have known." Finally, there is the familiar protest, "Guilt must not be imputed by anyone" before the Commission decides *but* " . . . there is nothing intrinsically impossible in the charges."

Guilt by association, by insinuation and indirection, the sowing of doubt and suspicion, and simple confusion by careful repetition of all the if's that imply crime are Saintsbury's methods. Their use is cool, deliberate, and skillful, though he does rely on some rhetorical tricks. Over and over again, during the year and more when Parnell made himself vulnerable by failing to demand an inquiry, the *Saturday* insisted that Parnell must prove his case; innocent men do not act this way. After Parnell did seek an inquiry, suspicion was kept alive while the larger guilt that the *Saturday Review* always assumed and the specific (unproved) guilt for the content and import of the letters blur into one—as intended. And the guilt was spread from Parnell onto all Gladstonites.

During the next year, the *Saturday Review* continued to hammer away sarcastically at Parnell's "frantic fear of investigation" and the inexplicable sight of "innocent" men acting as if they were "either desperately afraid of being found guilty or desperately afraid of being proved innocent." As Parliamentary debate on the Bill to establish a special commission to investigate Parnell dragged on night after night in July-August, 1888, the *Saturday Review* focused upon the increasing frenzy and hysteria in the House: "Injured innocence in screaming hysterics, conscious rectitude foaming at the mouth with the rage of terror . . ." and Mr. Parnell screaming about "loaded dice" and "poisoned daggers." The leader, "Mad or Guilty?" again asks, "Is this exactly the way in which an innocent man behaves?"

The final acts in the long drama were the Pigott confession and the fall of Parnell. When the commission called Pigott to testify on February 15, 1889, he confessed the forgeries, then fled to Spain and killed himself.[31] O'Shea had testified that the letters were written by Parnell, the court had refused handwriting experts, and Houston had named Pigott. The moment for the *Saturday Review* to cry, "We told you so!" had arrived. And Saintsbury does so in "The Wood and the Holloa." He challenges the view that Mr. Parnell has been "proved innocent." The Gladstonites had been spreading the delusion that "the whole connection of Parnellism and Crime turned on the letters," but he declares this is "totally baseless." They only *confirm* the case against Parnell and a whole party. This is certainly the "Fable for Parnellites" Saintsbury spoke of writing to cool the indecent Parnellite glee over the Pigott confession.[32] It may well be looked on as Saintsbury's political "diploma piece"—one worthy of the "Reviler" tradition—with its touch of that hubris political drama can inspire, especially when one holds the winning cards.

A strong reversal of feeling toward Parnell followed Pigott's confession, prompted no doubt by the English spirit of fair play. But the *Saturday Review* saw the shift from the cry of "crucify" to that of "Hosanna" as engineered by Gladstonites, "the real organizers" of a Parnell "boom," and concluded that these efforts to play upon maudlin sentimentality made Parnell's behavior seem a model of reserve.

When Parnell's troubles were multiplied by the divorce proceedings brought by O'Shea against his wife Kitty, the *Saturday Review,* protesting its reluctance, turned to the personal matter and accused Parnell of bravado in his decision to remain as Irish leader. The further suggestion was made that Parnell had decided that their cause, already scarred by violations of the Sixth and Eighth Commandments, would not be much uglier for a touch of the Seventh. The editorial ends with a typical Saintsbury rhetorical flourish gathering up all the "awful wrongs" of a decade.

> We are not against Home Rule because Home Rulers have been personally the most discredited and discreditable party of politicians that even Ireland has ever seen.... We are not against Home Rule because Home Rulers never won, with a few eccentric exceptions, a respectable advocate out of Ireland till they bought part of a party with the hope of office.... We oppose Home Rule ... because it is certain to cause disaster to this realm and this people....

No personal reforms would alter this judgment, because adultery is Parnell's lesser crime and his broader guilt is the main concern. "It is not more disgraceful deliberately to deceive Captain O'Shea than deliberately to deceive the House of Commons."

By 1880, the Victorians had arrived at a peculiarly unlovely hypocritical position on public and private morality. Though Lord Hartington and other well-known figures escaped, Charles Dilke had been put to the rack, and the Liberal Party, nursing its wounds, was vulnerable. For the Tory press it was a field day.[33]

The Kitty O'Shea–Parnell liaison had always been common knowledge in the Irish Party and among English Liberals, but Gladstone had stubbornly averted his eyes. When he finally repudiated Parnell in 1890, the *Saturday Review,* in "the Comedy of the Drumming Out," attacked his party's view of him as "morally sublime": "The moral sublime that waits to see how the cat will jump is not Himalayan in height or saintly in morality." Lighter in touch and affording some comic relief, "The Reappearance of the Irishman" is probably also by Saintsbury, a great lover of Charles Lever's novels. He uses Lever's *Charles O'Malley* to depict the struggle between Parnellites and the Justin McCarthy faction of the Irish Party. Freed from the "irksome restraints of a four-year alliance with an English party" and their "milk-and-water methods" of party warfare, "they break heads and fling mud at each other with all the buoyancy and abandon of fresh emancipation." The "rollicking" Irishman of Lever's fiction is thus patronizingly revived and, as the McCarthy faction battled with the Parnellites, the *Saturday Review* warned the English, "No one is bound to go to Donnybrook, but if he does, he is a fool to go without a shillelagh."

When Gladstone returned to power briefly in 1892, the *Saturday Review* greeted the new government in a familiar metaphor (such as Saintsbury loved) as a ship "with doting egotism in the captain's cabin, double-dealing and office-seeking on the quarterdeck, greed and ignorance in the forecastle." And the Unionists were warned, they should be flogged if they do not sink it! The next year, with a satiric Ibsen title, "The Political Master-Builder" and a parody of Polonius for good measure, Saintsbury hailed Gladstone's destruction of "stately edifices, the habitations of a living nation" to "run up his wretched jerry-buildings," tearing down the English constitution to build "the miserable shanty of an Irish Legislature and Executive." Finally, when the Lords killed the bill and Home Rule, Saintsbury offered a ceremony of interment for this "monster begotten six months ago by personal ambition upon party selfseeking."

By comparison with W. T. Stead's crucifying campaign against Dilke, the *Saturday*'s handling of Parnell is a model of calm, rational criticism—sophisticated, confident, smugly self-righteous and cruel but posing as impersonally judicious. And the attitudes toward Ireland and Parnell are more sober and less extreme than those voiced by Lord Salisbury or by the more vituperative daily press.[34] The tone is rarely personal, rarely abusive despite the large doses of sarcasm and the hammering repetition. The *Saturday Review* wanted to maintain its image as "written by gentlemen for gentlemen." It even suggested that the press, generally, could have shown more charity and grace over the divorce decree. But the satirist in pursuit of his quarry is enjoying the chase and sometimes reflects more faith in the laugh than the bludgeon. He shows some skill in "letting people make fools of themselves," be it Tipperary priests or Gladstonian Liberals. Saintsbury delighted in such things.

Since the aim was to shatter public confidence in the Liberals' Irish policies, the Tory organ could not afford the luxury of sympathy for the Irish peasant or the bedeviled Parnell, and, like Saintsbury, its readers probably felt little. They could not afford to admit Gladstone's idealism except as a form of moral hypocrisy, and opposing change as they did, they had to ignore the realism of his belief that the Irish people and their will must ultimately be reckoned with. Gladstone's "innocence" they chose to see as cunning—with some justification; his only motives seemed to them to be ambition and party interest. There are few moral grays; all is black and white. The fears aroused by violence are matched by fears of sentimentalism. Force and order, coercion or emigration, are the familiar traditional solutions proposed, none of which ever worked. A hundred years later it all seems too familiar.

The London press during these fifteen years (1880–94) was overwhelmingly partisan. E. L. Godkin of the New York *Nation*, surveying the scene in 1887, could discover no sources of impartial coverage of English politics.[35] Preoccupied with this virulent partisanship, he missed the fact that the press became more and more anti-Gladstone until, as Arnold pointed out, the Tories carried "the mind of the country" with them in resistance to Home Rule and many intellectuals registered their protest in periodicals. So the *Saturday Review*'s stand became more and more representative. The extreme view that Godkin deplored is there. The other side is portrayed as ignorant, stupid, foolish, or capricious and corrupted by the desire for political power. The Liberals, all those strange bedfellows—Whig politicians, statesmen, nonconformist Puritans, Birmingham Radicals, and Irish Nationalists—lent themselves easily to such attack, and the *Saturday Review* had a long history of taking the high moral tone in lashing its victims. Tricks of fate and timing (as with the O'Shea divorce) helped invite the trial by press that Saintsbury conducted.

Having the *Saturday Review* as his outlet, he could exert a steady influence anonymously. W. P. Ker told Saintsbury that his articles helped convert him from a Gladstone upbringing to anti-Gladstone views.[36] Clever and trained in his function, loyal to his side, often astute and shrewd but rarely inspired, useful therefore to any side in a mediocre political era, Saintsbury offers nothing lasting as political literature or distinguished in style. But he is truly "Mr. *Saturday Review*" in the last decade and a half of its power and influence, when it was still at least an index of Conservative opinion. These Irish articles afford one more window opening on that perpetually intriguing drama of Parnell and the struggle for Home Rule in Ireland—a typically Tory one.

CHAPTER 7

London Life: Reviews and Biographies

Saintsbury's family was settled in Kensington for the first decade of his strenuous, seventeen-year journalistic career in London. In 1882, they purchased the lease on a house just being built, one that had special amenities because it was used to advertise the other houses in the row. These included an elaborate bath with shower and an odd machine to produce waves ("more ingenious than effective") and a larder that the owner could convert to a very satisfactory wine cellar. Despite his claims for its modesty, the dimensions of its twenty-five stone bins indicate it held hundreds of bottles, casks, and jars, all lovingly selected.[1] The time Saintsbury spent on this hobby, snatched from a very heavy work schedule, gave him an important and much enjoyed form of relaxation and an escape from many pressures. Much time went to the study of wine lists, attendance at sales and consultation with wine merchants. Some of these became long-standing friends, notably the Harveys of Bristol. Finally, the storing of the wines and liquors and the choice of those that would grace their formal dinners were all done with meticulous, almost compulsive attention; acquiring the knowledge necessary for all of this took many more hours. Saintsbury describes his cellar in the 1880s as that of "a hardworking journalist." It staggers the imagination to picture those crowded days and nights—the editorial work with long days and a long walk home, the steady flow of book packets for review after long nights of reading while the more lasting work for essays, prefaces, and surveys was also going on. One should not wonder that we hear little of his growing sons, nothing more of family holidays, or of any real involvement with his family. When was there time?

Saintsbury refers to very little home entertaining before 1895, and his home from 1887 on was outside London, but *Notes on a Cellar Book* includes four dinner menus from 1884–86, one country one of 1888, and a later selection from Edinburgh—one a "fourteener"

115

in company, with ten courses from soup to savory, eight wines, and a champagne Jeraboam, Dagouet 1874, wreathed in primroses and violets, as a centerpiece. For two of the Edinburgh dinners Saintsbury used a French chef, Gregoire, who both "sent out and superintended dishes" and was famed for sublime dessert soufflés. He mentions that his wife shared in planning these dinners. Looking back in 1920, he admits that these menus were "overelaborated," as was then the custom. In his later view, "two entrees are quite enough." A dinner in June, 1886, with M. Beljame as guest included nothing French except the wines and introduced the Frenchman to "Iced Gooseberry Fool." A file of these somewhat Lucullan feasts with guest and wine lists included was destroyed with other personalia.[2] Three, five, seven, even eight different wines were served at each of the recorded dinners. Much about these occasions no record could capture because Saintsbury regarded dinner as "not so much to eat . . . as to drink, to talk, to flirt, to discuss, to rejoice 'at the closing of the day.'"[3]

For the night worker and night reader he was, such occasions must have been infrequent at best. Kipling recalled breakfast in the Albany with Walter Pollock and Saintsbury, who "produced some specially devilish Oriental delicacy which we cooked by the light of our united ignorances."[4] J. M. Dent tells of a "deliciously choice" dinner Saintsbury prepared for him in his Great Ormond Street rooms accompanied by the appropriate array of wines.[5] When Dent confessed he took no wine, Saintsbury was dismayed but carefully selected a cigar for him. When Dent began to light it with a wax lucifer, his host was "horrorstruck" and found a piece of wood to light it, explaining that the stench of wax would spoil the enjoyment of a cigar. He added that he had always tried to find the best in everything, material and spiritual.

These bachelor occasions, the only ones recorded, occurred in the years when he spent four nights a week in Great Ormond Street. W. P. Ker was a neighbor in Gower Street and, in 1892, they began an intimate friendship, one of the few Saintsbury cherished. Though idiosyncratic, Ker was, according to Saintsbury, "a rare man of the most varied likableness," brilliant in conversation, "if brief and broken," learned, and a lover of long evenings of talk. He was a born gift giver,[6] a bachelor devoted to his nieces and nephews, and, like Saintsbury, a great walker. Their companionship was a warm and happy experience, first in Great Ormond Street, Gower

Street, or at Reading, less often at Edinburgh where Ker had much earlier been a lecturer, and most satisfying of all, weekends when Saintsbury was Ker's guest at All Souls, Oxford. Ker's more exact scholarly mind and keen critical sensibility, his habit of understatement, and his disdain for history and even for poetic analysis[7] were a foil for the enthusiastic, more productive but less discriminating Saintsbury, with what Grierson calls his "clean-cut, strong-held prejudices and not less humorously exaggerated edge with which he stated them, and the out-of-the-way accurate knowledge which lay behind them."[8] Each of the pair knew much the other did not, yet their common ground was great. Ker read practically all Saintsbury's proofs after 1894 and they advised mutually on their books until Ker's death in 1923. Unfortunately, none of their correspondence survives.

Clubs, the typical Englishman's retreat, played their role for Saintsbury in the London years. He was at the Savile almost daily, including Saturday. The Omar Khayyam Club, "a cheerful hospitable society," once invited him to an "excellent dinner plentifully furnished with Omar's beloved liquor," but lacking "a tulip-cheeked creature" to sit beside one.[9] The Rabelais Club dined about six times a year, with no speeches except one toast—to "the Master." The intellectual side of the feast lay in "leaflets, verses, and all kinds of literary triflings" eventually collected in *Recreations of the Rabelais Club*.[10] Among these was a multilingual game in which a brief stanza in German in praise of Beethoven's symphonies by Sir Frederick Pollock went into Latin by Sidney Lee, French by Walter Pollock, then English by Besant, then Greek by Saintsbury.[11]

Saintsbury knew none of the earlier Victorian literary giants personally except Arnold and him only casually. He lacked Gosse's craving for "lions," literary or social. He speaks of Henry James and Meredith personally and recalled that both talked naturally rather than in the style of their books. He had two luncheons with Gosse at which James was present in the early 1890s. Saintsbury admired and enjoyed Hardy in club contacts and saw him last at the dedication of the monument to Henley (1907). He thought Hardy's gracious simplicity accounted for his greatness.

The New York *Critic* began a review of Saintsbury's *Elizabethan Literature* in 1888, with a pretty accurate description of the London literary scene.[12]

England swarms, just now, with competent critics of the second class, such as Gosse, Dobson, Lang, Dowden, Saintsbury, Symonds, Stephen, Traill, A. W. Ward, T. H. Ward, and Morison . . . able to turn out in six months a neat and praiseworthy history of English or French literature, a selection of lyrics, a neat edition of a classic, a biography, or an edited series, with perhaps an original poem or novel thrown in; while Mr. Churton Collins and the *Quarterly* lie in ambuscade. Mr. Saintsbury, in his preface, is forewarned and forearmed.

A flow of handbooks, anthologies, and new introductory editions of the "classics" came steadily from the press in the 1880s, done singly or cooperatively by men of letters, journalists, and academics. It was the start of a new industry, then amateur, but increasing in professionalism and in quantity ever since.

Parallel with his work on French literature and like it sandwiched into his busy life as journalist and editor, Saintsbury from 1880 on was represented in every category of English literary studies, establishing himself as a critic of some authority and as a literary historian. This work, though then less in volume than that on French literature, explains why he was an object of attack for W. T. Stead and Churton Collins in 1886 and why he knew he would be. His first published volume on English literature was a biography of Dryden. Essays, prefaces, and surveys quickly followed, all against the background of constant anonymous reviewing.

Reviews

The hundreds of reviews Saintsbury wrote from 1874 to 1895 deserve very brief consideration, ranging over every subject as they did and none of them distinguished. A born reviewer, he enjoyed the work; he never tired of it and returned to it in his last years.

Saintsbury did the criticism of all minor poetry for the *Academy* from 1875 until about 1883. He examined "probably not less than a thousand, certainly not less than five or six hundred volumes, finding the true poetic spirit in not more than two or three"[13]—staggering evidence of his tolerance for mediocrity and of the amount of it available. Among a dozen reviews of poets no one today ever heard of, he did Dobson's *Proverbs in Porcelain,* three volumes by James

Thomson, two each by S. H. Hodgson and Thomas Gordon Hake, but he does not overpraise these frail blooms of a pretty dead poetic season. Although stated *Academy* policy was to gibbet mercilessly what is bad, one finds little gibbeting.[14]

Saintsbury also read thousands of bad novels to unearth a few gems for the *Academy*. He was paid for reviews, not for volumes scanned, and the *Academy* was notably poor.[15] Perhaps only Saintsbury's sense of humor and his need to be constantly reading saved his sanity, as his comment on a best-seller of the 1850s suggests: "Any clever cub, in the prentice stage of reviewing could make columns of fun out of [*Emily Wyndham*]."[16] No one has more warmly recalled the fascination and pleasures of reviewing. But he also held "the memory full of fright of many a double-volumed night." He enjoyed slating, and he speaks of one book that made the "reviewer's fingers itch to smash."[17]

Saintsbury had no illusions about the overall quality of current book reviewing. In 1891, he described it as "on the whole the most lightly assigned and the most irresponsibly performed."[18] He admitted there was too much reviewing, too much butter and too little slating, and he knew that any man with a reputation for reviewing in London could write for a dozen papers and would be asked to do so.[19] As a result, the practice had lost a good deal of authority. He considered a man was not underpaid who received three pounds ten "for work which should on average take him an evening to read, and not the whole of the next morning to write"—the overnight break helping to tone down and order his impressions and shape a judgment.

In his 1896 survey of twenty years' reviewing, Saintsbury noted that the University Honors Programs helped prepare the reviewer—a "critic in little"—who should know the history of criticism and have a large experience of reading.[20] Like most of his contemporaries, he did not think a specialist's knowledge essential. Reviewing he saw as an art, not a science, and "the perfect reviewer," as "second best in everything."[21] The reviewer's business is with the way an author does his or her work and with the question, "Is this ... a fair addition to the literature of the class it intends to reach?" He *must* judge—not "shilly-shally." He must tell "the general congregation of decently educated and intelligent people," (the audience he aimed at) whether the work is worth their while. Saintsbury took pride in telling people what and how to read, and he felt that, with reviews, authors occasionally gain valuable censorship to offset mere popularity. He thought the journals he had written for imperfect but useful. "They have as a rule set their faces against prevalent follies and faults; . . . their strictures, even when harsh, have been wholesome in particulars . . . insisting that Literature is an Art, and the Man of Letters an Artist; that to admire bad art is a disastrous and terrible thing." And everyone with some effort can rejoice in the good.[22] Though this is rather an overestimate, such a faith strengthened the self-respect of the reviewer and fed his hope that the next batch of books would bring a fine surprise, such as Saintsbury experienced when he received Morris's *Voyage of Maeldune* or Tennyson's and Browning's swan songs. Unfortunately, he was not ready to rejoice when other surprises came to hand—Zola, Tolstoy, Ibsen, or *Tess of the D'Urbervilles*. And despite all this theory, too many of his reviews done too quickly are run of the mill. They came too easily.

Of the reviewing Saintsbury did for the *Athenaeum*, out of two hundred anonymous pieces only two score were on English writers. These include: the minor poets—Patmore, Stephen Hawker, Palgrave ("undigested"), Todhunter (who "never deviates into poetry")—also George Venable's *Bunyan* and Bayard Tuckerman's *History of English Fiction* (useless before Malory and inadequate on the nineteenth century), Disraeli's *Endymion* ("quiet, graceful English prose"), George Moore's *A Modern Lover* (the satire he thought woefully conventional). The *Athenaeum*, a staid and elderly journal under a not very colorful editor, Norman MacColl (from 1878 on), offered Saintsbury little challenge. Many of the reviews were only paragraphs. It was probably Saintsbury who gave judgment on Yeats's early *Wandering of Oison* in the *Guardian* as rough and sometimes unharmonious but with promise and a "touch of vision" second only to Tennyson's.[23] Rather patronizingly he concluded that, if Yeats put in such hard work and self-correction as the Laureate applied, "we ought to have some excellent poetry from [him]." With less need to prophesy, Saintsbury is more favorable to Meredith's *Reading of Earth*. Meredith he places in "the sparsely filled front row of our living men of letters" despite his willfully eccentric language. Longfellow, despite "hideous" Americanisms, is an exquisite and delightful poet "good for bringing children at one stage to poetry." But Mark Twain's *A Connecticut Yankee in King Arthur's Court* has no redeeming virtue.

In the *Saturday Review* he condemned some well-known current works, notably Mrs. Humphrey Ward's *Robert Elsmere*, as he did the French naturalists. This, and a more favorable review of James, illustrate the kind of influence he was exerting. *Robert Elsmere* is "on the wrong track" and exhibits the faults of two contemporary schools. Mrs. Ward is "as much a slave of documents" as any French naturalist and as much the slave of "analysis" as William Dean Howells himself, and she fails to add saving action or character interest. Her novel is far too long. In the same review, Edward Bellamy's *Looking Backward* is damned as "a stupid book," its "frame of fiction" being too slender and lacking in interest to offset "the solid muddle of dull purpose" and silly "didactics."[24] Saintsbury thinks *The Princess Casamassima* "worth a wilderness of *Washington Squares*" because James "has made a real story and invented . . . characters in whom the ordinary reader who enjoys Scott and Dickens and Marryat" can be sincerely interested. Despite too much talk and too much analysis, Saintsbury welcomes the romance in the novel and rejoices in Millicent Henning as a "cockney *pur sang*" and "a capital study"; he hopes James will continue in this vein.[25] Story, character, and romance are what he demands in all fiction, while he misses what really distinguishes James.

In Saintsbury's brief association with the *New Review* (1893–95), he dealt with several friends' works, Traill's *Lord Salisbury,* Lang's *Blue Poetry Book,* and Henley's *Lyra Heroica.* He wrote on Wilde's *House of Pomegranates* as "the best thing Mr. Wilde has yet done," Morris's *Glittering Plain* as "pure delight," and James's *Lesson of the Master* as proving James to be at his best as a teller of short tales; also on Kipling's *Naulaka* and *Many Inventions* (praise by a confessed jingo), Gosse's *Secret of Narcisse,* and Ibsen's *Master Builder* as translated by Gosse and William Archer. The Ibsen play was a fortunate choice. He finds it a "worthy work" by a man of genius, though he allows himself to laugh at Ibsen's worshippers and at Ibsen's own absurdities while stressing his "strange excellences," those of vast romantic fancy and true appreciation of the irony of life, "the two greatest things in all literature." He liked the *Wild Duck.* He does Ibsen far less justice in *The Later Nineteenth Century* in 1907.

Saintsbury wisely chose to reprint very few reviews. A handful reappeared in two posthumous collections. But he made a real mistake in judgment with *Corrected Impressions* (1895). Twenty-two slight papers (a pair for each of ten major Victorian writers and two on

"Three Mid-Century Novelists"), most of them done for the *Indian Daily News* and the *New York Critic,* were put into a volume in the "lean year" before Saintsbury's appointment to Edinburgh. They are by far the weakest part of his *Collected Essays.* Called "Impressions" in the preface, they are no more than this, being loosely organized, rambling, written in a tone of literary chit-chat more often associated with Gosse. They mingle personal reminiscence with an account of the subject's changing reputation as Saintsbury purports to trace the "development" of his personal opinions of that subject. Reviewers were quick to spot the irony, and Saintsbury himself laughingly quotes a contemporary's remark, "He never changed a first impression in his life." The corrections are negligible.[26] Saintsbury later did better with all these figures elsewhere. Before 1895 he had written at length only on Carlyle.[27] These feeble essays suggest a truth Saintsbury never faced. Compulsively writing too much, he also read too much mediocre and bad stuff; this was inevitably corrupting. Henley was perceptive when he declared in 1883 that Saintsbury wrote so much it was a wonder that he so often wrote so well.[28]

Until 1887, when Saintsbury's first survey of English Literature appeared, a host of reviews, the essays and prefaces just considered, one biography, and the large body of writings on French literature were the basis for his authority and reputation. These were what the English reader knew when, in 1886, the *Pall Mall Gazette's* guns were turned upon him.

Biographies

Saintsbury's first published volume on English literature was a life of Dryden. The evidence that Saintsbury enjoyed knowing and interpreting the lives of writers almost in spite of himself colors all his work and especially the essay "Some Great Biographers" (1892). Biography is for him of two kinds—the "editing" and the shorter, "digested" kind where all the material "passes through the alembic of the biographer," and the latter is artistically the most perfect. In the first kind he dared think that Lockhart outdid Boswell. Moore's *Byron,* with all its faults, is his other example. The subject tells his own story within a framework built for him by "an architect" who has "a perfect conception of the subject," who exercises his art in "severe but masterly selection" but skillfully effaces himself. The end product is "a finished picture, a real composition."[29]

At the extreme end of the digested type Saintsbury places Carlyle's *Sterling* because the weak subject, made romantic, almost vanishes in the brilliance of the writer and his re-creation of his world. This brief work he thinks a masterpiece but not strictly a biographical one. At the other extreme he places Sir George Trevelyan's *Macaulay*, a faithful unvarnished picture of the man as he actually was. In different ways he thus suggests how he might have reacted to the imaginative methods of Maurois, Strachey, or Guedalla. Decades ahead of them he protested against "the pathless deserts of four volumes" with "their cataracts of undigested documents and facts" that Victorian hagiography dumped upon their "devoted readers." He praised Lockhart not only for plan and selection, but for avoiding excessive praise or blame and for "the art of the advocate in making the best of it."[30] His own efforts in the field were all brief volumes each done to order for a series.

John Dryden, the first of Saintsbury's five biographies, he did for the English Men of Letters Series edited by John Morley in 1880. It had its inception in the reading he had done at Elgin, in a rejected series of articles, and in four lectures, "Dryden and his Period," he gave at the Royal Institution in the spring of 1880. It is his happiest attempt in the genre. A dearth of biographical material allowed him to concentrate on the literary development of this, "the greatest craftsman in English letters," as he saw him. His admitted indifference to the theatre narrowed the focus further. His prose is terse and direct and his personal judgment is firmly stated. He did no fresh research, though visits to the birthplace and other Northamptonshire spots Dryden knew helped him give a sense of reality to the available details within the limits necessary to this popular series.

Saintsbury disposes quietly of hearsay and of libels on Dryden's life as he traces the pattern of his literary maturing and his development of a modern, workaday style. He helps the reader see Dryden as "a typical Englishman of his times," "the most representative" but well in advance of his contemporaries, influencing everyone in all the literary forms of his day. One is reminded that this is a Victorian biography chiefly when Saintsbury laments the impossibility of quoting some of Dryden's artistically fine lyrics because of their "license of language" and by his dismissal of the comedies as vulgar and indecent.[31]

The question of Dryden's political and religious changes of mind and allegiance is dealt with in a sympathetic, commensense fashion acceptable still: Saintsbury sees them as the actions of a man passionate only in devotion to literature, one who, perhaps fed up with the Puritanism of the Protectorate, gave himself intensely and well to the argument of the moment—never having regarded consistency as a supreme virtue in anything. As for his conversion, Saintsbury asks one terse question: "Is Dryden's [present day] critic... prepared to question the sincerity of Cardinal Newman?"[32] He is unwilling to challenge that of Dryden.

As a whole, the volume reads easily. Dryden comes to life, and students getting their introduction to Dryden from it would not be misled on essentials, though they would need some supplement especially on the plays. Dryden the critic gets less emphasis and less clear-cut placing than in the later *History of Criticism*.

Attitudes that have become familiar in Saintsbury's reviews and essays are everywhere in this volume. He judges poetry by treatment, not by subject. A poet is great if he or she has "the power of making the common uncommon by the use of articulate language in metrical arrangement so as to excite indefinite suggestions of beauty." Dryden has this power in enormous range. Admitting he shares the romantic preference of his generation for "Kubla Khan," the "Ode on the Intimations of Immortality," and the "Ode on a Grecian Urn," Saintsbury nevertheless insists that Dryden is one of the great poets, one who shares the virtues of Aeschylus, Lucretius, Spenser, Shelley, Heine, and Hugo (a revealing list).[33]

He defends his minute attention to Dryden's style as essential, however out of fashion or unrelated to "criticism of life" it may be, thus anticipating but disagreeing with Arnold's "classics of our prose" judgment.[34] He places Dryden's prose style well in relation to other seventeenth-century prose, though he does not mention Thomas Sprat or the Royal Society. He credits Dryden with the first sure sense of the sentence as an organic unit and is sound in emphasizing that his was the first achievement of prose as an instrument absolutely reliable and clear when applied to any and every topic.[35]

Romantic though he is in so many ways, Saintsbury responded fully to the normal, "healthy" blend of classic, neoclassic, and romantic that was Dryden. Though he gave minimal space to ideas, he respected his subject. All this helps to explain why T. S. Eliot dedicated his *Homage to John Dryden* to Saintsbury.

The Saintsbury-Scott Dryden

The immediate outgrowth of the Dryden biography was Saintsbury's first major job of editing, that of the Walter Scott edition, the only complete *Dryden* then available. These eighteen volumes, somewhat a labor of love, were not a fortunate venture.[36] The admiration Saintsbury felt for Scott's editing worked fatally as he determined to do only what Scott would have done with only whatever advance the seventy-four years between might give, and to avoid "purely literary criticism" as much as possible, as well as philosophy, archaeology, and other things he thought "ancillary" to literature.[37] These limitations alone doomed the work.

Condemnation came soon and has continued ever since. The Dryden editors, John Sargeaunt and Montague Summers, condemned Saintsbury's efforts severely, then in turn challenged each other and have since been challenged by others.[38] His generation, which made so many medieval, Renaissance and seventeenth-century texts available (Grosart, Bullen, Arber, etc.) and offered the public such useful series of texts as the Mermaid and Muses Library, performed a ground-breaking task however amateur their methods. All of Saintsbury's editing (Dryden, Fielding, Sterne, Smollett, Peacock, Balzac, Thackeray, the Caroline Poets, and many single volumes headed by his Donne and his Mermaid Dryden and Shadwell) belongs to this era of amateurs.

Establishing an authoritative text of Dryden has proved so difficult that the work is not yet satisfactorily complete despite modern developments in textual scholarship and the cooperative efforts of groups of trained specialists. Saintsbury brought no such special training to the job, and he was undertaking work of a type where his competence was never high. A temperament alien to textual scholarship, poor eyesight, and lack of training all played their part. He always worked far too rapidly for meticulous editing, and the lack of technical knowledge that he shared with Scott could only compound Scott's errors.[39] His indifference to standards of precise accuracy only made things worse.

To consider all the specific charges that have been leveled against the Saintsbury-Scott Dryden would not be profitable. A great expense of energies was misdirected and hence wasted. Unrealistic in his eagerness to make all of Dryden available to the "general," with a self-confidence many critics have mistaken for cocksureness, in producing this huge unsatisfactory "monument," Saintsbury did Dryden a disservice except in its keeping the whole corpus of his work available.[40]

The inadequacies of Saintsbury's editing show most plainly when set beside W. P. Ker's two-volume critical edition of Dryden's *Essays.* Ker also wanted to provide a workable edition for the general student and the result is excellent.[41] He acknowledged Saintsbury's help but tactfully omitted all reference to Saintsbury's editing. Saintsbury recognized Ker's accomplishment graciously: "No one has vindicated Dryden better against the half-witted blunderers."[42]

Saintsbury's Mermaid Shadwell (1905) is a competent appendix to his work on Dryden. He admits the irony that a "professed servant of Dryden" should rescue Dryden's enemy from the literary oblivion to which he had been dispatched by Dryden's lampoons. There had been no edition of Shadwell since 1720, and the selection of plays was difficult because dullness, coarseness, and a general ineptitude run through the seventeen plays. Shadwell "could do anything but *write,*" as his famous enemy had proclaimed, but Saintsbury credits him with technique, a power of acute observation, a command of comic incident, and with bringing actual life onto the stage.[43]

The second of Saintsbury's biographies was that of Sir Walter Scott. No work could have been more congenial for him than this brief one put together rapidly in 1897. His respect and affection not much this side of idolatry were supported by knowledge and lifelong acquaintance, all demonstrated elsewhere. Lockhart's views seemed to Saintsbury wholly sane, but he made use of the *Journal* that Lockhart had omitted, believing it to be "one of the most pathetically interesting things in biographical literature." The painful mystery and "colossal irony" of Scott's financial ruin had a special fascination for him. He concludes that Scott might have been saved from his "not so very slow suicide" had he been willing to sell all that "vampire" of possessions that sucked his lifeblood instead of choosing bankruptcy and the dreadful writing marathon.

"Scott could tell a story as few other men could," he asserts, and

on this judgment he founds his great praise of both verse and novels—without ever answering the question why so few people read
Scott. His faith in Scott's greatness never swerves and he fails to
question the depth of Scott's knowledge of human nature as he commands, " . . . read, enjoy and admire."

Saintsbury was right in seeing that Scott's real importance was his
setting the pattern of the historical novel, but he refers his reader to
his essay, "The Historical Novel," where the method is well defined.[44]
Good as the essay is, the biography would have gained by the inclu-
sion of some of these insights, in place of the prize-giving commentary on the novels offered with its emphasis always on the characters.
One suspects that, like Gautier and Balzac, Scott will not again find
many to "read all of him" as Saintsbury wished.[45] The passionate
coda that closes the biography is one of those finales that become
familiar in Saintsbury, so eloquent that one feels a little ashamed not
to have read more Scott.

In the late 1890s, Blackwood invited Saintsbury to write the life of
Arnold for the Modern Writers Series. He was obviously pleased with
the assignment.[46] He used only the official source, *The Letters* edited
by George W. E. Russell (1896), who selected from the letters as they
were preserved by the family after excisions. Saintsbury did not go
much beyond them. At its worst, his slim volume is a perfunctory
running commentary on the letters, among which the early Arnold-
Clough correspondence was not included.

This short biography had virtues as well as serious weaknesses.
The first part gives useful detailed analysis of the prosody of *The
Poems* of 1849 and 1853, and the best of Arnold's poetry is recognized as such with contagious enthusiasm. The 1853 *Preface* and 1865
Essays are hailed as epoch making and as the roots of a new critical
movement—valuable even when one disagrees with them. Saintsbury
writes eloquently on Arnold's "Heine" and his later essays on Amiel
and Scherer, and he grasped the importance of *A French Eton.*

But on Arnold's prose as a whole the work fails, the low point being
reached in the chapter on the religious essays, "In the Wilderness."
There is too much negative criticism, too ready use of the terms
will-worship, wilful, caprice, and the like. His blindness on *Culture and
Anarchy* is more serious. He grants it is well written and "studiously
moderate," but the crusade it began he regarded as a waste of talents
and the results as "dead seafruit." *Literature and Dogma* and its great

popularity he could scarcely stomach. All his disagreements, whether on miracles, Ireland, education, or social programs, contribute little to any positive grasp of Arnold's later prose. Untroubled by his inconsistency, Saintsbury just barely redeemed himself by the eloquence and soundness of his conclusion that, despite his prejudices, leaves no doubt that he knew Arnold's worth and importance and knew them well.

One review of the biography was entitled "Pidgeon-holing Mr. Arnold"—a characterization not quite fair but understandable. Reviewers were embarrassed by the Tory High Churchman's querulous protests and his "imperfect sympathies,"[47] his cocksure flippancy, and a style one described as "a menace to good letters." Another critic found "too much of Mr. Saintsbury . . . and far too little of Matthew Arnold."[48] Saintsbury wished to do Arnold justice, but the lifelong conflict of literary father and son stood in the way of success, and he committed the very sins he cited in bad biographies.

Saintsbury's other two biographies, *Marlborough* and *Derby*, were "task work" done conscientiously by a busy journalist. Courage was needed to tackle the controversial figure of Marlborough in brief compass and give an impartial and judicious account of his life in the face of all the crimes charged against him by Whig historians, including Thackeray and Macaulay. Saintsbury examined the correspondence of the Duke and that of the Duchess Sarah, Coxe's *Memoirs* (1818–19), and Mrs. Creighton's brief study (1879). Because earlier works concentrated on the period of Blenheim, Saintsbury thought the question of Marlborough's "treason" to both James II and William was the sole justification for a new biography. Also, since he thought Sarah and Abigail Marsh had occupied too much space in history, they appear only when necessary.

Saintsbury's experience as a reviewer of military books had prepared him for his concentration upon Marlborough's military and political career, and he handles the campaigns clearly and succinctly, in a way that Lord Roberts at least approved.[49] He sensibly chose to quote Marlborough's modest and brief accounts of his first four victories from his letters to Sarah. There is no whitewashing of the Duke's moral character as he is judged guilty of "treacherous baseness" in his dealings with James and William. His informing James of the attack to be made at Brest is judged indefensible because of the high cost of English lives that directly resulted. But Saintsbury points to extenuating facts, practical not ethical ones: in a climate of self-interest and avarice the Duke was not alone in "always playing to win." Saintsbury paints a vivid portrait of a man who he thinks "had in perhaps the greatest measure of any Englishman every practical quality of the English character, except unflinching honesty and truth." In a final patriotic salute, he sheds the mask of objective historian. Later, more highly trained historians, while supplementing his facts and deepening some insights, have not quarreled seriously with the brief work—achieved by "competence and common sense."[50]

The Earl of Derby (1892) came closer home to a Victorian Tory who had spent his youth in the world where a rash and wayward amateur, the fourteenth Earl of Derby, played his undistinguished role and was thrice prime minister. There had not yet been a full life of Derby, and Saintsbury admits his Tory bias. He sought no private materials, brought out no new facts, and gave no bibliography. Though critical of Greville, he relies a good deal upon him for the facts before 1860 and occasionally for the later years. He also used what he himself had heard. The brief work is fair, frank, and politically shrewd. The final portrait is a wholly negative image of a near failure, the best Saintsbury could do for his subject. The result was a *tour de force* enlivened by anecdote, literary allusion, some slang, and some irony.

Saintsbury's five short biographies suggest that Lytton Strachey's violent assault on Victorian biographical whitewash perhaps deliberately overlooked the shorter works in such series as the English Men of Letters, where honesty and competence often match their brevity and offer little to tempt the debunker. Saintsbury, like other authors in those series, had learned from Lockhart and Carlyle as well as Boswell to give truth and frank judgment in vivid though brief detail, without the imaginative license of a Maurois or the satire of a Strachey.

CHAPTER 8

The Essayist and Historian of English Literature

In the early 1880s Saintsbury produced a series of twenty-odd signed essays on English writers for *Macmillan's Magazine*. The topics mostly proposed by its editor, his old friend, Mowbray Morris, were minor figures of the English and Scottish literary worlds of 1780 to 1860. He felt that they all had been neglected and none had yet been properly placed. He had discussed Lockhart in the *National Review* in 1884 and Susan Ferrier in the *Fortnightly Review* in 1882. All these essays he preserved in his *Collected Essays* and justifiably so. Having demonstrated in the *Fortnightly* essays on French novelists that the essay was his special forte, now with minor English writers he had found his most congenial subject. The results are good.

Typically, Saintsbury tells us what he did and did not read. All the minor prose writers wrote prodigiously; for Southey, Sidney Smith, and Cobbett the quantity is staggering. Susan Ferrier, with just three novels, is the happy exception. Many of these writers were shadowy or unknown to most English readers of the 1880s. Some were hard to come by and many were badly edited. Hence, the aim was to point out not only what was still readable but how to read it, and to bring the authors to life. Discussion of reputation is included and earlier critics' judgments afford a point of departure (e.g., Hazlitt on Crabbe, Carlyle on Wilson). The biographical sketches are concise but specific, occasionally witty, and rich in insight. Saintsbury's enjoyment as he traces character and biographical detail is greater than he liked to admit. He was eager to clear up misunderstandings and to put the writer in fair perspective, and he does not avoid judgment of character. He is severe but sound on Landor, Hunt, and Hazlitt and is concerned to relate the author's personality to the writings.

Their lives, ranging from the erratic and Bohemian to the well ordered and responsible, are made to seem relevant and interesting.

The group associated with the *Edinburgh Review,* the *Quarterly Review* and/or *Blackwood's Magazine* (Lockhart, Wilson, Hogg, Maginn, Jeffrey, Southey, and Smith), as presented, illuminate each other and bring the reader vividly into that cultural world of Edinburgh just before and after 1800 that they helped to shape. Others are linked by similarity of style (the humorists in verse and the writers of ornate prose), by their connection with the *London Magazine,* or by their friendships (Hazlitt, Hunt, and DeQuincey). These unifying elements, joined with Saintsbury's sympathy for earlier "gentlemen of the Press," helped make the essays a patterned drama. The literary life of an era is played out by a cast of journalists, with the major protagonists (Scott, Coleridge, Wordsworth) lingering in the wings in a way not done elsewhere. This work incidentally helped Saintsbury to know the Scottish world he was to enter in 1895.

Saintsbury shows how this era differed in taste from his own. Readers no longer welcomed the spontaneous horseplay, high jinks, or "cap and bells foolery" that many of the earlier men delighted in—ranging from bad to brilliant, from the rough jokes of Hogg to Sydney Smith's truer wit, and the verse punning of those eternal undergraduates, Praed and Hood. Similarly, the extreme, slating criticism of Wilson or Jeffrey, or the acrimonious and often ignorant impudence of Cobbett had gone out of fashion. But Saintsbury emphasizes the good things to be found in all of these men. He also offers his own rather adolescent and dated delight in Hood and the *Ingoldsby Legends.*

Today these essays have almost unique value because they set these men before us alive; they define each writer's faults and his peculiar virtues, and give judgment on his relative merit. More practically, they indicate the selective reading essential if one is to find the gold buried in the immense dross of these prolific and unequal writers. To have covered all this ground and erected the signposts is no mean service. On Borrow, Cobbett, Jeffrey, Wilson, Praed, and Hunt, it is well done and still deserves attention from students and thoughtful readers. In most instances, it whets the reader's appetite, though Edmund Wilson was led to Peter Pindar and his fellow satirists only to be disappointed. For the many who have missed Sydney Smith or were not brought up on "Lalla Rookh," *The Ingoldsby Legends,* or "The Curse of Kehama," Saintsbury arouses curiosity. One hopes to find the buried aperçus he promises or to "laugh till one's sides hurt" as he has done, or have one's blood stirred by the great English war songs. One may seek out one or another as students of mine did Sydney Smith. One may long for the anthology of these joys he never compiled or simply read him with gratitude.

Though Elton rightly complained that Saintsbury's critical handling often lacked finality, this is not true of these essays on minor writers. Subtle and sound distinctions are made, and the few overestimates, those of Hood, Tom Moore, Barham, and Sydney Smith, merely stamp his taste as mid-Victorian. He does not overvalue the two popular humorists, Maginn and Hook, and what he tells us of them is all we need to know.

He is less successful than he should have been on DeQuincey because he gives few signposts to guide the reader through the fourteen volumes of the Masson edition and is too much preoccupied with personality, as he seldom is. The essay on Southey is badly proportioned. Having devoted thirty pages to biography and three to poetry, he realized he had little space left for the dozen to fifteen volumes of prose that make Southey's real claim upon us. This illustrates something probably too frequent in Saintsbury's way of working—his leafing through and making running comments with little plan. Fortunately, these two essays are exceptions to the high quality of the series, and even these have their useful insights and their own quality of contagious enthusiasm.

Two of the best and most durable essays are those on the eccentrics, Borrow and Peacock. The job had not yet been done and Saintsbury does it well, making real the qualities that give these writers a hold on the few rather than the many. Nothing has yet replaced these perceptive studies or the prefaces to Peacock's novels that followed.

These essays, despite unevenness, are good criticism in their warmth of appreciation, in their sense of balance, in their catholicity, in their reflection of the critic's personality (he is truly at home here), and in the choice of vivid samplings. Saintsbury theorizes little, yet casually he drops some important ideas (e.g., on the vagaries of humor, on the relation of prosody to music, on the nature of genius). One must accept occasional overuse of superlatives as exaggerations of the moment. They belong to his "this-is-the-best-of-its-kind-any-where" syndrome and are matched by his "no one is more unequal or uncritical," applied first to Crabbe, then Cobbett, Hunt, and others. He failed to realize that he was simply defining the nature of any second-rate but vast producer—including himself.

Saintsbury does not overestimate the reader's familiarity with his subjects as he had sometimes done with major writers, and interest does not flag. The essays leave no doubt that he is at his best on minor writers and uniquely good on them.[1]

Along the way the reader may cherish the well-turned ironic touch, the whimsical response, a flash of wisdom or commonsense. Madame de Stael appears as "that second-rate leader-writer in petticoats." Of Sydney Smith's early struggles he says: "It is indeed not easy to live on invitations and your mother-in-law's pearls." One of Cobbett's crazes is neatly summed up: "Tea, the expeller of beer, the pamperer of foreign commerce, the waster of the time of farmers' wives is nearly as bad as the potato." The description of John Wolcott (Peter Pindar) was written by a confessed cat lover: "His best literary mood is that of a cat—not a cat in a rage, but a cat in a state of merriment purring and mumbling and rolling about. . . . You may look out for a shrewd scratch or bite shortly as part of the game." Faced with Dickens's disavowal that Skimpole was a caricature of Hunt, Saintsbury brooded, "with this, I am afraid the recording angel must have had some little difficulty."[2]

Those who enjoy local color may delight in Saintsbury's knowledge that the "leadless duel" between Moore and Jeffrey took place at Chalk Farm or that Praed's childhood was spent in John Street with the trees of Coram's Fields and Gray's Inn at the end of it and the associations of the Bedford Row Conspiracy and of Sydney Smith close by. One also catches the feel of Edinburgh with the subtle social differences between Moray and Buccleugh Places and the environs of Holyrood.

Saintsbury's habit of comparison, frequent here as elsewhere, usually justifies itself despite a sometimes negative emphasis. Landor's "marmoreal" prose is distinguished from Wilson's more flamboyant and DeQuincey's controlled and always appropriate ornateness. Peacock is matched with his "literary ancestors" (Aristophanes, Horace, Lucian, Rabelais, Montaigne). Jeffrey is presented on a large canvas amid all the critics of his era—with Arnold added for good measure, showing virtues he had and they lack.[3] A century has added new materials and new studies of the more major of these men (Hazlitt,

Lockhart, and DeQuincey, in particular), but these essays are still valuable, as are his best prefaces to English works, most of which were the work of the early 1890s.

The preface, a form of introduction incorporating a brief biography and criticism, had long flourished in France, and Arnold had successfully urged its revival in England. In Saintsbury's words, it "flourished to the modest advantage of the public men when vexed for want of pence." Convinced of its usefulness, he suggests what it requires. Since few readers have the information they need and few know the whole of an author's works or previous estimates of them, the introducer must supply these.[4]

In 1884, Saintsbury compiled *Specimens of English Prose Style* (a parallel to his *French Specimens*). The preface gives a historical survey of English prose style and includes his earliest definition of its rhythms, one later expanded in his *History of Prose Rhythm* (1912). He reminds the reader of his 1876 essay on modern prose and adds that his views have not changed.

Some of his prefaces rank among Saintsbury's best work. They have advantages over the literary survey because they allow more space for critical interpretation, for tracing the individual's development, and for those "literary filiations" and comparisons that are, for Saintsbury, "the most interesting things in literary study."[5] As introductions, they invited the appreciative vein with the stamp of personal flavor bolstered by fact. Often they seem less capricious, more carefully planned, and have more of the finality Elton wished for than his essays or surveys, perhaps because they are focused on a specific work or group of works rather than ranging over the whole corpus of the writer's often huge output. The tone is less "off the cuff," the style more polished. The result is memorable though seldom ground breaking, as were some of the essays on minor prose. His knack of summary and his skill in distinguishing quality also stand him in good stead here.

The preface to Donne's *Poems* is ground breaking, and one can easily agree with Elton that Saintsbury reached a peak of critical performance there.[6] Christopher Morley once suggested that Saintsbury's description of the provinces of thought where Donne was master be read "amorously." He does predate the whole twentieth-century exaltation of Donne, and he expressed the fear of having seemed "an unreasonable lover"; a charge not likely to be made today. Saintsbury analyzed the rare "union of the sensual, intellectual, poetical and religious temperaments" expressed in Donne (above all in *The Second Anniversary*), thus anticipating T. S. Eliot on Donne's "unified sensibility." He also found in Donne a pessimism paralleled only in Ecclesiastes and the paradox of "spiritualized worldliness and sensuality" typical of the Renaissance spirit that he defined so well in his preface to the *Heptaméron*.

There are shortcomings in his critique. He speaks of Donne's "roughness" of style as the result of lack of revision and thus somewhat underestimates the deliberation and conscious artistry it probably reflects outside the *Satires* where, as Saintsbury knew, it was conventional. He claimed for Donne some lyrics since rejected, but his general interpretation is a landmark as well as a hint of things to come.[7] The merits of this preface are of a different order from those of the longer, much more philosophical, and more scholarly one of his Edinburgh successor Grierson, for the Oxford *Donne* (1912), which was to become an ideal in scholarly editing. Saintsbury's, nineteen years before, had served an earlier, wider, less knowing audience.

Three of Saintsbury's prefaces of the same period, one for selections from Herrick, one for his anthology *Seventeenth-Century Lyrics*, and one for *A Calendar of Verses* are less important. Herrick had been a favorite choice for such volumes for a century. All these prefaces are brief and their emphasis is on prosody. In *Seventeenth-Century Lyrics* (1893), Saintsbury limited himself to things "singable to music" and his chief principle, he admits, was to please himself. Hence no sonnets.

The larger number of Saintsbury prefaces to English eighteenth-century fiction form a unified group, along with a few essays on later novelists linked by the emphasis on what he calls irony and the analysis of the various types of irony he finds in these writers: the quite subtle art of Swift at his best, the pure irony of Fielding's *Jonathan Wild*, the histrionic "humors" and the "snigger" in Sterne, the quaint satiric vein in Borrow, the peculiar Puckish humor of Peacock, Susan Ferrier's hard dry sarcasm, and Jane Austen's insatiable and ruthless delight in roasting and cutting up a fool. When he edited Thackeray (1908), he also defines his satirical mode. In all this, Saintsbury's use of the term *irony* is too loose and all-inclusive, his analysis too superficial. Relying too much on generalization, he recognizes and labels but does not probe the many characteristic styles. Everything from light humor to the sardonic, satire, wit, and sarcasm come under the name of irony. As in all his discussion of fiction, structure is little attended to, the lifelikeness of characters is too much emphasized. In almost all of the writers, he saw the ironic vein as the source of their strength amid the conventions of fiction of their time—giving each his or her individual stamp.

The prefaces for Peacock are models of their kind. Nine years after his essay on the subject, they gave Saintsbury the opportunity to "expand and reason out" views expressed earlier. He resists the temptation to quote the good drinking songs included in his essay and expands upon Peacock's development of technical mastery. He sees growth from "exaggerated burlesque to the right satiric verisimilitude" in portraiture and the maturing into a more austere irony. Peacock is judged "no mean scholar," but Saintsbury is severe on his unfair and unamusing treatment of the "lakists," especially Southey. The verse is not neglected, and frequent references remind even "the Peacockian" to look more closely at things he or she may have neglected amid the charms of Peacock's "piquant talk" and persiflage. The audience is recognized as "the fit though few" who can laugh at themselves and who believe almost nothing is beyond satire. Though he would agree with many readers that *Crochet Castle* is the best of his novels, his own favorite is *The Misfortunes of Elphin*. His enthusiastic comment on Seithenyn sent the present writer to an immediate rereading—to savor again "his demonstration that he is not dead."[8] The present-day student may still profit from this introduction to an eccentric writer.

In the same period, Saintsbury's grasp of Swift was twice demonstrated: in prefaces to *Gulliver's Travels* (1886) and to *Polite Conversation* (1892). The latter has special value not only as an effort to place and to recommend this most good-humored of Swift's works but also as another analysis of what Saintsbury held to be the true vein of Swiftian irony, "the quiet abstracted" as against the "broad and loud." These dialogues and Swift's introduction to them Saintsbury saw as a neglected anticipation of the novel that was about to blossom in the four masters whom he also edited.[9] These prefaces also have some lasting worth. The evaluations have scarcely been challenged despite the new knowledge that almost a century has brought and shifts in criticism that have increased concern with structure and given less attention to character. Fielding, Smollett, Richardson, and Sterne are presented soundly, Sterne somewhat less sympathetically than the others.

Eleven of Saintsbury's works fall into the category of English literary history: two overall surveys (the *Short History* and *A First Book of English Literature*), surveys of three periods (the Elizabethan, the eighteenth and nineteenth centuries), histories of the English novel and of English criticism (a selection of material from the larger *History of Criticism*, with additions and some revision), the histories of prosody and prose rhythm and the *Historical Manual of Prosody*. Together, these represent a wide range of legitimate historical focus. All were pioneering; some were firsts of their kind and the last group have little parallel. The last of his English histories, *The Peace of the Augustans* (1916), is an idiosyncratic and personal product of the elder literary statesman, popular and significant but better considered in the frame of his retirement.

The English reader of 1876–95 knew Saintsbury as a literary historian only of French literature and Elizabethan English (as far as full surveys are concerned), but his reputation as a historian certainly also derived from his prefaces and essays, his *Britannica* articles, and his *Dryden* when he came under attack by Churton Collins and Scherer, and then Symons. Though he had been at work on *Nineteenth-Century Literature* and the *Short History of English Literature* before he went to Edinburgh, they appeared after his arrival there (in 1896 and 1898) when the focus of his writing was shifting to the larger, European literary scene.

The general nature of Saintsbury's practice as "critical historian of literature" had become evident in his work on French literature. He found and approved, in Thomas Hurd, "that wider study of literary history which is not so much indispensable to literary criticism as it is literary criticism itself,"[10] history being, for him, "the root of the critical, as of almost every other matter. To judge you must know."[11] Despite the tendency of later critics to see Saintsbury only as the appreciative critic or impressionist, the evidence proves him to be one of those for whom "the best thing produced is better if they are enabled to understand its origin" and for whom no single literary work is as fascinating as "the marvelous map" of all literature.[12] The value Saintsbury puts upon the "indefinable . . . but indispensable" historic sense that saves one from anachronism is everywhere apparent.[13] He tends to use, almost interchangeably, the terms *critical historian* and *historical critic*. He hoped to explain things without getting into the "quicksands of theory." In Wellek's terms, it was a "strange empiricism":[14] philosophy without theory, perspective without definition of terms. He isolated literature when he refused to include history of thought or society and when he refused to give such subjects as science, politics and education, stage history, or philosophical trends and their bearings on literature any real place in his historical surveys and critiques.

These arbitrary limitations support Nichol Smith's view that, in Saintsbury, the critic was born, the historian made or rather "forced by circumstance,"[15] though this view does not altogether match the facts. Nichol Smith valued Saintsbury's literary judgments and believed that, in writing histories, Saintsbury developed on the spur of the moment methods and emphases other than those of purely appreciative criticism. When Saintsbury began his historical works, there were few models. The amateur bellettrist reigned. But it was no accident that he conceived of the large historical scheme of the *Primer, Short History,* and *Specimens of French Literature* in 1876, or later the *Periods of European Literature,* the *History of Criticism,* and the *History of Prosody* and *Prose Rhythm.* These were all his own innovations in the historical treatment of literature. When he looked back over thirty years of writing literary history in 1912, he claimed correctly to have always avoided any "parade of systematic theory" while exercising a unifying point of view.[16] As Wellek and Warren noted, he is proud of his refusal to define terms and willingly accepts vague concepts of periods without analysis.[17] He claims to work "a posteriori" and to require "a wise passiveness" before the facts.[18] While generalizations must result, Saintsbury increasingly protested the "generalizing mania" of Taine, Buckle, Comte, and Spencer and the confusion of history, sociology, politics, and literature in Quinet and Michelet.[19]

Wellek, who has done more perhaps than anyone else to define the relations of critic and literary historian, does not dismiss Saintsbury as a literary historian, however unhappy he may be about some of his assumptions or lack of them.[20] His own historical and logical perspective and his deep and wide knowledge make him fully aware of the primitive state of literary history a century ago, and he stresses the groping that characterized the early historians. Gradually, ideas of systematic historiography were spreading from France and the English began to try more systematic approaches.

The evolutionary concept was being applied to all moral and social phenomena. John Morley had argued for it in 1874 in his essay, "On Compromise."[21] By 1893 it was familiar enough so that Pater refers to "the idea of development, of degrees, of a slow and natural growth" as "the illuminating thought which earlier critics lacked."[22] Green's *Short History of the English People* (1869–74) had done much to popularize the idea of a nation as a growing organism, and, in 1886, John Addington Symonds published two essays, "The Philosophy of Evolution" and "On the Application of Evolutionary Principles to Art and Literature."[23] He coupled Darwinism and Taine's determinism with a few dashes of Comte and Spencer; these ideas, not very fully analyzed or developed and never fully applied by Symonds, had little immediate influence.

In 1895, W. J. Courthope's massive history, *English Poetry from Chaucer to Scott,* began to appear.[24] Its explicit assumption was that literary developments are influenced by national economic and social life. A trend had begun, and Gosse, always susceptible to fashion, announced in his *Short History of Modern English Literature* (1898) his intention to apply Spencer's evolutionary principles, to look at literature "as part of the history of a vast living organism," and to ask of each writer not only what he is worth critically but also "where, in the vast and ever-shifting scheme of literary evolution, does he stand . . . who are his own kith and kin?"[25] That Gosse gave promise rather than performance with this ambitious proposal is generally admitted. He lacked the knowledge and discipline to write such a survey.

Meanwhile Saintsbury had written not only his French surveys but two English period ones, and this *Short History of English Literature* came out in 1898. In 1889, he had explicitly rejected strict evolutionary theory as applied to literature because whatever truths they tell "are always made to extend too far and too widely and to apply far too absolutely."[26] Saintsbury's common sense led him to distrust all rigid systematizing and all strict evolutionary formulas, product-of-circumstance determinism,[27] and theories of race and of progress alike when applied to art. Faith in progress he regarded as one of the vainest of delusions.[28] Not that he denied continuity or connections between writers or periods. Indeed, the age that turns its back upon its forbears he insisted is subject to "the unalterable law of nature, to dwindling, starvation, sterility,"[29] one of his vague anticipations of T. S. Eliot's view of tradition. As demonstrated in his French surveys, he traced developments of language and style but retreated repeatedly to "the incalculableness of literary progress"[30] and other metaphors to describe literary connections. "The wind of the spirit blows where it lists. . . ."[31] The phrase "revolution tempered with permanence," he repeated at least three times.[32] Seeing new and old side by side, one waxing as the other wanes, he could not accept the idea of predictability that went along with Symond's assumption that the individual cannot alter the sequence.[33] He recognized that men at the end of a great period are often under "a curse," the shadow of their predecessors, as he argued in "The End of a Chapter," yet he believed that genius may at any moment emerge unheralded.[34]

Aware of contemporary theories, Saintsbury sought some commonsense middle ground. He saw no "*easily calculable* ratio of connection" between the causes and effects literary histories were emphasizing.[35] Influences must be dealt with cautiously because literary changes are often "in the air" and they often appear simultaneously in more than one person of genius or talent.[36] Another of his favorite explanations is the familiar figure of "the man and the hour," which he used to account for the pressures of an age or "the desires of the time."[37] Granted all this, he says, "the principle of sane literary determinism, drawn from large induction" will often make one refuse to try to say why.[38] Writers are influenced and they do reflect their world, and "the spirit of the age" is a reality. But having made his protest, he was as ready as anyone to use some biological analogy—of seed-time, maturation, and decay.

An ideal pattern of literary historiography in all its many phases is still unachieved, and the battle between antihistoricism in criticism and those who would keep the functions of critic and historian together is still very much alive—from the New Critics to the New Historians of the 1980s.[39]

Saintsbury would agree with Wellek and Warren's view that the first task of the literary historian is not to theorize or classify but to establish "the exact position of each work in a tradition" and that literary periods should be established "by purely literary criteria." He would agree that, in period or genre, unity is only relative and that the historian is tracing the gradual realization of norms in various writers as well as "the decay of one convention and the rise of a new one." He would have welcomed their recognition that explaining literary change is a very complex problem and that satisfactory histories of genre and periods, of specific literary elements such as diction or prosody, and above all, of national and international groups of literatures are still only remote ideals. Any more precise, even scientific definitions and concepts he distrusted as much as they dislike the vagueness of his own. He would have been dismayed that they lump his work with that of Elton and Gosse as collections of critical essays, *not* histories.[40]

Other modern critics have questioned Saintsbury's theories and practice of history in other terms. For George Watson, Saintsbury's is a "narrative kind of history" and his lack of conviction about the importance of biography helped prepare the ground for the anti-historicism that dominated criticism between the two world wars.[41] Similarly W. K. Wimsatt and Cleanth Brooks argued that Saintsbury and his contemporaries—Raleigh, Elton, Quiller-Couch, and Garrod—weakened literary history by their lack of theoretical concern and their emphasis upon critical appreciation.[42] Saintsbury theorized more fully than the others, though not systematically or in depth, and he insisted on the historical frame and process, but his practice and his tone account for the impression Wimsatt and Brooks shared with many writers that the critic predominates over the historian.

Elizabethan Literature

So much for theory. Like his French surveys, those of English literature exemplify the little theorizing he did. The Elizabethan and nineteenth-century surveys were part of a cooperative, four-volume history.[43] Their chief value is not in theory or systematic historical analysis but in scattered passages. *Elizabethan Literature* (1887) had as its scope the century from *Tottel's Miscellany* to the Restoration but surprisingly included Milton and other later writers "who produced great work in the anti-Restoration styles." At that time, no survey of the period had been done with any success. Gosse's lectures on individual writers, *From Shakespeare to Pope*, were available. Saintsbury promised a thorough literary prospectus in which minor authors but not merely late imitators would be stressed. His prefatory remarks were an open challenge to Churton Collins, since he admitted that his dates and biographical details here as elsewhere were second hand and declared that, on matters that are not strictly literary history, he is indifferent to minute accuracy.[44]

"Nothing if not critical" was the theme of at least two reviews of this volume. C. H. Herford would have liked something closer to Taine or Arnold, that is, cultural history, and less of the manner of the reviewer.[45] Sidney Lee, though generally more favorable, regetted the omission of scholarly data.[46] These judgments are correct on the whole. Critical interpretation does predominate. The author frequently argues with other critics and is concerned with the changing reputations of writers, as he often was in his essays. Eight years later, in his *Nineteenth Century Literature,* the "I" is less frequent though personal judgment and idiosyncracy are there. References to other critics are fewer and the balance between critic and historian is better maintained, though that survey, too, has occasional erratic neglect or overexpansion as well as some odd judgments.

In the *Short History,* the "I" becomes "some critics think"—a difference that is not merely stylistic. Its preface explains that critical opinion is to be less prominent and the writer will give facts, "a sufficient chain of historical summary," and "critical learning" on which opinion can be built.[47]

Nevertheless, the Elizabethan survey emphasizes development, that of the growth of a language finding its way toward mature mastery, though the Elizabethan era as such is not clearly differentiated. Within this loose frame, Saintsbury writes good, brief critical essays: one on Spenser, one on Shakespeare's sonnets and lyrics and on his general quality (restraint, universality, and humor), and, best of all, an eloquent "apology for Caroline poetry" that anticipates his later *Minor Caroline Poets.* He is good in discussing the Authorized Version of the Bible, in exploring Marston's sincerity, and in defining the flagging genius of the Caroline period (he saw a parallel to his own day). He is weakest when he generalizes upon Shakespeare's plays without giving evidence or analysis, when perversely he "talks down" Milton because he thought other estimates "unduly high,"[48] and when he relies upon quotation alone to represent the quality of lyric or sonnet. The space given to the pamphleteers and to the later minor poets is disproportionately large simply because he enjoyed writing about minor writers.

Comparison of *Elizabethan Literature* with Saintsbury's *Short History* reveals some contrasts apart from the reduction in the amount of subjective opinion. The treatment of Donne and Herrick in the *Short History* is briefer and better.[49] He had also made a new evaluation of Crashaw and Vaughan and offered fresh evidence for it. The result is a fairer estimate. Having reread all of Shirley, he had come to think better of him. Comparison of the two works shows once again Saintsbury's gift for putting old things freshly. Saintsbury's style in *Elizabethan Literature* is comparatively clear and rarely lapses into the complex parenthetic pattern that later became infamous. The plan and order of each chapter is almost too explicitly spelled out. He is too kind to the tiresome, overworked conventions of the Elizabethan sonnet and tends to classify and rank continually. One must go elsewhere for the larger view of what the Renaissance meant.

Nineteenth-Century Literature

Though a volume dealing with contemporaries was bound to suffer lack of perspective, Saintsbury's *Nineteenth Century* is more substantial and reflects personal taste more often than the Renaissance survey, but it is the least well written of all three. Distortion results from his genteel habit of not judging living artists. The increase in the number of figures to be covered made selection difficult, but his mere listing of the *numerus* serves no useful purpose.

The bias toward the romantic lyric, always evident in Saintsbury, has its special outlet here. This is *the* age of the lyric and he places Shelley at the head of the romantics (one of the first ten or twelve of all poets in his ranking); Byron is "too rhetorical" (he calls this a very personal estimate). His overestimate of Beddoes is lyrical enough *almost* to convince, and the querulous dethroning of Wordsworth could appeal only to a thorough anti-Wordsworthian.[50] Victorian taste is reflected in the overvaluing of *The Princess* and *The Idylls of the King*. Tennyson gets the fullest discussion. Other prejudices play their part; he found the "mania" of purpose and obvious mannerisms marring the later Dickens, and *Middlemarch* is not discussed at all.

Saintsbury is preoccupied with the "decadence" of later decades and their "too literary" character, where books are the standards both of nature and of life. As in France, so in England, literary forms, even older manners and thought, seem to him "near exhaustion"—with resulting imitation, exaggeration (e.g., ornateness in prose that could go no further), and "the uncertain and eccentric quest for novelty."[51] Saintsbury was too close to all this to decide reliably whether it was transition or decay, too conservative intellectually to realize that the security of faith and tradition was gone, though he knew that the older literary conventions were dying or dead. He sensed new strength in no one but Yeats and that very faintly. He even considered the need for "a holiday from literature," but his lifelong faith reasserts itself in a final note of hope: more knowledge of more literature may help.[52]

Short History of English Literature

New in design, as Nichol Smith said, Saintsbury's *Short History* is no simple recension of earlier work.[53] Its brief conclusion reinforces his prefatory promise of less criticism; he calls its attitudes "'a reasoned orthodoxy,' . . . with heresies repressed except when honor and conscience require protest." Differences of opinion are granted but not discussed and "endless questions of authenticity, integrity, date and so forth" are left to special studies.[54] Interchapters already used in the *Short History of French Literature* provide "a chain of historical summary" to indicate general lines of development. They contain some of his most memorable generalizations and some masterful, brief summaries. Often Saintsbury touched on a writer's quality more strikingly here than elsewhere, with a vividness that leaves the reader savoring the phrase and wanting to test the discrimination. There is Donne's "mysterious melody" and, in the Middle Ages, the slow, steady accumulation of new themes, handlings, forms, that grow from "scantlings" into the "stateliest and most elaborate of romance structures in Malory." One thinks twice as one reads: "An English literature without Sir Thomas Browne is a thing so impoverished as to be appalling to think of." One feels fresh awareness as one reads that the eighteenth century had "to create a sort of etiquette which should prevent even really fine poetic frenzy from describing the eyes of the Magdalene as portable baths and compendious oceans." One hears the inimitable ring of Dryden's verse described "as of a great bronze coin thrown down on marble" and sees Locke clearly when he is characterized as "eminently of such stuff as dreams are not made of."

The work as a whole is well proportioned, though the last of the eleven books, as the author admits, is hurried and lacks definitive characterization. Fortunately, more than two-thirds of the work is devoted to literature before 1660, freshly organized and offering interpretation of the Elizabethans, particularly on style. Saintsbury is better here on Shakespeare's dramatic development than in *Elizabethan Literature:* on Spenser he is briefer and less eloquent; his discussion of *Paradise Lost* becomes a mere listing of memorable passages. But an analysis of a passage from Burke is Saintsbury at his best. He argues persuasively for Bunyan's great literary powers and for *Pilgrim's Progress* as a novel, one of the first.

There is some gain in the forced conciseness of this volume, and the style is often distinctive. Transitions are often entertaining, sometimes facetious, occasionally forced. When he disagrees with someone he is too prone to the abrupt dismissal (e.g., "this is uncritical," "idle," or "silly"). Rather powerful insinuation adds to the personal tone, but new restraint is evident in some revised judgments.

As literary history, the earlier sections seem strongest. Where the maturing of the language and of style can be emphasized or where new forms like the novel or journalism are first blossoming Saintsbury can spot "premonitory symptoms," as he did in Lyly. Reviewers preferred the later sections as "fresh and new," but he rightly felt his perspective weakening. Each literary age comes alive, however idiosyncratic, allusive, and involved the style.

Some reviewers challenged the two later surveys. Herford again questioned the historical side and the lack of treatment of ideas while praising the criticism of style.[55] Symons reviewed *Nineteenth-Century Literature* with a patronizing contempt: Saintsbury, though too flippant, says "sensible and unimportant things which, in the main, are hardly worth saying."[56] Oliver Elton, having seen reams of Saintsbury's proof sheets, held him to be an accurate chronicler, who "made fewer mistakes than most historians who write on the grand scale."[57] On this scale only Daiches and Legouis and Cazamian parallel this survey in our century.

CHAPTER 9

"Logrolling": W. T. Stead and Churton Collins

Signed articles, larger and more frequent headlines, gossip and causeries, interviews, correspondence columns, virulent attacks, and melodramatic crusades were the marks of the "new journalism" of the 1880s. Some of these were introduced by Edward Levey in the *Daily Telegraph* (1883–90), some even earlier by O'Connor in the *Star* in the 1840s, and others most flamboyantly by W. T. Stead in the *Pall Mall Gazette*. It is Stead with whom Saintsbury was involved.

When John Morley left the *Pall Mall Gazette* for politics in August, 1883, he is reputed to have said, "As I kept Stead in order for three years, I don't see why I shouldn't govern Ireland."[1] In a fairer evaluation, he pictured Stead

> abounding in journalistic resource, eager in convictions, infinitely bold, candid, laborious in surefooted mastery of all facts, and bright with a cheerfulness and geniality that no difference of opinion between us and none of the passing embarrassments of the day could ever for a moment dampen.[2]

For all Morley's liberalism, the *Pall Mall Gazette* had been conservative. Gosse, Lang, Henley, and Saintsbury had all written for it regularly. To many it seemed stodgy despite the hand of Stead, whom Morley also described as "50 percent idealist and 50 percent showman."[3] Alfred Milner, one of Morley's subeditors, saw Stead as a blend of "Don Quixote and Phineas T. Barnum," but "fun to work with."[4]

The "showman" displayed himself even before Stead left Newcastle, where he had caught and cooked mice in the newspaper office, had eaten them on toast and went on eating them with purported relish, all from rather fuzzy radical motives.[5] Unlike Lord

Northcliffe (Alfred Harmsworth) and George Newnes (editor of *Tid-bits*, 1880), with whom he later worked, Stead, with all his scoops and stunts, cultivated sensationalism not chiefly for commercial profit but idealistically and also for practical ends, to get at the men who he believed were controlling the political, social, and literary situations he wanted to change.[6] Saintsbury and Gosse were two of these men.

Once Morley's hand was off the helm of the *Pall Mall Gazette*, Stead began a series of spectacular crusades culminating in the infamous "Maiden Tribute of Modern Babylon." He campaigned against poverty ("The Bitter Cry of London," 1883); he demanded a bigger navy; he interviewed General Gordon and argued with fatal success that he should be sent to the Sudan,[7] and carried on his long persecution of Charles Dilke. On July 4, 1885, in "A Frank Warning," he opened his most sensational campaign with a sensational promise. The next four issues, he said, will contain articles dealing with "those phases of sexual criminality which the Criminal Law Amendment Bill was framed to repress." This bill was to raise the age of consent from thirteen to sixteen. Stead announced (in a familiar come-on) that "the squeamish and prudish and all those who prefer a fool's paradise of imaginary innocence and purity, selfishly oblivious of the horrible realities which torment those whose lives are passed in the London Inferno *will do well not to read* the *Pall Mall Gazette* of Monday and the three following days."

In those articles, Stead estimated the number of prostitutes in London at over 50,000 (R. K. Ensor suggests a third of this number as more accurate). He castigated the public for its indifference and reported how he had posed as someone engaged in the white-slave trade and had purchased a young girl of thirteen for five pounds. He had warned the Archbishop of Canterbury, the Bishop of London, and Cardinal Manning of his plan and taken other precautions, but these were not sufficient to save him from charges of abduction and a three-month jail term. Much of the public and the press found it revolting, but, as he often did, he produced the results he wanted.

For ten days the daily press and the weeklies kept silent but on July 15th the *Manchester Guardian*, while approving of Stead's aim, denounced his manner as a "gross violation of public decency." A meeting in Exeter Hall on July 17th proposed a resolution demanding legislation, four hundred thousand copies of the articles were printed while Stead rushed about to meetings, and the bill, which had been stalled in Parliament, came to a second reading on July 10th and passed the House of Lords with strengthening amendments a month later.[8] Saintsbury was still writing for Stead and had found him not too difficult to deal with, but by the end of July, he, like Gosse and some other members of the *Pall Mall* staff, resigned in protest against the "Maiden Whore" campaign.[9]

During his imprisonment, Stead edited the *Pall Mall Gazette* from Holloway jail. Whatever other crusades he was planning, the attack upon Saintsbury and Gosse had begun. Gosse wrote to W. D. Howells on December 12, 1885, that he had come in for a "veritable vendetta of criticism."[10] Saintsbury wrote Gosse on December 15th: "As for Stead, he is Stead. It will not read badly in our Cronikles 'How Sir Edmund and Sir George helped in the great rescue of the Damsel [name illegible] from a Satyr that was habited as a Puritan; and how the Satyr did cast his filth at the knights and how wind returned it in [his] face'."[11] The *Pall Mall Gazette* had just panned his *Marlborough,* and worse was to follow.

The *Pall Mall Gazette* for January 15, 1886, carried a column-long article entitled "Half Hours with the Worst Authors." Signed "Oxoniensis," this was an attack upon Saintsbury's style and grammar in his essay on George Borrow in the January *Macmillan's Magazine.* A fortnight later (January 30 and February 2), two anonymous articles appeared with the titles "'Log-Rolling' in English Letters" and the "The 'Log-Rollers' Again." Both tone and phrase sound like John Churton Collins, a *Pall Mall Gazette* staff member who used "Oxoniensis" as one of the several pseudonyms he put on letters he planted in various periodicals to support his crusades.[12]

Whether the first of these three articles was by Stead or Collins or by Oscar Wilde (as one of his editors suggests),[13] the three pieces are the early guns in Stead's crusade against anonymity in literary criticism and the attendant evil of "mutual puffery in literary publications," as the OED defines "logrolling."[14] Stead saw the value of linking this attack with the campaign against academic critics and the universities that Collins had already launched in the *Quarterly Review.* With Collins on his staff, Stead, now out of jail, could leave this crusade in his hands when, in February, Charles Dilke looked like a more rewarding target for his own pen with more appeal for the audience that the "Maiden Whore" campaign had attracted.

The *Quarterly Review* was one of the oldest offenders in the savage anonymous tradition, and so well entrenched was that system that the *Pall Mall Gazette* attacked the practice under its protection. Collins battled away for more than twenty years, always from behind that mask or a pseudonym with the added support of hosts of letters he solicited from outstanding men, then published without indicating they had been solicited.

Collins and Stead were concerned more with excessive praise and mutual puffery than with the unfair critical attack possible under anonymity, as the first articles indicate. "Half Hours with the Worst Authors," the first of three focused on Saintsbury, offers "specimens of the prose of the future according to the *système Saintsbury*" and cites errors in grammar and "atrocities of style" that make the essay on Borrow "a disgrace to even magazine literature." What are these "atrocities"? Several failures in subject-verb agreement, some slips in logic such as "constantly right in general," the unnecessary archaism "unfriend" and "black beast" for *bête noire,* which the writer finds "abominable." All this to suggest that Saintsbury was overvalued. The language sounds like Collins rather than Wilde or Stead. Saintsbury, in his careless, rapid writing and inadequate copy- and proofreading, invited this kind of criticism but so far had escaped.

How fully planned this campaign was cannot be determined, but Saintsbury refused to fight back. It all might have ended there because, when Richard Garnett of the British Museum, an old friend and a *Saturday Review* writer, offered to "take up the cudgels," Saintsbury refused the offer.[15] But Garnett sent a letter to the *Pall Mall Gazette* declaring that he could no longer contribute to a journal that so malevolently attacked his friend and a former *Pall Mall Gazette* writer as well. Nothing could have served Stead's purposes better, and immediate, effective use was made both of this and of Garnett's subsequent letter in the two articles on "logrolling"—whether by Stead, Collins, or some other staff writer scarcely matters.

"'Log-rolling' in English Letters" (on January 30th) begins with an innocent-sounding reference to Arnold's desire for an English Academy as a means of improving the inferior quality of "journeyman's work" in English literature, an inferiority due "not to the absence of a formal academy but to the presence of an informal one," a "journalistic junta" or critical clique, a "journeyman's trade union." This "mutual admiration society" is an "offensive and defensive alliance against the rest of the world." "You roll my log and I will roll yours," is its first commandment. And so "Mr. S[aintsbury], Mr. L[ang], Mr. G[osse]. Mr. C. and Mr. W. [do these represent Henley and Rider Haggard as has been assumed?] praise and support each other," and thus, through a "merry kind of literary exchange," manage to prevent honest criticism of various works. Their methods are "boycotting, picketing and intimidation." Witness Dr. Garnett.

In his second letter, Garnett had asked why the *Pall Mall Gazette* had ever employed Saintsbury if he wrote so badly. He added fuel to the fire by asserting that both Saintsbury and Gosse had resigned from the *Pall Mall Gazette* because of their disgust over the "Maiden Whore" business. Thus he gave Stead a public excuse for revenge. This letter was reproduced in the *Pall Mall Gazette* on February 2d. The deliberate malice of the articles is carried in the commercial argot, but Garnett's charges are answered cleverly and well. The writer argues that the *Pall Mall Gazette* had reviewed both Saintsbury's essay "English Prose Style" and his "Sainte-Beuve" favorably, that the adverse criticism of his *Marlborough* was the work of a trustworthy military expert and hence justified,[16] that they had praised Gosse's lectures on "Shakespeare to Pope," and that "extraordinary as it may seem to the logrolling fraternity," the *Pall Mall Gazette* has no logs to roll and gives no instructions to its reviewers. Finally, he argues that Saintsbury *did* slip up, and when Saintsbury or Gosse falls short of his best ("*Corruptio optima pessima*"), "the very stones should cry out"— since they can do better. Only mere scribblers may be ignored when they err!

Continuing the commercial metaphor, the writer speaks of "a little knot of men who lord it over English criticism ... an unreformed corporation" and adds, "corporations have no conscience." Stead and Collins thus developed the theory of a conspiracy among this group of conservative professionals who could not deny they were all writing anonymously as well as with signatures for many of the same major journals and newspapers and, inevitably, as the chief contributors (Saintsbury and Henley were editors as well) exercised incalculable influence. They reviewed each other's works and often wrote more than one review of their favorites. At the same time, they were writers of literary surveys and biographies, essays and lectures, and the editors of classics in English and other languages being issued in quantity for a widening audience. But no proof of conspiracy was ever offered. Mutual praise and self-protection and dictation of taste under a cloak of anomynity, whether deliberate or not, were the *Pall Mall Gazette's* targets. They saw this small "literary establishment" given added power by anonymity and the "logrolling" this made easier. It was not the first time that its power had been recognized or questioned. The "Pléiade-cut-down-to-four" of the late 1870s had aroused antagonism, and in 1881, Mandell Creighton reported to Bishop Copleston in India, "Saintsbury, as you know, is the literary dictator of minor poets and novelists: they bend before him and he scourges them at his will."[17] Saintsbury himself noted that the *World* called him "dictatorial" in 1886.[18] Fair or not, these criticisms supported Stead's assumption that these men were looked to as authorities in literary matters and so were worth attacking.

Stead's objectives are clear, but who was Collins? He had been attacking literary figures for most of his career. He had been an acquaintance of Saintsbury for several years, a friend of Gosse, Symonds and Swinburne since 1875. An Oxford-trained scholar and a free-lance journalist, and an adult-education lecturer on literature, he also did some tutoring and had written three books. He was a devotee of the classics and something of a linguistic purist, a man ambitious for a regular university post in literature who was already disappointed and resentful. Like Saintsbury, he had been an unsuccessful candidate for the new Merton Professorship of English Language and Literature when, in 1885, it went to the Anglo-Saxon scholar Arthur S. Napier.

Collins's disappointment over Napier's Oxford appointment was rooted in personal envy but also in his passionate concern for university reform that would recognize English literature as a serious area of study and give that study formal structure. He had now found channels (the *Quarterly Review* and the *Pall Mall Gazette*) through which to vent his frustration and carry on his battle for what, to his credit, became the Oxford Final Honours School in English in 1893. Collins had a free hand while Stead stood in the wings. The team was a good one: Collins's learning and passionate devotion to his cause joined with Stead's courage and cleverness.

Yet it all would have died quickly if Collins, nine months after the "logrolling" articles, had not chosen to attack the highly sensitive and popular Edmund Gosse. Named Clark Lecturer in English Literature at Trinity College, Cambridge, in 1885, he was reelected for three years in July, 1886. Suddenly, Collins leveled his attack upon him in

October. A year earlier, in a long article on John Addington Symonds's *Shakespeare's Predecessors,* Collins had argued that the writers of all recent literary histories lack knowledge of "the classics of other ages and of other tongues."[19] He praised Symonds as a scholar but condemned him as a critic, as one of the Swinburne school and as an imitator of Swinburne's style. Neither Symonds nor Swinburne responded to this 1885 attack, believing, like most of the men at whom the "logrolling" attacks were directed, that silence is the best defense. Even Gosse seemed to hold that view until he was hit. Then all changed.

The real direction of Stead's campaign as well as his confusion of issues was revealed in the May 28, 1886, *Pall Mall Gazette.* Here, Stead had dredged up and praised Collins's *Quarterly Review* article on Symonds of nine months before. Collins's identity as the author of these attacks and the fact that he was crusading for Stead were quickly recognized by his victims. Saintsbury wrote Dobson on September 21, 1886, to explain why he was omitting acknowledgment of Dobson's services from the preface to his *History of Elizabeth Literature:* "I have abstained deliberately in order that there may be no danger of once more dragging you as you were dragged before into a quarrel where you had no interest. *Collins shall and will of course attack it and I don't want my friends splashed with mud meant for me.*"[20] In its mixture of defense, defiance, and indifference to petty cavil, the preface is an effort to anticipate and offset Collins's attack. Saintsbury says he has never delivered a second-hand literary judgment, though he does take dates and biographical facts from others. But he will not feel "deeply convinced of sin if it turns out that he has dated this poet's *Tears of Melancholy* in March, 1593, when the true date is May, 1595; or asserted that the poet's grandmother was Joan Smith, who is buried at Little Pedlington, instead of Jane Smith who was married at Kennequhair." These things, though interesting and sometimes valuable, are "ancillary . . . to the history of literature in the proper and strict sense," which is his concern.[21] All this sounds almost as if Saintsbury knew what Collins' main points of attack upon Gosse were to be the next month in a review undertaken months after the work had appeared and well after most discussion of it had ended.

Collins's "English literature at the University," in the *Quarterly* of October, 1886, was a review of Gosse's *Shakespeare to Pope.* Its original materials were the lectures Gosse gave in the United States in December-January, 1885–86, and again at Cambridge during early 1886. The *Times,* on October 19th, carried a letter from Gosse stating that he would reply to the attack elsewhere but denying the claims "from several anonymous quarters" of "these vile and secret arts of mutual puffery."[22] The last phrase linked Collins with the *Pall Mall Gazette* articles of the previous January.

Thus began what Gosse described as "the worst week of my life" and "the scandal of the year," as the *Critic* (New York) declared it. Gosse had taken the center of the stage, and the campaign against "logrolling," which first focused on Saintsbury, became for the next few weeks a battle between Collins and Gosse. Into this struggle a vast number of people were drawn. On October 20th, Saintsbury wrote Gosse to offer his help in making a "good or crushing reply." He added, less happily, that he had noted some of the errors that Collins cited, but he condemned "the animus of the whole and the positive literary dishonesty . . . of such misrepresentation as that about the *Arcadia* given your enormous library." Collins had charged that Gosse did not know whether Sidney's *Arcadia* was in verse or prose— implying that Gosse had never read it.[23]

As Gosse's biographer, Ann Thwaite, interprets the drama, the fanatical pedant Collins was right on Gosse, and Gosse's deep distress was the result of the fact that he had to acknowledge his careless and stupid mistakes and his overconfidence, but the immediate victory went to Gosse. His host of friends wanted to see him as the victim and the University of Cambridge could not afford to admit its mistake in appointing him. Collins wanted to keep the focus on the failure of the university and its press to maintain standards in allowing publication of a "literary charlatan." However, the attack was personally so abusive it overshot its mark, as Collins often did. Gosse's triumph was short lived. He put up a weak defense that lacked dignity and must have embarrassed his friends. J. M. Dent commented, "He's not quite sound."

Gosse's extreme discomfort had made him the center of attention, but what of the other "logrollers"? One looks for Saintsbury's attitudes in the *Saturday Review,* where *From Shakespeare to Pope* was favorably reviewed. More relevant are two articles on the Collins-Gosse quarrel.[24] Neither has the savage joy Churton Collins displayed. The tone is judicious though the editors admit they are "observers not exactly outside." They deplore the "extreme acrimony and the voluminous bulk of the controversy" and insist upon clarification of "some real issues which are in danger of being overlooked and confused." Friendship is termed irrelevant and Gosse's errors are granted. The summary of Collins's article is much like that Saintsbury had given Gosse in his October 20th letter.[25] Covering all the salient points of the quarrel, he speaks of their "peculiar jealousy for the honor of the art and mystery of reviewing and accuses the *Quarterly* writer of failing in the first obligation of a reviewer when he deliberately ignored proofs of Gosse's competence as a seventeenth-century scholar which he knew well. He thus committed "one of the most heinous offenses against the ethics of reviewing."[26]

Churton Collins's perfectionist complex made him concentrate on errors and inaccuracies which often prove trivial or are a matter of scholarly opinion only, and his passion blinded him to the common ground he shared with men like Saintsbury, Garnett, Gosse, and Lang. Stead must have found him less comprehensible than most of them did. Saintsbury's more flexible and tolerant temperament, Lang's casual, witty light touch and Gosse's worldly, gossip-loving nature only intensified Collins's anger and rigidity as did their success—above all, Gosse's university appointment. In contrast to Collins's deadly earnestness and Gosse's supersensitiveness is Saintsbury's self-assured comment: "I used to let Churton Collins accuse me of having misquoted Milton when I had correctly quoted Plato."[27] Similarly, when an Edinburgh student referred to Collins, Saintsbury "praised some of [Collins's] work, distinguished between the good and the less good, and said a word in extenuation of his critical misdemeanors." Another student called it "a lesson in literary good manners."[28]

Collins had not forced Saintsbury to fight, but he was not one to despair or fail in what he felt was his duty. Since Saintsbury had expected Collins to attack his *Elizabethan Literature,* he was probably not wrong in believing that it was Collins who persuaded Edmond Scherer to attack the third edition of his *Short History of French Literature* in 1887. Also, Collins reviewed the last three of the four volumes of essays Saintsbury published between 1889 and 1895; his crusade picked up steam in 1894, when Frank Harris, having bought the *Saturday Review,* hired him and gave him carte blanche in attacking "what he deemed incompetence."[29]

Now the tirades began afresh, this time at full tilt against the newly resigned *Saturday Review* editor—in its very pages. Other scholars who are attacked along with Saintsbury include Jusserand, William Rossetti, LeGallienne, and Gosse again. Collins included many of these attacks in *Ephemera Critica,*[30] among them that on Saintsbury's *Short History of English Literature,* "A Scotch Professor on English Literature" (1898). The reprinting identified this article, but Collins said nothing about the four earlier ones on other Saintsbury volumes that were unquestionably his. No one could mistake the sweeping denigration, the familiar acrimonious phrases, or gross exaggerations. Saintsbury "continues to chatter around and about his subject, without one word of real criticism ... no general ideas, no point of view; he represents in his bookish talk about books, precisely the average person...." Thus he greeted Saintsbury's most vulnerable work, *Corrected Impressions.*[31] Ten months later, just after Saintsbury's appointment to Edinburgh, reviewing *Essays in English Literature* (second series), a volume of distinctly higher calibre, Churton Collins attacked Edinburgh University as he had earlier attacked Cambridge:

> [One should find here] the qualifications ... to justify Professor Saintsbury's appointment, the great excellences that must have been required to outweigh the claims of such a teacher of English Literature as Mr. Churton Collins or so inspiring a critic as Mr. W. E. Henley.[32]

Unblushing, he proceeds to judgment: "an ephemeral farrago of straggling opinions ... without any definite plan or purpose," "pretentious ignorance," and "the pinchbeck generalizations so dear to the Literary Charlatan." The style will afford students "an example of what to avoid." A "budget of blunders" follows—none important, some mere quibbles on literary terms, but all in the same tone of self-righteous indignation and contempt. "A Blind Guide in Victorian Literature," a review of Saintsbury's *History of Nineteenth-Century Literature,* is similar. Every chapter "teems with blunders and misrepresentations"—a wrong date for Cobbett, Stedley for Smedley, a Goethe line miscalled "an axiom"—and worse, Saintsbury seems "utterly incapable of distinguishing vulgarity and coarseness from vigor and liveliness."[33] The acknowledged review of the *Short History* on December 3, 1898, again attacked Edinburgh University: "... work more discreditable to a University Professor never issued from the

press. . . . It has the worst characteristics of irresponsible journalism."
Still more irritating to Collins was its "cool assumptions of critical
authority."

Whatever the worth of Saintsbury's volumes, it is lost sight of in
the exaggeration, the neurotic intensity, the constant repetition of
Collins's attacks. Even his sound negative criticism evoked no response from anyone. Stead had long been off after other quarry and
the public had grown tired of this bludgeoning style. Saintsbury, who
did not share Gosse's supersensitiveness, meanwhile achieved the
scholarly and academic recognition Collins pined for. In June, 1895,
even before the Edinburgh appointment, E. K. Chambers hailed
Saintsbury as "a representative leader of critical opinion,"[34] and the
next year Arthur Waugh condemned those who disparaged him as
unable to make stick charges of "serious inaccuracy, an absolutely
false judgment, . . . *animus* or prejudice."[35]

Saintsbury was Churton Collins's major target for four years. What
was his response? When the first of these attacks appeared, Saintsbury (between jobs) acknowledged Collins in three brief, signed reviews in minor journals. Their tone is measured, polite, satiric, but
the implied judgment is severe. Collins always interests him as a critic,
though, or because he "rarely agree[s] with him" and because *Essays
and Studies* offers "an alternative for the 'I like it' school." Collins
knows the classics and at least some part of English literature very
well, but his "opinionatedness" is not just now fashionable. Rather
more acid is the comment, "Only critics pure and simple possess the
critical venom in its fullest perfection, of such . . . is Mr. Churton
Collins," but he is a tonic and is saved from the curse of seeming
"vague and vacillating."[36]

Collins achieved a university appointment at Birmingham in 1904
(having again drunk the bitter cup over Raleigh's appointment at
Oxford). He died in 1908, one would hope with some sense of accomplishment, though his personal diaries belie this. Gadfly he was,
learned and indefatigable, often right in some degree, but he lacked
the sensitive response to literature and the warm enthusiasm that
made Saintsbury, Gosse, and Lang popular despite their limitations.
The term *logrolling* had established itself, and, as anonymity gave way
to the signed article, some of the evils disappeared; others continued—with signature or without. Traill could ask in 1893: " . . . amid
all the vain and peevish chatter which goes on . . . about 'rings,' and

'logrolling,' and 'stabs in the dark,' ... had anybody yet come across a grain of solid fact?"[37]

Were they guilty? Since the logrollers were all friends and co-workers and all voluminous writers, one does not have to look far for evidence, though it is less clear-cut than the attacks lead one to expect. Henley's biographer, Connell, describes him as a "roll-a-log-and-do-a-good-turn, professional man of letters and respectable journalism."[38] This phrase suggests the standard attitude of the anonymous journalists of the days before Stead: professional, yet amateur to the modern view, casual in their willingness to praise, even overpraise, and to praise each other. Who was to know when the *Saturday Review*, the *Athenaeum*, *Longman's* or the *Manchester Guardian* praised Dobson's verse or Saintsbury's essays which of them had written the review? Indeed, who was to know but that the author himself had done the review, though little evidence supports that charge. Few of these men would have been guilty of such bad taste as that of Collins when he spoke of his own superior competence for the Edinburgh professorship in an anonymous review of Saintsbury. Lang admitted once reviewing his own *Encyclopedia Britannica* article and he reluctantly admitted authorship of a parody when Walter Pollock asked him to review it. Saintsbury goes to great lengths to speak vaguely and indirectly or with elaborate modesty when referring to his own work. The temptation was there, but usually these "Gentlemen of the Press" drew a line at anonymous self-praise.

The *Saturday Review* files during Saintsbury's editorship afford ample evidence of logrolling. Saintsbury thought that an editor should exercise "something like despotism provided it be vigilant and benevolent" and that he should allot books on his own judgment and be free to alter reviews so that all would blend and reflect the tone of the paper.[39] Between 1880 and 1886, when the Collins-Stead attacks began, his *Primer* and *Short History of French Literature*, and some of the works he edited were all favorably reviewed in the *Saturday Review*, though the *Dryden* was condemned for a "few mannerisms" of style. His *Britannica* articles were frequently singled out for praise, much of it deserved, and there was no quarrel with his editing of the Scott *Dryden* despite its grave weaknesses. In 1887, the *Saturday's* praise of his *Elizabethan Literature* had some qualifications, but the fulsomeness of the comment on his preface to *Specimens of English Prose Style*, on January 2, 1886, suggests what the *Pall Mall Gazette* was gunning for.[40] Whoever wrote it says, "No more can be done than to commend very especially the original and brilliant essay.... It well deserves the attention which the scholarly reputation of the writer is sure to obtain it." The editor's modesty did not stand in the way of this puff, and the potential irony in the last sentence may have struck Stead or Collins while their "Worst Authors" piece was in the making.

The *Saturday Review* notices of many Dobson volumes (all favorable) sound like Saintsbury, but Gosse, Lang, and Henley were equally enthusiastic about this delicate minor verse. Whoever the reviewer is, too much space is given to it at a time when more important new authors (Yeats, Shaw, Hardy, Wilde, for instance) were being scanted or ignored on the decision of Saintsbury, the literary editor. With justification, H. G. Wells charged him with having "very rarely brought his critical acumen to bear upon contemporary writing."[41]

Stead and Collins together focused attention briefly on the evils of logrolling. This was healthy, though Collins soon shifted the focus to the faults of the literary historians, and they did not prove any conspiracy. Yet they never concerned themselves with another evil of anonymous journalism, that of the same man writing on the same book in several journals simultaneously. Saintsbury admits having written as many as five reviews of the same book. He thought the practice undesirable, but he admits he would not blush "if all five were reprinted side by side," done as they were "by no offer or intrigue of my own, but simply because as many editors, unasked sent the volume to me."[42] He quotes Harwood's sound judgment: "If the reviews are favorable, it is scarcely fair to the author, and if they are unfavorable, it rather deceives the public."[43] Henley admits to three reviews of one James novel. Lang argues, less responsibly, "I cannot approve of reviewing in the manner of Briareus (who wrote in a hundred papers, having a hand for each), but if one has more to say than can be said in one review, why not bubble over into several papers, on a special subject where there are not many specialists?"[44] The practice, shocking as it seems, was supported by long habit and economic advantage—and hidden by anonymity. Combined with logrolling, it doubled the evil. One lone protest came from Henry James, in a letter to Robert Louis Stevenson condemning the "density and puerility" of contemporary criticism: "... Lang, in the D[aily] N[ews] every morning, and I believe in a hundred other places."[45]

At times, Saintsbury must have seemed omnipresent to those in the know since the subjects of his signed works so often paralleled those in the anonymous ones, and his style and attitudes easily betray their source. Economic pressures and the need to supplement his *Saturday Review* income cannot be ignored—the practice was pretty universal—but the result is Saintsbury speaking repeatedly on the same writer or work. The problem is not consistency (he has that) so much as the weight of the influence exerted—and its distorting and stultifying effect.[46]

The practices are now largely a historical curiosity since even the *Times Literary Supplement* has abandoned anonymity. Friends still praise each other, writers attack those they hate for good or bad reasons, the literary battles go on, and charges of bias have not ceased. Readers still say, "The *Times* has praised him" or "The *Atlantic* has damned him" whether the reviews are anonymous or signed. The authority of the journal carries weight, and even the position and length of the review has its effect on popular judgment. The story of logrolling and multiple reviewing in the last days of anonymous journalism is a chapter of literary sociology that helps define the climate of Saintsbury's writing in the 1880s and 1890s.

CHAPTER 10

"A Clock That Stopped..."

In 1891, Arthur Symons greeted Saintsbury's *Essays on French Novelists* and *Miscellaneous Essays* with the charge that they were "marking...time...by the record of a clock that stopped the better part of twenty years ago."[1] Writing anonymously, the young critic spoke for a new generation. He struck a similar note in regard to Saintsbury's other three volumes of essays on English literature issued during 1890–95.[2] The essays on French writers had their use, Symons grants, though they now seem "old-fashioned and obvious." Because the public has now accepted what had been novel fifteen years earlier, Symons thinks Saintsbury is no longer interested in giving them what is new. As he notes, Zola, Maupassant, Huysmans, Daudet, or even the older Goncourt brothers are not treated except in the introductory essay written in 1888. The critical insights of the essays he judges to be "of second-rate quality" that "never surprises but...rarely disappoints," journalism, not literature. He concedes that Saintsbury's Baudelaire essay was the "at once first and best, indeed the only good essay on the subject in English," but adds that the discovery was really Swinburne's, a fact Saintsbury often mentioned.[3] These are serious charges that must be reckoned with in estimating Saintsbury's role as interpreter of French literature to late Victorian England. Symons was an eager and thorough student in the field.[4]

What Saintsbury had done was simply to reprint the essays he did for Morley, who chose the subjects. He then added those he had written on Hamilton and Sensibility and his preface to Lesage. These gave the volume a strong effect of looking backward. He chose to add nothing on Zola, the Goncourts, and later fiction except the unsatisfactory introduction, "The Present State of the French Novel."[5] In his preface he said that the growth of naturalism since 1878 made this essay necessary. Otherwise, he found his own views little changed and he made additions only on Flaubert.

161

New materials had become available and he wanted to emphasize the gulf he saw between Flaubert and naturalism. In his 1891 note to the Flaubert essay, he presents him as "witness of the fatal error of the degenerate Realist and Naturalist school" that claimed him as one of them.[6] He describes the current French novel as "suffering under the yoke of Naturalism and pessimism." Unwisely, he risks the prediction that Zola "must pass away" because he lacks both style and "artistic presentation of matter." Negating the "first rule of literature" that reality must be transformed or "disrealized," he offers only a photographic copy and with his "wearisome nonsense" of "documents" leaves nothing to the imagination; he is also indiscriminate in choice of subjects.[7] The Analysts (American, French, or Russian) who by "elaborate dissection of motives and character" give not even part of the story are for him as bad or worse. He grants genius to Zola, Bourget, and Maupassant, but laments its waste because they deny art and are preoccupied with forbidden subjects. When they escape their obsessions, the result for him is Maupassant's *Pierre et Jean,* the best novel since 1870, by the most gifted of them all. With a hollow protest that he is "absolutely free from squeamishness" and still believes those who condemned Baudelaire to be "fools for their pains," he condemns the predominance of the dirty and nasty and the simply dull in Zola and others because it is unpleasant.[8] A familiar dodge. These views expressed in 1888 were unaltered in the 1891 volume.

Exhaustion is the keynote in Saintsbury's attitude toward most of those who write after 1880. Using this metaphor in 1895, he wrote "The End of a Chapter," an *ave atque vale* to French writers that picks up where "The Present State of the French Novel" left off. Opening with the by then familiar term *fin de siècle,* Saintsbury states his theme: "the literature of the nineteenth century in France has come to an end . . . there is now, in the first rank, nobody at all." After twenty-three pages, all too exclamatory, he celebrates with enthusiasm "the new worlds of imagination and expression" opened up by the writers of 1830–90. Actually, he limits these to the writers before 1870 and makes no reference to the naturalists. Then he repeats the theme: "We are sitting . . . at the side of the deathbed of one of the greatest periods of European literature."[9] Only Verlaine and Maupassant (d. 1893) of later men have first-rate genius. Others have the strong mark of influence and imitation, of "schools," and even of "unconscious descent." He cannot predict how soon a new flowering may occur.

Saintsbury had expressed these same attitudes toward contemporary French poetry in an 1890 essay, "The Frost of Poetry in France."[10] Mallarmé and Verlaine "have gone off into strange wanderings of 'decadence' and whatnot." Maupassant and others have turned to prose, and there have been no new poets since 1866. Imitation, revolt, and unconscious descent are here, too. The Parnassians are still active, but he fears that the French no longer read poetry, and their best critics (Faguet, Brunetière, Montégut) are largely indifferent to it. On this last point he was correct.

Whatever the French were reading while the symbolists were emerging, there was some audience for their poets in England in the 1890s. Both Verlaine and Mallarmé visited England in 1893–94, within four months of each other, lecturing and reading their poems.[11] Symons, who was involved with both visits, was now the chief interpreter of the later French school. He wrote "The Decadent Movement in Literature" in *Harper's Magazine* in November, 1893, and *The Symbolist Movement* in 1899. In the latter he discussed Gerard de Nerval, Maeterlinck, Mallarmé, Laforgue, Huysmans, Villiers de L'Isle-Adam, and Rimbaud, of whom Saintsbury had almost nothing to say.[12]

"The End of a Chapter" and "The Frost of Poetry in France," taken with the essays that Symons specifically attacked, indicated clearly that Saintsbury's sympathies had stopped with the generation of Gautier, Balzac, Baudelaire, and Flaubert. From Symons's point of view, he was playing safe. The forward movement in European literature after 1875 (e.g., Ibsen, Wilde, Shaw, Tolstoy, Nietzsche, James) now seemed to Saintsbury "topsiturvification" or "satanic pose," "easy tricks of inversion and unexpectedness," or literary pastiche, and he gave it little attention.

When he reviewed Max Nordau's *Degeneration,* he found Nordau's "lamentations" and "rantings" upon Zola, Ibsen, Tolstoy, Nietzsche and even Rossetti and Wilde merely amusing, though wryly so. He saw Nordau as uncritical and full of a "Teutonic doggedness" but praised his insight into the "fact" that, at the ends of periods or centuries, when schools of art lose their freshness, they "degenerate into caricatures of themselves" and offer violence as a substitute for strength or originality.[13]

Saintsbury now contented himself with loyalty to the older French writers and, at the age of forty to fifty, exhibited that hardening of the literary arteries usually suffered by much older critics. He deserved Symons's criticism. In the *Saturday Review* in 1890, for example, he takes a good deal of space to apologize for the injustice done thirty years before by that periodical to Banville's *Odes Funambulesques* (when he had been praising them in the *Academy*).[14] This minor poet still writes "such occasional verse as not a half dozen men now living in Europe could write if they would." He greets Maxime de Camp's *Gautier* as "a useful protest against the very noisy and motley crew of younger writers in France who affect to disdain Gautier's merely literary power."[15] For the younger writers, there is no praise.

Saintsbury wrote "The Present State of the English Novel" for the *Fortnightly* in 1888 and extended it for *Miscellaneous Essays* in 1892; it parallels his essay on current French fiction and confirms Symons's judgment. Everywhere the novel now seems to him sterile and less so in Britain only because the romances of Blackmore, Stevenson, and others give him hope that a new period of romance will breed a new growth of the novel. He maintains that the manners and characters that fed the Victorian novel had already seemed near exhaustion when he began reviewing two decades before and now, amid overproduction and a general bustle, the shadows of French influence lie heavily upon it all—the naturalist's documents, Bourget's analysis, and the Goncourt quest for the personal epithet. Genius is spread thin and no masterpieces have been produced. Ignoring Hardy, Meredith, Gissing, and James, he finds too much fine writing, oddity, license, and, worst of all, neglect of "a live story" not dissected or photographed but artistically "dis-realized" (always a key term indicating his impulse to escape reality). In his implicit fear of isms he exaggerates wildly as he proclaims that the novel must deal with "life not thought, conduct not belief, the passions not the intellect, manners and morals not creeds and theories."[16] He could not mean this literally considering the great novels he praises, but he is striking out blindly at ideas he dislikes. He claims that there are no forbidden subjects and that treatment is all, but his protests against Zola's subjects make one doubt that he believed it. Such generalizations come too easily.

Saintsbury's inconsistency on these matters mark him as that Victorian prototype described by Walter Houghton in *The Victorian Frame of Mind,* that paradox of hypocrisy who could condemn Pecksniff, Podsnap, Mrs. General, and Mrs. Grundy but "at the same time condemn any open description of vice."[17] A critic who "had no patience with the 'immoral prudery that will not face the facts of human nature itself, and falsified them to the young' was equally ready to complain about the present fashion of dwelling upon unclean topics and ugly things in the naturalistic novel."

This hypocrisy became an irresistible habit of evasion deeply and pervasively rooted in Victorian society. Those who attacked the hypocrisy returned to it repeatedly, and too often regarded the person who escaped it as a poseur, deliberately turning the world topsy-turvy (one of Saintsbury's increasingly favorite terms of abuse).[18] The rationalizations and contradictions involved a clash between reason and emotional responses, guilt and evasion, a fear of analysis and ambiguity, and a distrust of one's natural reactions, all woven into a web of conventional and personal threads difficult to disentangle. The result was compromise and confusion, contradiction and frequent shifting of ground. Saintsbury did not escape this pattern.

Saintsbury proclaimed himself "no prude" more than once; late in life he admitted that both King Arthur of the *Idylls* and Arthur Hallam were prigs and that he found, in Prince Albert, "hints" that he could not like.[19] With these he joins Aeneas, as an uninteresting, unheroic cad,[20] and Waverly, a "simpleton." He cherished the Victorian ideal of masculine virility evident in his admiration for the sane aggressive, robust, healthy temper of Fielding, Lockhart, and Scott, "the least prudish-prurient of men."[21] His impatience with "cheap altruistic sympathies" as part of the sentimentality of his day is not unrelated to this image of masculinity.[22]

In 1887 he wrote that only "very severe moralists... insist on applying the same morality without the least alteration to fiction and to fact."[23] He is straightforward and sound on Shakespeare's sonnets, the supremacy of their thought, their evidence of self-knowledge, their "clear vision" and poetic beauty, and he accepts the passion of a man for a man as a likely personal experience beautifully conveyed.[24] But when he deals with his own later contemporaries, the worst Victorian attitudes emerge, as in his reactions to the naturalists. The suggestion of Lesbianism in Compton Mackenzie's *Sinister Street* he says is "conveyed quite cleanly and not as Maurice Hewlett would have done it." In a letter to Hunt, he describes Hewlett as "tarred with that singular mixture of pose and not quite cleanness which disfigured so many men of his own particular generation," at its worst in Oscar Wilde, and from which Kipling is free. He claims to have liked Robbie Ross but, when making a contribution to a fund to aid him, he pities "the poor fellow," whose follies "have come home to roost."[25] He omitted Wilde from all his surveys.

How much Saintsbury knew of the facts recorded in Steven Marcus's *The Other Victorians* or how much he suspected or knew of the personal problems of such friends as Symonds, Gosse, or Lord Houghton is not discoverable, but even Symonds was cautious. Saintsbury knew Lord Rosebery, whose son committed suicide after an affair with Wilde, and was a friend of George Wyndham, who helped Wilde gather evidence for his trial. Yet apart from a contribution to *The Yellow Book,* he seems to have distanced himself from it all as he did with so much of unpleasant reality. When he reviewed Havelock Ellis's *The New Spirit*, he observed primly that Ellis seemed to know much about "things that other people do not know," but he accepted him as a not "offensive exponent of panting modernity."[26]

How did Saintsbury view marriage—and the eternal triangle? In *The Angel in the House,* that Victorian celebration of domestic love, he found beauty though it seemed to him "too fluent and sometimes a little pathetic."[27] More to his liking was *Yeast,* where Kingsley, disguising his own early life story, portrayed his wife in its heroine Argemone as a pure strong woman, worship of whom exalts both marriage and the hero as passion is spiritualized. To the satisfactions of married love, Saintsbury's most amusing tribute is one regarding Shakespeare's will and the second-best bed: "I've never had the slightest doubt that there were particularly pleasant associations for the pair with that bed!"[28]

As for adultery, Saintsbury's judgment of Parnell was severe but politically colored. Like Carlyle, he found Harriet Taylor distasteful; of Thackeray and Mrs. Brookfield, he betrays no suspicions though he edited Thackeray in 1908. On Dickens and Ellen Ternan he had too little information, but the public separation of Dickens and his wife may have confirmed his feeling that Dickens was not a gentleman. George Lewes's domestic tangle may have intensified his prejudice against George Eliot, though his dislike for her moralizing and his distaste for all bluestockings are sufficient grounds.

All these things reflect Victorian prudery and evasion, but Saintsbury tried to avoid discussing such matters in criticism and literary history. Writing of Queen Margaret de Valois and Clemet Marot he says: "Some excellent folk have ... tried to clear Queen Margaret of any scandal. Let us do better: let us not even consider the question."[29] In the same spirit, he wished, in 1927, that he knew less than we do about Sterne and Elizabeth so that he could refuse to discuss the matter. He once remarked that the biographer had a right to omit such facts, a questionable principle not put severely to test in his own biographies.[30]

Symons's anonymous attack on Saintsbury in the *Athenaeum,* for which Saintsbury had been writing for fifteen years, at first glance seemed not very representative. Despite Collins's and Stead's campaign and Scherer's attack, reviews of Saintsbury's work had been, on the whole, favorable during the 1880s, and he had a reputation and authority of some weight. But Symons's correspondence suggests that some change in attitude was taking place. In 1888, Symons wrote to James Dykes Campbell regarding a review of Saintsbury's essay on Borrow: "I think you are too hard on Saintsbury who is of course not a profound critic or a pattern pedagogue." He asks why Campbell called it "an awful exhibition" and as a "fervent Borrovian" says he had found it a "capital" popular résumé. Three years later, after his own attack on Saintsbury, Symons expressed surprise at Gosse's negative reaction to his review: "It seems to me so scrupulously accurate [and not] substantially different from what I have heard you yourself say." He thinks his view is lenient when compared to that of his friends, with whom he has had to defend Saintsbury. Dykes Campbell and George Moore, he says, "can see absolutely no merit in his work." Symons sees merit in it, but he had never heard of anybody who considered him a great critic. He adds that he would be sorry to have Saintsbury know he wrote the review, although he has no doubt that Saintsbury would recognize it as "perfectly true."[31] On this last point he is probably right. He was certainly confident as he attacked an established critic and editor twenty years his senior. He was aware that Gosse had crumpled under similar but more violent assaults and that Gosse, a long-time friend of Saintsbury, had devalued him when talking with writers interested, as they both were, in contemporary French verse and fiction. It is the kind of Gosse behavior that led to Saintsbury's breaking off their friendship a decade later (Gosse "played monkey tricks," he told Hunt).

Like Saintsbury, Symons and Moore were devoted to Gautier and his principle of the autonomy of art ("The perfection of form is virtue"). Both praised Banville and Baudelaire, and Balzac was an acknowledged strong influence on Moore. Symons embraced the Goncourts, Flaubert, Zola, and Leconte de Lisle as realists with whom he also finally placed Baudelaire rather than with the symbolists. But his interest in the naturalists and his deep appreciation of Rimbaud, Verlaine, Laforgue, and Mallarmé left little room for patience with anyone who dismissed so much of their work as Saintsbury did. New to the critical fold as he was, Symons was right in seeing that this failure marked Saintsbury as less than a great critic.

Treating Saintsbury at some length in *The Rise and Fall of the English Man of Letters* (1969), John Gross raised again the question Symons had posed, that of Saintsbury's relation to the aesthetic movement.[32] Placing him accurately as a first generation aesthete, Gross charged that Saintsbury denied the progeny he had helped earlier to foster and argued that his "clumsy" aestheticism had been merely "a pigheaded reaction to the equally pigheaded moralism of the previous generation." Gross adds the contemptuous label "aesthete on paper" because Saintsbury never thought of applying the aesthetic creed to practical living (as the decadents did), a choice also made by others who did not embrace Huysmans or *Dorian Gray*. In 1904, Saintsbury concluded that he had exaggerated the art-for-art's-sake position and stated half-truths in early reviews, but even at that remove he justified his doing so as "necessary . . . almost desirable" to offset the then all-too-incessant intrusion of opposite theories into current criticism.[33] It had been more than a "pigheaded" reaction. By 1890, Saintsbury no longer felt the necessity to exaggerate as conditions were beginning to reverse. But he never gave up his belief in the primacy of form, though for the rest of his career he limited his role to that of a critic-historian with a focus on earlier literature. One must regret that the clock had stopped, as Symons said, but this does not cancel out his early battle for attention to form and against the didactic heresy or his lifelong appreciation of Gautier, Baudelaire, and Flaubert.

A footnote to all this is the fact that the first issue of the *Yellow Book* carried "A Sentimental Cellar" by Saintsbury.[34] Along with contributions by Gosse, Garnett, A. C. Waugh, and William Watson, this little chat by two wine lovers provided a genteel facade to offset the more daring Aubrey Beardsley, George Moore, Max Beerbohm, and Symons, but it did not prevent the attacks that focused on Beardsley.

Symons had sensed what Gross failed to realize, that Saintsbury's reactions to contemporary writers differed markedly from his response to older ones. However, Symons did not explore the reasons why Saintsbury rejected the dirt and scatological detail in Zola while he rejoiced in Rabelais and Swift. The clues lie in his phrase for Rabelais, "time-deodorized,"[35] and in his complaint that Zola's works are not "dis-realized." For him, distancing in time and imaginative handling separate Rabelais from modern realism and documentation. An element of dream or fantasy does it for what Saintsbury thought was the best of Balzac and Flaubert as it does for all romance. Helen Waddell learned what she called "the historical attitude" from Saintsbury and explained it to her old friend and father-figure, Dr. George Taylor, who feared her having too much exposure to the Renaissance.[36] With this attitude distancing her from the work, she gradually got used to Rabelais's grossness and, realizing his great humanity, came to enjoy his work that had earlier repelled her. She saw this process chiefly as a matter of the reader's attitude, but Saintsbury, when he rejected Zola, preferred to explain it as due to Zola's lack of artistic handling. He thus avoided facing his wish to escape the uglier realities of his world or the security he found in the past even when it was ugly. As a result, when he later tried to deal with realistic contemporary literature in *The Later Nineteenth Century*, he went terribly wrong as he never did on Rabelais.

While the drama of the 1890s was unfolding around him, Saintsbury, showing no awareness of Symons's judgment, took stock of his own critical methods in "Kinds of Criticism," the preface to the first volume of his *Essays on English Literature*. He never republished this essay though he believed the method it defined gave unity to the five volumes of essays he published from 1890 to 1895 and was peculiarly his own. Along with the introduction to Scherer's *Essays* of 1889, also never republished, this essay is a brief statement of his critical theory, which Saintsbury later thought that he had covered in the *History of Criticism*, but these two essays are useful as earlier statements of his critical method.

In "The Kinds of Criticism," Saintsbury dismisses three types of criticism then in vogue: the sayer of fine things, with his or her concomitant "gush"; the scientific critic ("a contradiction in terms") with his or her generalities or "product-of-circumstances" theories, who is powerless before "the splendid mystery of the idiosyncrasy of the artist"; and the purely impressionistic critic who, though superior to the other two, misses "the full and proper office of the critic," that is, to judge.[37] Mere obiter dicta or personal responses are not enough, although he here tells us nothing specific about what the standards are to be. The critic must try "to render the whole virtue of the subjects," compare them with similar and dissimilar ones in the same and other languages, analyze the literary causes and effects, then place and value the work. These five steps must be supported by wide knowledge of all literature so that the critic may make the many comparisons central to the process. To the range of comparison there should be no limit.

This process should lead to generalizations and steady continuing revision of these generalizations. All this, he believes, should strengthen one's power of distinguishing good work from bad and save one from rigid formulas and dogma, from delusions of progress and mere random impressions. If they also keep their focus upon the literary character of the work (style and treatment), critics will avoid extraliterary prejudices and be on the high road to true literary criticism. Saintsbury suggests practical tests: what idea of the original would the critic give to a tolerably instructed person who did not know the original? Has he or she placed the subject in the geneal history of literature and that of its own language and department? What has he or she done "to aid the general grasp of that literary sum?"[38] The emphasis on the historical is strong.

It is a large order, not strikingly original, but in Saintsbury's view it is his own and is essential to sound judgment. He admits that his efforts to do it all may have been faulty. He adds a few other points. Sainte-Beuve welcomed "subjects possessing but qualifying merits,"[39] and the serious critic will gladly take up the challenge to appraise the minor and the second rate. In this, Saintsbury faithfully followed the master. Further, the critic will judge old and new alike, being, as Saintsbury judged Scherer to be, "as independent of the charms of novelty as of antiquity."[40] For the classic and the contemporary, the same methods and standards should work.[41] A sound ideal but one Saintsbury was now proving himself unable to live up to. More than simply playing safe, he was afraid of the new and radical.

In the Scherer preface, he also offered a portrait of the "perfect critic."[42] He or she will possess "in about equal parts the intimate grasp, the universal range, the everlasting tolerance of Sainte-Beuve, the literary grace and girlish charm of Mr. Arnold, the intuition of Hazlitt, the sympathy of Lamb, and, lastly . . . solid manly argumentative power, not hesitating if necessary at dissolving analysis." To these, Saintsbury added, in another comment, independence, flexibility, love and enthusiasm, "gusto," the ability to "give the reasons for the faith that is in you," and plain common sense. Ruling over all will stand the primary duty—always to compare.

What omissions are there in this manifesto? Saintsbury elsewhere had been far more insistent about primary attention to form; also he often reiterated the "law" that the critic shall not dislike A because it is not B, no matter how fine B may be, and that he or she must judge by intention and result, then check his or her reaction by rereading many times. Equally significant are his more calculated omissions of those things he regarded as not strictly literary: history of ideas, social relevance, cultural history or the philosophical temper of an age. He believes that critics are required neither to influence the artist nor to lead their age other than as a purely literary guides.

Unsystematic thinker that Saintsbury repeatedly proves himself to be, one comes to feel that this kind of general, somewhat vague statement was made too readily and that writing so much and so steadily he rarely took account of all his precepts. Rather, he worked spontaneously with certain basic impulses directing him: to share his pleasure, to express appreciation for it, to define the virtues of the work, to afford others access to what gave him pleasure, and, in the process, to place it all in its historical frame, a purely literary one.

The method Saintsbury defined in "Kinds of Criticism" he had demonstrated to readers for almost two decades—impressionistic, appreciative criticism, full of personal enthusiasm, undogmatic but, as he indicates here, checked and (he hoped) regulated by the use of historical knowledge for constant comparisons. He had faith in the process, and he saw in contemporary impressionist criticism a growing need to correct and order its impressions "into some coherent doctrine and creed."[43] Distrusting abstract theory, he believed knowledge and comparative analysis would do the job, never seriously questioning their adequacy, never feeling you could read too much. Later, in the *History of Criticism,* he defined criticism, his kind and what he believed to be Pater's, as "an endless process of correcting impressions—or at least checking and auditing them till we are sure that they are genuine, coordinated, and (with the real if not the apparent consistency) consistent."[44]

Independent as he liked to think himself, the influences that shaped his view are pretty clear: Swinburne, Arnold, Sainte-Beuve, and Pater, above all. In the mid-1860s, only an insensitive undergraduate of Oxford could have failed to respond in some way to those influences. Saintsbury's enthusiastic reaction to *Poems and Ballads* and his echoing of the more rebellious statements of Swinburne were the roots of the young man's faith in art-for-art's-sake as the way to save criticism from the heresies epitomized for him in Arnold. Yet when he wrote a life of Arnold twenty-odd years later, he spoke of him as "the master of all English critics in the latter half of the nineteenth century,"[45] a view confirmed by T. S. Eliot at Harvard in 1933. "In quite diverse developments it is...the criticism of Arnold that sets the tone: Walter Pater, Arthur Symons, John Addington Symonds, Leslie Stephen, F. W. H. Myers, George Saintsbury—all the more eminent critical minds of the time bear witness to it."[46]

Sainstbury's working critical attitudes throughout his life offer a paradox: no man more fully influenced him than Arnold; there was none with whom he more frequently argued, but he never underestimated his influence. In some respects he feared it; in others, he knew it to be good for his time though in ways different from those Arnold himself most hoped for. The important thing about the relations between them is not the fact of influence, because scarcely a cultured man in England after 1860 escaped that influence, but the varied ways Saintsbury reacted to it. Every serious literary student since has been scorched by those oft-repeated phrases burning into his consciousness. Saintsbury is a special case.

The more one reads Saintsbury, the more frequently one meets the phrase "criticism of life," which, as a "misleading" definition of poetry,[47] became a kind of obsession. He could never rid himself of this or the other Arnoldian catch phrases and controversial ideas. He condemns, qualifies, approves, questions, sometimes just growls. He recognized that Arnold "raised the stature of literature" and gave criticism a dignity and importance with the public that it had not had theretofore.[48] He believed Arnold to be serious and honest in intention, a champion of new ways in criticism, "a real and valuable corrective," but also a threat to literary values, one who could go wrong and who should be followed only with caution.

Saintsbury saw Arnold in dozens of roles and wrote about him more often perhaps than he did about any other English writer. His frequent contradictory references come to sound like those of an ambivalent son, embarrassed though still affectionate, irritated by the very paternal teachings that had most impressed themselves upon him. He fights them with various tactics, and all this makes him representative of the varied impact of Arnold on his age. At one moment, he complains of Arnold's caprice in judgment and of his too narrow range of knowledge;[49] at another he acclaims him as a very good force set against "ignorance" and "insularity, the neglect of comparison . . . undisciplined impression and 'irresponsible indolence.'"[50] Both things are true: Arnold set some ideals he could not fulfill and thus inspired his literary progeny. Saintsbury always felt his grace, though he deplored the "jaunty air of infallibility" with which Arnold trespassed on grave political and theological subjects.[51] But Saintsbury also missed much as he turned away from Arnold's main ideas.

Saintsbury knew Arnold personally though not well. He recalled just one conversation with him, one in which Arnold "good-humoredly" objected to Saintsbury's overvaluing of some French poet.[52] With some accuracy, Saintsbury says " . . . though an accomplished, he was by no means a complex character,"[53] but he had "a singularly agreeable presence."[54]

What were the main points of contention? A clue to these and to the conflict within Saintsbury himself is his response to Arnold's view of Emerson as "a friend and aider of those who would 'live in the spirit.'" All such views, Saintsbury remarks, are personal.

> To some, Gautier, with his doctrine of "Sculpte, lime, cisèle" as the great commandment of the creative artist, has been a friend and leader in the life of the spirit: to Mr. Arnold he was only a sort of unspiritual innkeeper. To Mr. Arnold, Maurice de Guérin, with his secondhand Quietism, was a friend and leader in the life of the spirit; others scarcely find him so.[55]

This 1889 retrospect throws one back to the 1870s and Saintsbury's early reviews.

The main bone of contention is his belief that, for Arnold, "insistence on the character of the subject was his critical being's end and aim."[56] This idea, first developed in Arnold's preface to the *Poems* in 1853, led inevitably, as Saintsbury saw it, to the controversial definition of poetry as a "criticism of life." Always "one of its most decided and irreconcilable assailants,"[57] Saintsbury never lost the need to reverse it or at least to qualify or neutralize it. In one early, hopeful moment, he pled that Arnold must have knowingly exaggerated;[58] in another, he accepts it as a "half-truth";[59] again, as something present in poetry but not of its essence. Again being haunted by "the insidious neatness" of this "unlucky and maimed definition," he tries rephrasing it. Poetry is "passionate interpretation" or "re-creation" of life or "the passionate experience of life (which is a different thing from the 'criticism' of it)."[60] Off on another tack, Saintsbury says one side of poetry was "crudely and wrongly stated but rightly indicated, in Mr. Arnold's formula"[61]

Saintsbury went on being irritated and troubled to the end and was hampered by the effects it had upon him. It encouraged him to exaggerate the formal side, as he admits, and less consciously it strengthened his tendency to dismiss the "criticism of life" in any specific work without analyzing it, as if it spoke for itself.

Examples of Saintsbury's reaction to other Arnold phrases abound. For instance, "Classics of our prose," that blundering Arnoldism for Dryden and Pope, became a point to protest in Saintsbury's early appreciative treatment of Dryden and elsewhere.[62] He deplored Arnold's "Grand Style" as too narrow a conception to fit anyone but Dante and devoted three lectures to this style in Milton, Shakespeare, and Dante and broadened the concept.

More important is what Saintsbury did with Arnold's definition of the function of criticism. "To learn and propagate the best that has been said and thought in the world" afforded Saintsbury a point of departure for his own demand that the critic learn and propagate "all the good." This quarrel colors all Saintsbury's writing: how can you know what is best if you do not try first to know all? Why derogate the value of the minor and second rate if, in even minute measure, it can give us literary pleasure and worth? Indeed, is not critical treatment "more telling, more needed, more interesting" with minor writers? The great will make their own way with fit readers. So the critic must "read everything" and (adapting Arnold's words) must "endeavor to find, to know, to love, to recommend, *not only the best, but all the good,* that has been known and thought and written in the world."[63] To know all the good was the goal of unlimited range Saintsbury had set himself as an undergraduate many years before Arnold set down his famous definition, and he apparently never feared the blunting of one's power to discriminate by too much reading of the mediocre (as Arnold did). Increasingly, this obsession with reading all literature became more compulsive both for himself and as a recommendation to all readers. Read all a man wrote, all minor writers, all literatures, he urged.

"The current of fresh ideas" Arnold wanted criticism to produce is for him an extraliterary concern and "the calculus of profit" that he thought Arnold had wrongly adopted from Goethe is "the pure Philistinism of culture itself."[64] He anticipated T. S. Eliot's objections to Arnold's use of poetry as a substitute for religion, as he also lamented all the energy Arnold expended upon excursions into politics, religion, and theology, energies he thought (probably wrongly) could have been channeled into poetry.

The hold of Arnold's cliches upon Saintsbury did not end here. In his famous preface to Ward's *English Poets* in 1880, Arnold had introduced, along with "the criticism of life," the touchstone device, the "classics of our prose" formula and that neat triad, the "historical," the "personal," and the "real" estimates. Arnold dismissed the first two of these estimates as critical fallacies because they might lead to the overvaluing of the mediocre or obscure and even to the neglect of the truly excellent. Unlike Saintsbury, Arnold felt there are limits on what the mind can absorb. But the underrating of literary history and historical perspective and of the personal response bred profound distrust in Saintsbury. He even once stooped to a sarcastic reading of Arnold's motives, arguing that it was convenient, "enabling him to skip periods, authors, literatures, that he did not care about, and . . . fortifying him in . . . secure and extremely one-sided generalizations."[65] This attack, a blot on his otherwise good essay on Scherer, was but one of many ways Saintsbury defined his own position by reacting against Arnold.

Having been led to study French literature by Arnold and having become its historical interpreter on a scale Arnold may never have envisioned, Saintsbury, with his vast range, had doubts about Arnold as a guide to French writers. He never quite forgave the attention

Arnold gave the Guérins or Senancour, and he deplored Arnold's failure to appreciate French poetry in general and the power of the Alexandrine in particular. By his own work, he challenged Arnold's role as a major guide to French literature though he would probably not have denied that his initial inspiration had come from Arnold.

Thus, to pursue our metaphor, father and son stood embattled—with Saintsbury doing all the battling and chronologically having the last word though Arnold's greater stature carried his impact to new generations after he had fertilized his immediate literary progeny. In Saintsbury's terms, Arnold had been "a germinal influence" as he continues to be.[66] Though he often blew hot and cold and could, at one stage, tick Arnold off as "that angelic but ineffectual rebel against romanticism,"[67] Saintsbury's acknowledgment of Arnold's accomplishments is finally just and gracious—in the biography and the *History of Criticism,* in *The Later Nineteenth Century,* anonymously in the *Saturday Review* at the time of Arnold's death, and a few months later when *Essays in Criticism,* second series, appeared.[68] He even offered backhanded praise of Arnold's "serene self-confidence" because it helped him drive home truths that Englishmen needed driven home. He was able, in Saintsbury's favorite phrase, "to give a reason . . . for the faith that was in him, to connect his private likes and judgments into an organic whole," and was, finally, one of "the greatest stimulators of the thoughts of others."[69] One must conclude that the Arnoldian yeast worked in Saintsbury all his life as a major energizing force and stimulus—jostling as it did that of Pater and others.

The influence of Pater can be stated more briefly. It is important but limited. Saintsbury knew Pater better personally than he did Arnold though never intimately, and he felt that their similar Oxford experience gave him special understanding of Pater's ideas. He was referring almost wholly to *The Studies in the History of the Renaissance,* where he found a definition of his own way of criticism. He endorsed Pater's philosophy of "the moment" and the highly sensitized receiver of them as the aesthetic ideal way of living and felt this way of living was possible without one's suffering the moral damage Pater had feared when—"rather unwisely" in Saintsbury's view—he withdrew the Conclusion from the second edition of the *Studies* in 1877. He called Pater an ethical hedonist, but argued that his doctrine was compatible with "the extremist orthodoxies of the best kind" though it could be degraded. He thought its abuse had been encouraged by "unscrupulous satire"—Mallock's *New Republic,* Burnand's *The Colonel,* and Gilbert and Sullivan's *Patience,* but also by the example set by "false brethren" and by "the natural inertia and gullibility of the public mind."[70]

Far less subtle in intellect and artistic consciousness than Pater, Saintsbury responded to his concern for style and artistry and thrilled to the importance of the refining, sensitizing process by which the critic and reader become capable of filling their moments with the ecstasy art proposes. He lacked Pater's philosophical mind, and being a person of compulsive activity had far less self-knowledge. After *Studies in the Renaissance,* there were many trails on which he could not follow Pater.

Saintsbury's 1906 essay on Pater is a warm tribute and proves his continuing discipleship after the 1890s had shown how Pater's initial creed could be exploited by those who forgot Pater's insistence on the constant refining, purifying, ennobling of one's interests and one's receptivity. It is not easy to define the influence of the quiet Oxford recluse upon the ebullient young literary journalist he met first in 1873 and whom Pater later called "that admirable scholar of our literature." Pater praised Saintsbury's *Specimens of English Prose Style;* he appreciated Saintsbury's recognizing his concern with the paragraph, but protested his too great separation of form and matter as well as what (mistakenly) he thought was his dislike of ornate prose.

In his Preface to *Studies in the History of the Renaissance* (1873) Pater borrowed Arnold's "to see the object as in itself it really is" as the aim of criticism but stated that for the "aesthetic critic" the only means of achieving this is to "know one's own impression as it really is."[71] Like Arnold, he rejected abstract theorizing. The critic's job is "to disengage the virtue" by which a work of art produces its impression of beauty or pleasure and "indicate what the source of that impression is," a process he compared to that of chemical analysis. To disengage he defined by the terms "to distinguish, to analyze and separate from its adjuncts." Saintsbury's paraphrase shifts the emphasis significantly:.

To feel the virtue of the poet or painter, to disengage it, to set it forth—these are the three stages of the critic's duty.... Expose mind and sense to them like a camera, assist the reception of the impression by cunning lenses of comparison and history and hypothesis; shelter it with a cabinet of remembered reading and corroborative imagination, develop it by meditation, and print it off with the light of style.[72]

Pater's emphasis on analysis is gone and Saintsbury has substituted for Pater's analogy to chemistry that to the newer art of photography and thus reduced the analytical process to passive reception, while adding the lenses of history, comparison, and hypothesis (these were in his own definition in "The Kinds of Criticism"), meditation and "corroborative imagination," all things only implied by Pater. For Saintsbury, this *is* the modern critical method and his own. Elsewhere he had added judging, but he knew that, for Pater, truth to the impression is all that is possible in a world of flux where each of us is "a prisoner in his own dream of a world." Saintsbury hoped historical and comparative attitudes would limit this subjectivity.

Saintsbury attributed to Pater more faith in the saving grace of knowing and reading everything than either Pater or Arnold ever aspired to. It is his own faith speaking out, rooted in his own temper, but it reflects the spirit of his prespecialist era and its ideal of omniscience. It encouraged superficiality but, in Saintsbury, it was strenuously pursued and utterly sincere. With absolute standards gone, his generation, like Arnold's, Pater's, and our own, had to find ways of shoring up its judgments.

Beyond these two major antithetical influences of Arnold and the early Pater upon Saintsbury, one could find evidence of many others. Yet with someone as soaked in the history of criticism as he was, many of these might better be seen as parallels that he enthusiastically recognized: Longinus on the Sublime, Joubert on the "poetic moment," Hugo's great critical question, "L'oeuvre, est-il bon ou mauvais"? as the central one (in the Preface to *Les Orientales*). *The History of Criticism* is full of such evidence.

With Sainte-Beuve and Gautier, influence was early and strong as already noted. The Hazlitt parallel and influence are more mixed but strong. Saintsbury's high opinion of Hazlitt is most evident in his essay of 1887, where, in an enthusiastic exaggeration, he calls him "the greatest critic England ever produced."[73] In Craik's *English Prose* he says most specifically why he rates him so highly. Hazlitt is one who "can see the whole of his author most clearly, can place him in due relation to other authors most exactly, can formulate his idiosyncrasy in the most effective manner with the fewest words."[74] Though too sweeping, this sounds like Pater and like Saintsbury himself in "Kinds of Criticism" and in the conclusion of the *History of Criticism* on the true method. It leaves out the energy and great enthusiasm, the "personal love of literature," Saintsbury treasured in Hazlitt and shared with him. It also downplays the prejudices, the lack of system and of range he regretted in him. He especially valued Hazlitt's "circlings round his subject," as he perceptively calls them, where one of his insights "will hit the nail on the head and drive it home . . . there is little method but the reader is carried by assault, mass, variety, repetition."[75] The two critics have often been compared and rightly so. Saintsbury here anticipates Daved Daiches's judgment of Saintsbury himself as "the great amateur."[76]

> The critic . . . shows no method at all. . . . [His is] a personal, unsystematic eclectic kind of criticism, creating as it moves a highly literary atmosphere . . . relaxed and discursive . . . but a civilized exchange of opinion. . . . Only a generation secure in its possession of a rich and stable literary tradition can afford to be so relaxed. . . . When that security ebbed, the connoisseur gave way to the analyst.

No one has bettered this verdict, whatever additions one may make. It is the verdict of a later generation with a perspective Symons lacked. But in his concern for Saintsbury's neglect of contemporary literature, Symons was right. To know all the best had come to mean to Saintsbury the best of a past two decades away. To fight Arnold's values in 1890 was not to engage in the main battle. It was a retreat broader than Symons recognized.

CHAPTER 11

Ends and Beginnings: "The Lean Year" and the Man

The *Saturday Review* held its place as the leading Conservative London weekly for thirty-nine years. This era ended abruptly in 1894 when Frank Harris purchased the paper and began a new regime of his own, short-lived but distinctive. The seven years between the death of Beresford-Hope in 1887 and the debacle of 1894 had been years of uncertainty and of some decline. The thundering against Gladstone and the Irish continued to the end; reviewing was kept up to a pretty fair standard, but the original vigor and initiative were fading. As Henley commented to Charles Whibley in 1889, "the *Saturday Review* is dwindling and pining à vue d'oeil."[1] A sad picture with five years to go, and Saintsbury says very little about it.

Behind the scenes, the sense of insecurity was steadily increasing. Saintsbury admitted in 1892 that there was now no certainty that mail addressed to staff members at the offices would be received. The root of the trouble was that Beresford-Hope had bequeathed the paper to his older son, Philip, rather than to the younger, Charles, who had a real interest in it and to whom it had been promised. His father simply neglected to put it into his will. Though Charles became manager of all but the finances, Philip's extravagance soon fatally crippled the enterprise, and in 1892 he sold it to Lewis Humphrey Edwards. Walter Pollock and Saintsbury continued as its editors while rumors spread about its fate. "Dying of dignity," was one pundit's verdict as it was "hawked round for sale at almost any price in all the literary marts in England."[2] Circulation had dropped until, in 1894 as the final blow fell, it was quoted at little over £2,000.

On November 2d that year the sale to Frank Harris took place, and having made a clean sweep of the entire staff, Harris assembled his own, for the most part a young, brilliant one including G. B. Shaw, Max Beerbohm, D. S. MacColl, Chalmers Mitchell, Cunningham Graham, W. Hamilton Fyfe, H. G. Wells, and Churton Collins. "It was the twilight of the academic, a revolution," said Wells, facetiously. "I gathered that our fortunes were made ... that Oxford and the stuffy and the Genteel and Mr. Gladstone were to be destroyed, and that under Harris the *Saturday Review* was to become a weekly unprecedented in history."[3]

Unprecedented it was, to a degree, for three brief years, *and* vigorous, with its new, original talent. It was also as uneven and unpredictable as its new owner-editor Harris always was. And "of course it didn't pay," as Hamilton Fyfe put it.[4] Fresh from eight years as an editor of the *Fortnightly Review,* Harris had his own view.

> The *Saturday Review* was evilly notorious as the most poisonous critic of all lost and all new causes. I told my contributors ... I wanted the *Saturday Review* to become known as the finder of Stars and not the finder of faults.[5]

Fyfe thought Harris "gingered up the *Saturday Review,* once a power in politics and literature ... now sunk into lethargy; Harris galvanized it into vigorous life.... Everything was well-written."[6]

Whether there could be any real freedom under such a maverick as Harris was a question, but the new *Saturday* had a brief literary success and was a good deal discussed even if it never became a power in the arts or politics. When Henley was asked by Harris to write for him, as he says, "*at a salary* and—so far as I can judge—at his dictation," he refused.[7] Gosse's picture is more graphic and typically more gossipy: "The *Saturday Review* has been bought by a wild kind of Sioux or Apache called Frank Harris, who has driven the old staff out into the street with cuffs and kicks, and is trying to run it with young braves and scalphunters of his own." Gosse fails to add that he continued to write briefly for Harris though he does say, "Many of us are taking refuge in a new weekly called *The Realm.*"[8]

Though the cuffs and kicks were verbal, the whole process could only have been painful for the staff, and particularly for Saintsbury, even though, having been warned by Gosse of the threatened takeover, he had resigned a week before it occurred.[9] Walter Pollock had gone earlier—"evicted," as his brother Sir Frederick described it. Edwards carried on an "editorless proprietorship" with Saintsbury remaining as subeditor after he wisely declined the editorship. We do not have his reasons, but he wrote Gosse of his refusal and of his efforts to find other income as early as September 7th. Saintsbury's immediate role was that of acquainting the owner, Edwards, with "the gifts and graces" of the old staff members who, he believed, should continue to write. He urged Gosse to see Edwards but to let him know in advance so that he could "sound the trumpets and beat the drums." For Walter Pollock, Saintsbury expressed great sympathy and some grave doubt about the practicality of his plans. The "Literary Gossip" column of the *Athenaeum,* on August 25, 1894, said Pollock planned a paper on new lines (could this have been *The Realm?*), and "a most influential and distinguished following" was predicted.

On September 1st, the same column reported that Saintsbury would resign at the beginning of November; the following week it apologized for its error based on a report "from what seemed a trustworthy source," and on November 3rd, the *Athenaeum* announced the actual resignation and the subsequent sale of the *Saturday Review.* The September 1st leak had alerted friends to Saintsbury's situation; Gosse, in addition to warning him against Harris, seems to have made a very generous offer of aid. Saintsbury replied that he would never forget this "spontaneous friendship," but assured Gosse that he was in no immediate need.[10] There are changes at the *Saturday Review,* he admits, "and I don't much like change," but none so far seemed objectionable. After this tactful understatement, a postcard to Gosse on November 1st ending, "So now hey for a Hincome!" confirms the fact that Saintsbury had acted on his "kind and friendly warning."[11]

A postscript to all this is supplied by another letter to Gosse, written from Edinburgh on February 18, 1896 (thirty years after his first letter to Gosse from Elgin had spoken of his sense of exile and his longing for the world of journalism).

> ... it is a great thing to work only in the matter one loves best. Also you do not and cannot overestimate the blessing of being free of journalism in the better sense ... though the mind sometimes feels inclined to cry "Give me the daggers" as of yore. ... I never thoroughly enjoyed writing for anything but the *Saturday Review* and even that in the latest years was necessarily labor and sorrow.[12]

"Labor and sorrow" is a revealing phrase from the reticent Saintsbury, who had loyally played the game to the end and, at forty-nine, faced the most difficult and uncertain of his professional years. Oscar Wilde wrote Harris in 1898, the year Harris sold the paper:

> ...though you do not blow through all the horns and flutes, or beat on *all* the drums, still I feel you are there, just as in the old days there was always the aroma of poor old lady Pollock's weak tea and literary twaddle—"the five o'clock" of their reminiscences and butter....[13]

Saintsbury passed his fiftieth birthday in Edinburgh on October 23, 1895, a week after he had delivered his inaugural lecture at the University. A major meridian point of life for most people, for him it was a break between two "half lifetimes." The move from London to Scotland, from journalism to an academic chair, marked the division between two worlds. The end of a half-century of his own life seemed to him to coincide with the end of a literary and social era.

At this point, when he shifts careers and moves into new duties and new contacts, in a new setting, it is fitting to pause with his fiftieth birthday as a *point de repère*,[14] to size up the man as a personality and project oneself into his state of mind as one looks backward and forward. Thirty-seven years of his life span lie ahead, twenty of them at Edinburgh, all of them save the last with book and pen, proof and print, in hand—always reading and writing but almost entirely about past literature.

The "lean year" before Edinburgh (Saintsbury also called it "one of the vacant interlunar caves of my fortunes") forms a kind of inner frame of the portrait affording clues to the man as he copes with this crisis in his career. Saintsbury's resignation from the *Saturday Review* in 1894 made immediately pressing the insecurity that had threatened since the death of the elder Beresford-Hope. To many a man of fifty, after twelve years as an editor wielding more power and influence than the title of subeditor would imply, the experience of being suddenly on the pavement "incomeless, disestablished and disendowed" would be shattering.[15] Saintsbury's reactions express his character.

Saintsbury had given his time more and more completely to the foundering *Saturday Review* and had thus deprived himself of other connections; being suddenly thrown upon the market was therefore the harder. The miscellaneous journalism and editing of this year and two small books on the cooking of partridge and grouse indicate his need to increase and vary the outlets for his vast energies as well as a sturdy confidence that he could make a go of it as a free-lancer. He had a partially invalid wife and two sons in their twenties who never earned enough to subsist without an allowance from him. Since 1891, he had had a house in Reading, then in Cambridgeshire, where he joined the family on weekends, and rooms at No. 34 Great Ormond Street, London. His accounts show a minimal number of income-bearing investments as reserve against the crisis.

Traumatic as the break must have been, the months after the lonely dinner that he treated himself to at Greenwich on the night he went out of a job show him, with typical courage and initiative, developing new projects and working compulsively. He wrote for new periodicals;[16] he worked on large cooperative projects like Ward's *English Poets* and Traill's *Social England;* he read government civil service examinations and university ones for Victoria University, Manchester; he did some copyreading for Heinemann and Dent and added to the editing he was already doing. He began the Pocket Library of English Literature for Rivington and projected twenty volumes. After six volumes (*Seventeenth-Century Lyrics, Political Verse, Political Pamphlets, Tales of Mystery, Elizabeth and Jacobean Pamphlets* and Defoe's *Minor Novels*), the series was abandoned as unprofitable. Prefaces for *Pride and Prejudice,* a condensed *Sir Charles Grandison,* Marmontel's *Moral Tales,* J. B. Nichols's *Words and Days,* and *National Nursery Rhymes* each brought in its few pounds while the editing of Fielding, Sterne, Smollett, Peacock, and Balzac proceeded apace. Other projects begun then, jettisoned when salvation came from Edinburgh, included a book on cooking hare to accompany those on grouse and partridge, a wine book, never completed, and a volume of "Tales of the Century." This last was planned to illustrate political and social matters—an uncongenial one for Saintsbury suggesting some desperation. He had appealed to Kipling and Hardy for contributions.

Of all the schemes, the most ambitious was the one Saintsbury proposed to William Blackwood, which was to absorb much of his time and energies for the next fifteen years. In a letter of November 24, 1894, to Blackwood, he writes of his break with the *Saturday Review* and adds, "if you have any literary work in which I can be of service to you, that service is very much at your disposal."[17] Four days later, he acknowledges Blackwood's typically prompt response and plunges into his ambitious proposal: a history of "critics and criticism" from Aristotle to the modern and "a series of 'Periods of *European* Literature' dealing with the contemporary and comparative in the different countries." Wide knowledge would be required in the editor, but, disclaiming arrogance, Saintsbury promises he "would make something of them."[18]

By mid-March, 1895, planning for the project was under way. An April 20th letter specifies the twelve volumes he would include in the *Periods* series and provides a list of possible authors. He refers to work in hand, some of it "the 'pot-boiling' kind" that leaving the *Saturday* had forced upon him. Much too hopefully, he names Christmas, 1897, as a date for completing the Criticism "volume" and closes with the reassurance: "I am rather famous, I believe, for punctuality and moreover I always like to take a long day."

The next letter to Blackwood (June 21, 1895) refers to Saintsbury's candidacy for the Edinburgh Chair—a turn of events that was to postpone completion of the big project long beyond the date anticipated and make things difficult for Blackwood. In September, one year after leaving the *Saturday Review*, Saintsbury arrived in Edinburgh to begin his new academic career.

A View of the Man

If Saintsbury exists visually for the mind of a modern reader, the image is probably that of the William Nicholson portrait done at Bath when Saintsbury was seventy-seven (1923), that now hangs in the Buttery of Merton College (fig. 1). Skull cap, long wispy beard, lined face, and wistful, even melancholy expression behind the small, oval, steel-rimmed glasses suggest the weariness of age and experience with all their strains but tell little of the vigor and massive strength one finds in the writing of this man at forty, fifty, even seventy-five. "My natural countenance is not, except when I'm deliberately grinning, a very lively one," was Saintsbury's comment, but he thought it "a picture and not merely a 'Portrait of Gentlemen.'"[19]

Five photographs and the full-length cartoon that appeared first in 1904 and several times thereafter in the University of Edinburgh *Student* otherwise comprise the visual record. All the photographs are from the two decades he spent in Edinburgh. The earliest, by Moffatt

George Saintsbury by *William Nicholson, 1923,
original oil painting at Merton College, Oxford, print by
Goupil Galleries, London, courtesy of George Kitchin.*

George Saintsbury, print from portrait photograph, ca. 1912, Lafayette, Ltd.

of Edinburgh in 1895, appeared again in the *Student* in 1916. Saintsbury least liked the one of 1900, done by flash for a series, "Contributors to the *Encyclopedia Britannica* in Their Homes." The other three,
one by Lafayette (fig. 2), two by Elliott and Fry of Edinburgh, are the
best. One of the latter is a three-quarter-length study—in a velvet-
collared, gray-black great coat, with his hands thrust into the pock-
ets.[20] It catches his strength and portly bearing and the direct keen
glance of rather near-sighted eyes behind small, oval glasses. The
eight-inch beard, fine, thin, and graying, and a fuzzy moustache hide
the mouth; strong, straight white hair lies back, center-parted, from
a broad, high forehead. One is left to imagine the ruddy cheeks and
the red of the large bulbous nose that Henley celebrated. The car-
toonist, in his full-length sketch (fig. 3), exaggerated the baggy
though narrow trousers and long, squared-off jacket, the slightly
stooped but powerful shoulders, the large, well-shaped head sunk
between them, the five-foot eleven carriage, and—most prominent
of all—very large feet. This was how the students saw him. The photographs all preserve what one student called "the determined
strength of his figure," "the massive power of his face," and "the
positive manner." The genial charm that others report and what
Elton calls "the kindly, sagacious and expressive eyes" are barely suggested.[21]

A verbal portrait by Sir George Chrystal brings all this into three-
dimensional reality as he recalls seeing Saintsbury "breasting the east
wind" through Edinburgh mists, a "burly figure" with "a truly So-
cratic homeliness," walking "sturdily and rather stiffly, with something between a stride and a strut... [with] a suggestion of closed
fists and pugnacity about his hands, one of which always grasped an
umbrella very firmly."[22] His high-pitched voice and rapid speech
complete the "motion picture." Several witnesses insist that his writings carry "the authentic rhythms of his speech" and "the native
idiom of the speaker ... in his talk and letters and thought."[23] Grierson remembered him as a "brilliant conversationalist" whose rich,
allusive "flow of talk" had the range of his writing. His more sweeping
statements were likely to take on a more genial tone in speech. Hence
he was "a delightful guest."[24]

Blyth Webster, with the advantage of more than two decades of
acquaintance, made several attempts to define Saintsbury the man.
He found him in Meredith's Dr. Middleton, "an Englishman of the

*"**George**," cartoon of Professor George Saintsbury,
University of Edinburgh Student, 1904.*

day before yesterday" combining "piety and epicureanism, learning and gentle manliness."

He saw him also as a secular counterpart of Pusey, for whom Saintsbury had a personal veneration. Webster called them "great gentlemen, devout and heroic lovers, and impressive figures in their prime . . . indefatigable in study and productiveness." He thought they outlived the opposition and the polemics they provoked, to enjoy "the love of many and the respect of all," also that both had sturdiness not style and that they did much to further "the practice of sanity and sobriety across years of confusion and experiment, of doubt and desertion."[25] Webster's adulatory tone is that of a loyal assistant writing a memorial.

But Webster felt that Saintsbury was even more like his friend Mandell Creighton. Expanding Bishop Copleston's description of them both as "profoundly convinced that unintelligent acquiescence in opinions was immoral and dangerous," he says both were sceptical and felt the irony of things, both had practical intelligence and common sense, the historic and comparative sense, a vast range of allusion, wit, vivacity, and, at times, flippancy. Webster also found something of the Regency, the eighteenth century, and the Victorian mingled in Saintsbury. He cites his "gay courage" and said he was "English in solid weight, in self-trust and sufficiency, and in reticent expression of feeling."[26] Elton is more succinct: "He has much depth, and even fierceness of temperament."[27] Saintsbury admitted to a quick temper and impatience, not suffering fools gladly or easily, and to contrariness as a besetting sin. He could be difficult and dogmatic, and seemed terrifying to his daughter-in-law and her children.

In Gautier, Saintsbury early recognized his own "unconquerable appetite for work, the sovereignest cordial for any tendency to pine for what is not."[28] His need to be busy and always conceiving vast new schemes was compulsive. He once compared himself to a friend who "was never happy unless she had a child inside her."[29] There was some economic pressure; his family needs as well as his tastes made his income insufficient. But the drive was complex and internal. His desire for omniscience and the compulsion to work are, in their intensity, neurotic while all too familiar. It is not surprising that a perceptive Edinburgh student, thinking of all of Saintsbury's books, asked when he had time to think.[30]

But the steady compulsion to read and write was no grim stance of frustration. When he saw the lack of joie de vivre in contemporary French literature of the 1880s, Saintsbury quoted the maxim, "What you do not do with relish you do not do well."[31] The joy, the enthusiastic relish and appreciation are rarely missing from his pages. Enthusiasm was never incompatible with Victorian earnestness and, in Saintsbury, the enthusiasm always prevailed.[32] The big books he wrote at Edinburgh were done, he says, "not for coin but because I like to do it and because I think it is really part of a fairly paid professor's work."[33] After his wife's death in 1924, though ailing himself, he speaks of work as salvation and as the best anodyne.

Saintsbury wrote too much to do it all well, but the compulsive writer often *must* do too much or nothing. The compulsion was as real and as strong as in any Victorian devotee of Carlyle's "gospel of work." Many a Victorian used work as defense against intellectual doubt, perplexity, and depression. In Saintsbury, defenses were built early. One never hears the note of depression or doubt, though there was a strain of pessimism in his temper. The drive for omniscience, hard work, aesthetic enjoyment of beauty, wine, foods, the vicarious life of fiction, the retreat into past literature, and religious and political dogmatism are all elements of which his defenses are compounded. Whether as a result or a mere concomitant of these, self-confidence helped him to initiate and carry through large projects even when health problems mounted.

Saintsbury never clearly expressed the personal sources of self-doubt. Most fully admitted was the need to compensate for his early-acknowledged inability to do creative things in literature by leading others to the best--his goal as a critic. One may also suspect that his obsessive work ethic compensated for some lack of satisfaction in his marriage and family life—and even in his family background. Books substitute for something. He used them as a retreat from boyhood on, as he cut himself off from closeness to other people, even family.

How did Saintsbury relax? After he got to London there were occasional evenings of good food, wine, and talk, hours at his clubs, work on his wine cellar, walking, and reading. He records his pleasure in several pets: the "ferocious" St. Bernard puppy "apprehended" at Elgin for annoying ladies, the bulldog "Cherub" of the early 1890s, and the Scotch terrier "Bounce" who, in quest of a rat in his Edinburgh cellar, was "o'erwhelmed by the debris and foaming floods as two magnums of champagne fell and broke."[34] He confesses to adoring cats and bulldogs, and in discussing the poet Gray, "adds his tears to the waters that drowned Selima."

Saintsbury's one athletic pleasure was walking. His record is a strenuous one even for an Englishman: forty-three miles once in a day; twenty-five to thirty miles in an average day; a record of seven miles in one hour, twenty-seven minutes, and thirteen-and-a-half minutes to the mile until past the age of forty; "five hundred miles in twenty days and one pair of boots without training, and with a heavy knapsack." Breaking a bone in his foot in the 1880s ended all this, but he continued to take constitutionals and loved his nightly London walks with Lang, Henley, and Gosse. He walked to and from work in both London and Edinburgh, up to three miles each way. His extensive walking tours were all cherished memories: he had walked, at one time or another, the whole circuit of Britain between John O'Groats and Land's End and had enjoyed following all Borrow's trails as set forth in *Wild Wales*. He rejoices over five hundred miles in twenty days,

> ... discovering something, on this and many other occasions, some-
> times alone, sometimes in company, of the secret of the sea and the
> lessons of the land from Scilly to Skye; from Land's End to Dover;
> from the Nore to the Moray Firth; from Dartmoor to Loch Aber;
> and from the wealds of Sussex to those Northumbrian lakes that
> lie lonely and rather uncanny under the Roman wall.[35]

Finally, it comes back to the open book—to reading and writing—if one is to define Saintsbury's life pattern. He tells one more about his reading habits and ways of working than has ever been recognized. In 1938, Sir George Chrystal said that Saintsbury had become "more and more completely absorbed in the 'adeption' [sic] of literature." Earlier he had quoted the charge that Saintsbury was guilty of "keeping to the page and missing the dogfight."[36] These charges fit the elderly man but, in his earlier political writing and editorial work, he had to be much in the world as observer and commentator. Saintsbury knew the dangers of which Chrystal speaks. He warns against "literariness... encroach[ing] on life and substitut[ing] itself therefor."[37] Nevertheless, he admits to being one of those fortunate persons "to whom the world of books is almost as real as the other two worlds of life and dream."[38] The term *dream* is significant here. As his energies dwindled and illness became more constant, he spent more time with books than with people. Toward the end he had increasingly to ration himself on both but could still dream. He praises "that infinitely happier system of conversation by books, which anyone can enjoy as he likes and interrupt as he likes at his own fireside" and "the silent companionship of the library."[39] He also confessed, "I like poetry better than anything."[40] The range of his literary enthusiasms is enormous. An all-embracing literary passion gave him a "contempt for anyone who can't get excited over paper and print."[41] He did not "envy a man who can read 'Requiescat' for the first or fiftieth time without mist in his eyes and without a certain catch in the voice."[42] At the other extreme, he asserts "there are no dull subjects (except perhaps bimetallism)."[43] His literary faith becomes a kind of chant: "Books are cheap . . . they are infinite; they are inexacting . . . they need no partner to exact their enjoyment; they interfere with nothing; they help everything."[44] The same intense feeling provoked his comment, "I do not regard reading as work!"[45] There are times, he once said, when "one must read or die"—on a wet evening in a country inn or in prison.[46]

Saintsbury writes a good deal about his habits of reading and writing. Most of this has been largely ignored. Ben Ray Redman refused to believe those who, when faced with his errors in dates and quotations, accused Saintsbury of faking.[47] The present writer believes that he read all he said he did (putting aside for the moment *how* he read), and that he had a remarkable but not infallible memory. The scattered clues he gives about *how* he read explain much.

Solitary walker as he chose to be, Saintsbury was also a solitary reader. He speaks of Cowper's "detestable habit of reading aloud . . . murderous to talk," yet he sometimes had to read verse aloud "with accompaniment of handbeat."[48] He believed himself "a rather unusually rapid, without being a careless or unfaithful reader," with a faculty for seeing "at a glance whether anything on a page needs more than that glance."[49] He identifies with those "who read very fast, who like to read more than once, and who are pleased to meet old friends in constantly new situations, and [who like] long books."[50] He even records how fast he read. He estimated half an hour's reading time for a short story or, with the style of a Gautier or Mérimée, a couple of hours. *Les Trois Mousquetaires* should require "no more than half a day."[51] "A tolerably rapid reader" should get through *Nightmare Abbey* in an hour or so and Carlyle's *Sterling* in one sitting.[52] This is fast reading with little time for analysis. The sixteen volumes of Walpole's letters would demand a month of leisurely evenings' reading for "slow savoring."[53] He could not be reading every page.

More useful than these statistics is Saintsbury's defense of Scott's way of reading, and probably his own, assimilating books "with a distressing inaccuracy in particulars, with a general and genial fidelity of which the pedants do not even dream and could not comprehend.[54]

It was such inaccuracy that Churton Collins and many modern scholars (not pedantic like Collins) have charged against Saintsbury. The defense offered by loyal friends—that every critic or historian cannot do everything well and that Saintsbury's strength was in judgment—hardly disposes of the issue. To see how he read does not dispose of it either, but it does illuminate it.

The main explanation of how he read and reread so much is in his own phrase, "Skim and Skip and Dip." Conscientious about reading and rereading all the material pertinent to anything he was writing upon, he knew when to skip. He warns that skipping should occur only when necessary, but only a prig or a pedant will disallow it.[55] *The French Novel* is full of "confessions" of skimming and about books he would not or could not read. These stand side by side with claims regarding the marathons he performed: the *Grand Cyrus* and forty volumes of the *Cabinet des Fées,* and forty days for twenty volumes of continuous reading of *Astrée,* labeled "collarwork."[56] In reading Thomas Amory's *John Buncle* skipping-cum-skimming was necessary.[57] No one could have had more need than Saintsbury for this art, but the habit grew on him and, combined with reliance on his remarkable memory, brought its disadvantages in inaccuracy. At the same time, it saved him from being bored by millions of pages of dross and preserved his capacity to spark when he struck pure metal. Any competent, mature reader skips judiciously, but Saintsbury's frequent references to the practice suggest a self-conscious awareness of the habit and perhaps guilt, defensiveness, a naive egotism, some sense of inadequacy, and a compulsive need to record such detail.

Saintsbury's habit of parading his reading has irritated some readers. Others see this mannerism as endearing evidence to support the legend of his having read more than anyone else in a world of men whose range was vast. They rejoice in the knowledge of whatever feats they happen to recall: the claim that only he and John Morley had read all of Diderot; *Pickwick*, Peacock, *Wuthering Heights, The Antiquary,* Southey's *The Doctor,* Jane Austen, Thackeray, and so forth *all* reread once a year; the *Earthly Paradise* read twenty times with unfading delight; *Gulliver* a hundred times; three hundred volumes of Gautier; all of the *Anti-Jacobin; The Anatomy of Melancholy* read twice through (it "was not easy"). These parallel the legend that, for fifteen years, he read a French novel every morning before breakfast. He saw himself as "one of those who seldom find anything that resists their devouring faculty."[58] "Getting over tiresome things" he describes as "literary mountaineering"[59]

Those who enjoy these boasts smile when Saintsbury admits that he has not read all of Dumas or Soulie or Restif de La Bretonne, that he has not read Boyle's *Parthenessa* and never intends to, that "It is enough to have read Sainte Madeleine of the Ink-Desert herself, without reading bad imitators of her."[60] But as one smiles, one realizes afresh the immense range of his knowledge and the inevitable price—superficiality.

Saintsbury's reading habits correlate with his working habits. His account of how fast he wrote helps explain his slapdash work. Referring to Balzac, he speculates: "A thousand words an hour is anything but an extraordinary rate of writing and fifteen hundred by no means unheard of with persons who don't write rubbish."[61] He calculates that even "rather dilatory writers" such as Thackeray might write "a couple of hundred pages of one of these present volumes . . . in little more than six weeks."[62]

Saintsbury took pride in his own speed, but he observed Lang writing much more quickly than he could and able to work under the most unaccommodating circumstances, as he could not. He, on the other hand, never could stay in bed after 8:00 A.M. and liked a long day—preferring 2:00 A.M. as bedtime, but he admits, "Not every constitution will stand an eighteen-hour day."[63] He usually wrote all morning, sometimes in the afternoon, and reserved the evening for reading.[64]

Legends regarding Saintsbury's illegible handwriting are many. Any sampling of letters, account books, or typed copy (overlaid with "dreadful insertions of script") proves that the legends exaggerate little: A nervous breakdown among typesetters, Macmillan's committee formed to decipher his letters, family conclaves working over scrawled specimens received (and some of them never deciphered), and Grierson's report that he never wholly made out all of the kind letter Sainsbury wrote him on his appointment to Edinburgh. His malformed hand produced a scraggly, half-formed script and, typing with one finger of the left hand, he did it badly.[65] He admitted this to one of his editors and spoke of his absolute rule "not to let anything appear in a book without seeing a proof. Typewritten copies are no good. . . . Until one sees what one has written in actual print one never knows what it is."[66] Such practice would make any modern editor blanch.

One typical Saintsbury manuscript proves his feeling to be justified.[67] Seven and a half legal-size pages of the lecture "Specialization" have heavily penned corrections superimposed, about six to the line; omitted letters are filled in; spelling is corrected and punctuation supplied; and there is transposition and actual revision of text. Any printer would have had to correct a dozen errors on the first page alone. The miracle is that errors were so few since he usually wrote this way at great speed, in one draft, then revised in proof. Of one article, he says he took "some trouble with it even to the extent (rare with me) of making a rough draft and rewriting."[68] He admitted, in 1895, "My eyesight in correcting small type is none of the best."[69]

Of equal interest are the ways Saintsbury prepared for the actual writing. Long journalistic experience played its part. He wrote on the flyleaves of books and marked passages as well. He describes the flyleaves of the letters of Sidney Smith as covered with references. When he reread Hazlitt in 1887, he found innumerable passages marked for reference; and for his essay "English War Songs," the six-volume *Pills to Purge Melancholy* was "plumed with paper slips."[70] In the *History of Criticism* he complains, " . . . so always: the very plethora of one's notes for comment warning the commentator that he is lost if he indulges rashly."[71] But he did it all himself. Unlike Gosse, he did not rely on copyists or research assistants. Once the slips were set in a text or the marking was done, Saintsbury, with a general plan in mind, leafed through the volume or volumes—sometimes commenting seriatim as he does on Dodsley in *The Peace of the Augustans* and often running out of space before he has exhausted his references.[72]

The method was unsystematic in the extreme, yet the plans of the large surveys and the interchapters and conclusions indicate a structure carried in his head. Some disproportion was the obvious result, but the whole procedure went along with an immense capacity to order his days, to do fantastic quantities of work on schedule, and to keep numerous disparate projects going simultaneously. If he promised an article in a week, he met his schedule, and he was often ahead of his deadline. When reading proofs, he planned so that he could give a half-hour per day to this and be done on time. He once asked an editor, "If it should be convenient to me to send you the copy before April 1, I suppose you would not object? One sometimes has a gap in longer work, which it is useful to fill up with shorter."[73] Such was the pressure he imposed on himself constantly.

CHAPTER 12

Edinburgh Professor, 1895–1915

The struggle to establish the study of English literature in the universities that Churton Collins spearheaded in the 1880s only intensified when Napier was named to the Merton Professorship in 1885; Oxford having settled again for more philology. But the Scottish Chair of literature was over 130 years old when Saintsbury went to Edinburgh, and such universities as London, Liverpool, Victoria, and Glasgow had Chairs of English. The Universities Commission of 1889 made provisions for establishing Honors Schools. Honors in English began at Edinburgh in 1892; at Oxford in 1893. The first two Honors candidates at Oxford took the examination in 1896; David Nichol Smith was Edinburgh's first in 1895.

Oxford was to have no real literature professor in English until Raleigh was appointed in 1904; the Cambridge King Edward VII Professorship came only in 1911, with its first occupant, A. W. Verrall, almost immediately succeeded by Arthur Quiller-Couch. Professor Edward Freeman's objection was typical of older university men's attitudes toward English studies: "We cannot examine in taste and sympathies." Others argued that no one needed to be taught their own literature or that the study of English was not useful and could not be scientifically taught.[1]

Meanwhile Scotland, with its long tradition of democratic education and its strong respect for rhetoric, had professors of English literature at all four universities. Alexander Bain and Minto at Aberdeen, William Aytoun and then David Masson at Edinburgh, and John Nichol at Glasgow had already given the Chairs great distinction. The older, Scottish tradition of general education with a balance between science and literature and with a special emphasis on "moral philosophy" was gradually giving way to the Oxbridge concept of specialized university training.[2]

The Scottish Universities Act of 1858 introduced English literature into the Scottish curriculum and expressed the goal of assimilation to the English system because Scottish University graduates were failing Indian Civil Service Examinations, which included English literature. In 1872, control of Scottish education was transferred to London, and the Universities Commission instituted certain reforms in 1889. The old general degree retained for local use was "fossilized," while the more specialized Honors program, free of "moral philosophy," was set up to prepare students for "Imperial Jobs" and Civil Service competition. The Ordinance of 1892 established entrance examinations for the four universities under a joint board of examiners and admitted women on the same terms as men. Professors were put on regular salaries, pension funds were set up, and university lectureships were created.

In 1892, G. Gregory Smith, a Balliol graduate who had been Masson's assistant at Edinburgh since 1889, became assistant lecturer in English and, because Masson was uninterested, undertook to establish the English Honors program. In 1895, Saintsbury found this program satisfactory and altered it little.[3]

The Chair of English Literature at Edinburgh is a crown appointment. When David Masson (1822–1907), who had held it since 1865, resigned in the late spring of 1895, the appointment fell under the shadow of the political changes of that June. When the Lord Rosebery government, just sixteen months old, resigned on June 24, Lord Salisbury formed a new government. The General Election of July brought in 342 conservatives and 71 liberal Unionists as against 177 Liberals and 82 Nationalists. The Edinburgh University appointment would obviously be conservative, and Saintsbury moved quickly to become a candidate.

Saintsbury asked Blackwood for a testimonial; it carries the date of June 24. The next day, thanking Blackwood, he explained some details: "If our people really come in [in the Election]," J. N. B. Robertson, as Rector of the University, will have a "consultative voice" and has already been approached. About the Marquess of Lothian, who had been Secretary for Scotland from 1886 to 1892 and might hold that office again, Saintsbury has some doubts, but Blackwood's writing him might help.[4] The secretaryship went to Lord Balfour of Burleigh.

Saintsbury sought six other testimonials.[5] A representative and effective selection—state, church, science, education, letters, journalism, and publishing—included, in that order, A. J. Balfour, the new First Lord of the Treasury and Chancellor of the University of Edinburgh, who sent four lines of positive support stressing Saintsbury's knowledge and catholicity; Saintsbury's old Oxford intimate, Mandell Creighton, now Bishop of Peterborough; his school and Oxford friend, W. T. Thistleton Dyer, now the director of the Royal Gardens at Kew; A. W. Ward, Vice Chancellor of Victoria University (who speaks of Saintsbury's experience in lecturing and examination reading); Andrew Lang, writing (typically) from Lord's Cricket Ground; Henry D. Traill, and William Blackwood. Lang and Blackwood, who could speak for Scottish interests, gave assurance that Edinburgh would be well served. All except Blackwood spoke out of twenty to thirty years' acquaintance, some from intimacy. Dyer, who brought a scientist's perspective to bear, wrote the best and most substantial of the letters, praising "the balance of sympathy and judgment, the sanity and lucidity of Saintsbury's critical activity" that had earned him the respect of scientists.

As for competition, Saintsbury had made certain that Lang and W. P. Ker were not among the candidates before deciding to stand. Lang had been offered the post and had refused. In a rather long list, Henley, Walter Raleigh, and Saintsbury were the chief contenders throughout the three months until the choice was made. Others included Churton Collins, William Sharp, C. H. Herford, Rev. Eric S. Robertson, C. E. Vaughan, William Symington McCormick, Hugh Walker, and G. Gregory Smith.[6]

The story is an amusingly human one. Raleigh's role is the most admirable; Henley's, the most amusing. Raleigh wrote to his mother that he wanted the chair because Edinburgh, unlike commercial Liverpool, was a milieu he understood. He asked W. P. Ker for a testimonial. Ker, an intimate friend of Saintsbury, was put in an awkward position, though Raleigh's request was most good humored: " . . . if the Edinburgh Chair had to be fought for in a jolly-boat by Henley, Saintsbury and myself, I should be crippled by my respect for both. But . . . the Crown may want a simple lecturer, or junior, or an inferior man—who knows what the Crown wants, or why?"[7] When Ker refused, Raleigh wrote that he appreciated his attitude and humorously described his difficulties. Among the people who might write are those who are standing, "those who back *Another*," those who don't answer letters, others who cheerfully "give mangey documents to all," and those who will "freely and cheerfully testimonialize your servant." On July 27, he reported the odds as 3 to 1 on Lord Balfour's gardener's son, 4 to 1 against George Saintsbury, 25 to 1 against Henley, and 1,000 to 8 against himself.[8]

Henley, having greeted the suggestion that he become a candidate as preposterous, adding that he would hate it and was unfit to do it, was persuaded by his friends to stand and, by August, was totally preoccupied with the matter. He reports Savile Club betting at "6 to 1 on the Saint, and no takers." His guess is Raleigh but " . . . the Saint and his partisans are cocksure; and if I'm to be beaten by him, I shall have something *not* nice to say to the men who ran me against my will."[9]

While rumor ran wild in London, Saintsbury was off to Scotland for the last two weeks of August. From Dundarrock he reported to Blackwood by postcard: first, that he had no direct news but understood Henley was his most formidable rival; later, that Lord Balfour had asked him to call and that he understood Lord Balfour "is a man who likes to 'decide for himself.'"

The decision was made—in Saintsbury's favor—rather late. He learned of it through Blackwood's congratulatory telegram and the morning papers on September 27. Henley wrote to Whibley on October 8, "The Chair *was* a moral for the Saint. . . . For myself, I do not care a d——n. But I am sorry for my friends." In another letter to Whibley, his real feeling is more evident: "The Red-Nosed one gave his first lecture today. I wonder what he made of it. I hear that both the University and Town are furious that it wasn't either Raleigh or I."[10]

Saintsbury was not a Scot and he was not an academic; he was a Tory journalist, a literary critic and historian; the last two characteristics he shared with most of the contenders. How much politics had to do with it cannot be determined. His career in journalism was probably not an advantage, though Masson also had come out of that world. Saintsbury's critical reputation had some authority though chiefly on French literature and he had a minimal experience in lecturing and examining.[11] He had been thought of by T. S. Minto for a post at Aberdeen in 1881, had stood for the Glasgow post, and, like Lang and Churton Collins, had been a candidate for the Merton Professorship in 1885. Linked with Gosse as he had been in the Stead-

Collins attacks earlier, he again became a prime target for Collins. Nichol Smith told me, on what he regarded as good authority, that Lord Balfour saw some risks in his choice.

The die was cast, and the London journalist of twenty years went back to Scotland and into the most prestigious Chair of English in Britain, to be at the center of academic life in the North for the next twenty years. He took his commitment seriously, as the notice he provided for the *Athenaeum,* October 12, 1895, suggests: "Mr. Saintsbury is withdrawing from all literary work not closely connected with the subject of the Chair at Edinburgh to which he has been appointed." He thought a professor of literature might write for magazines and reviews but should not be a regular reviewer for daily or weekly papers. Later, he decided this was foolish, even arrogant, and made it less easy to keep up with current literature.[12]

Saintsbury was, according to Grierson, "the most vivid personality in the Scottish Universities of those years," and "No one ... had anything like the range of his knowledge."[13] But there were many giants in those days, a gathering such as Edinburgh would perhaps never see again. S. H. Butcher (1882–1903) who had come from Cambridge via Oxford; Sir Ludovic Grant (1890–1922), Regius Professor of Public Law; Alexander Mair in Greek; Joseph Nicholson in Political Economy, and Sir George Protheroe (a friend of W. P. Ker) in History. A Balliol contingent included Sir Richard Lodge in History (1899–1925); James Millar in Constitutional History (Lecturer, 1900; Professor, 1909–25), and William Ross Hardie in the Chair of Humanity (1895–1916). The two Pringle-Pattisons—James in Moral Philosophy (1898–1924) and Seth in Logic (1891–1919)—were "a kind of family concern or monopoly," according to Stephen Potter, and there were two German-trained scholars, Eggling in Sanskrit and Copeland in Astronomy.

Two Principals served in Saintsbury's time at the university: Sir William Muir (1885–1903) and Sir William Turner (1903–16), and he liked them both. A. J. Balfour, already a friend of Saintsbury, was elected chancellor in 1891 and served until his death in 1930. Lord Balfour of Burleigh, who had chosen Saintsbury for his post, was Rector of the university, 1896–99, and George Wyndham, a London friend of Saintsbury, was Rector, 1908–11.

From 1896 to 1901, the university had an average enrollment of 800. In 1906, the number passed 1,000, and from 1906 to 1914 it

averaged 1,200 (half were women). Everyone benefited from the
$10,000 gift from Andrew Carnegie to the Scottish universities in
1900. Edinburgh Honors degrees in English, 1892–1914, totaled 89
men and 56 women, with 42 percent Firsts, 46 percent Seconds, 12
percent Thirds.[14]

The Scotsman cited Saintsbury's established reputation "of the highest order" earned specially in the field of French literature and noted
that he was welcomed with "keen and critical expectancy" by the
Scottish public.[15] The Cooking of Grouse and The Cooking of Partridge
(1894) and "The Sentimental Cellar" in The Yellow Book may have
made some sterner Scots wonder, but for students who had known
"the redoubtable stalwart" Masson, the prospect of either Henley or
Saintsbury "seemed to augur a regime of unprofessional liberty and
excitement."[16]

The inaugural lecture by Saintsbury, on October 15, 1895, attracted "one of the largest crowds in the history of the University,"[17]
perhaps because he was the first Englishman to succeed to the Chair
of Blair, Aytoun, and Masson. The accent of the high-pitched Southern voice was for years mimicked by students chanting, "Blaah . . . my
predecessor in this chaah."[18] Sir George Chrystal summed up the
effects of the lecture: "No one who heard him . . . could have seriously doubted that he knew his business or . . . that he could produce
prose of excellent sobriety and poise."[19]

After paying due homage to his predecessors, Saintsbury launched
into praise of Scottish contributors to "the joint stock of our literary
treasure"—especially when, twice in history, the Scots "came to the
rescue" and revitalized English literature, first with the Scottish
Chaucerians, later with Burns and Scott. About his duties, Saintsbury
was clear—not to champion modern education against the classical,
but to "expound and illustrate those common principles of literary
art . . . found alike in Aristophanes and in Swift, in Aeschylus and in
Shakespeare . . . . For the city of literature is a true . . . city of the
world." He defined rhetoric as coextensive with the whole art of
literary criticism—the method of which literature is the result—in
fact, the whole art of writing. Literature and criticism offer limitless
pleasures and advantages but desultory reading will never make a
student. So without the German kind of specialization that often results in "a catalogue of syllabic lengths" or of "the sex of animals in
Shakespeare," he will try "to point out and illustrate the universal

laws of literary expression" and act as a guide through the "vast . . . province of their application"; he will construct with the students a map of literature—a never-ending job and a perpetual delight because "no bloom is taken off by the most careful and critical literary study."[20]

There was nothing revolutionary in his words. The emphasis on universal literature and the value of a literary mind map are familiar tenets of his. Nichol Smith recalled the "precise and rapid utterance." The *Student*, the weekly paper, noted a final winning graceful gesture: when three cheers broke out for Masson as Saintsbury left the room, he turned back and "waved his mortarboard in the air to lead the applause." On November 21, the *Student* spoke of his misfortune in not being born a Scot, then welcomed him as an expert on French literature and an already-known guide to English from whom common sense might be expected—but "no style!"[21] Ordinary class lectures were characterized as clever in speech, enthusiastic and rapid—delivered without notes, by a lecturer "forgetful of a hundred and fifty poor note-takers . . . struggling with an unfinished sentence five minutes behind the eloquent lecturer." This is the first hint of the ordeal of the making of a professor out of a fifty-year-old journalist.

Saintsbury's retrospective view of his new situation is highly favorable. He saw it as "an almost ideal combination of vocational employment, with varied residence and opportunities for vocational work and play."[22] To the London journalist, a twenty-week session seemed to leave an immense spread of time for the other work he regarded as a serious part of his commitment. Colleagues ragged him because he had earlier described the Scottish professor as one who, once his lectures were on paper, "had nothing to do for the rest of his life but collect bundles of pound notes at the beginning of every session."[23]

Things had changed by 1895, and he found himself very busy. He began the first of his 150 lectures of the first year within two weeks of his appointment. He gave 5 per week until January when he began to give 10. On October 25, he wrote to William Hunt, "I am still in the throes of conceiving a lecture every AM and being delivered of it the same afternoon." And he was still furiously house hunting. On Christmas Eve, 1895, he wrote, "The first year of a Scotch professorship is no child's play. I don't think even Churton Collins would find it so." Later he recalled that he had been warned that "the University of Edinburgh does not scamp work." He chose to think that the Senate at his retirement recognized his efforts "to keep up the tradition."[24] He made things more strenuous by his determination not to deliver written lectures, not to repeat himself, and to strive for originality.

The letters Saintsbury wrote to Hunt and Dobson from Edinburgh all reflect the heavy work load, much of it self-imposed beyond the university schedule, as well as his absolute and prompt conscientiousness in regard to paper reading, testimonials, letters, and so forth. The labor was not all joy. Letters contain the occasional not untypical academic reaction to a new term: "The Gates of Hades open tomorrow." This note was more frequent in the last years, as ill-health and family anxieties piled up and weariness was constant—so much so that, in 1915, when he was seventy, he seemed to George Kitchin suddenly "a very old man."[25]

The university calendar, 1896–97 outlines the course of lectures. Before Christmas, in three lectures a week, a survey of style in poetry and prose from Chaucer to the nineteenth century; after Christmas, a "general History and Contents of the Subject from the earliest texts to the present day"; on the two other days of the week, the lecturer was to discuss the prescribed texts; some, page by page and line by line. Rhetoric was the topic of some lectures with DeQuincey's essays and Whately's *Rhetoric* for illustration. Like the famous "Beowulf to Hardy" survey required of most American students in the 1920s and 1930s, this was for general students who had four other subjects. One might, with the professor's approval, pass to the Honors program. The number of Honors graduates grew slowly from three and four up to 1903 to twenty and twenty-one in 1913 and 1914.

To this Honors group, Saintsbury gave fifty lectures a year— "twenty-five before Christmas on the Higher Rhetoric or the theory of prose and verse in English, including a sketch of the history of criticism from Aristotle onwards"; and after Christmas, twenty-five lectures on a special subject in the period chosen for that year: for 1897, "The Study of Nature in the 18th Century." The English Language lectures were given by Webster and George Kitchin.[26]

Textual analysis in class was a Saintsbury innovation and one he decided was popular though he knew Masson's students were accustomed to "moralizing and general history and *personalia*."[27] Saintsbury, who never dealt with living writers in his surveys, offered as his excuse for omitting them: one must not thrust oneself between the student and a contemporary writer.[28] But students recalled quaint references to "my friend" Kipling, Stevenson, Jusserand, or Gaston Paris. Religion and politics were rigidly excluded, but "there was a run of allusive asides, and shrewd criticisms of life and character were casually dropped." The manner was not impressive or meant to be, but cool and useful, without platform tricks, if somewhat unemphatic; with few pauses and "some tumble and disorder."[29]

More than one student reported Saintsbury as formidable and he may have grown more doctrinaire as the years passed, but he wanted students to react directly to literature, and on rhetoric he was liberal. As he put it, "Some of us warn our students that if they treat what we say as gospel we shall 'mark them down' for it." Hugh Blair, 130 years earlier, would have resigned if he had thought two opinions possible.[30]

Saintsbury thought examinations a necessary evil, and some of his crotchets, his wit, and his special concerns color essay topics. For an Honors three-hour essay, "Trace and Value the influence of Longinus on literary criticism. In a history of prose style, how would you treat John Bunyan? The interaction of modern literatures. The probable effects of an English Academy of letters." And, for a shorter essay, "Somewhat different views have been held of the style of Hazlitt. Give yours." For the Ordinary class, "How far are the deficiencies of Wordsworth's writing sheltered by the definition of poetry as a criticism of life?" (Shades of Arnold.) "Without saying, 'It became a trumpet in his hands,' say something about Milton and the sonnet."[31]

George Kitchin recorded his first impression of Saintsbury:

How he would trail his coat for an unruly element to tread on! The ritual of his entry, the high-pitched voice, the rapid delivery. . . . There would be no lowering of his flag, one felt. But how good it was for us![32]

A Scot who had been an undergraduate in English, Kitchin suggests the problem faced by the new, "alien" professor as does the *Scotsman* obituary of Saintsbury in 1933 (January 30): " . . . he overcame obstacles in the way of his complete success, including an evil tradition of rowdyism, which was apt to break out with special virulence on the the opening day of the session. . . . But long before the end of his time, no department of teaching in the University was better organized or controlled."

One does not always know how it strikes the contemporary student, but as a Scot once put it to me, "They have long memories in the North." The recollections of twenty-five of Saintsbury's students given in interviews and letters reveal how Saintsbury won through those first years of alienation to a position of warm respect and affection.[33]

The files of the *Student* tell the story. After welcoming Saintsbury favorably, the *Student* began reporting the slips of tongue all students delight in: for example, "Syatt and Wurrey," the judgment that Mrs. Browning "sometimes came near to being a poet," and the quip, "A pound of reading is worth an ounce of discussion." The first hint of trouble (January 21, 1897) was the report of Saintsbury's pursuing a student who had left his fortnightly examination before its end. "Is it another exhibition of 'his own way?'" asks the reporter. Unhappily, the inexperienced Professor rose to the bait with the comment, "A fortnightly is not a holiday," and precipitated an explosion of what perhaps had been fourteen months of simmering antagonism. "Flippancy... nonchalance... superb egotism... supercilious superiority..." were some of the charges now leveled against Saintsbury. Unwisely, he lectured the next week on discourtesy, and the *Student* labeled this fairly enough as a "storm in a teacup" by a public man who must expect his actions to be judged.[34] The writer called Saintsbury's *Nineteenth-Century Literature*, just published, "a mausoleum of inaccuracies." He was perhaps merely echoing the young Nichol Smith, who had just read the proofs and as he recalled, corrected errors on almost every page.

The next autumn Saintsbury was reported as having "the largest and noisiest audiences of any professor on the Arts side."[35] Two years later he had perforce "called out his reserves in the persons of two servitors... to quell disturbances."[36] In 1903, rumpuses were reported in all first lectures but, in Saintsbury's class, five hundred men had appeared and were put out by the university police force, who decided it was a shame to rag a professor on that scale.[37]

Such boorishness, traditional in Scottish universities, lasted into the 1960s,[38] much of it the product of invaders from other faculties intent on mischief. It was custom, but Saintsbury's manner was some provocation: the too rapid, high, thin, "squeaky-voiced" delivery, the accent of the South, the level and load of learning and allusion poured bewilderingly over the heads of students seated in an ill-lit room who felt he "lived and worked on Olympian heights . . . not to be approached by the average student."[39]

This academic baptism by fire gradually cooled with the turn of the century. Later attitudes are described by John Purves, an Honors English scholarship student, who noted Saintsbury's growing reputation, including the transatlantic one.[40] He found that persiflage and expression of personal preferences saved the Ordinary lectures from being dull, and there was common sense and the recognition "that life is wider than Art." Saintsbury's jokes, his "polyglot sallies," and "the glittering shower of verbal cut, thrust and parry,"[41] even his scathing irony were beginning to be understood and liked, and his occasional sarcasms were less resented. At first he had failed to recognize what both Kitchin and Geddes knew as students ("We were so crude and unpolished . . ."). But both sides were learning. "The Beowulf Matinee," when Saintsbury annually presented Beowulf as John Bull, became a tradition. And biographical quips were remembered: John Gay "liked to be taken charge of by people"; as for Landor, "All of his friends with whom he did not quarrel held him to be the most amiable of men."

The *Student* shows the change of mood and an awareness of his interest in wine. In "A Very Imaginary Conversation" between Peacock and Saintsbury (December 19, 1901), two dozen bottles of Port are consumed between dinner and dawn and Saintsbury tells Peacock not to say Scotch for Scot, then adds, "the Scots are perverse but I like them for it." "An Apostrophe to Professor Saintsbury" (1907) is a parody of Milton.

> Come . . . pensive man, well-read, cocksure,
> Sarcastic, witty, yet demure . . .
> Teach me to correct impressions . . .
> [A play on Saintsbury's book title]
> Thy quips and cranks and wreath'd frown
> That made thee dear to us o' the gown . . .

Best of all, is a parody of Chaucer on the Clerk of Oxenforde (1904–5).

> A Clerk there was of Edwin's Burg also
> That unto English had long ygo.

Discreet he was and of greet reverence . . .
Of words would he speak more than was need.
And out of books he would much rede, . . .

Ending after 20 similar lines:

A better Clerk I trowe nowheer noon be
Than him men clepen George le Seintes Burie.

Thus, after a decade, the "alien" Saintsbury was becoming a cherished monument—and a legend—whose eccentricities were cause for raillery.

The cartoon "George" (see p. 190) appeared three times between 1904 and 1913, with increasingly affectionate comment. The first verbal sketch creates a vivid image of the great "lyrical" outpouring in his lectures:

. . . the forward-set figure loose-clad in the gloomy gown, the tight-crossed arms enswathed in the robe, the upcast chin, the face gleaming between the lights in the cold half-lit room . . . not a dull moment in the hour . . . always in a hurry . . . younger and jauntier every year . . . with his genius for interesting, annoying and instructing his hearers.[42]

And in February, 1913:

This is George. He is paternal and peevish. He has a wonderful beard and lectures into it; therefore his beard is infinitely wiser than his pupils. He loves the Restoration Dramatists and thinks the Modernists are a set of—ahem—fools. His feet are really much smaller than the artist has drawn them.

One later tribute in the *Student* is of special interest. A. S. Neill, the since-famous radical founder of Summerhill School, was the *Student* editor in 1912. An Honors candidate in English at 28, he was a rebel at heart, getting his education by reacting against Saintsbury and his methods. Having discovered Ibsen, when asked for an essay on *Hamlet,* he wrote a criticism of Shakespeare for not being a realist and was called up by Saintsbury for "such nonsense." Nevertheless, his 1912 editorial praised the professor as "always approachable, always considerate, always humorous, occasionally a little dogmatic, occasionally a little fierce, a little like his favorite Dryden, a little like Dr. Johnson, and a great deal like himself—a 'real good sort!'"[43] When Neill wrote again for the *Student* in 1916 (January 26), he saw Saintsbury as "the System," but admitted he was "the most kindly fellow in the world... the most perfect gentleman of criticism... sort of a father, remote and preoccupied, but potentially paternal."

On November 11, 1962, this the most distinguished and individual of Saintsbury's students generously wrote me a retrospect of fifty years, less genial yet eminently fair. He now termed his three years under Saintsbury "A narrow education... reading books about books," but he granted that Saintsbury gave him "a strong belief in the plain style." In modesty, he concluded, "He was a great scholar and I never became one, hence my opinion of him must be a limited one."

These tributes take us a long way from 1897, but students do not vary greatly over the years; so it is not surprising that one of the first, who had also known Masson, felt in Saintsbury's lectures "a conversion, a rebirth, an awakening into a new world," that of literature. He also sensed two sides in him, "stern to a degree, impatient, somewhat overbearing, but... quite exceptionally kind, accessible, and helpful."[44] Saintsbury had mellowed and they learned not to try to take it all down. They now took pride in Edinburgh's possessing so eminent a professor. They admired the "courtly dignity of eighteenth-century politeness" that to the earlier generation had seemed arrogant, "foreign," and patronizing—as the manner of a shy reserved person may do.[45] Almost all those with whom this writer spoke, all then in their late sixties, seventies, or eighties, still possessed their handwritten testimonials from Saintsbury—in itself a moving tribute. "There are some good 'seconds,' too," he said to one. "I once got a second," he wrote to another. He came to understand them.

Mary Martin, an Honors First in 1915, recalled "the brightness and humor of his eyes as he shared something good with us" and admitted that she treasured the early image he had painted of himself, "in a linked line of uproarious students chanting the intoxicating lyrics of Swinburne down the 'High.'"[46] Arthur Mowat, also a 1915 First, recalled Saintsbury's objecting to Meredith's "metaphysical vein": "Gentlemen, I like my whisky and my metaphysics neat!" He also remembered the "whimsical raising of the eyebrows in parentheses, the occasional glint from thick lenses in the sally... the urge—urge—

urge—to see, hear or feel for yourself . . . it would surprise you how unsqueamish 'George' was."[47] These later recollections support the citation for Saintsbury's Edinburgh D. Litt.: " . . . the freshness and zest with which he taught." When taken together, all the individual student responses so generously given to me created the impression that, however remote or awesomely learned he seemed, Saintsbury did get to many of them and influenced them to read and to enjoy literature. To all of them he seemed a gentleman.

He had come to accept the whistling and shuffling of feet; he had learned to enter in step with the tapping out of "O Come All Ye Faithful," and to accept the good-humored "foot applause." They now came from other Faculties as to a kind of "cultural exhibit" and some stayed to praise.[48]

In 1911, an English Society was formed and student productions (*The Knight of the Burning Pestle* in 1913, *Hamlet* in 1914, and *The Shoemaker's Holiday* in 1915) gave the Honors group closer touch with Saintsbury—and to them he did not betray his distaste for theatricals. To some he seemed old-fashioned and the Fabians, knowing his views, longed to hear what he thought of Shaw and Wells, Dowson and Masefield, but were disappointed. In 1916, Saintsbury wrote Hunt that his successor, Grierson, "wanders off to Ibsen, Maeterlinck and Tolstoy and expects them to follow . . . . We are all 'priests who slay the slayer and shall be slain.'" The last years brought the cloud of war and the weariness of age and ill health, but he had made his mark in the academic world and his reputation grew as the larger works appeared. Many honors followed,[49] the most cherished being an Honorary Merton Fellowship in 1909 and an Oxford Litt. D.

Saintsbury, never a man for organizational life, had refused Walter Besant's urging to join the Authors' Society several times, but, in Edinburgh, both professional groups and the invitations to lecture were unavoidable and irksome. "Their lust for lectures here is something frightful: I never wanted to hear a lecture in my life," he wrote to Hunt in 1896. There were the Burns Nights (Saintsbury gave the toast in Edinburgh on January 16, 1896, and at least once later—at Greenock). He became vice president of the Scottish Text Society and lectured to them in 1902 as he did to the Bronte Society at Huddersfield in 1899. One of his best lectures, "The Permanent and the Temporary in Literature," he delivered at Birmingham in 1910.[50] Saintsbury also made a few contributions to the Edinburgh *Student—*

"The Chair of English," "Sir William Muir as a Man of Letters," one on Scott as a student, and "Bakespearism"—on the Baconians.

In the larger business of the university, Saintsbury played his role and was bored by committees. Though he spoke seldom in Senate, the official minutes at the time of his retirement struck a frank note: "He held strong views on matters of University and public policy, and was prepared on all suitable occasions to express them in forcible terms" though always with courtesy and "temper unruffled by debate."[51]

With the Honors program already established, it was time for consolidation rather than innovation in the university—a state congenial to Saintsbury's temperament. He feared the multiplication of examinations and of higher degrees, and of the new "gig" universities, as he labeled "redbrick" (in response to an appeal for funds for Southhampton). He feared the watering down of university standards and of the whole educational system.[52] He favored an increase in tutorials and leaving the students as free as possible to read. His own Oxford training remained his ideal, but he accepted the Scottish emphasis on English. The Senate noted his special contributions in 1933, terming him a "scholar after the liberal fashion current before our era of specialization" and credited him with enlarging the horizon of English studies throughout the British universities "by laying stress on the unity of literature" and by drawing upon classical and foreign critics.[53]

When the new chair of English Literature was created at Oxford in 1904, Saintsbury seemed the likely candidate, but the choice fell upon Raleigh, whom Lord Balfour had named to the Glasgow Chair in 1900. So Saintsbury remained in Scotland, official Oxford having finally blasted his hopes of a return. Raleigh, he said, made English "a going concern" though he seemed "more interested in men than in books"—[54] the reverse of the charge often leveled at Saintsbury himself! He showed little jealousy of Raleigh except in a pathetic, half-joking remark made several times: "You are holding what I ought to hold." He repeated it to Nichol Smith when Smith succeeded Raleigh in 1924. His heart remained with Oxford, and he once confessed that, for his bones, the North was always "the place not mine own."[55] His deeper feelings found voice when he received the Oxford Litt. D. in 1912: "I own it was pleasant to stand at the foot of those remarkably steep stairs with the Public Orator speaking *Magnificen-*

tissime of one in Latin (thank heaven not modernly pronounced) and then ascend right among the doctors. Academically where can one go higher?"[56]

Saintsbury's life in Edinburgh had its social side. In 1895 he leased Murrayfield House, a large, handsome, rambling, eighteenth-century house with a fine view, set in a large wooded tract of land at the eastern end of the city. Its style answered well the dream of a gentleman squire and had room for a large wine cellar. By November 15, the family had moved in, and they were soon busy doing it up. He tells more about this shared activity than he ever did any other aspect of domestic life. He and Lewis, who had a knack for such things, did the dining room and studies; Lewis and his mother, "the more frivolous rooms"; Christopher (now twenty) helped with the cellar in the evenings as he had begun work in the University laboratories. Six weeks were given to restoring the books in the library.

Saintsbury entertained at Murrayfield until 1899, when he bought (for £3,000) Professor Protheroe's house at 2 Eton Terrace, at the end of South Bridge. This smaller, fine, four-story, eighteenth-century town house was more convenient to the University and to Blackwood's, at 45 George Street.[57] He liked continuing the long tradition of the professor of Rhetoric's dropping in there.

Edinburgh menus contained in Saintsbury's *Notes on a Cellar Book* reflect some elaborate entertaining. Sir George Chrystal observed that Saintsbury "soon became a prominent and popular figure in Edinburgh society" and his hospitality "embodied and expressed his interests in some of the material elegances of life."[58] Chrystal lunched once at Murrayfield with Dobson. Nichol Smith argued that Saintsbury did not "bother" with society, as such, but kept to the "University set" and found many colleagues congenial. He entertained chiefly at luncheon. Kitchin recalled a butler serving at student luncheons, and the "servants' strike" that Saintsbury described as overshadowing Christmas, 1912, suggests a fairly elaborate staff—not unusual in those days.[59]

Saintsbury enjoyed some club life in Edinburgh. "Always join two," he jokingly told Kitchin one day after a fire at the University Club, "then you can go along to the other—as I did—for coffee!" He had joined the University Club and the Conservative Club in Prince's Street on arrival and became a member of the Pen and Pencil as well. He took little part in civic life, and his view of "dining out" is damning: "The most hospitable but the most speech-loving of peoples simply inundated me with invitations to come and propose or reply to 'Literature.'" From six until midnight, as a guest and "English hostage . . . always at the mercy of your neighbor" he suffered—once with the Edinburgh Border Counties Society (1897), yearly at Holyrood "under the grim portraits of the Gaelic Kings," with pipers skirling among unhappy Stuart ghosts.[60]

He preferred intimate, quiet evenings with one or two congenial friends like that when he, George Protheroe, and Lord Kincairney, a judge and "quaint Pict . . . full of letters and fun," Tories all three, dined at Murrayfield and did "fair justice to a '78 Leoville."[61] Or the evening at the University Club when George Wyndham, Saintsbury, and his close friend and colleague J. H. Millar decided over dinner that W. P. Ker, "the most sociable of persons," would make a perfect fourth.[62] Grierson tells a story of the quarter-centenary at Aberdeen in 1906 when the Saintsburys were his guests. Knowing Saintsbury to be an epicure, Grierson had procured a sheep from his brother in the Shetlands to offer them presalé mutton. Saintsbury, who could not have known of his effort, said when asked that he never took mutton if beef was available.[63]

By 1910, entertainment was much curtailed and Saintsbury had come to dine out rarely because of his wife's illness and his own worsening health. But he had been warmly welcomed by colleagues. Butcher, Hardie, and Protheroe he labeled "good fellows" though Hardie seemed to him shy and Butcher, "the most nervous man I know."[64] The older, "Scottish lot" were most cordial, and he surmised that Masson had "trumpeted [him] *magnifé usuré*." As a friend of the Pringle-Pattison brothers he enjoyed the "vast cellars at the Haining, Selkirk."[65] In 1900, he spent a fortnight at Dunkeld ("so beautifully Celtic"), and other holidays were spent in the Trossachs, at Saltburn, and also in Yorkshire, at Harrogate. But he cherished most the weekends at All Souls with Ker, visits to Merton (1909, 1911, and 1912), working days at the British Museum, and holidays at Bath.

External examining took Saintsbury to Manchester, Liverpool, and Belfast (to all three in 1914), and Gregory Smith returned to Edinburgh from Belfast as external examiner from 1906 to 1910. University Joint Board meetings brought Saintsbury to Aberdeen (to the Griersons) and to St. Andrews, where he and Grierson were sometimes joined by Lang. Grierson, who says, "To read his books is to hear his voice," describes Saintsbury's flow of interesting talk—in company or à deux—and his courtesy, which unfortunately forbade his using a typewriter for letters to his friends. Grierson, who had finished university just when Saintsbury's *Elizabethan Literature* appeared, then thought of Lang and Saintsbury as "the two most authoritative critics of current poetry."[66]

Elton, Ker, and Gregory Smith read proofs on all Saintsbury's major volumes from 1898 to 1916—evidence of Saintsbury's confidence in them and their generosity in performing this mighty labor. Saintsbury did some of their proofs in return. Much friendly interchange must have accompanied the process, and they must have come to know him well. Elton, in his six-volume *Survey of English Literature,* acknowledges Saintsbury's "valuable advice," his encouragement, his reading of the proofs, and his always making "generous allowance for differences in our critical views."[67] Ker and Gregory Smith both noted his helpful advice and their dependence on his "public works."

In 1904, Saintsbury was elected to the Athenaeum, and "Pallas" became a place for London rendezvous with Dobson, who had proposed him and whom he asked to act "as Pandarus-Mercury" to introduce him to the club's mysteries. One failure to meet Dobson there inspired an amusing parody of his favorite among Dobson's verse, "Rose kissed me today." When the porter said, "Mr. Dobson lunched here yesterday," the result was the verse "I lunched here today . . . ."[68] Saintsbury grew fond of the Athenaeum—"not a young man's club of course," but with "an air about the place," where one "meets half the people one has known at different times."[69]

With younger colleagues at Edinburgh, Saintsbury had less to do socially than with his contemporaries, but Kitchin recalled Sunday afternoons (1912–15) when he and Blyth Webster went to Eton Terrace to plan the week and Saintsbury would "break out a bottle" of some good vintage. Of the two, Saintsbury preferred Webster for his flair and rather dramatic style. He thought him "one of the best" lecturers in Scotland, and predicted a brilliant future for him.[70] The more stolid Kitchin had studied under C. W. Firth at Oxford after his undergraduate days at Edinburgh and, after eighteen months in Bombay, was summoned back by Saintsbury to be his assistant. Saintsbury described him as "full of brains." A shrewd, slightly malicious man who understood Saintsbury's preferences, Kitchin recalled him warmly for me in 1962, as he had in his 1933 article: "What talk there was about the right food and the right drink, and the right poetry, and the wrong legislation, education and religion . . . and the perpetual play of wit and spirit!"[71]

As an Honors student, Kitchin had been invited to "the famous student lunch parties," which he later recognized as an effort to bring sophistication of taste to the rude young Scots and to civilize them. "We were proud of him," Kitchin confessed, "and we liked the full rigor of the game, the last punctilio of ceremony. His quick wit saved him and us from any embarrassment." Kitchin looked upon it all as a glimpse into the pre-Reform world. Others, too, recalled the luncheons, with their haute cuisine and superb vintage wines, with great delight. Inevitably, legends grew up around them. The most persistent one, recalled for me in 1962 in several different versions, concerned a teetotal Scottish student (one, some, all, or "a large Highlander") refusing wine and Saintsbury's requesting his wife (or the maid or the butler) to "bring a glass of milk for the gentleman" (or gentlemen). One former student dismissed the tale: "The *bon viveur* could be waspish in the lecture room but not at his own table."[72]

Because of Saintsbury's prejudice against "Reminiscences," the record of his personal life at Edinburgh, as elsewhere, is sketchy. The fullest, happiest part of this record, though clouded by anxiety over his own and his family's constant ailments, is the steady flow of letters that went from Edinburgh to Hunt and Dobson. With Hunt there is always a run of Tory political comment, often angry or satiric, some report of university life and of his writing, as well as occasional judgments on people. None of the letters are long.

Dobson, faithfully sending his newly issued volumes of verse and manuscript for criticism, afforded Saintsbury much comfort. Often he reports anticipating the best release he could desire—an evening spent over the contents of the newly-arrived package: "Yesterday I was weary and 'overworked' and to be candid, rather cross. And there came a parcel . . . and I sat in my chair and read *Vignettes* and blessed God and the giver and was at peace."[73]

There is talk about Saintsbury's *Caroline Poets* and his *Prosody* and an appeal to Dobson for verse to illustrate the *Manual of Prosody* with the request, "You'll be silent to Gosse about this?" They discuss the editing of Thackeray, as Saintsbury decides how to give a "natural display of Thackeray's growth and genius. May his spirit guide me!"

With his typical apology, "speaking as a fool," he says Thackeray might have liked his introduction and adds, "but without you what chance should I have had at this most honorable chore?" Saintsbury is most in his element when he gives Dobson asked-for criticism of his verse: " . . . it seems to me never permissible to slur a French final *e* in English verse. . . . I've been berating my beloved William Morris in my *Prosody* for doing this." Other lines he finds "a little half-achieved and vague in phrase"; offering a few revisions, he concludes, "I shall put some . . . cake and fizzling salt in the fire to expiate the lèse poésie. Saintsbury often wrote from Bath when on holiday. In 1913 he asked Dobson to "write a rondeau on the gold fish that have naturalized themselves in the old Roman Bath and revel in the hot water—as I do," and, sharing his amusement over a new sign, "Bath Cat Shelter," he recalled Mrs. Thrale's description of herself as a "regular Bath cat." While he was reading for Honors lectures on Pope, Dobson sent him a picture of Martha Blount. He reports that he is coming to half like her. "And every man of sense must now approve her who makes a critic even half a lover."[74]

The other side of this happy friendship is eloquent in Dobson's modest reply to one of Saintsbury's criticisms: "You have delighted me by your kind words; for at seventy-three one easily comes to think one has fallen below the level." On January 12, 1915, Saintsbury wrote, "I am getting very old and very tired: but one must cultivate the garden." On August 29, he wrote to say that he had retired.[75]

Edinburgh had an amateur repertory theater run by Fenella Angus and her sister. Mrs. Saintsbury became a patroness of this group, "The Tragic Comedians," and at one time was its president. Unlike her husband, she shared her sons' enthusiasm for this activity. Lewis, who acted with them in 1907, married Fenella. Lewis had a taste for the theater, if not the ability that made his cousin, Harry A. Saintsbury, a famous comedian. Lewis toured in 1907 in America with Sir Frank Benson's Company; he also once toured in *Monsieur Beaucaire* with Lewis Waller's Company though, as his father put it, he was not very good at "roughing it." Lewis's wife Fenella, an amateur actress, was a descendant of Mrs. Siddons and a relation of the Kembles. She had a private income that became the chief support of their family, which included two sons and a daughter, Elizabeth, born in 1914. Elizabeth went to Oxford and then became an Anglican teaching sister, and lives now in Devon. Of the two sons, one disappeared into

Canada; the other, George, born in 1911, became a Roman Catholic convert and a Catholic schoolmaster after some slight experience in acting. Still later he became a Catholic priest, and now heads a religious institute near London. Just before Saintsbury retired, Lewis and family moved to Godalming in Sussex. Lewis sank into invalidism and died in 1922.

Saintsbury's younger son, Christopher, was for a time a pupil of an Edinburgh architect, Sydney Mitchell; briefly again, in 1904, he was "architecting," this time with Champneys and Eustace Balfour in London, but he never qualified professionally. According to his father, Christopher tried many jobs from which he was regularly sacked. After a time in the Scottish Sea Scout Patrol, he suffered in an army dock-job (1914–18) for which he was not fit. Never married, he remained in Scotland when his parents left in 1915. He spent his later years at Crail, in Scotland, posing as a sort of Scottish laird (even to the kilt) and speculating in the local effort to create a kind of Scottish Brighton. In Saintsbury's last years, when Christopher came to Bath to care for him, he was making and hoping to sell amateur calendars with scenic photographs he had taken. These won his father's somewhat pathetic praise. He shared his father's tastes in wine and foods and little more. He died in 1959.

One remembers Gosse, Ruskin, and Samuel Butler as sons, Dickens and Browning as not very successful fathers, as well as other Victorians who were emasculated by Victorian mores and by family attitudes. The self-made, successful, hard-working, authoritarian, upper-middle-class father expected his sons to repeat his pattern but often managed to prevent its happening. Saintsbury had some companionship with his father until he was fourteen, when his father died, and he was thrown on his own resources with help from his mother and sisters. His sons were close to their mother and had little contact with him. Had they been girls, perhaps the story would have been different. Saintsbury had always wanted a daughter.

Gregory Smith had left Edinburgh in 1908 to become professor at Queen's University in Belfast. In 1911, he invited Saintsbury to serve for three years as external examiner in English there. Saintsbury recalled that, in 1914, he went to examine at Liverpool, then on to Belfast "with a horrible cold and sense of overwork and hardly the faintest premonition of what was going to happen." He was invited to dinner on the evening of June 19 at Gregory Smith's home to meet the young Helen Waddell, whom he had examined at her *Viva* for the B.A. in 1911 and for her M.A. in 1912. He had seen her M.A. thesis on Milton in rough manuscript and made largely illegible notes in its margin. These indicate his awareness of her promise and help justify his 1917 testimonial, in which he says he had known her since he examined her in 1911 and noted "the altogether exceptional ability and orignality as well as knowledge" shown in her papers and again in her work for the M.A. He adds, "For appreciation of literature and power of expressing that appreciation it would be difficult to find a superior to her." This belief in her unusual abilities and scholarly potential he shared with Gregory Smith, but the unfolding romantic relationship begun at Gregory's dinner was theirs alone.

As she sat beside him in white satin overlaid with a mist of yellow chiffon, the mutual attraction was immediate and "electric." He stored up every moment of her Irish charm, her youthful wit and gaiety, in long-lasting remembrance of the short hours till she left at 10:30 P.M. with the wish it might be prolonged till 10:30 A.M. During a brief time in the apple orchard, as he later writes to her, her "gracious shoulder" touched his and "set us off (though you did not know it at the moment) to Samarkand"—and thus started the fantasy romance they carried on for eighteen years. He called the next evening at her home and stayed on after other guests, as she writes to her sister Meg: "Top hat and frock coat and all. If he had any idea how my very soul revolts at them he'd give them to an 'old clothes'...." As she packed away some children's toys he kneeled beside her, handed her things, and looked at her "with wistful beaming spectacles." She continues:

> He told me he was growing homesick for the Paris boulevards—the uplift of heart and gaiety of it... [and added] heavily, "You are too young. I wish you were older." Meg, is he going to keep doing sentry between this and Edinburgh till I've sense to eat what's set before me?[77]

"A game we played"...a kind of seventeenth-century lovemaking,...what he thought to be "the great, the beneficient, the much abused art of flirtation."[78] Or, as she writes in 1917, "our extravagant and very delightful game" in which "it pleased me to have beguiled some days that might have been duller; but after all, I was only a variant of the fairy tale that you have been telling yourself forever—I think the dates are your own—seventeen to seventy." She addressed him as "Excellency" and "My Lord," and only at times faced the depth of his "passion in absence," that of a "Greedy Lover," as he called himself. He later tells her he had waited half a lifetime for her and it was worth it. She was 25, he was 69, and they would meet again only once—in 1931. But for him, life had taken on a new and treasured glow as he returned to Edinburgh.

In September, 1914, Saintsbury wrote the first of his many letters and asked her for a photograph. His second letter indicated her refusal. He was to remember her as he'd seen her by candlelight. He chided her cruelty teasingly, and in one of three P.S.'s said, "My eyes tell my heart what to love and my heart tells my eyes what to delight in."

He was at work on *The Peace of the Augustans,* his last book on English literature, and, as he told her, wrote several passages especially for her. The remainder of the year in Edinburgh saw increased weariness and ailments, his wife's increasing helplessness, and the strains of packing and moving, all offset by the pleasure of their correspondence. More than thirty letters written in his difficult script and many of her replies written before he settled in Bath in 1916 testify to this.

For Helen, 1914 to 1916 were hard, even heartbreaking years as she lived through the loss of two much-loved brothers and the constant anxiety of nursing her selfish alcoholic stepmother to whose care she devoted herself until the woman's death in 1920. She postponed her dream of going to Oxford despite the urging of Gregory Smith and Saintsbury and did research at Queen's. She relieved the stress first by producing her *Lyrics From the Chinese.* This fine poetic translation of thirty-three sixth-century songs was published successfully in 1915 by Constable, and she sent a copy to Saintsbury on Gregory Smith's urging. Meanwhile, she pursued her research on medieval women, directed by Smith, whom she called her "literary Father Confessor." She was strenghtened by her steady correspondence, also begun in 1914, with Dr. George Taylor, a missionary in India who became a kind of spiritual father until his death in 1920. Beside these two guides, Saintsbury took his place as literary mentor and became the fairy-tale lover. As his more than three hundred letters prove, it was for him a deeper, strangely fulfilling liaison, make-believe yet very real, that ran through the rest of his life, a story still to be traced.

References to Saintsbury's ill-health after 1895 have been numerous enough to deserve explanation. Before leaving London at fifty, he had not complained—as far as available records show—except about the leg injury that ended his walking tours early in the 1880s, and the arthritis and gout that curtailed wine drinking to a degree in the same period. In 1917, his admission to A. R. Waller that one cannot, as he used to think, always work as hard as one likes was not merely a septuagenarian's normal recognition that the wheels drive more slowly.[79] It reflected the price that Saintsbury paid for the compulsive pressure and drive to overwork that he had imposed upon himself for fifty years. This pressure rapidly and drastically took its toll after he was fifty—but without noticeably slowing down his production for another twenty years. In 1913, at sixty-eight, Saintsbury admitted "it takes more trouble to do little things than it used to do."[80] In 1911, he had written to Hunt, "Too much work and too little health and I am sick of it." And in 1912, "I sometimes feel seven hundred, never seventeen."[81]

His ailments after 1895 were varied and serious. The most serious was vertigo. It has long been generally known that, in his last twenty years, he suffered dizziness, probably due to Ménière's disease—along with gout, rheumatism, weakening sight, and throat and bronchial distress. That these had been almost constant accompaniments of his daily labors at Edinburgh during most of his two decades is evident in his letters.

All these problems, accompanied by high blood pressure and recurrent gastric troubles that led his doctors to forbid wine or beer and eventually made eating no longer the great pleasure it had been, would have reduced many a man to inactivity. The squeaky voice—a joke to students—was the result of a weak larynx unaccustomed to lecturing and suddenly subjected to that constant strain and to the cold, damp air of Edinburgh winters. "Who could be well?" he wrote when downed by a cold in 1900. Recurrent hoarseness, coughing, and sore throats ("throat wars") "made lecturing difficult . . . smoking impossible."[82] He knew that lack of practice in public speaking and lack of training had helped the strain, but he seldom complained. Little wonder that he feared drafts, worked in a "sealed" study, and gave up dining out at night.[83]

Saintsbury's dizziness, though it had been occasional for two or three years, came on in 1904 in two very sharp attacks that laid him up for a week ("the first time in ten years"). The doctors thought the causes both gastric and aural, and heavy, steady reliance on bromides became necessary as well as catheterizing of the nose and Eustachean tubes to relieve obstruction. He refers to the problem frequently in letters thereafter: "... my persistent thorn in the flesh," "... an annoying return of my old giddiness but I hope it will go"; "... giddiness always hovering," "Slightly vertiginous" or "giddiness never far off me... I find bromides still a fairly sure stronghold." In 1905, he reported to Hunt: "... free from my main enemy for two months but rheumatic as if the poison must break out somewhere. But I'd much rather have rheumatism than vertigo!" In 1917, the doctors told him he had overbromided himself and had better "bear the thing." He learned to deal with attacks by sitting down abruptly or leaning over the back of a chair. But with all the uncertainty this condition brings to its victims he labored on, began new projects, and joked about it and other related matters, such as the "cures"—massage, baths, douches, and one hilarious session at Bath that required a "four-pound bag of shot which one rolled over one's abdomen while lying on one's back." He tells Hunt, "I shriek with laughter as I do this."[84]

In the last years at Edinburgh, the struggle against weariness and all these ills, with his wife now also helplessly rheumatic and having to be lifted, must have been Herculean, yet he continued to write and publish. When the decision to retire came, it was his wife's health that he stressed as the major reason. Admitting that he had been working "against the collar" for some years and was getting "croaky," he nevertheless insisted that he would have hung on, indeed that he would have liked to continue until he was eighty, had his wife been equal to housekeeping.[85] There is pride and a good bit of rationalization here in a man of compulsive work habits. He wrote Helen Waddell on April 29, 1916, the most explicit statement available regarding Mrs. Saintsbury's condition: "Besides bronchitis, sciatica, and gout and some other ailments [she] has a very weak heart. They say there is no positive organic disease but such weakness that it is very unsafe to apply strong remedies to the other complaints." The many illnesses of husband and wife are very similar, but, with her weak heart, hers were more debilitating and they must have been painful. Increasingly, she required a good deal of nursing as she became much overweight and unable to move about.

Since they would go into rooms and do no housekeeping, he planned to liquidate everything, a difficult task in the midst of war. He would have liked to settle in London or Bath, but since his wife disliked both, they decided on their birthplace, Southampton. Adjustment was not easy and probably contributed to the physical collapse he suffered soon after the decision was made. He spent two weeks in bed in July, 1915, and two more on "graduated rations." His condition was exacerbated by a tumble from his library steps—he gashed his head—and by "the unbelievable worry of rummaging and sorting and destroying and keeping and packing and arranging and selling and traveling and unpacking and other occupations of the Devil." Only the compulsive Saintsbury would find it "curious" that he then felt an "inability to work hard and an indisposition to work at all."[86] At seventy he seemed worn out; yet he had seventeen years of writing ahead, accomplished by an iron will and a pretty strong constitution.

Saintsbury's application for retirement was approved by the University Senate on June 14, and his pension was set at half-pay, £450 per year. When Grierson's appointment to the Chair came in August, Saintsbury bestowed a qualified accolade: "...though I think Gregory Smith ought to have been it, Grierson has a strong radical influence...he has done very good work at Aberdeen and some of it in books: and he is a gentleman and a good fellow, though a Radical."[87] He had shared with Helen Waddell the hope that Gregory Smith would be chosen. Smith refused the offer of Grierson's chair at Aberdeen and remained at Belfast until retirement.

One day late in October, 1915, J. L. Geddie stood outside Waverly Station with George Kitchin and pointed to a tall, muffled figure in old-fashioned square bowler hat just entering the station and remarked, "That's the last you'll see of old George Saintsbury."[88] The trip south, made by invalid carriage because of his wife's helplessness, was punctuated by five ghastly hours shunting about London; they arrived in warbound Southhampton at 2:00 A.M. and settled into a hotel, The Polygon, in rooms too small for all their impedimenta. A nephew lent Saintsbury a pleasant study in Portland Terrace "with a view over trees to the water and the New Forest," where, by April, he ws "forging ahead" on his *History of the French Novel*. He planned to lecture on Shakespeare at Nottingham on May 4.[89] But Southampton proved unsatisfactory for reasons never given, and, by November, 1916, the Saintsburys had moved to the four rooms at Number

One Royal Crescent, Bath, where he lived for the remaining sixteen years of his life.[90] The apartment was the first at the east end of the crescent and had a view south over the gardens. Their meals and housekeeping were provided by the landlord and his family. The entrance was through a small wicket gate. The small circular tile on the front identifies the house as the one he lived in from 1916 until his death in 1933.

CHAPTER 13

The Widening Range:
"The New Hallam"

This and the following chapter—"The Widening Range" and "The Narrowing Reach"—are concerned with Saintsbury's writings on European literature and criticism and his work on English prosody and prose rhythm, the major works of his years in Edinburgh. The Blackwood venture is one that can only strike terror to the heart of any publisher, with problems the editor of any cooperative history will recognize. William Blackwood had been impressed with Saintsbury's competence and authority when he received his proposals in 1894. The conception (entirely Saintsbury's) was European in range, comparative in approach; the periods survey to be done cooperatively under Saintsbury's editorship; the history of criticism to be his own. Like his earlier French project, this encyclopedic idea has his typical ambitious sweep. As a free-lance writer in 1894, he had reason to believe that he could devote his major time to it, and Blackwood had the plan in hand before Masson announced his retirement.

It was not the demands of Saintsbury's office in the University but rather problems with his cooperating authors that delayed it. His own three-volume *Criticism* was completed in 1904, and he wrote three of the twelve volumes of *The Periods of European Literature*. The hope that the whole series would appear in proper chronological sequence had to be abandoned early, and the compromises on quality and scope were serious, as was the drain on Blackwood's resources. The scheme had been wildly overoptimistic. Saintsbury was fired by a new vision, "the study of comparative literature." It was then, as he told Blackwood (1903), an embryonic field of study and not understood by most people. That year the new *Journal of Comparative Literature* began in the United States; professorships were "already working in France," and he accurately pleads: "Ours is literally the sole textbook of the subject: and if we could only have gotten the volumes out quicker and more together ... it would already have made its way. As it is ... we have a start which it will not be easy for anyone to catch up...." It *was* a first and embodied a dream born in Saintsbury's Oxford days—to know and make accessible all European literature.

But eight years after the start, with half the volumes not yet out, the financial record was in the red and Blackwood hinted at abandoning it all. C. E. Vaughan, Ker, and Grierson were still trailing with their *Periods* volumes; the *Criticism* had grown from one to three volumes and the first two had as yet made no money; and, a poor deal on the U.S. rights was limiting the profits from there, for which Saintsbury had had high hopes.[1]

Saintsbury, who tended to judge by his own capacity for work and discipline, wanted the best men to do the job. So the headaches began. Ker alone stayed the course. The other men on Saintsbury's original roster all refused or withdrew along the way. Three others that he approached later refused.[2] Finally it was Ker, Hannay, Snell, Elton, J. H. Millar, Gregory Smith, Grierson, Vaughan, Omond, and himself. Most of these men he had come to know after he entered the academic world and some were as harried by university business as he was. They were scholars, not journalists, for the most part. Some had special personal problems; some simply dragged their feet.

One year after his inaugural, Saintsbury was reading proof on his *Flourishing of Romance*. He reported to Blackwood that Traill's hands were too full and he must drop out. A few months later he expressed a hope that he might get S. H. Butcher for the first volume of the *Criticism*. Since he wrote it all himself, clearly that hope had been short lived. In 1898, while in Aberdeen to receive an honorary degree, he gained Grierson's consent to do a *Periods* volume; later that spring, while "fixing" Snell's volume, he complained to Blackwood that a man of full leisure is "less to be depended on and more troublesome than a busy 'hack' with twenty irons in the fire at once."[3] By October, he had decided to do *The Earlier Renaissance* himself. All the roots of weakness in the series and the basic superficiality of his encyclopedic approach are painfully clear—especially to a modern specialist's eye.

In 1900, Omond's *Romantic Triumph* (following on the *Flourishing of Romance*, Elton's *Augustan Age*, and Snell's *Fourteenth Century*) occasioned some adverse criticism in the *Scotsman*, and the weary Saintsbury writes: "The 'office boy' who does the reviewing" thinks that "absence of competence can be atoned for by impertinence." He then confesses, "I tick off each week of work as a get through."[4]

During 1901, the financial strain on Blackwood's led Saintsbury to suggest that, instead of receiving £50 for editing his own volumes as he did for others, he would get some friend to give "a responsible revision for £20."[5] When, in the autumn of 1902, *The Earlier Renaissance, Criticism* vol. 2, and Millar's *Mid-Eighteenth Century* came out, Saintsbury assures George Blackwood that his own *Later Nineteenth Century* is ready and "is sure to sell" but *must* come out last. Fearing again that Blackwood will abandon the series, he pleads: " . . . until the series is complete, we can hardly expect it to make its way. One volume calls to another. . . . "[6] Vaughan's and Ker's volumes were in print in 1903, and Saintsbury glimpsed the end, the "penultimate erring sheep having come home" in 1905.[7]

Despite all the trials, his editing had been meticulous, detailed and prompt. Elton recalled with gratitude "many a penciling in the proof margins; a comment on a fact ('surely no?'), or a judgment ('ça porte malheur!') which made us think hard, once we had deciphered the cryptic handwriting."[8] The huge project made no money and Saintsbury spent more time and money on the *Criticism* than he could possibly be rewarded for.[9] It was a labor of love. His self-discipline probably saved his sanity, though he overworked compulsively and learned much about the vagaries of scholars working on a cooperative project. Yet his faith in it all was strong. Having written three of the volumes himself, he came to believe that he might have done all twelve faster himself (as Gosse had urged him to do). Once, in a moment of despair—with his own copy ready and others still not in hand—he exploded to Blackwood, "I never realized till now what sort of rotten reeds men are in almost the majority of cases. . . . Some people seem to have no method, and others no energy. . . . Excuse the grumble!" This rare outburst after more than twenty years' experience as an editor reflects his own obsessive drive to work, a trait that distanced him from many writers.

Both *The Periods of European Literature* and the *History of Criticism and Literary Taste in Europe* assumed a kind of literary confederation of Western Europe, expanding and multiplying its interactions as the individual literatures develop singly and simultaneously from the Dark Ages to the beginning of the twentieth century.[10] Saintsbury knew the problems. Such a survey could not be exhaustive and it ran the risk of superficiality. Each volume was to be handled by one author because he believed a survey is satisfactorily made only by one pair of eyes, and it is by *one* mind that the "general literary drift of the whole of Europe during the whole period" can be kept in focus while separate simultaneous developments are traced. The price was the sacrifice of specialist knowledge, since none of the authors could know thoroughly all the literatures even of his own period. Scholars had not been trained in this horizontal view—a problem that has not vanished even as this approach has flourished. Saintsbury looked for men "thoroughly acquainted with the literature which happened to be of greatest prominence in the special period," but with adequate general literary knowledge and critical habits.[11] A compromise but a practical necessity. He reasoned that such an overall view was increasingly necessary because, as individual studies of the many separate European literatures rapidly widened and deepened, "a deeper and wider ignorance could accompany the deeper and wider knowledge."[12] This foresight was correct, but Saintsbury seemed not to realize how superficial the results had to be. Certainly they did not provide deeper knowledge. But his faith in literary mapmaking and inclusiveness made him think his goal was attainable.

The scheme of each volume of the *Periods* is identical according to Saintsbury's own "jointed map," and the twelve volumes were dovetailed and linked under his guidance, then drawn together in the final volume, his own *Later Nineteenth Century,* where he explained the general plan, some of the difficulties encountered, and the omissions found necessary. He deplored the inevitable neglect of minor literatures and apologized for having relied upon translations for the Icelandic, Russian, and Norwegian. He waived his former rule of omitting all living writers and was thus able to include such major European figures as Zola, Ibsen, Nietzsche, and Tolstoy, a sound decision defeated by his prejudice against them all. He did not include Wilde or Shaw. He hoped the series would be useful in the higher forms of schools and in universities.

Separate treatment was not given to ancient literature in the *Periods* because, as Saintsbury explained, as *live* influences they had to be dealt with in every period. Contemporary Latin Literature is included wherever it is an influence on the vernacular.[13] Any hope of including Byzantine, Arabic, or Oriental literatures Santsbury dismissed at the start as impossible, though he dreamed of that range too. The overall goal was "a connected, critical, and comparative view of the 'Literature of Europe'"—a literary atlas. The period divisions are reasonable, though necessarily arbitrary.[14]

"We may call consciously comparative thinking the great glory of our nineteenth century," wrote H. M. Posnett, an Englishman, in 1886.[15] He acknowledged the concern of Frenchmen such as Ampère, Villemain, Sainte-Beuve, Taine, Demogeot, and Scherer with both comparative study and the study of the influence of foreign literatures on French literature, and he insisted that English literature "cannot be explained by English causes alone." He suggested the creation of chairs of comparative literature.

The idea of comparative literary study reaches back into the eighteenth century to Bodmer and Breitinger in Germany and Diderot in France; it was suggested by Herder, applied by Madame de Staël and Chateaubriand before Hallam; also by Noel and Laplace in *Cours de la littérature comparée* in 1816. Later men who used the term and the comparative approach, each with a difference, include Joseph Texte, Gaston Paris, Jusserand, and Brunetière.[16] In 1894, C. M. Gayley, an American, called for the founding of a Society of Comparative Literature, and, in 1899, Columbia University instituted its University Studies in Comparative Literature. In 1903, G. E. Woodberry began the *Journal of Comparative Literature;* it had just four issues. The International Congrès d'Histoire Comparée des Littératures was held in Paris in 1900, three years after the first volume of Saintsbury's *Periods* was published.[17]

The human sciences had all gradually become comparative; philology was the first, in the eighteenth century, and scientific influences on literary history were increasing. These sometimes aided the comparative approach and sometimes hampered or restricted it, as with Taine's determinism, Hennequin's scientific criticism, and Brunetière's rigid concept of genres. Some of the best work came from scholars in minor nations for whom the study of their own limited literature seemed insufficient (e.g., Georg Brandes, Edouard Rod, and Marc Monnier).

In 1921, Baldensperger reviewed the various directions that "la littérature comparée" had taken.[18] Parallels and contrasts, influences and interrelations, evolution of theme and genre disregarding national lines, or simply emphasis on a knowledge of literatures other than one's own—all these and more the omnibus term *comparative literature* has encompassed as its works have proliferated in the century since Posnett wrote and Arnold urged the English to study French literature. Baldensperger, while acknowledging their contributions, complained that Loliée, R. G. Moulton, Manzoni, Pavolini, Saintsbury, and Engel used a method that worked on apparent results, not facts, and gave inadequate attention to causes and development. He also stressed the need to treat minor authors and to deal with changes in reputation and taste, both things Saintsbury considered important (though the scope of the *Periods* allowed them little place). *The History of Criticism,* in its concern with changing literary taste and fashions, was to supplement the *Periods.*

Hallam's *Introduction to European Literature* (1837–39) had covered only the Renaissance and the seventeenth century, and since Hallam's chief interest was the progress of learning, subject matter and especially philosophy got his chief attention and he showed little literary sensibility.[19] Saintsbury reversed the situation by emphasizing the art, the style and structure, prosody and rhythms, and the overall shaping of language to their ends as well as critical evaluation of all these, thus maintaining the same focus and limitations he had kept in his earlier literary histories, English and French. In his *Criticism,* he traces the development of literary history, both national and comparative, and measures the scope of the critic-historian's range. He finds these too slight in early adherents of the comparative method, better in Montégut and Texte, though the latter had the fatal weakness of "generalizing and abstracting too much."

Saintsbury argues that the practice of Sainte-Beuve and the doctrine of Arnold "canonized the idea." "Regular academic and other sanction" had been achieved only in the decade before he wrote this in 1904, but, for him, the comparative method had seemed "the 'via sola' of literary safety" for almost forty years. In his French and English surveys, the critic and historian had merged into one in both theory and practice as he insisted that "*the whole drift* of European literature and criticism and taste" must be the lenses through which "the New Critic" sees the poem, play, or novel.[20]

It was a noble ambition, and Saintsbury deserves recognition after eighty years that have seen his vision fulfilled and extended to embrace the study of global literature, however inadequate and outdated are his results. Unfortunately, these years have also seen the failure of depth that such extended horizontal range precipitates, side by side with the critical ills that arise from the dominance of the specialists.[21] For some of these ills, criticism has sought the correctives of "close reading" and analysis of many kinds, linguistic and structural, some brilliant, some verging on the absurd. The horizontal range of the *Periods* and the *History of Criticism* has not been attempted on the same scale since, but the point of view has been established and the vision is reflected in more limited and specialized surveys, critical and scholarly studies, anthologies, and university courses. Saintsbury did not even dream of the ethnic ramifications recent decades have seen.

In actual accomplishment, the *Periods*—not surprisingly—are very uneven from one volume to another and within the single volumes as the writer's ability to deal with several literatures varies. The best and one still valued is W. P. Ker's *Dark Ages*. Elton's *Augustan Age* and Grieson's *First Half of the Seventeenth Century* are also distingushed. To rank the others is not necessary, because all are pretty much superceded. Their importance lies in their being parts of this pioneering survey that made clear the need for more knowledge of their materials and challenged the student to know all the literatures of Western Europe as interrelated. The three volumes Saintsbury wrote illustrate the typical faults and strengths of the series as a whole as well as his own individual virtues and weaknesses.

The Flourishing of Romance was the best of Saintsbury's three volumes. Some of its weaknesses resulted from Saintsbury's lack of specialist knowledge of literatures other than English and French; others from the conditions under which he wrote, crowding these three volumes into an already full university schedule, as well as from his faith in the value of the brief, superficial survey he offered. Only occasionally does he stop to recreate a poet, a single work, or a character as he does the *Dies Irae*, the "very human" Guinevere of the original Arthuriad, or Renart (in a comparative analysis of the French, German, and Flemish versions).[22]

The Flourishing of Romance was rooted in Saintsbury's lifelong enthusiasm for medieval romance begun with his boyhood adoring of Arthur, Guinevere, Lancelot, and Sir Bors. He had treated the romances in his short histories of French and English literature and was now at ease dealing with them in the comparative manner he preferred. He also shows a familiarity with the German poets. He had a warm feeling for Wolfgang von Eschenbach and makes clear the charms of Walter von der Volgelweide's two hundred songs with their occasional "dactyllic swells" so "intoxicating after deserts of iambs."[23]

The last two chapters of the The Flourishing of Romance, one on Icelandic and Provençal and one on the literature of the Peninsulas, are too slight to be useful. Like the final pages on the late Greek Romances as representative of the Scriptores Erotici and a "dying literature,"[24] they illustrate the irresistible impulse Saintsbury felt to include everything, however inadequately dealt with.

The specialists Saintsbury had unsuccessfully approached to do The Earlier Renaissance had been fearful of each other in relation to various subdivisions of the material. Doing it himself, he avoided theoretical controversy because he had no interest in the complex question of the the nature of the Renaissance.[25] The first chapter is rewarding in its discussion of the various ways Latin served in this transitional period. He gives a rather long, lively section to Macaronics and the somewhat neglected work of Folengo, and with equal relish offers a "flying sketch of some of the Epistolae" to illustrate a variety of comedy "essentially modern."[26] Comparative method is illustrated as Latimer is set against Colet, the developments in the sonnet form in the various languages are contrasted, and the pervasive influence of The Courtier is traced.

The Later Nineteenth Century (1850–1900) is so faulty as to rank as Saintsbury's worst work. Its first four chapters lingering over "giants" of the mid-century are supererogatory, and the last hundred pages, where he tempts "the fate of Moses if not of Icarus" in an effort to focus and unify the story of more than a thousand years, make a too superficial survey even more vague. Between this and the English and French material lie three inadequate chapters: one on German literature, one on "the Southern Literatures" including a thirteen-page insert on Portuguese written by Edwin Prestage, and a chapter on "the New Candidates," an omnibus sketch of Belgian, Scandinavian, and Russian literature. These Saintsbury should never have touched; he manages only to demonstrate a total failure of sympathy with the modern literary mind. Anyone who knew his essay, "The End of a Chapter," was prepared for this, but it did not justify his failure rooted as it was in his fear of what he sensed were profound new intellectual forces changing his world. Unfortunately, he felt he must complete the vast scheme he had conceived. As an orginal attempt at an all-encompassing comparative literary history of Europe when taken with the *History of Criticism,* the work is a landmark. He knew the direction literary history should take and foreshadowed later developments.

By the time he wrote his *History of Criticism,* Saintsbury's few vague principles expressed in "Kinds of Criticism" had been applied for almost three decades. These critical ideas are reaffirmed within the massive *History.* As early as the 1870s he had sought, in vain, some historical treatment of his critical predecessors for his own guidance. Then, characteristically, he decided to provide it himself. Meanwhile, the "controlled impressionism" that he advocates at every turn had dominated his own critism. This appreciative, enthusiastic interpretation and placing of a literary work he continues to assert as the only way one achieves true catholicity and "universal criticism."[27] Saintsbury had himself condemned the mere "impressionism" of which Irving Babbitt was to accuse him in 1912.[28] The critical process, as he examines it in the *History* in many exemplars, is, at best for each critic a long, slow, endless one of forming, then refining and correcting one's generalizations and thus ordering one's impressions (though he himself seldom corrected his own). In criticism, he argues, "one must make many mistakes . . . before one comes right."[29] At the same time, he sees literature itself in its development altering tradition, a hint that anticipates T. S. Eliot in "Tradition and Individual Talent."

> . . . every generation and every country adds . . . fresh supplies of matter . . . which must sooner or later get added to [the total] and may affect conclusions drawn from [it] as vitally as did the work of Dante or that of Shakespeare.[30]

But he fails to apply this insight to his own era.

Saintsbury's basic values and prejudices color the whole history. He spots even in ancient critics the first faint efforts at a horizontal and comparative view of literature, the first enthusiastic reporting of actual works, and every early attention to form and treatment as the critic's main concern. He lights with joy on the first critic for whom music and transport are primary in poetic effect or for whom poetry and verse are inseparable. Conversely, he detects and deplores even the slightest hint of a moral preoccupation or rigid rule and he ignores philosophical ideas, thus limiting this work as he did others.

Saintsbury's first assumption—and a sound one—is that the true critic must *love* literature. This love he found in large measure in Lamb, Hazlitt and Hunt. Its fatal lack he regrets in Swift, Voltaire, and Schiller. He also assumes that a "natural appetite toward poetry and literary delight . . . exists more or less in all but the lowest and most unhappy souls." Saintsbury never lost sight of these two assumptions, which sometimes get lost in modern specialized or technical criticism.

Saintsbury's inconsistency is very human as he strongly denies progress, stressing ebb and flow and flux, but at the same time discovers a steady forward development toward appreciative evaluation, away from a priori rule and generality, toward judgment "by the result," analysis of actual works and, above all, attention to form and style. His explicit aim is to view everything *sub specie aeternitatis* and to maintain catholicity, but he is his own man with his own somewhat vague aesthetic, his own enthusiasms and prejudices. This gives the work its vitality as well as its limitations. There is a discrepancy between his avowed catholicity and his vigorous, forthright pronouncements, such as that on Goethe's "calculus of profit," *er kann nichts mehr helfen,* as "mighty disgusting" and "mighty dangerous" and as "the root of much of the bad criticism of the world."

"The Devil take all theories," the motto Saintsbury chose for the title page of the *History of Criticism,* has been generally accepted as a key to the definitive weakness of the work. Evidence to justify protest is everywhere, despite his assertion that "this delivery unto Satan of all theory . . . is of course intentionally hyerbolical." Efforts to investigate the why of literary pleasure he believed too often draw the eye of the critic away from the text itself.[31] He was more than willing to leave all such theory to as sane and reasonable a contemporary as Bernard Bosanquet, whose *History of Aesthetics* (1897) he regarded as a sound complement to his own *Criticism.*[32] Feeling that the two kinds of criticism—judgment and theory—must not be confused, he kept his eye chiefly on critical practice, an attitude opposite to that of much later twentieth-century criticism, where theory tends to predominate.

The preface makes clear the limits set: he would trace "the reasoned exercise of Literary Taste," that is, "the function of the judgment which busies itself with the goodness or badness, the success or ill-success, of literature from the purely literary point of view." Interpretation and "the general judgment" or implicit taste of various ages have their place, but conjecture and criticism by the critic do not, and rhetoric in its more practical sense will have little or no attention. Philosphers such as Descartes, Rousseau, Hegel, and Kant, in whom the critical point of view of their age is so often rooted, receive too little mention.

As always with Saintsbury, the handling is erratically disporportionate.[33] *The Frogs* is here seen as a shrewd critique on actual texts; the ten volumes of the Greek Anthology were examined in a fruitless search for literary comment, as were the autobiography of Aelius Aristides and the letters of Dante and Erasmus. Some medieval writers not professionally critics or rheticians—St. Augustine, Apollinaris Sidonius, Themistius, and Julian the Apostate—are touched upon, but strangely not St. Thomas Aquinas or John of Salisbury. J. W. H. Atkins praises Saintsbury for "hewing a path through a strange country" in the Middle Ages.[34] But Spingarn, the best judge of the handling of the Renaissance, noted shortcomings as well as a failure of "philosophical unity" and a neglect of recent research; then he added graciously, "While I am carving my cherry pip, he is rearing a vast cathedral to heaven."[35] As the quantity of material mounts, selection is more arbitrary and reflects Saintsbury's romantic bias, though it is not as crippling as Irving Babbitt charged.[36]

The work has all the signs of Saintsbury's typical practice. He tried to reread the texts but sometimes trusted to memory and blundered in summary. Notes testify to his search for obscure and scarce texts as well as to fresh impressions gained from rereading. But with his lack of system, indifference to ideas, and casual method, the work falls far short of modern standards.

The work of Longinus, "the critical masterpiece of the ancient world," dominates the first volume as the first pure aesthetic criticism. In some of his most eloquent pages, Saintsbury portrays Longinus as one who looks at "literature as a whole," recognizes as "the true and only test of literary greatness—the 'transport,' the absorption of the reader," and sees beautiful works as a main means whereby this effect is produced. He also was the first with a comparative view as he dealt with Greek, Latin, and Hebrew. Without overestimating this fragmentary but seminal work, Saintsbury makes one feel the power of this unknown critic to whom no other Ancient refers. Longinus is claimed for the romantic camp, rescued from Boileau, to Irving Babbitt's dismay, and given his first modern appraisal, one approached later only by the efforts of Allen Tate and Elder Olson.[37] There is no better introduction to the text of "On the Sublime."

The second volume of the *History of Criticism,* carrying critical development through eighteenth-century neoclassicism, gives major attention to English criticism because Saintsbury thought it superior to all other criticism of the time. It clearly reveals his romantic bias as he searches out evidences of taste, of a poetic or literary sense, and of enthusiasm. He asks of every critic, does he think verse necessary to poetry?—a test wholly passed by no critic before Coleridge. He had dealt with all the English and French critics earlier and there are no surprises. Dryden emerges head and shoulders above every other figure, "a source and model forever," as Saintsbury does more justice to his role as a critic than he had done earlier. But this second volume seems otherwise largely negative because "The Dissolvents of Neo-Classicism" and "The Reconstruction of Criticism" are reserved for volume three.

Saintsbury's evaluation of Samuel Johnson is the occasion for one of his more important statements on what makes a great critic: "a sound critical calculus rather than a caprice," a solid, reasoned body of critical judgment, and a judgment "we can never justly disable," however much we disagree. He understood Dr. Johnson's blind spots and gave full value to *The Lives of the Poets.* The failure of the "streaks of the tulip" dictum is memorably illustrated. By this standard, Lady Winchelsea's horse in the twilight, Tennyson's ashbuds "in the front of March," and Keats's perilous seas through magic casements must all be rejected. He is amusing on Dr. Johnson's distrust of Gray: he suspected "the romantic snake in Gray's classically waving grass. . . . He spied the great romantic under the Pindaric and Horatian muffler—and he did not like it."[38]

Throughout volume three of the *Criticism,* as he spots landmarks in the progress of criticism toward his own ideals, Saintsbury sounds like an explorer exclaiming, "Here at last!" The new lights of criticism provoke a rash of exclamations: "the *sine qua non,*" "the acme," "the cardinal principle," "the epitome," "the new charter," or "one of the last secrets" of modern criticism. These overlapping superlatives allow for little analysis and show a lack of discrimination.

He omits literatures other than English, German, and French because he thinks their criticism is unimportant for general history and, more practically, because treatment would have had to be based on translations, a kind of limitation he would have been wise to have imposed in the *Periods* survey. Saintsbury celebrates Diderot as the first critic who submits himself to a work of art "as if he were a 'sensitized' plate . . . absolutely faithful to the impression produced" (the figure he later used for Pater). This, for him, is "the 'idea' of modern criticism"—a contact of subject and critic "intimate, physical, uninterrupted and resulting in conception and birth."[39]

Romantic as his own bias was, Saintsbury was beyond his depth with the more philosophical romantic critics—the Germans, Coleridge, and Wordsworth. On the minor English romantics, he does less well here than in his earlier essays and surveys, offering only a kind of guidebook to local beauties and a catalog of memorable passages. To Sainte-Beuve here (as elsewhere) he does fair justice; with Arnold he continues his long quarrel. As already noted, he puts Pater at the head of the modern school, praising the impressionist, not the philosopher whom many scholars have increasingly valued. He complains that an amateur everyone-can-judge-for-himself attitude characterized the periodical criticism he grew up with and critics forgot that subtle pleasures of style require "intelligent, sympathetic, and to a certain extent submissive cooperation on the part of the person who is to enjoy them." Later he commented, "I have never myself understood why it is godliness to gulp and sin to savour."[40]

At the end of this long journey through the ages, Saintsbury saw the whole as "a story, a history, a chain of opinion and comment on opinion," in which no great critic becomes obsolete. He found time to express several of his guiding beliefs. He assumed a "consensus of good criticism with which any man has the right to disagree . . . at his own peril" and holds that critics have some responsibility for literary taste in their age. They should promote "the intelligent appreciation, the conscious enjoyment of literature" and, while recommending all the good that has been written, should let the public know if they are not getting as good poetry or prose as they should. He also argues that the "*ethos of true criticism*" once grasped should never fail the critic, and that this "adeption and fruition of literature," innate to a degree, can and must be cultivated. At the end he reiterates his lifelong faith: knowledge of the history of criticism assists this cultivation, "by pointing out past errors it prevents interference with enjoyment; . . . it shows how to grasp and enjoy; . . . it helps the ear to listen when the horns of Elfland blow"—his final tribute to "the tenth muse."

Like all his work, the *History of Criticism* has Saintsbury's personality stamped on every page. Whatever its many limitations, it is still readable and, at times, amusing with its slangy paraphrases and the flashes of that academic jocularity with which not all critics have been happy. Saintsbury's defense is unanswerable: "To those who pronounce a task impossible the best answer is to go and do it; for those who hate jokes and literary allusions one can only say, God help them!" He knew that there were blunders and that specialists would disagree. For his indifference to philosophical ideas he had no apology.

The *History of Criticism* was more widely reviewed than most of Saintsbury's works. It came at a time when he was established academically and had achieved authority and influence comparable, as one reviewer noted, to that of Brunetière in France.[41] Reviews by distinguished scholars, among them W. P. Ker, H. O. Taylor, Emil Koeppel, Ferris Greenslet, and Joel Spingarn, were favorable on the whole.[42] They regarded errors and inaccuracies as inevitable in a ground-breaking work of such scope. They praised the courage of the undertaking while deploring the neglect of research and aesthetic theory. Some reviewers objected to his romantic leanings. One found him guilty of the art-for-art's-sake heresy; another charged that his romanticism invalidated his claim to impartiality; another called him a "formalist in the apparel of an aesthete."[43] Babbitt added Saintsbury to his list of degenerate followers of Rousseau; he accused him of having led men into aesthetic anarchy and concluded that his reputation proved "that the English are not critical."[44] The most thoroughgoing criticism was that of Spingarn and Croce, who both deplored the lack of a philosophical conception of criticism and of purpose and method.[45] Raleigh called the work "a prolonged assault on all systems, rules, standards and principles."[46] Much later, René Wellek lamented the haziness and poverty of Saintsbury's concepts and criteria but admitted that he "does constantly discuss theory of literature, poetics, rhetoric and metrics and generalizes very freely about periods, trends, schools and movements in literary history." He acknowledged Saintsbury's great influence, both good and bad, and the role he played as a mapmaker though he "may not have furthered the cause of criticism in the abstract."[47] A less stern judgment was that of T. S. Eliot, who found the *History* "always delightful, generally useful and most often right."[48]

Superceded in part by the surveys of Wellek and J. W. H. Atkins and others, Saintsbury's *History of Criticism* still has its uses after almost a century of development in criticism. It still surprises with moments of insight and eloquence where the subject is sympathetic.

Loci Critici (1903), an anthology compiled to "illustrate the drift of criticism in modern Europe," grew out of a conversation with C. M. Gayley and the advice of other authorities.[49] It became a handbook for Saintsbury's Edinburgh students and for several generations to follow in Britain and the United States. The selections and the proportions bear the editor's stamp as do the "bare interpretations" he allows himself. Like the *History,* it had few competitors until the post–World War II flood of anthologies and critical discussion. The excerpts, more of them brief snippets than modern standards allow, reflect Saintsbury's faith in the isolated critical aperçu; and all his favorites are there, including most of the classic statements of critical truth. An occasional judgment is thought provoking, such as that on Dr. Johnson's possessing that "association of contradictories which often does (and perhaps should) mark great criticism." In 1912, Saintsbury compiled the *History of English Criticism,* adding a summary of the ancient critics to the English chapters of the larger history.[50] Meanwhile he had turned his attention primarily to prosody.

CHAPTER 14

The Narrowing Reach
and the Formal Bent

Having extended his range to all European literature and criticism, Saintsbury narrowed his focus to the limited matter of literary rhythms and produced his most unique work. In the last volume of the *History of Criticism,* he began to feel his way explicitly toward the narrower subject and, dealing with the end of the eighteenth century, he omitted prosodic matters, promising to treat them elsewhere. At that time, he proposed the *History of English Prosody* to Macmillan, and the firm authorized it before the last volume of the *Criticism* was in print. *The Prose Rhythm,* only a hint there, had become a promise by the time he finished the *Prosody; A Historical Manual of English Prosody* (1910) came between them. These five volumes are truly "the last word and logical outcome" of Saintsbury's formal bent, carrying to a climax interests that predominated in his very first writings, when he preached that primary attention to form is a sound critical attitude and a protection against moral preoccupation and excessive subject worship.[1]

Prosody and the rhythms of poetry and prose have always been as controversial a subject as theology and have become more so as linguistic science has increased its scope and variety.[2] A service discipline sometimes threatening to become an end in itself, prosody has often confused the reader when it should have been helping him or her to read and enjoy poetry as poetry and it has never commanded a large audience. Because Saintsbury chose this neglected area for his last large literary project and because he is still uniquely the historian of both English prosody and prose rhythm, an account of his work is necessary, though it requires a plunge into highly charged and murky waters.

Saintsbury was glad to have learned "to read scanningly" as a schoolboy and often reverted to that method of reading aloud "with accompaniment of handbeat."[3] He says he was never taught any system of English prosody and formed his ideas solely by reading English poetry.[4] He had an unusual ear that heard feet and line divisions,[5] but he tried to remember that some ears do not hear the feet,[6] though such recognition seemed to him basic. In 1923 he went further: "We do and must make [a sensible division between lines] though the time occupied by this division is the smallest that will 'divide'"[7]—a difficult and controversial requirement but one relevant to Saintsbury's prosodic analyses and scansions.

As one of the personal origins of his system, Saintsbury recalls an evening at Oxford in the 1860s when, as he was reading the Song of the Sirens in the *Odyssey*, a "Slap" (a group of street musicians) outside played the popular "slow voluptuous" waltz "The Cornflower." Suddenly he thought how little truncation one of the lines of the *Odyssey* would require to be "adjusted—*spaced*—to the waltz time itself, different as it is from that of the natural hexameter."[8]

He more than once refers to prosody as akin to dancing and also says he did much of his thinking about prosody while walking, "the two 'modes of motion' physically or metaphysically suggesting each other."[9] Scansion for him did not require reading aloud; he preferred "that *inarticulate* but exactly proportioned following of actual delivery which is necessary for rhapsodic appreciation."[10] One recalls those undergraduates in the Merton College gardens in 1866, reading Swinburne's *Poems and Ballads* aloud with their hypnotic flowing rhythms, then turning to Baudelaire and the Parnassian poets. Also, for forty years, Saintsbury enjoyed discussing prosodic problems with Dobson and with other friends.

Devoted as he was to comparative literary study and French poetry in particular, he insisted on the prosodic independence of each language, each having "the prosody it deserves," each growing out of the language to which it belongs. Since he believed you cannot imitate the prosodic effect of one language in another successfully, he did not write a comparative prosody.[11] Saintsbury traced the influence of French forms upon English in the early medieval world, but his exclusion of all other foreign matter from the *Prosody* led W. P. Ker to protest the omission of origins and of the impact of the foreign "Mothers"[12] on English forms. In his *Short History of English Literature* (1898), Saintsbury made clear his view that there is a break between

Anglo-Saxon and later English prosody, thus disagreeing with Guest and Skeat.

Saintsbury's earliest statement of what constitutes the foot appeared in 1878 in a review of a Coventry Patmore essay on prosody: English verse is to be scanned both by quantity and by accent, and "no verse is really good which does not answer this double test."[13] This statement anticipates that more specific one given in 1910 in the *Manual:* Whatever "*makes* the difference between 'long' and 'short,' it...*exists*, and is felt at once whether it is due to accent, length of pronunciation, sharpness, loudness, strength, or anything else."[14] Verse cannot exist without it and it is "in English rather largely created by the poet," though it is "conditioned by certain conventions of the language."

Preparation for *The History of Prosody* was prodigious, and as was his habit, Saintsbury says so. His aim was to show how the manipulation of the foot "has effected (or, to be entirely impartial, has coincided with) improvement, or deterioration, or stationary quality in English poetry."[15] Or, to quote one of his frequent biological metaphors that made some critics unhappy, he wished to give "the natural history of metrical evolution." His method was to be analysis and scansion according to the foot system. He would rely on "the mind's ear," not the eye or fingers. A subsidiary purpose, but a quite militant one he admits, was "to wage truceless war" against Skeat's view of stress, accent, or beat as the sole secret of meter. Saintsbury's defense of the foot system is frequent and forceful. Typically, in the *Manual,* he claims that it adjusts to the whole history of English verse, "bars nothing, carves, cuts and corrects nothing; begs no questions; involves no make-believe." His quarrel was with Guest and Bridges as well as Skeat.

In concluding the *History of Prosody,* Saintsbury explained that he had tried to make it not a mere chronicle or tabular conspectus but "a possible and logical life history of English verse." He added that this could be done only on the metrical system, and that the chief fact expounded is the foot, though he had refused to say precisely what differentiated "long" and "short" as its elements.[16]

Saintsbury made many statements similar to this defensive one throughout the *History of Prosody,* the *Manual, The History of Prose Rhythm,* and, finally, in the preface to the second edition of the *Prosody* in 1923—some of these in response to reviewers' demands for clarification. The last was his most successful and fullest attempt to define the constituents of the foot. He specifies three sources of quantity or syllabic length or shortness in English as in classical languages: vowel value, position, and stress (that of ordinary "accent" or the poet's special emphasis). These work together in varying, complex ways and to a varying extent, but the range of "commonness" is very great in English. The standard is that of syllables as "spoken by the best tongues and heard by the best ears"—open to debate as that may be.[17]

This last effort at clarification did not solve all Saintsbury's problems, but it filled a gap in the original work and it makes clear why Saintsbury's system cannot be labeled simply a stress theory.[18] While offering this last effort at redefinition, Saintsbury expressed genuine puzzlement at the need for it. He had never admitted to himself that his aims and basic assumptions had not been clearly stated though numerous reviewers asked, some wistfully, some impatiently, What, for Professor Saintsbury, *is* a foot? How does equivalence or substitution work?[19] Some readers found clarification in the *Manual*, which Saintsbury organized on "a new principle." For others, the problem remained unsolved.

Saintsbury undertook the *History of Prosody* in the belief that "no authoritative body of doctrine on the subject" existed and that he would have to create methods as he went. His pragmatic method produced his best definitions only at the end and again in 1923—too late for many readers. Also because of his strong distrust of theory and abstraction, he wished to stick to "the facts," not realizing that the facts prove insufficient when these involve both technical elements and individual aesthetic responses.[20] Other problems grew out of Saintsbury's lifelong preoccupation with rhythm as a literary value and his unusually sensitive ear (a gift akin to that of perfect pitch for the musician). These led him to expect too much technically in other readers' responses to poetry and made him assume that others heard what he did. But any ear less sensitive than his demands more guidance, more analysis, and clearer definitions.

With scansion as the prime method of his history, Saintsbury raised problems both mechanical and psychological, and one needs to follow every clue he gives to judge his results. But his faith in the method and in his own readings was unshakable. He tells us that he freshly scanned all of Shakespeare and all of *Paradise Lost* along with his other preparation. He warns the reader that, without scansion, no one can understand prosody. But many readers have had to put the device aside. Rupert Brooke even pictured him as drowning in his "false feet."

Saintsbury's insistence on scanning created problems even when he treated the earliest period. He admits that scansion is only "dimly visible" in Anglo-Saxon verse, that the struggle toward feet "creates a conflict of accentual and metrical" in Layamon, and that verse of the alliterative revival cannot strictly be scanned. Langland he finds "potentially metrical," a view based on his surprising and radical determination to treat effects without regard to intention and to discuss "latent scansion not present to the mind of the poet," effects that justify his scansion and can be detected and systematized in "a community of slowly developing order."[21] This view, which also produced the anapests he found in early verse and the trisyllabic feet he heard in *Christabel*, is certainly controversial.

Other points show Saintsbury's flexibility. He admits it is possible to adopt very different foot divisions for any one line in scanning English poetry. He often shows two alternatives (because of the frequency of common syllables in English), but he believed the effect of each alternative is different. He also assumes silent and extrametrical syllables. Distrustful though he was of spondee and amphibrach, unlike some prosodists he allowed them as possible in English. He accepts a minimum of elision and refers with approval to Dryden's rule that you must not elide what you pronounce. Every line in Shakespeare, he asserts, can be scanned iambically if one remembers that not every line is a five-foot line.[22] In scanning, he marks off feet with bars, usually without indicating long and short except where substitute feet are marked to indicate equivalence.

Criticisms of this highly technical survey include, in addition to that of a failure to define, those of vagueness and diffuseness at one pole and of too much analogy to biological development at the other. Saintsbury argued, probably with justice, that some diffuseness was inevitable if the work was to be more than a history of the mechanics of verse. Since he insisted that no one quality distinguishes the "long" from the "short" (not time, not accent, not quantity, etc.), but rather that some or all these things and more produce the result for the ear, he had to discuss them all. This added confusion for minds desiring precision and for those with ears less sensitive than his to the values he detected. But many readers, including the present writer, have found that one of the rewards of the history lies in the discussion of "fingering" or "rhetorical prosody" and have wished for even more attention to things such as vowel music and alliteration, pauses and enjambment, cadence, and verse paragraphs.

In treating literary rhythm, Saintsbury thinks more in terms of an organic history than in any of his other surveys. He sees maturing and decay, relapse and recovery, even (as in the extreme figure he applies to the transition from Anglo-Saxon to early English verse) impregnation, fertilization, crossing, hybrids, and self-propagation.[23] He sometimes exaggerates, but Harvey Gross, the modern editor of Saintsbury's *Manual,* is wrong when he condemns this as "moralism, a besetting fault of historians" and as inappropriate to technique. The decay or the health, the growth and the bloom, the good and the bad, that Saintsbury is tracing are not moral but literary facts, facts as the ear hears them, not related to moral decadence or the dissoluteness of poets.

The breakdown of blank verse, for example, though it happens to accompany the moral license and decadence in Jacobean drama, has no causal relationship and Saintsbury claims none. Gross uses the phrase "the dialectical swing of English prosody"[24] to avoid the biological metaphors that Saintsbury enjoyed and perhaps used too freely—and sometimes mixed wildly. But Saintsbury's figures do emphasize the continuity of prosodic development as he wanted them to, while they also give prosody a kind of life of its own.[25] Once he spoke unwisely of "the personalities" of feet, though he warns against overstressing the individual character of iamb, trochee, et al.

As one moves through the *History of Prosody,* one grows more and more aware that, for Saintsbury, prosody was meaning in a very real sense and sound is "the life" of poetry, or as he put it, "It's the 'riding that does it.'"[26] Meaning is richest for him when the marriage of sound and sense is most perfect, when the versifier finds and fuses the perfectly appropriate form with his meaning and blends the prosodic, rhetorical, and poetic elements into full harmony.[27] A poet may be important prosodically though not great poetically (e.g., Leigh Hunt and Matt Lewis), but the best poets are the best prosodists and the most successfully innovative.[28] The proportionate attention and the valuation Saintsbury gives to poets here differ from those in his other works because the innovator, not the most competent versifier or the master, often has greatest significance for prosodic development.

"The Mothers," the first chapter of the *History,* though too slight to please W. P. Ker, depicts what people of 1200 would have had in their ears and points out that the vernaculars adapted accentual Latin poetry to their own accent. Saintsbury sees alliteration disappearing by 1200, and "prosody by feet with rhyme" established with some equivalence and substitution evident. Having described Layamon as the experimental laboratory of English prosody, he emphasizes Chaucer's mastery not in originating but in adapting and improving all prosodic means. He concerns himself with some interesting distinctions between rhythm and meter and describes a "splendid piece of cadence" at the beginning of *The Parliament of Foules* and "The Swing and Sway" of "The Nut Browne Maiden." The relation between quantity and accent, which Saintsbury never quite satisfactorily defined, enters into his thinking again and again.

He is good on *The Pearl* and on the appropriateness and variety of rhythms in the York and Townley cycles. He is devastating, even funny, on the disease of quantity that struck all Europe and compares the jarring effect of Campion's English elegiacs to the noise made when "the tension of a typewriter goes wrong, and the carriage drags against the teeth of the rack."[29] His comments on the unity and variety of prosodic texture in *The Faerie Queen* challenge one to reread just for that. The appendixes of the first volume are important to the main text of the whole survey because they deal with essential matters such as equivalence, the pause, rhyme, and alliteration.

Saintsbury's discussion of stanza forms is brief but generally sound as it is, for instance, on the social achievements of the Spenserian stanza, the potential of the verse paragraph, "the drawing power" of the couplet, and the assistance that "artificial measures gave to the establishment of English meter." In the hymns of the eighteenth century, he saw a "strange power of *disciplining* the general ear." Thus, prosodic development as organic action and interaction within the culture is well handled without rigid theorizing. The summaries he gives of the essential qualities of various forms, though personal, challenge one's ear. On Shakespeare's absolute prosodic mastery he is convincingly specific.

Through the seventeenth century Saintsbury moved confidently, battling Bridges on Milton, being thoroughly at home with the Caroline lyrics, including those of the minor poets he was then editing, and concluding, "These men can do almost anything." He rejoices in

Dryden's ability to develop the full range of possibilities in one form, but on Pope's technical skill he is more blind, put off as always by what he calls "the curious jointed-doll character of the metre." No such antagonistic feeling checked his eloquent but somewhat exaggerated praise of Smart or of Blake for his "hardly surpassed power of fingering, of giving life to every metre that he touches."

With *The Ancient Mariner,* his enthusiasm explodes in wild metaphors celebrating "the match that kindled the torch of revived true English prosody, the knife that set the prisoner free, the mallet that knocked the block from the dogshores and sent the ship careering into a sea hitherto silent, soon to be full of magical voices." Amid a continuing rhapsody on Coleridge, Shelley, and Tennyson, he struggles with crowding examples while chiding himself, "This is not a book of Beauties." His personal bias betrays itself in negatives as well. Wordsworth is "prosodicaly uncritical"; Byron, careless and often "shoddy" in contrast to Shelley, who in *Prometheus Unbound* gives the greatest prosodic beauty and variety in all English poetry.[30]

Saintsbury holds to his often-expressed belief in the supremacy of his own period in poetry and, above all, in prosody, in "the triumph of the foot system with equivalence and substitution," in variety and freedom with order. He gives O'Shaughnessy an unjustified amount of attention, and the limitations and derivativeness of other contemporaries become virtues for him though he recognizes that even Swinburne was no innovator. His passing references to the living, to Bridges, Yeats, Kipling, and Hopkins, are wholly inadequate.

As he ends this "life-story" of prosody, Saintsbury raises the question whether any system of analysis adds to appreciation but shows little doubt that this work as a poetic anthology will do so—the one virtue most readers of the *History* have acknowledged. The poets do speak in their own voices despite the scansion and the comment. Both the technical and the human protagonists of the drama—the feet, each with its own individuality; the meters, each with its own prosodic pattern; and the poets, each with his distinctive prosody—come alive in the historical procession, and the rich complexity of the long development is never lost sight of despite the focus upon the metrical foot. Discursive, biased, fluid, and sometimes confusing within its large, loose structure, the *History* can be faulted on many scores; yet its richness will probably never be matched in more scientific and specialized ages. It has the peculiar value that a special single focus can give to any survey of poetry as it expands on matter that existed embryonically in his earlier histories. The full harvest is nowhere else. Today's student can profit from his special forte: presenting what his keen ear heard.

For most readers, the concise *Historical Manual of English Prosody* (1910) is easier going than the three-volume *History*. Intended as an abstract of and introduction to the *History*, presented chronologically and rich in illustrations, it too has the charm of an anthology. Harvey Gross found it "singularly complete," with its practical metrics, its account of prosodic theory and the history of versification, a glossary and even a list of poets "according to their prosodic quality and influence."[31] Saintsbury vowed, as in the *History*, " 'to load every rift' with prosodic fact." The analytical organization makes the principles stand out clearly when taken with its one hundred pages illustrating English scansion on the foot system, all useful for students.

"The Heart of the Matter" is book 1, chapter 6, "Rules of the Foot System" where principles of the system, as stated in the *Prosody*, appear in boldface. These include the constitution of the foot, the basis and limits of equivalence ("confusion of base must be avoided"), and the nature of rhyme; also included are discussions of pause and line arrangement, vowel music, and "fingering."

The *History* and the *Manual* are together a monument to his "narrowing reach," the concern with form above and beyond the matter as the climax in Saintsbury's lifelong love affair with poetry. Since he wrote them, poetry has moved out in many directions in both theory and practice, yet the *Concise Cambridge History of English Literature* (1970) still carries George Sampson's judgment that Saintsbury's histories of prosody and prose rhythm are "the standard and necessary treatises."[32] George Fraser likewise judged both the *History* and the *Manual* as "the greatest work in English on the subject."[33] Wellek and Warren, while welcoming the idea of such specialized works, dismissed Saintsbury's result as poor and arbitrary because of his "strange empiricism" and his failure to define his principles, a charge less justified here than in regard to his other works. Wellek regarded the meter and rhythm on which they were based, as "unclear and obsolete conventions" that vitiated the results.[34]

Harvey Gross, a more sympathetic American critic, found all the works on prosody "charmingly sensible" and "authoritative."[35] He valued Saintsbury's scansions as the product of a very good ear despite his "self-contradictory dogmatics," his occasional old-fashioned moralism, his "naive teleology," and a "minimum of formal preconception." On the more crucial question of the basic principle of scansion and Saintsbury's refusal to define "long" and "short" precisely while rejecting pure stress and classical quantity, like the present writer, Gross maintained that Saintsbury's ambiguity and flexibility are sound and desirable in such a controversial area. Gross noted that Saintsbury's method is supported theoretically by Wimsatt and Beardsley's brilliant essay, "The Concept of Metre,"[36] and is made timely by the revived use of scansion by contemporary prosodists and the return of many poets to foot scansion.[37]

Saintsbury found a place for and did justice to strong stress verse and vers libre though he insisted that the first, having shown no promise, "broke off" in the Middle Ages, and that the second is a hybrid lying somewhere between prose and poetry, at best leaning toward the latter. He accepted the innovations of Whitman and, later, of Hopkins; he could not have known those of Eliot or Pound when writing his Prosody; nor could he have foreseen the mingling of strong stress and syllabic stress meter that were to develop later. Like Eliot, he was certain that "the ghost of some simple metre should lurk behind the arras in even the 'freest' verse. . . . There is no escape from metre, there is only mastery."[38] As late as 1923 Saintsbury discussed free verse as a main feature of the previous two decades, and, while deploring the term free because he could not acknowledge any "slavery" in meter or rhyme, he admitted there is "room for a-metric and unrhymed but symphonically rhythmed verse and for hybrid forms between this and other forms" such as recently had been tried, an attitude that promised sympathy for future experiment.[39] Elsewhere he called free verse "the pretty and pleasing mistress" allowed to the poet whose true wife is metre.[40]

In Saintsbury's later years he did an occasional review on prosody as well as two papers for the British Academy, "The Historical Character of the English Lyric" in 1912, and "Some Recent Studies in English Prosody" in 1919.[41] Neither of these papers makes any new contribution and both suffer from a lack of specific references. Saintsbury also did the chapters on English prosody for the *Cambridge History of English Literature* (1907–16)—a standard source for several decades.

Some remarks within the *History of English Prosody* indicted that the narrowing reach was to extend its focus to prose. When Saintsbury found a "bastard rhythm," not quite prose or poetry, in Blake's later work, he suggested that Blake should be treated in a history of prose rhythm.[42] Whitman's free verse, which he terms a "hybrid" poetry-prose form, raised the same question but was dealt with grudgingly, then relegated to an appendix of the *Prose Rhythm* under the title "Stave-Prose Poetry—Ossian, Blake, Whitman, etc."[43] Saintsbury lived long enough to see this "debatable land which is much more poetic than prosaic" extend widely, but he still felt that it should be set off from prose because of the "constant observance of a definite 'stave-end,'" different from "the closes of clauses and sentences," making a paragraph of every versicle. He argued that such versicles cannot otherwise be paragraphed without blurring their best, most distinctive effect.[44]

In the preface to the *History of English Prose Rhythm,* Saintsbury said that the work carried out lines laid down a good deal earlier than those of the *History of Prosody.* Its tone is far more tentative and less dogmatic, and Saintsbury emphasizes its "entirely exploring and pioneering variety." It aimed "less to arrive at definite conclusions—still less to lay down a cut-and-dried system—than to give a rationalized survey of the facts" and to share his delight in them. Not finding any regular development in prose rhythm, he tries only to indicate "advances and changes in the proportion and character of the rhythm itself generally."[45] A wise choice of limits for an experiment that had no forerunner and no real successor, and one that was likely to command an audience even smaller than that for the *Prosody.* A few more limited studies have appeared since.[46] In 1928, Herbert Read stated that the study of prose rhythm was still "very much in its infancy" despite Saintsbury's "very complete and provocative history," and he approved of Saintsbury's refusal to classify those rhythms.[47]

Signposts along the road that Saintsbury traveled toward the *History of English Prose Rhythm* are his essay, "Modern English Prose" (1876), and the preface to *Specimens of English Prose* (1885), essays in which he does not use scansion. In the years between them he had systematized his ideas. His early view is expressed in an 1881 review: "*The differentia* of poetical rhythm is that it is metrical, of prose rhythm that it is not. Metrical prose is bastard prose; unmetrical poetry is not poetry at all."[48] Wrong and outdated as such a view now seems, it was his point of departure—reinforced by the words of Quintilian placed on the title page of the *History.* These views are reflected in the thirty-seven introductions he wrote for Henry Craik's *English Prose* (5 vols., 1890–96) and in all his works thereafter.

He says that he was stimulated by regular professional study of the remarks of Aristotle and Quintilian and others on prose rhythm and that his interest was focused early by Henry Mansel's Oxford lectures and sermons, the fine rhythms of which remained in his "memory's ear."[49]

Saintsbury assumed "the omnipresence, in speech and writing alike of at least the materials of rhythm, contrasted in a fashion which something like the *communis sensus* of Europe has agreed, until recently . . . to call 'long' and 'short.'" He set up four classifications, though typically he did this only after two-thirds of the book was finished: metrical and unmetrical poetry, "strictly rhythmical prose," "prose in which rhythm, though present, is subordinated to other considerations," and the "standard prose" dominant since the late eighteenth century. This last type, which should prevail in ninety-nine cases out of a hundred, scans only in sections (not feet) if analyzable at all. But for rhythmic prose, the "great law is that every syllable shall, as in poetry, have recognizable rhythmical value. A list of classical feet precedes his text. Prose feet may have up to five or even six syllables.[50] He is specially concerned with monosyllabic feet because of the great number of monosyllabic words in English. As in the *Prosody*, he often scans passages.

The most eloquent section of the *History of English Prose Rhythm* is that on the Authorized Version of the Bible. On its 300th anniversary in 1911, Saintsbury had written severely on the shortcomings of the Revised Version and of the educational system that by its inadequacies seems to make "journalized versions" necessary in every century—a practice he characterizes as "to meet dropsy by giving drink."[51] In the *History*, he exalts the 1611 King James Bible as "the best words of the best time of English, in the best order, on the best subjects."[52] By comparing the phrasing in the Vulgate, the Rheims, the Douai, the Geneva, the "Great," the "Bishop's," the Coverdale, and the Tyndale with the Revised Version of Isaiah 60:16–20, he illustrates "the polished perfection" of the Authorized Version. One sympathizes as he deplores the substitution of "love" for "charity" and the revision of "in a glass darkly," "one of the literary catchwords of the English language" in Corinthians I, 13:57. On aesthetic grounds, his position is almost unanswerable; other arguments for or against new translations are not relevant, given the stylistic basis of his judgment.

Saintsbury moves deftly among the other Renaissance peaks of the rhythmic landscape, offering great passages from Raleigh, Donne, Taylor, and Sir Thomas Browne, and praising all those triumphant voices of ornate prose that any reader might rejoice in. To the Latin influences—Attic or Ciceronian—he gives minimal consideration, believing that Latin cadences do not transfer to English.[53] In this earlier ornate prose and in that of his own time, Saintsbury faced the problem of rhythm so dominant as to distract attention from meaning. He praises the balance achieved in standard Georgian style, "the adjustment of cadence and the symphony of matter," and cites Southey as the most perfect example of this adjustment though he never really feared that the study of rhythm would detract from attention to meaning. He fully appreciated the "quietly exquisite" style of which Newman was one of the world's greatest masters, but his enthusiasm for the more ornate and flamboyant De Quincey, Ruskin, and Swinburne is infectious even if one wishes for stricter discrimination than he shows in handling their excess verbiage and rhapsodic flow.

Saintsbury did well to keep his handling brief, tentative, and as little systematized as he did. The scansion he uses to analyze prose rhythm is even more controversial than that in the *Prosody*. He is more rewarding in discussing other elements that contribute to the effects, and the questions themselves still afford illumination. The chief rewards of the volume are in suggestion, in the focusing of attention on the subject, and in the sharing of effects where his ear and his taste rarely go wrong. Charges of diffuseness brought with some justice against the *Prosody* bore fruit in the brevity here. For so special a matter as the work treats, the audience will always be small, but for that audience it still has value.

For his own prose, as always, Saintsbury makes no claims: "Cluvienus and myself" he cites as extreme examples of the clumsy and the awkward, and anticipating criticism, he repeats his lifelong plea, "You may criticize without being able to create."[54]

As Saintsbury carried his primary concern for form to its logical conclusion in these works on rhythm, he must have enjoyed the work as much as any he had ever done. For six or seven years his energy and literary feeling were absorbed in attention to the music of verse and prose and closely related stylistic elements while he was largely freed of the obligation to dwell on matter. While he enjoyed his work and believed it worth doing, he knew that such narrow concentration upon form would provoke further condemnation. Hence he makes self-conscious and defensive references to such criticism, as in the preface to *The Peace of the Augustans:* this book, he says, may escape the usual charge because with the "standardization" of form in its period it requires less attention to style than any other.

As late as 1926, Saintsbury expressed his pride in having championed the accentuation of the importance of treatment over mere subject for half a century. Such charges had always been made against him, including Pater's mild protest against "a tendency to regard style a little too independently of matter" in the 1880s and A. C. Bradley's more serious attack in 1901.[55] Saintsbury had said that, in Wordsworth's "Our noisy years seem moments in the being of the eternal silence," the poetic beauty was added and quite independent of its meaning though assisted by that meaning. Accusing Saintsbury of a lapse into "the heresy of the separable substance," Bradley generously assumed this to be a momentary confusion that reduced the substance of a poem *not* to its subject but rather to "a supposed invariable material."[56]

In *The History of Prosody*, Saintsbury foolishly picked up Bradley's challenge, then ten years old, thus proving that his statement had been no momentary lapse. He rephrased the Wordsworth line in clumsy prose: "Our loud-sounding (clamorous) twelve-months seem seconds (minutes) in the existence of the unending soundlessness," and argued that all the rest is what Wordsworth has added to the meaning.[57]

Later, in *The History of Prosody*, unregenerate in his extreme formalism, Saintsbury again made the simplistic kind of "separation" (one that he had used on Whitman thirty years earlier). Discussing William Morris's political verse, he dismisses the meaning as "mischievous rubbish" and embraces the form with the absurd suggestion:

What does meaning matter when you have . . . such verse as "A Death Song"? It must be a singularly feeble intellect and taste that cannot perform the easy dichotomy of metre and meaning . . . . You pour the poison or the ditchwater out; you keep, and marvel at, the golden cup. You can refill it, as far as meaning goes, at your pleasure with the greatest things . . . but you cannot make the cup. . . .[58]

Saintsbury had probably seen a remarkably close parallel to this odd notion in Swinburne's *Blake* in 1868.[59] Fifty years later he applies it to Swinburne's "Song in Time of Revolution." The matter he thinks is rubbish, the form superb, "and it is the form that is the poetry." Changing the matter would leave the poetry unchanged.[60] At the close of the *Prosody* he spells out his conviction more reasonably: "The formal part of English poetry . . . is to me the life of poetry—a life which, like other lives, is mysteriously and inextricably blended with other things, but which is still, in a way, separable."[61]

In 1924, he protested that few things surprised him more than "the objection of some who are *not* fools, to the separation of form and matter in literature." This principle, he goes on to insist, is "a necessary axiom of the study of Art, and especially Literature."[62] Examples of the principle applied are legion in his writing from the time when it emerged first in his early art-for-art's-sake crusade in reaction against Victorian subject worship.

This naively superficial view of form as separable deserves attention only because Saintsbury returned to it so often. He had not grasped or had forgotten that those he followed in exalting form did not espouse the separation except in a momentary exaggeration, such as Swinburne's in his *Blake*. Flaubert may have once aspired to write about nothing, but Gautier and Pater were equally firm on the reverse. For Flaubert, "C'est comme le corps et l'âme, la forme et l'idée; pour moi, c'est tout . . . un. . . . "[63] For Pater, in perfected art "the end is not distinct from the means, the form from the matter, the subject from the expression; they adhere in and completely saturate each other."[64] Saintsbury would have been saved from his heresy if he had adopted this more profound, more organic conception of the process of art, but he stopped short with the early Swinburne and failed to take warning even when Pater chided him.

His fear of the neglect of the way things are said even led Saintsbury in 1889 to challenge Pater's view that what distinguishes good from great art is not a matter of form and that great art must have "something of the soul of humanity in it," and must "find its place in the great structure of human life."[65] Saintsbury labeled this "hedging" and regretted it as a lapse, failing to recognize that, sixteen years after his *Studies in the History of the Renaissance,* Pater had worked out his carefully discriminated modification of ideas on which he had agreed with their master Flaubert.

Saintsbury, in the vast range of his writing, also "hedged" on the final question. He too admits that "the greatest poet must show the most knowledge of human nature."[66] In discussing Arnold, he concedes that though all does *not* depend upon the subject, yet of two poems equally good in other ways, that which has the better subject will be the better."[67] Unless Saintsbury, like Pater, had come to this sound view in practice he could not have been right as he usually is on the greatest writers. It is not for form alone that Aeschylus, Sophocles, Shakespeare, Dante, Milton, Donne, Swift, Spenser, and Shelley are for him supreme. One can only regret his inconsistency and his tendency to exaggerate and to seek refuge in separation when the marriage of form and content was not perfect.

During the first decade of this century, when he was most absorbed in his technical works, he occasionally looked back with some perspective on the early crusade. As the 1890s carried things beyond what his generation had intended or envisioned, he began to see that the doctrine of art-for-art's-sake was "half truth and half nonsense."[68] A decade later he commended Gautier because, in his defense, he had kept it within reasonable bounds.[69] Other of his qualifications have already been cited. But he never doubted that the doctrine had been needed as a reaction against subject worship and nineteenth-century "commercial and material tendencies." The protest, he argued in the *History of Criticism,* "must be allowed in the High Court of Historical Criticism."

In 1923, when he looked back at his long battle and his loyalty to such men as Baudelaire and Flaubert, he denied having neglected their matter and continued (echoing Flaubert): "Form *without* matter, art *without* life are inconceivable—or conceivable only like the jejune conceptions of mathematics. What we fought against when we carried the banner was the meddling and muddling of the two, the inability to distinguish them." He adds, "Let no one suppose that this danger is passed."[70] This retrospect, though weakened by a loose use of terms, does not cancel his more extreme statements or his contradictions. To remind "those who think of meaning and subject only" that there is something else in literature is, as he once said, not to be "a blasphemer of 'the subject' and a rebel to meaning," but he found himself sometimes not unfairly condemned as such.[71]

Over and over again, Saintsbury's vague use of terms causes confusion and defies analysis, as critics have complained. One is often not sure whether by form he means style in the most limited sense of sound, image, and word choice, style within the paragraph, or overall "artistic presentation." When this uncertain and shifting terminology joins with exaggeration (as it often does), is supported by his vaunted indifference to "general ideas," and is then linked with his belief in the "moment of transport" as the chief test of poetic effort, his formal bent becomes his greatest weakness with inevitable results. On the positive side, it led to his constant concern for artistry and careful workmanship and made him sensitive to carelessness, though his romantic temper made him likewise value spontaneity and fear "the smell of the lamp."[72] It gave us the *Prosody* and *Prose Rhythm* but it also led him to make vast claims for the power of artistic treatment, for example, "I have never given up the doctrine that *any* subject *may* be deprived of its repulsiveness by the treatment of it,"[73] a view he lived up to with respect to Rabelais but not to Zola.

In more restrained moods Saintsbury could warn against extreme formalism. He admitted that Hugo's exalting of form overlooked thousands of years of literary experience that shows that some subjects are "more difficult and thankless than others, that they are *practically* impossible."[74] His focus on form had other results. It is the reason that he exalted Shelley and Spenser above other poets and could not acknowledge Crabbe as a poet. As it dictated his preoccupation with sound and rhythm, it led to his neglect not only of philosophy, total design, and structure, but even of such formal matters as connotation, image, metaphor, verbal irony, and ambiguity. Since, for him, the ear is more important than the eye and more attended to than "the whole soul in activity," the phrase and the moment—"jewels five-words-long"—are overvalued.

Saintsbury's concern with form also motivated his three lectures on "the Grand Style."[75] He wrested the concept from Arnold to make it his own and developed it in the lectures on Dante, Milton, and Shakespeare that epitomize what Wellek calls Saintsbury's "radical formalism."

As Arnold defined it, "the Grand Style" was a high and special, rarefied thing, the "sublime" not in Longinus's broad sense of the term but as the eighteenth century narrowed it to mean exalted formal expression appropriate only to the highest, most serious, even exclusively religious matter. Focusing on Arnold's statement that "the Grand Style arises . . . *when a noble nature, poetically gifted treats with simplicity or with severity a serious subject*," Saintsbury argues that the term thus defined applies fully only to Dante, not to Milton or Shakespeare.[76] Appropriating the term and equating it with "the sublime" of Longinus as he saw it, he applies it in turn to each of the three masters.

To differentiate "the Grand Style" of Dante from that of the other two, Saintsbury cites "the inevitableness" of his phrasing; in Southey's terms, the expression is "necessary, voluptuous and right." There is "a quietness and confidence" in it and its rich allusiveness, its minute accurateness of detail, and the constant "suggestion of things not said" makes for total adequacy.[77] In Milton, he finds just one form of "the Grand Style" but one more fully sustained than in anyone else—"affectation transcendentalized and sublimed," the "consummateness-in-the-circumstances" of expression. Its sources include Milton's rich music, his use of names, the superb handling of word order, of apposition, of figures, of alliteration, and, above all, the "Miltonic vague."

Turning to Shakespeare, Saintsbury once more offers a fresh definition, broadening his term to include "perfection of expression in every direction and kind" to a degree that "transmutes the subject and transports the hearer or reader."[78] He emphasizes that such style cannot be continuous, noting as the differentia of Shakespeare his absolute command of such style coupled with a readiness not to use it when it is not required, what he calls Shakespearean ambidexterity.

Because Saintsbury widened the term Grand Style so much, these essays do not add any precision to his views of poetic style. But one need not agree with Wellek's view that the term, as Saintsbury uses it, "is merely another term for the poetic moment."[79] Saintsbury offers some fresh insights and an appreciation of the differences among the styles of the three masters at their best. On Shakespeare he is least satisfactory, largely because the term there becomes so all-embracing, but in all three lectures he leads the reader back to the poetry and relieves the phrase "Grand Style" of Arnold's narrow and moralistic sense.

Saintsbury gave one more evidence of his "narrowing reach" in his editing of *The Minor Poets of the Caroline Period*, a task begun while he was still at work on his massive surveys. Planned in two volumes and extended at his request to three by the generosity of the Oxford University Press Delegates, it contained the verse of seventeen minor poets—and a list of nine others he was forced to jettison. Of their importance to the understanding of English literature, Saintsbury had no doubt: "Neglect of minorities is a serious, and may be a fatal mistake," he says in the introduction while recalling afresh that Arnold, Mérimée, and Goethe all had disparaged the study of minor writers. The student and the reader need to know the evidence at first hand; they need to see the enjambment, the "unbridled overlapping" lines in their blank verse, the typical Caroline cadences and the aureate diction, their indulgence in "familiar and slovenly forms of speech and the games they played." All this they need in order to correct, at one extreme, the "determinism of the Taine school" and, at the other, that individualism that refuses to "look at filiations and groups and *milieux* at all." Only by knowing such things is the student turned into "a scholar who can appreciate, and a lover who can understand."

Wellek rightly points out that Saintsbury's appreciation of the baroque in Donne and the other Metaphysicals accounts for this work that, as Saintsbury explains it, deals with the metaphysical run to seed.[80] He wished to provide for others those minor sources of poetic pleasure that he so much enjoyed and that were not readily available. This pleasure, mainly a formal one, is evident in his brief introductions to the individual poets. William Chamberlayne's appeal is "for those who enjoy 'the poetic moment,' the 'single-instant pleasure' of image and phrase and musical accompaniment of sound." Sir Francis Kynaston gives intense "poignancy, that ever-repeated pang of peculiar pleasure . . . fanciful, metaphysical, conceited, decadent, what you will; but . . . intensely and essentially poetic." Sidney Godolphin "wears the Caroline rue with a more than sufficient difference," and within his narrow range, John Cleveland ("he knew no mood but abuse") seemed to Saintsbury "a curious and memorable figure"—one who "was . . . what he satirized in a literary way" and who "caricatured himself," not intentionally perhaps. Henry King's "Tell me no more" is "faultless and perfect," embodying "the Caroline essence."[81]

Though eager to share all his enthusiasms, Saintsbury resisted the temptation to write at length. Even so, the first two volumes of *The Minor Caroline Poets* appeared in 1905 and 1906, but the third was delayed until 1921. Because of eyestrain he gave up modernizing the spelling and extensive revising of the text and sought the help of Percy Simpson and G. Thorn-Drury, who did more with *apparatus criticus* and comparison of manuscripts than he had planned. He undertook this large task at Edinburgh because he believed a person in his position "should ... do something, in unremunerative and unpopular ways, to make the treasure of English literature more easily accessible."[82] Because poor eyesight had prevented his studying paleography, he planned to use only printed sources, but it proved difficult to find copies of the poems that could be used for printing.

This vast project does not meet modern standards of editing. It predated Grierson's Donne, that 1912 landmark of literary editing and a model for all editors of sixteenth- and seventeenth-century poets. Saintsbury not only lacked training in paleography but, as the Scott-Saintsbury Dryden had painfully demonstrated, his was not a temperament that could produce thorough or precise editing. In establishing his texts, he usually relied on the last edition published in a poet's lifetime, and any collating of editions or manuscripts was casual or nonexistent.

Nevertheless, *The Minor Poets of the Caroline Period*, unlike the Scott-Saintsbury Dryden, was not a waste of scholarly and critical energies. It filled an important gap by providing texts for a group of poets who were condemned by conventional nineteenth-century taste, few of whom have been edited since. The attitude of the modern editors of Cleveland—Brian Morris and Eleanor Withington—realistically offers a sensible and sound reaction to Saintsbury's work. They grant the limitations of earlier editing, as anyone must. Acknowledging the debt all editors owe to Saintsbury, they express their intention only "to continue and elaborate the work so well begun by their predecessors."[83]

This last, specialized product of Saintsbury's formalism still stands as a respected and substantial contribution to literary scholarship, probably worth the vast labor put into it. Had Saintsbury's concern for subject been greater, the task would have been less congenial.

He was able to dispose of the imitative quality of much of the material with a sane and good-humored comment on plagiarism hunting as "only one degree higher than worrying cats."[84] He did not overestimate these lesser figures; he points out their weaknesses, but his unfailing responsiveness to poetic quality made him alert to their individuality, their representativeness, and their historical significance. The work remains a treasury for those who enjoy the odd corners of literature. It may still set them exploring, as Helen Waddell was inspired to do.

Saintsbury, in his "sober academic role," in the twenty years between 1895 and 1915, carried his most obsessive lifelong convictions to their ultimate conclusions: in one direction, literary omniscience widened to embrace all Western European literature while moving away from the writer and the text to criticize the critics and map out their history; in the other direction, preoccupation with form narrowed to focus on rhythm—proving him a true worshiper of "the Goddess Prosodia."[85] Pioneering in both areas, he became more his own kind of critic-historian, just when he was enjoying a reputation as a major figure in English criticism. The scene would change with new writers, the New Criticism, semiotics, structuralism, feminism, Marxism, political and ethnic concerns, new theories of history, and new intensive methods of scholarship and editing, but these vast works, flawed and inevitably dated, pointed the way. They stand as a challenge, and some of them have not been superseded. Widening and narrowing the focus of his interest, they reflect the conflicting impulses native to his temperament.

CHAPTER 15

Other Writing, 1895–1920

Though Churton Collins continued his dissenting note until his death in 1907, the public grew accustomed to hearing of Saintsbury as a leader of criticism,[1] or as Arthur Waugh put it in 1896, as "the soundest, most authoritative, and most just critic among our contemporaries," adding that his reputation had been established "almost exclusively as a reviewer." He regarded omniscience as Saintsbury's "foible" but rejoiced that Edinburgh had freed him from too much miscellaneous editing.[2] Dobson reminded Saintsbury in 1896 that reviews of *Nineteenth-Century Literature* were good considering how many men had their knives out for him.[3] Complaints continued in the *Academy* and the *Saturday Review* regarding his art-for-art's-sake leanings;[4] "'Parnassian' rejection of everything in literature but its technique," the *Saturday* reviewer (probably Collins) muttered in 1904.[5] In 1912, Irving Babbitt declared Saintsbury to be "almost the official critic of England" though he could not rejoice in the fact, and in 1916, Robert Lynd referred to Gosse and Saintsbury as "the two kings of Sparta among English critics of today."[6] Meanwhile, as John Gross points out, in 1900, "Mr. Balfour let slip a complimentary reference in his Romanes lecture, Lord Morley paid tribute in his presidential address to the English Association," and Saintsbury was fair to becoming "the doyen of academic critics, the nearest thing to a Critic Laureate."[7]

Few universities that put a premium upon the publishing side of a professor's labors have ever gotten better value. Saintsbury once admitted, "I don't consider books 'grind.'"[8] While doing the big books he continued editing, did some periodical writing, and contributed to such works as Chambers's *Encyclopedia of Social England,* and the *Cambridge History of English Literature.*

During the early 1890s Saintsbury dabbled in the flourishing arena of literary popularizers headed by Robertson Nicoll and his *British*

Weekly. He wrote for Clement Shorter in the *Illustrated London News* (1892–95) and did a few short pieces for *Atalanta,* Mrs. Meade's magazine for girls, and for the *Minster* in 1895. In 1901, he wrote the section on English literature for the special issue of the *Illustrated London News* that commemorated Victoria's reign and Edward VII's accession. In his last two years at Edinburgh he wrote eight essays for the short-lived *Everyman,* a magazine that aimed to "make the man in the street realize what... makes a particular book a permanent classic."9

Saintsbury had a number of writing commitments when he arrived in Edinburgh: he had finished the editing of Balzac and Smollett for Dent, but the Sterne and Peacock were still in process; the *English Literature of the Nineteenth Century* was in proof; and he was at work on the *Periods of European Literature* and the *History of Criticism*—more than enough for one full-time professor for decades. Other books already discussed followed quickly: twenty-two volumes in twenty years done by the occupant of the Edinburgh Chair of Rhetoric who typed with one finger of one hand.

The English Novel, in the Channels of English Literature series, is brief, student-oriented, and casual in tone. It rapidly traces "principles of development." He claims to be the first to use such a focus to give his work structure and notes the lack of any other complete handling of the subject: Dunlop stopped too soon, Lanier is sketchy, and Sir Walter Raleigh stopped with Jane Austen.10 Bradford Booth accurately evaluated his attempt in 1964: "Saintsbury ... opened no new approaches and advanced few ideas that would have surprised David Masson or Frederic Harrison... the work is darkened by plot summaries and the enumeration of beauties." Saintsbury had none of the claims to pioneering that Walter Besant or Henry James, with his *Art of Fiction* (1884), had. The change from Victorian "appreciation" to modern, disciplined critical evaluation was, as Booth correctly sees it, the work of James, "who penetrated beyond plot and characters into meaning and the artful techniques by which meaning can be conveyed through the subleties of suggestion and indirection."11

Saintsbury's views of fiction remained largely traditional and not well defined. Since he made no advance on his earlier handling of fiction, this survey is less important than his prefaces and essays. His innovations lay only in his concern with minor novelists. Even Booth omits Borrow, Peacock, Henry Kingsley, Robert Louis Stevenson, and others with whom Saintsbury dealt. No one would have deplored the omission more than he, but he persuaded no one.

His methods and values are all familiar. Looking at the beginnings of fiction, Saintsbury points out story and character interest where they first emerge and finds in every romance "the germ of a novel and more" and "at least the suggestion and possibility of romance in every novel that deserves the name." In *Pilgrim's Progress*, Saintsbury finds "the romance interest of quest, adventure, achievement ... the pure novel interest of character and conversation," vivid and sufficient scene painting and setting. But he hails Defoe and Swift as the first in English to have the true "knack of *absorbing* the reader—the knack of telling a story." Thus typically, Saintsbury refuses to go beyond interest and absorbing to define the grip of good fiction. Again he points to the blending of the novel and romance in Scott, in the Brontës and Dickens, in Blackmore's *Lorna Doone,* and the later Stevenson.

Few praised Jane Austen more highly than Saintsbury; few will praise Scott as fully, but most critics will more readily accept his evaluation of Austen and her consummate irony. In Scott, he continues to confuse intention and influence with the total quality of the novels. As always he is disproportionately severe on Dickens's faults and his praise for Thackeray is supported by little analysis. He overpraises Bulwer, neglects the Brontës, and assumes the reader has read it all.

Succeeding chapters show a loss of perspective, a less firm grasp, and errors of judgment appear as in his other histories; he portrays a kind of decay in the novel delayed only by the appearance of Hardy and Meredith—this in 1913.[12] When he complains, "there ought to be no need of sitting down before the thing with tools and dynamite like burglars at a safe.... It is the first duty of the novelist 'to let himself be read'—anything else ... is a bonus, a trimming, a dessert ..." one knows the moderns he has in mind.

In conclusion, Saintsbury again spells out his hedonistic priorities: " ... the proof of the art of the novelist is that—at first hand or very shortly—he 'enfists,' absorbs, delights you. You may discover secrets of his art afterward with much pleasure and profit." He valued as the greatest gift of novelists that of "conceiving and projecting character." Characters must be capable of being loved, hated, admired, or despised, "lived with" in short.[13] Thackeray's Barnes Newcome we can both enjoy and detest and we need not psychoanalyze him. Saintsbury is happiest with the inner life revealed only through the largely external means used by the great classic realists—omniscient description and comment, soliloquy, the epistolary mode, or irony. He failed to recognize how far the Brontës, Dickens, even Thackeray had carried the revealing of consciousness and its ambiguities, and such revelation in George Eliot and Meredith made him uncomfortable. He ignored the symbolism in *Bleak House* and elsewhere as well as the many flashes of psychological insight in the later Dickens that are now valued most. He underrated both *Wuthering Heights* and *Middlemarch*, preferring *Jane Eyre*, *Silas Marner*, and *The Mill on the Floss*, as we might expect. All this reflects his fear of any deep exploration of "the buried life." He was not ready for James's sublety or his concern with point of view or for the advances in inwardness he met in Dostoyevski and elsewhere. As a whole, the volume is pedestrian and outdated.

Saintsbury draws on his experience as a schoolmaster and professor in his *First Book of English Literature* (1914) and on the practice he had had in his *Primer of French Literature*. Recalling errors made by examinees, he insists on an early grasp of a "mind map" but also of details—names, dates, versification, and diction. He intends to be "as little as possible quotable!" His aim is "to teach them how to read," though not in the analytical way a modern reader has come to expect. He offers an outline of literary development but minimizes political and social matter. And he concludes: "For the history of literature is the history of expression."[14] The beginner, he says, needs to know about but not to read until later such things as *Gammer Gurton's Needle* or *Gorboduc*.

One doubts that a page on Shakespeare should have been sacrificed to ruling the Baconians firmly out of court, but the new Elizabethan note of intensity and universal curiosity is well defined by references to the personality and subjects of Marlowe. Dryden is convincingly presented as "the central hinge on which the new framework of English literature turns."[15] As always, the crowded later pages on the Victorians are less happy and the generalizations somewhat misleading.

One novel feature of this primer is the description of a typical English library of each period (1066, 1400, 1577, 1600, 1660, and "a little before 1800"), a novel device that gives perspective. Beginning students, though they had to look elsewhere for substantive comment on ideas or on the structure of larger works and for other estimates of major figures to set against Saintsbury's more eccentric ones (e.g. negative on Milton and Wordsworth, very positive on Shelley), would have come away with a brief "mind map," and an alertness to forms of versification and to the developing qualities and various levels of poetic and prose style. They might have gained some eagerness to sample Langland, the romances, Spenser, and Swift—and would not feel talked down to. The style is clear, lively, economical and not heavily allusive. Finally, Saintsbury's hints about differences of judgment among critics should have stimulated them to make up their own minds—something Saintsbury hoped for in his Edinburgh students.

In October, 1915, Saintsbury wrote a preface for his *Peace of the Augustans: A Survey of Eighteenth-Century Literature as a Place of Rest and Refreshment*. With the unifying focus expressed in the subtitle, he hoped the work would attract the general reader. Taking "a literary hedonist" point of view, he planned a guidebook to those pleasures of "the Middle Paradise" that are typical of the eighteenth century. He promised attention to "matter and thought and temperament" more than to form. He applied to the whole century an attitude he believed that Thackeray, Dobson and Besant had taken toward parts of it. He hoped to offset the indifference, even denigration, the "taking-for-granted" attitude toward this literature that he thought had been dominant since 1800. He wanted to foster understanding and appreciation of its virtues, to give access to its quiet, not too intense or too involving pleasures (what it gives us, not what it enjoyed), and, thus in this "haunt of peace," to offer rest and refreshment to both intellect and feelings, and by its contrast to the present to serve as an alterative or specific for our "modern measles."

Written in the first years of World War I, the work makes almost no reference to it and none to Saintsbury's decision to retire. Yet the choice of the Augustan era for its sense of order and measure, its restraint, and what Saintsbury thinks is its "curiously pervading good nature" expresses a weariness and a real need to retreat from the present. He complains of too much fuss, whining, rotting, and effeminacy. His alienation from the world of the previous forty years is clear, despite the warm, intimate, lively sharing of what he treats. The work is selective in terms of its theme, not exhaustive like his other surveys. Burke and Blake are not discussed for different reasons: Burke offers little to the Tory author that rests and refreshes, while Blake has escaped "the Happy Valley" of Rasselas and possesses those supreme qualities of wonder, dream, and the sublime lacking in the eighteenth century but present for Saintsbury in the greatest literature. The selection and the omissions along with the recommendations for how and when to skip in order to avoid the boring in such collections as Chalmers's forty volumes of British *Essayists* and the ten volumes of Dodsley's *Poets* help to emphasize literature's power to amuse and divert, and to refresh at various levels.

The impressionist critic prevails over the historian as Saintsbury defines the virtues of individual works, praises, compares at length in his usual plus and minus fashion, and then judges. In its relaxed, conversational yet enthusiastic tone as well as in method it epitomizes his critical style and perhaps best illustrates what gave it its appeal. It became popular probably because he shares his pleasure and justified it in eloquent passages—notably on Swift, Walpole, and Collins, and in less predictable ones such as that on "the triumph of technique" in Pope, his minority report on Dr. Johnson's letter to Chesterfield, or his description of Lady Mary Wortley Montagu's verse as "flashing with the very best paste in Dodsley."

He shares his amusement at the "staple literary refreshment stall" of the novelists with a fresh zest and repeats little of what he had said elsewhere. He again analyzes the special delights of the four masters, Richardson, Fielding, Smollett, and Sterne, because he feels that they had been neglected by the twentieth century. He tempts the reader to seek out Amory, Graves, and a few minor women novelists of the later 1700s, but he warns against many others who belong on the rubbish heap. He reminds his reader that the novel did not begin here, and that Esdaile's *Catalogue of English Tales and Romances Before 1740* runs to well over three hundred pages, much of it in translation.

Among the poets, he gives Collins much space, pointing up his strengths and weaknesses and quoting passages that "you can murmur to yourself for luxury and consolation." He wants Percy's *Reliques* to be read intact and uncluttered by scholarly notes so that the reader may share the excitement of the 1765 reader over the novelties of this great "mishmash." Similarly, Chatterton's Rowley poems are to be read with the original weird spellings (they are essential to his aim and fool no one), not in Skeat's modernization, and the critical reader should study Warton's *History of English Poetry*, preferably in the original. All this in order to get some feel of the century's mind. He deplores reliance on anthologies where bits and pieces are "cut and dried and tinned," though he does not push his read-everything dictum here as he does elsewhere. You may avoid the boring minor poets and novelists on this trip.

Low-key and "middling" as many of these pleasures are, Saintsbury nowhere wrote more eloquently of Swift. The rest and refreshment he offers, both intellectual and spiritual, are profound, and Saintsbury's insight is deep and true. The greatest of his century, and in English literature, second only to Shakespeare, Swift is for him a voice of genius with passion, love, humor, yet "always quiet" even in its most terrific satirical truth and sardonic strength. In his variety and great range of interest for both child and man he "never wearies." A critic, Saintsbury says here, must adjust the judging to the liking. On Swift he does it triumphantly, and any reader should be better attuned to the Dean after this eloquent introduction whatever more he may ask. There are illuminating passages on the Yahoo in every man, a fine analysis of *Jonathan Wild,* and a moving comment on the *Journal to Stella* with its lines on "Only a woman's hair." This last went into the *Oxford Book of English Prose.*

On Dr. Johnson, Saintsbury is less rewarding. He assumes too much knowledge on the part of the reader as, without citations, he prescribes Johnson's wisdom and wit as a cure for the ills of the twentieth century. On these ills he is specific and biased: pose, self-conceit, contempt for the lessons of history, fads, affectations, "paradox and mirage," crankery and quackery, all to be offset by escape into the common sense of the earlier period. He pauses to argue, at too great length, against the "myth of Grub Street" fostered by Pope's spite and crystallized in Macaulay, contending reasonably that the early journalistic and publishing world generally rewarded those who really worked, including Johnson, and was not responsible for Johnson's misfortunes.

The alienation from his own world that erupts a number of times in Saintsbury's *Peace of Augustans* is in line with his increasing rejection of that world already noted in the forty years of his maturity and his whole professional life. He had been making such charges and had rejected new writers and movements since he first came to London as an adult. Whatever appeal this Augustan "Peace" had for many in the grim war years, his querulous attitude could not have attracted younger readers. Anyone who knew the life of the trenches and the casualty lists of 1914–18 must have resented being told that the earlier century was "a school that bred *men*," an age that "could play the game and face the music, and win a victory without crowing too much, and take a beating without whining at all." It is shocking even today and mars an otherwise fine work that won many readers and can still lure readers into the literature it celebrates. One may overlook the complaints and still wonder how he could so distance himself from the terrible toll of that war. But the habit of evasion was very strong, and he gives no evidence of ever having grieved over the dead.

Though Saintsbury hoped to appeal to the general reader, he says that the book was addressed to "the gentle chosen ones." He also told Helen Waddell he wrote for her, especially, the sections on Swift, the footnotes on the Duchess of Queensbury and *Polite Conversation*, parts of the Thralia, touches in the pages on Prior, and a passage on the poetry of Gray.[16] He enjoyed it all, one can be sure, and he proved himself able to write well about the Augustan literary world with a new slant despite his lifelong devotion to lyric and romance.

Saintsbury's unsympathetic attitude toward his age was fast hardening. It bursts out often in letters to William Hunt, himself an archconservative. Asquith, Lloyd George, Woodrow Wilson, and Winston Churchill all get their share of the verbal whiplash that Gladstone had suffered earlier. Saintsbury wrote fairly often to the *Times* and projected longer articles that were not accepted. Gavin understandably refused one for the *Observer* on current events in 1917, and Blackwood discouraged him on current topics he proposed soon after leaving Edinburgh. Saintsbury told Hunt that when Northcliffe took over the *Times*, they shut its doors to his letters. Fortunately he turned his waning energies to more congenial tasks, and his next work, *The French Novel*, shares the positive virtues of *The Peace of the Augustans*.

The war contributed to the difficulties of retiring just as it had conditioned his view of the eighteenth century in *The Peace of the Augustans*, which was published before he left Edinburgh. At sixty-nine, tired and ill, he was more ready for retirement psychologically than he liked to admit. Yet he was already planning new projects, including the two-volume *History of the French Novel*, his last major work. In 1912 he had predicted to Hunt that *The History of Prose Rhythm* would be his last book, but the compulsion was too strong, and he continued to write until his very last month. This fact makes more poignant his reports in the 1920s of finally, with regret, having to refuse requests for articles and prefaces.

Except for *The French Novel,* what Saintsbury wrote on French literature proper after 1900 is almost wholly on writers who wrote before 1870. This was fortunate, considering the way his mind had closed to new developments. He edited Mérimée and the plays of Molière and delivered the Taylorian Lecture in 1904 on Gautier; he wrote a preface for Rabelais and reviewed some works on Balzac. In *The Later Nineteenth Century,* he was cavalier on the writers of the 1890s and in the *History of Criticism* he ignored them. Rewriting his survey of French literature for the *Britannica* in 1909–10, he called Verlaine the greatest poet of the past half-century, "with wonderful command of sound and image-suggestion," Mallarmé a "true poet in his way" but "the victim of pose and trick," and Villiers de L'Isle Adam eccentric but with "a spark of genius." Rimbaud is ignored.

Written in retirement without the pressures of academic or editorial status, *The French Novel* allowed Saintsbury to discuss most writers at greater length than he had done before, while giving free rein to personal opinion and prejudice. A pleasant record of his lifelong devotion to French fiction, it also contains a reappraisal of some of the novelists. There are too generous plot summaries, some lively interpretation, and some notable passages, such as the long, eloquent chapter on Rabelais, where he parallels earlier tributes with a fresh assessment. These are worth reading today. His own library had been dispersed and he was living in Bath, away from the resources of London and Edinburgh, but he made a great effort to reread much of this fiction. Being rereadable had always been an important standard of judgment for him; he now tests it and notes the results. Comparison to English works seems more frequent than earlier.

Three-quarters of the first volume is concerned chiefly with romance. He inadvertently omits Marie de France and protests the recent exalting of Chrétien de Troyes but does justice to the Vulgate Arthur. On the *Heptaméron* he is less good than in the earlier preface. He gives more credit to Despériers than previously and adds a long enthusiastic footnote on a forerunner, Hélesenne de Crenne. He justifies his too extensive handling of *Le Grand Cyrus, l'Astreé,* and the *Cabinet des Feés,* by claiming they were "the seedbed of the novel," but he admits they are better taken at second hand by most readers. In the preface he promised to keep to the "principal things," but he could not resist the temptation to share lesser figures and gives them too much space: for example, too much on Crébillon fils and Hamilton, who, with all their license, create "the most elegant scandal in the world," too much on Pigault-Lebrun because he was the French "novelist-tradesman who first made novel writing a business," too much on Paul de Koch and Alexandre Dumas fils (whose synthesizing of character was in accord with the theory he condemns), too much on Hugo, almost all negative because he thought Hugo contributed nothing to the art of the novel.

Surprisingly for Saintsbury, he shows critical strength in his reworked treatment of Flaubert, Zola, and Maupassant. His effort to repeat as little as possible is successful as he adds new insights and "corrected impressions," and offers some sound judgments still deserving attention. He recognizes the artist and the genius in all three. Mrs. Grundy is looking over his shoulder as always, but he manages to put the grime, the obstetrics, the boring adulteries, the floods of technical detail, and other repulsive ugliness out of mind. Forgetting the theories he thought wrong, he does Flaubert fresh justice and admits the value of Zola's practice where, for him, it came right as in the Blake-Turneresque nightmare scenes of *Travail*. He acknowledges Maupassant's power to "sublime" repulsiveness by the force of art comic, tragic, or romantic and to create vignettes of great power. Despite all his earlier grumbling and his distaste for naturalism, his capacity to respond to great artistry triumphs. Unfortunately, this success did not include any more adequate treatment of Stendhal or prevent his damning of Laclos. Wellek regards the two volumes as Saintsbury's best historical work,[17] and T. S. Eliot praised it; few critics otherwise have rated it so highly, but most readers enjoy the enthusiasm and liveliness of the work.

Looking at Saintsbury's work on French literature as a whole, it is best to estimate him by his positive contributions rather than belabor the older generation, as is too easily done. Inspired by Arnold, he was the first systematic interpreter in English of *all* French literature for a generation who had no other such English source. Ruth Temple argues that, unlike Gosse, he assumed too much knowledge of French literature in his readers and so may have reached a less wide audience.[18] The historical surveys and the *Encyclopedia* articles, even the *Essays on French Novelists* with their large proportion of fact and summary and their enthusiastic appreciation do not support this argument; nor does his reviewing or editing. Apart from the new verse and fiction of the last decades of the century, Saintsbury was everywhere among French writers before 1890 dealing with the classic, the middling, and the trash, with the permanent and the wholly perishable. The sheer volume of his writing must have worked its influence. Despite his prejudice against the naturalists, in range he had no competitor in English. He could be eloquent and persuasive, and his enthusiasm has a contagious quality. The French government would have done well to recognize his as a service of wider range than Gosse's and of comparable value. He deserved and never received honors such as Gosse courted and won. The tribute of the *Mercure de France* obituary stands alone as grateful recognition—too little and too late.[19] Fortunately, Saintsbury seems not to have looked for such recognition. Gosse embraced contemporary vogues well into the twentieth century; Saintsbury did not—a real defect in a critic and historian. Yet the effects of Saintsbury's work may have been as great as that of Gosse, since popularizing French literature among an audience in England beyond that to which a Sainte-Beuve or a Saintsbury spoke was a dubious task at best.

John Gross damns Saintsbury for his "refusal to learn" about the literary future as he saw it in the making. But Saintsbury knew the facts of older French literature well and understood its importance for the English reader. Even Gross recalls that Arnold praised him for insisting upon the importance of those facts.[20]

According to a Hunt letter of 1918,[21] there was some talk of Saintsbury's being named to the Oxford Chair of French Literature. It was too late for that, but his surveys have been reissued and are not wholly replaced, while the dust has settled on Gosse's essays and Symons, unfortunately, is largely out of print. Saintsbury's failure to move with the age was a serious limitation, but he offered his age much of French literature for its intrinsic worth and because he believed it is "the best suited to qualify the study of our own, correct it, and preserve it from flaws and corruptions."[22] He built a cultural bridge and a foundation for responses to literature he could not enjoy, and, in so doing, more than anyone else he fulfilled Arnold's expressed hope for increased attention to French literature. For writers later than Flaubert, the balance would have to be redressed by younger critics led by Symons, Pound, and Eliot.

On another French art, wine making, Saintsbury did not falter. "Saintsbury is in this matter of Burgundy, so profound, of such high Bacchic smack of discernment, that upon my word, we cannot exclude him." Thus George Meredith, in 1883, was an early voice in a long line of wine connoisseurs who have reveled in the author of the *Notes on a Cellar Book*.[23] Some of them had probably shared wine talk with him at the Savile Club and elsewhere. On March 28, 1920, Saintsbury wrote Dobson (a teetotaler), "I am writing a wicked little book on wines," and Dobson replied, "I find in it more meat than drink! I am delighted with the autobiographical touches that sparkle through it . . . full of good things, it impresses me as always with old wonder at your range and variety."[24] The slim volume, concluded at Bath on Easter, 1920, was a substitute for the larger *History of Wine* that Macmillan had requested and Saintsbury had long wanted to write.[25] Much to his regret he no longer had the energy or the research facilities for this undertaking, though he had preserved his notes from fifty years of study and enjoyment of wines and other spirits (their kinds, their merits, and their innumerable, world-ranging associations in life and literature, in history, and in society).

The smaller work, based on the personal cellar book he kept from 1884 to 1915, is a running commentary ranging from sherry, Madeira, and port through the French and German light wines, to spirits, liqueurs, beer, cider, and "mixed liquors" (chiefly punches and cups), "Bottles and Glasses," "Cellar Arrangements," and some fifteen menus.[26] Calling himself an amateur, he hopes that "a little preciseness" may help this "ghastly thinfaced time of ours" beset by Pussyfoot and teetotal movements and by the spectre of Volstead and U.S Prohibition. Of the liquors recorded over the half-century, he says:

> They pleased my senses, cheered my spirits, improved my moral and intellectual powers, besides enabling me to confer the same benefits on other people . . . the grapes that yielded them were the fruit of that Tree of Knowledge which . . . it became not merely lawful but incumbent on us to use with discernment.

The book began as a series of articles requested by a short-lived periodical, the *Piccadilly Review*. When the *Review* expired, two chapters had been published and four more were in its "dying hand"; all were restored to the author to go into the book.

Valued most by the connoisseurs of wine and spirits, this account of a lifelong devotion to Bacchus is embroidered with personal crotchets, a host of literary allusions, and warm nostalgic associations. Here is the boy who learned his first wine lore from his father, with whom he shared "the almost intellectual as well as sensual interest of wine." The boy carried his interest and knowledge to Oxford but bought his wines from a London friend of his father. From Guernsey years, he recalls his first acquaintance with Hollands, the "exceedingly grateful comforting" taste of *vin brulé* on Christmas and the New Year, and a rich and inexpensive variety of wines. At Elgin he was introduced to whiskys direct from the distilleries, unblended and so good they spoiled his taste for brands later available elsewhere.

Holiday trips yielded memories of whisky and milk on Skye, the newest of ales (but delicious) at St. Davids, the fresh ciders of Devon and Somerset sampled on early walking tours, the best genuine hock he had ever drunk (at Kings Lynn), a light porter drunk at the foot of Rosebery Topping in Yorkshire out of big stone bottles like champagne magnums, white whisky drunk only at the hospitable Ulster Club in Belfast, and his own punch known as "*Saturday Review* cup."[27] The occasional rumble of his disgust with "Pussyfoots," Prohibition in the United States and temperance advocates is matched by his dismay when he learned, in 1920, that no Oxford college any longer brewed beer within its walls.

Saintsbury describes the *Cellar Book* as paying his literary respects to Dionysius as he had done all his life to Apollo. He is celebrating both the pleasures he had had and "the state of well-being and capability for well-doing that alcohol induces." In its pages, wine taster and literateur are never far apart in parallels, associations, and the intermingling and interplay of the two. Critics have often seen Saintsbury's literary criticism as a kind of wine tasting, a savoring of poetical effects very like his enjoyment of the bouquet and flavor of wine, sometimes even cast in the language of the lover of the grape. Examples are easy to find. Perhaps the most extreme is his reference to Sterne as a liqueur, *not* "the good strong Ale, and generous Port, and subtly flavored Claret and wisdom-giving Amontillado, and inspiring Champagne and ineffable Burgundy of Fielding and Scott and Miss Austen and Dickens and Thackeray and other great novelists."[28] The reader is left to sort out which is which in this one of the many flowing lists he could not resist.

The Cellar Book offers similar comparisons and associations. The good clarets of 1888 and 1889 remind him of Browning's "A Pretty Woman." The red wines of the south of France are "Hugonic in character" and congenial to Hugo's novels. Sparkling Moselle is the more pleasurable because Ausonius celebrated it fifteen hundred years ago. But Marsala fails to inspire his enthusiasm "in spite of all the literary and historical associations of Sicily from Theocritus to Nelson."

Saintsbury's first wine was Marsala, and he tasted a 1790 brandy before his father's death in 1859. The sale of his Edinburgh cellar in wartime he termed "a disaster," but he gallantly drank a toast to it. Because his steady, large consumption of liquor was just about over by 1915, his later reports are almost all reminiscence and the associations with persons, places, and, above all, with literature are part of the remembered experiences. As associations enhanced the pleasure of the moment, allusion preserves it. He never missed or forgot a writer's reference to drinking, personal or fictional. Scott, Lamb, Hazlitt, Peacock, Thackeray, Marryat, Dr. Campbell and his thirteen bottles drunk at a sitting, Mr. Pickwick with his beloved hot brandy and water, and many others jostle each other in the pages of the *Cellar Book,* and such references are frequent in all his other works as well.

The methods that Saintsbury employs to criticize wine and spirits often resemble those in his literary works. He constantly compares and ranks the bouquet, the taste and flavor and texture of vintages and defines various types of liquor by their differences. Port strengthens and gladdens as no other wine can do, but it lacks "the feminine grace and charm of Claret, the immediate inspiration of Champagne, the transcendental qualities of Burgundy and Madeira." How he loved such lists, whether of critics, poets, or wines.

Just as he wanted to read everything and could find pleasure in minor and second-rate writers, so with wine and spirits he wanted to know them all, always exploring and experimenting, filling out a mind map. He spoke once of knowing fifty or sixty kinds of port, and the pleasures of rereading are matched by the repeated enjoyment of good wine and whisky. One might even see a parallel between his pleasure in the details of literary history and prosody and the friendships he had with merchants such as the Harveys of Bristol, with whom he shared knowledge and judgments. As readers have asked how did he read so much, one may wonder how all the time spent building, stocking, and keeping his generous cellars fitted into his strenuous life. He read so much, wrote so much, drank so much, he deserved the title he cherished from the address on a cask of Bass's ale, "Mr. George Saintsbury. Full to the bung." As one reads of the Rabelaisian quantity and variety of his drinking throughout the days and evenings—wines, beer, ale, whiskey, rum and gin, liqueurs, punches, flips, cups, and bedtime toddies—one must marvel that he functioned so well and so long.

The pleasures of alcohol are both intellectual and sensual, Saintsbury asserted several times. In his more than seventy-five years' experience they were also certainly emotional and imaginative. One must sip and savor slowly, never gulp, fingering the stem of the glass (therefore stemmed wines are best), meditating on the "wine moment" as one does on the "poetic moment." The idea of wine simply as a thirst quencher he rejected out of hand. No good wine should be used for that purpose. The pleasurable effects are relaxation, refreshment, and comfort. "Rum is the most carminative and comforting of spirits," and all spirits create a euphoria that he refuses to see as toxic or in any way harmful.

But Saintsbury's claims for alcohol's virtues go much farther than this. "The greatest of medicines," he insists, it has produced much of the world's imaginative work, and it stimulates the moral and intellectual powers. He dismisses the scientists who support Temperance and Prohibition as hypocritical or as quacks and labels Hogarth a good artist but poor in intellect because by painting the evils of gin he hurt its reputation.

One need not pass moral judgment on Saintsbury's perverse blindness to dangers he did not wish to see in order to recognize the rationalizing typical of the enthusiastic drinker. It is he who reports that he had to give up port in the 1880s, then claret, then burgundy because of gout, rheumatism, and various stomach problems. But he never mentions what must have been the worsening effects of all the liquor he imbibed on the dizziness and imbalance that Ménière's disease brought to the last three decades of his life. He never gave ground on the virtues of the bottle. He enjoyed the memories as he had the reality and admitted that he allowed himself the occasional forbidden drink in his very last years. He also complained fiercely about postwar prices and taxes on liquor.

The social evils of drink he could be expected to ignore or deny as he had rejected the ugly realities that Zola depicted, and his refusal to acknowledge the relation between alcohol and his various illnesses is part of the pattern I have traced throughout his life, that of an obsessive escape or evasion: the past not the present, romance and the medieval world, form rather than ideas in literature, fiction and the friendship of books rather than people, fantasy and dream in art and in love, the rejection of naturalism in fiction, of change in church and state, and always the solace of wine and spirits, never their drawbacks. Granting all this, a reader can still share Saintsbury's pleasures in the pages of *The Cellar Book* and, thus, know him better.

The attractive little volume went into several editions and enjoyed a popular reception that seemed ironic and not altogether welcome to its elderly author. This feeling helps explain his lack of gratitude when, in 1931, a group of wine lovers founded the Saintsbury Club. As the wine expert André Simon relates it, this tale has its ironies.[29] At a luncheon on February 5, 1931, while those assembled were enjoying a fine Chateau Brion 1874, J. C. Squire remarked that Saintsbury as "a fine apostle of good wine" should be there to enjoy it but was, in fact, living "sightless and friendless in Bath." Sympathy for this somewhat distorted image inspired those present to plan a dinner in his honor for April 23, the birthday of Shakespeare and Saintsbury's Saint Day. Their invitation being twice refused in Saintsbury's almost illegible script, the dinner was finally held on May 28 at the Connaught Rooms and was attended by a large number of his male admirers. After tributes to the Professor and wine lover, the Saintsbury Club was formed, to meet twice a year (April 23 and October 23), to keep his memory alive and to discuss new vintages and new books.

Unaware that Saintsbury, though not poor, friendless, or completely blind, was confined by his last illness, they elected him "president in perpetuity." The first club dinner was held at Vintner's Hall on October 23, 1932, Saintsbury's eighty-seventh birthday and three months before his death. The oration was delivered by Hilaire Belloc, who next day recalled not a word he had said. A fine testimony to the vintages sampled, but thereafter the orations were recorded and a number were privately printed in limited editions.[30] The club still meets; in April, 1988, the session was held in Paris.

To these admirers, Saintsbury seemed perversely ungrateful, a view André Simon never relinquished.[31] As he wrote in 1957, "Pro-

fessor Saintsbury was ungracious to us to the bitter end." Unfortunately, their ineptitude also continued—to his grave. Four of the
faithful, Simon, J. C. Squire, Ian Campbell, and A. J. A. Symonds,
wishing to pay final tribute when Saintsbury died, impulsively traveled down to Bath with a wreath, only to find "he had himself buried
at Southampton." Meanwhile, their view of his suffering, poverty,
and distress built into a kind of legend as begun by Squire after the
visit he paid Saintsbury in 1927 and continued in his *London Mercury*
obituary in 1933. Dorothy Margaret Stuart was one of several who
felt the need to correct the picture.[32] As she noted, one is scarcely in
poverty on a Regius Professor's pension.

In 1924, Saintsbury wrote a charming miniature sequel to his *Cellar
Book* for *The Book of the Queen's Doll House* in which he commented on
the dozens of *tiny* bottles of spirits that were dontated to the wine
cellar of the doll's house.[33] One of the miniatures he gave to the little
daughter of his Bath landlord.

CHAPTER 16

"La Princesse Lointaine"

During the year that Saintsbury spent in Southampton before finally settling in Bath, his correspondence with Helen Waddell became regular. Having given up Oxford to nurse her alcoholic stepmother, she found the incessant demands of the task made research difficult and writing unfruitful. In 1915, out of concern and as a kind of therapy, her close friend, Maude Clarke, persuaded her to join her for an August holiday and to collaborate on a novel. They found a cottage at Larne on the Antrim coast, and Helen teasingly invited Saintsbury to join them in the project. He replied "in six illegible pages" with a promise to criticize the results.

During the next year Sainstbury followed the novel's progress. He was amused and flattered at being portrayed as Tavernier, a friend of the main characters whose resemblance to Helen and Gregory Smith was unmistakable. He also enjoyed the many allusions and literary puzzles put in for his and Gregory Smith's edification. Neither of them found any serious fault in the short fiction, though Saintsbury anticipated that the suffragette incident toward its end would insure its rejection. When it was turned down, his praise consoled Helen. Claiming critical objectivity, he wrote that it was the best novel he had read in sixty years. His personal pleasure came chiefly from Elizabeth, the heroine into whom Helen had put so much of herself. He wondered whether Elizabeth ever wrote a love letter, then admitted that criticism and love making, though not incompatible, cannot be done at exactly the same time. The implied question he asked Helen elsewhere: Had she ever loved him for thirty minutes at a time, indeed had she ever really loved anyone?

He received regular reports of suitors who proposed (five of them in 1918) and were regularly refused. For one he expressed sympathy and wondered was Helen making a habit of rejecting legacies, jobs, and suitors as she had recently done. He speaks as he had before and

283

would again of "his unselfish and cross-grained notion that she ought to marry," reasoning that if anyone can add to the intense happiness of the world they should do so and that she could do it well. These remarks undoubtedly masked deeper desires he knew to be impossible of fulfillment. Like the physical distance always kept between them, this was a kind of safety curtain to cover impassioned feeling while they both wrote of meetings planned but never carried out. She toyed with the idea of marriage after each proposal and wrote to Saintsbury that she thought of herself as born for children and a home but had come to realize that, unlike her emotions, her mind would always remain single.

As the years passed, Helen received Saintsbury's complaints on wartime shortages and the difficulties of shopping for one who thought of fish and meat as the only welcome food, also of too much "amateur nursing" and the aggravation "especially where there is no pain"—a surprising statement in view of Emily's multiple illnesses and his report that she was too ill to be left alone. But Helen, amid her own trying duties, comforted and cheered him and teased him too. He was consoled, as he wrote her:

> Balm of Gilead is nothing to balm of Helen. How do you manage to write so that something spreads itself like balm between the skin and the flesh of the soul, and trickles through its veins and changes the marrow of its bones? For the soul has all these things, you know, just like the body.

His physical metaphors here and elsewhere signal the somewhat strange and complex satisfaction he gained from his fantasies, fed by Helen's not altogether innocent game playing. In one of her letters, he found "much to please body and soul" and he recalls again the cherished image of her in Greg's garden in the heliotrope dress and Samarcand shoes, "like an angel with half outstretched wing-sweep," a picture "refreshing to the joints and marrow." On June 23, 1916, he wrote:

> You cannot think how it pleases me to have pleased you. I feel as if I were a youthful Homeric hero and you a maiden in a chiton boiling me in a beautiful tripod of warm water and then anoint-

ing me with the sweetest oil, and clothing me with white and pur-
ple, and then feeding me with goat and pig and the best of
wine. . . .

In another mood he adds, "Yes, beloved, when you and I are not in
Samarkand, Camelot and Joyous Gard (and Carbonek) are the places
for us. But one cannot always be in any of them."

Helen wrote Dr. Taylor that Saintsbury had a theory that a young
girl, like radium, "radiates delight without losing anything thereby."[1]
Later, after some trick of hers, he adds a new figure, "Is there such
a thing as a she-leperchaun? If there is, you are one and I'm sure I'm
very glad of it as I am of everything you are. . . . I am more sure than
ever that you and I were at sometime united in a star (probably Poe's
El Asraaf)."

In October, 1920, he wrote, "Circe, I love you, Circe. I am
infinitely grateful to *you* for loving *me*." The next month, Helen sent
the photograph Saintsbury had pled vainly for five years earlier (see
fig. 4) and he rejoiced, "It would set one craving to see the face if one
had never seen it and raving at the idea of it if one had." He found
her arms "fascinatingly childish" and confessed that he had looked
at the hair with a magnifying glass. Shadow and substance, these
sexual fancies he pleased himself with and reported to her!

In the last year of the war a practical note was struck when Helen,
shuddering at the thought of baconless breakfasts, sent off to Bath a
nine-pound Limerick ham, a gift so welcome Saintsbury shared the
news with Kipling who marveled in envy. Helen wrote Dr. Taylor of
Saintsbury's kindness and humanity. Saintsbury also sent gifts and
he never forgot a birthday. A succession of books included his edition
of Herrick, *The Peace of the Augustans,* and his *French Lyrics,* this last
with the envoi:

Go, Book, to her in whom do meet
All wealth of wit and witchery.
And when thou comest to her feet
Say, Lady I have brought for thee
What once was worthless but behold
Since thou didst deign to ask for me
It were more precious far than gold.

Helen Waddell, *studio portrait, ca. 1920, print courtesy of Stanbrook Abbey, Worcestershire.*

He enclosed three labels ranging from formal professional to warm friendship and was pleased when she used all three. At other times, he sent a pressed flower, money to buy a moonstone to replace the opal she had lost in Gregory's apple orchard, and, crowning all, after he had received the ham, he sent a pair of shining paste shoe buckles. This occasion is captured in Helen's letter of thanks, full of that flirtatious youthful fun he loved in her. Here she is Eve, Cleopatra, and Millamant in turn.

Excellency,
    This is the minute before the packet is opened, just to caress you. But Eve is barefoot and dreadfully impatient.
Ten minutes thereafter
    She has it—on black velvet, strapped sandal fashion under the eiderdown so that by virtue of one foot she is no more Eve but Cleopatra. You don't know how it glitters.
    But to her mind it looks nicest on—do you remember black and green brocade shoes with very high heels that I wore that night in Samarcand—the night I lost the opal thing under the apple trees? They have been worn little since. They were waiting for these. Now they are Millamant's shoes. I know they were Millamant's buckles . . .
    So she distracts him to a new question: is the buckle to stay where it is all night, or is it to be kissed and put under the pillow with its fellow?

Yours Helen

But Excellency, how did you know? Years ago I told Miss Anne that the one thing I coveted was old paste buckles. But that I wouldn't buy them for myself because it's the kind of thing only the right person should give you. Do all things come if one waits?

A copy of the limited edition of Swift's *Polite Conversation* with Saintsbury's preface (now in the University of London Library) is inscribed, "Helen from G.S. for the 31st of May, 1923, in the 31st year of its life—at Bath."[2] A letter pasted into the volume reads: "Faire as the years go on. There is not much of Miss Notable in you, there is more than a little of you in Miss Notable . . . as how should there not be seeing that she is charming. . . . Take this, Cherie, and

like it and all good luck go with it. Yours ever, George Saintsbury."
This Swift volume was just one of the small gifts marking Helen's
birthdays. In 1919 she described to Dr. Taylor Saintsbury's gift of a
Brussels lace handkerchief and quoted his message, "...peradven-
ture to make it more precious you will carry it on your wedding day,"
and an accompanying "scrap of pastiche" as he called it:

A toi trentième
A Ma Lointaine Princesse
Moi, je t'adore
Bien plus encore
  sans cesse.[3]

The year before this, Saintsbury had sent Helen an odd volume
he called "the Pig Book," so named because it was enclosed in a
pigskin slip case he had had made with her name engraved in gold
on its front. In this blank-page dummy of *The Peace of the Augustans*
he had inscribed, in the early pages, a series of quotations from love
poetry including all his favorites: Donne, Dryden, Herrick, Dante,
Gautier, Baudelaire, Musset, Tennyson, Morris, Beddoes, O'Shaun-
essy, and others.[4] Among the quotations was the line from Rostand,
"Moi, j'aime la Princesse Lointaine," which echoes through Saintsbury's later letters. A note at the front of the book dated May 19,
1918, reads, "Tis Helen's now: who is twenty-nine. No age in girls is
more charming...." Succeeding lines, not all legible, express his
hope that Helen will fill in the blank pages, something she never did.
An enclosed letter states that it is a long time since he had had a letter
from her and asks, "Is man's life so long that he can afford such
partings?" This is a somewhat puzzling remark since the years from
1914 to 1919 are those of their most regular and frequent correspondence.

None of Saintsbury's letters are very long. Their salutations have
the greatest interest as they express the playful fantasy and the literary quality of the relationship: "Beloved and Fair," "My Lady," "Mi-
gnonne," "Circe," "Daughter of Zeus," "Vivian mine," "My Lady of
Dreams," "Cleopatra," and most often "Incomparabilis." It is a fantasy, a game for him as for her. But he tells her, "Dreams are the best
things in the world after all" and asks whether she believes, as he
does, that "Romance ... once one has it ... survives all physical aging,

in sickness or health, etc. and never withers away." Thinking of her
youth, he tells her that though he is old in body he has never been
"less than twenty or more than five and twenty in the not-body."

In 1921 Saintsbury wrote, "O Princesse toujours lointaine . . . What
a once that was when you were near." And the next year, "How sorry
I should have been if I had never had you, Helen." At times he quotes
verse:

> Oh let me love, if I may not possess,
> Let them enjoy, I grudge not nor demur.

Another set of lines appears twice in separate letters, translated from
the Latin. He says the original is much better.

> If this my love be pain
> If this my pain be love
> Of these two things I know not
> If this my pain is love
> A joyful thing is pain.

In 1926, he speaks of "that other Valley of pleasures that never have
been."

The letters are not all romantic dream or make-believe. There are
occasional misgivings and more realistic feelings. Many letters deal
with Helen's work and Saintsbury writes as a teacher rather than a
lover. Helen told Dr. Taylor that Saintsbury had delighted her and
stimulated her as a critic long before they met, that he was like a
"galactic battery," and that she had felt "sheer gratitude" for this.[5]
In 1916, he set her reading Elizabethan and Caroline lyrics, and she
pleased him by her enthusiastic responses to Campion, Carew, Suck-
ling, and Browne, the meter of Dryden's "Farewell ungrateful trai-
tor," and, above all, Donne. He claimed she was the first person he
had ever got to feel with him about Carew and Dryden and that he
had failed even with his friend Robert Bridges. He concludes, "They
shrink beside Donne but who doesn't?" Helen had written, "I don't
think you have any idea though your students in Edinburgh may
have let you know something of it, of the magnitude of your gifts to
the likes of me."[6] What some of those students said to me in 1962
confirms her view.

In 1918, Saintsbury and Gregory Smith urged eighteenth-century French and English prose upon Helen because they felt that her style had deteriorated. They soon saw results that justified their advice. Meanwhile, she reported her reading of *Manon Lescaut* (one of Saintsbury's great favorites). She had finished it "in a hot anguish." Thirteen years later she did her fine translation of *Manon* for which Saintsbury wrote his last and very fine preface. Reading his *French Novel*, she tells him he "illuminates history." When he sent her *Nepenthe*, a work of the minor Irish poet George Darley, in 1917, she chastized her own generation for "being cock-a-hoop over people like Rupert Brooke and letting this argosy be sunk"; then, with more discrimination, she added, "He's not one beautiful stone, like Blake. He's rather a dingy, no *crazy* is the word, treasure ship with lots of rubbish to bury his good things. Did you ever see—out of Keats— such awful adjectives?" Saintsbury enjoyed these signs of her shaping taste and her frankness.

A turning point in Helen Waddell's life came in 1920. Her stepmother's death in June set her free (at thirty-one) to live her own life and become the scholar she longed to be. Under the strains of round-the-clock demands she had felt herself grow old and there was much she wanted to forget, as she wrote Dr. Taylor. When he died suddenly in February of that year, the loss to her was heartbreaking. In July, she wrote Saintsbury that she felt human again for the first time and gradually seemed less fatigued. During weeks spent in the healing atmosphere of her sister's family she began to plan. Then she sold her house. She had never been happy there, she told Saintsbury, except when writing to him.

In the autumn of 1920 Helen went to Oxford as he had urged her to do, rented rooms there six flights up, and began reading at the Bodleian. As a member of Somerville College she started work for the B. Litt., then the Ph.D that she never completed. In March, 1921, she went to Italy with the Somerville Classical don Hilda Lorimer and shared it all with Saintsbury in letters, especially Torcello where she gathered flowers for him on a day she described as "like the colour of your moonstone." The next year she wrote him that he made love "in the grand manner, with that undercurrent of irony not for the mistress but for himself."

That autumn she was invited to deliver eight lectures on the Mime in the Middle Ages under the auspices of St. Hilda's Hall. An outgrowth of her Queen's University research and an anticipation of *The Wandering Scholars,* these were enthusiastically received, but she was restless and did not feel at home in Oxford. She left in June for London, which was to be her home for the rest of her life.[7] With his deep attachment to Oxford, Saintsbury must have enjoyed her accounts of it, and his recommendation undoubtedly had a share in her receiving the two-year Suzette Taylor fellowship from Lady Margeret Hall in June, 1923.

Soon Helen was in Paris at the Bibliothèque Nationale deep in research on the scholars vagantes. Letters to Saintsbury reflect her intense involvement as she read all that the scholars had read, the scholars themselves, and the 217 volumes of Migne's *Patrologia.* One evening she returned home and read Donne, then wrote Saintsbury confessing, "I like 'Full nakedness, all joys are due to thee.'... Perhaps it's because this art is so aware that it just took off its clothes a minute ago." In December, 1924, she was back in London completing *The Wandering Scholars.* When she submitted chapters to Constable's, Otto Kyllmann, the editor, pressed her to finish it and, in April, 1927, published the work. That same day he offered her a place on the staff, first in the office then later as a consultant and advisor on medieval matters. This gave her time to translate Latin lyrics and to write the novel on Abelard she projected. On these she reported regularly to Saintsbury.

The Wandering Scholars was an unexpected success. It went into three editions in the first year and was enthusiastically reviewed. She had brought the obscure early period of the Middle Ages into vivid life and had made the Fathers and their world three-dimensional and human, and had done all this before any of the major works on medieval culture (C. H. Haskins, E. K. Rand, F. J. E. Raby, etc.) had appeared. Like others, Saintsbury reviewed the book (in the *Observer*) with praise. He cited the way she had diligently mapped out the whole province of Latin medieval literature and illuminated the influence of Latin on the whole literature of medieval Europe.

During 1921–27, exciting years of growth and creativity for Helen, Saintsbury faced increasing strain, worry, illness, fatigue, and sorrow. At times she must have seemed very far away, faithful as her letters were, but they gave him many moments of consolation. In 1923, he wrote of his "poor patient's worsening condition" and the exhausting demands his wife's illness made on his own ailing constitution. When he wrote of Emily's death in 1924, Helen's reply from Paris struck exactly the right note since it made him feel that she alone really understood what he described as the violence of his passion for his wife over a half-century and his grief, his fatigue, his illness, and his need for work as an anodyne. Helen had written earlier that year to her sister Meg that she had come to feel their relationship "had all gone hollow—the bubble pricked as with the 'sharpness of death,'" but suddenly with the reassurance his letter offered, she realized "how deep her feeling for him had gone apart from play-acting," and she felt the old relationship was real again.[8]

One must pause to wonder just how this fantasy liaison related to the rest of Saintsbury's life during those eighteen years with the flow of letters and gifts, most of them before Mrs. Saintsbury's death. Shut up alone together as they were most of the time in Bath, Emily must have felt very much alone. One son was dead (in 1922) and the other was in Scotland; her husband always reading or writing and sometimes asking, "And what is it now, Emily?"[9] How much did she know and think or feel? She must have eaten the ham. One hopes she never saw the letters. Later, when Christopher came to live with his father, he thought Miss Stuart was closer to him than anyone and after 1926 he was probably right, if one judges by visits and the letters exchanged.

From the start, Saintsbury spoke and wrote of Helen Waddell as a remarkable young scholar he had seen just once. To Hunt, he described her as a "delightful creature." He also told Kipling and Sir Frederick Pollock about her. Later he told Helen and Dorothy Margaret Stuart each about the other. When Miss Stuart wrote about his later years, she referred to Helen's friendship with him as like her own. This public image he fostered, and it sufficed apparently to protect the secret of the "passion in absence" he kept alive and often confessed to Helen—with only the occasional reminder that the "undying flame" perhaps went one way, not both. Once he wrote to her that someone might wonder how he could love his wife so much and yet write to a girl as he did. He wrote this close to the time when he confessed to wanting Emily more when he saw her in her coffin than ever before—a strangely confused set of feelings at best, if true, but something he felt compelled to tell Helen. She wrote, in 1933, that "he married young: he had Prospero's island of enchanted lawn at the beginning of his life instead of at the end, and all his years were transfigured by it." This is the picture he gave her, but it is only a part of the truth, the part she chose to believe. Sometime early the romance with Emily had faded; he retreated and then gradually avoided all domestic intimacy and developed a pattern of escape that climaxed in his deep attachment to Helen, disguised as a friendship of student and teacher. After the 1914 "seduction over coffee," as she once described it, he never kissed her or held her in his arms, but he imagined and dreamed of doing so and reported such moments to her, often with some literary allusion.

As late as 1931 Saintsbury wrote that he had dreamt of kissing her. He had told Miss Stuart he could never kiss her since he had vowed on Emily's death never to kiss another woman, and he made her feel that his grief for Emily was very real. But with Helen it was different, as lines translated from the Chinese of A.D. 818 and sent to Helen with "the Pig Book" indicate.

> In absence now I gain . . .
> That I can catch her
> When no one can watch her
> In some close corner of my brain.
> Now I embrace and kiss her
> and so I both enjoy and miss her.

He may never have wanted more than this. Certainly he made no real effort to have the physical reality.

CHAPTER 17

"On the Shelf":
Friends and the Daily Round, 1916–33

Never a great letter writer, in retirement Saintsbury revived contact with some old friends—notably Kipling, Bridges, and Gosse. Along with the Waddell correspondence, the steady flow of letters between him and William Hunt affords the best account of the last years. Saintsbury's brief notes offer a running commentary on his work, his problems, and his griefs and joys, continuing even when he increasingly had to discourage visitors and was "submitting to solitary confinement quite placidly."

In 1923, he wrote to Hunt of Sir Frederick Pollock's being in Bath and of his seeing him "in my usual flying manner." He was still hearing from Walter Pollock and he reported visits by Kipling and his daughter, who brought as a gift a three-volume edition of Kipling's *Poems*. He defends Kipling against Hunt's criticism and ranks him with Yeats as "far the best poets of their generation."

Saintsbury reports his work on *The French Novel* and the publication of the second volume in May, 1919, and Alfred Balfour's letter of congratulation. One learns that the tenth edition of *Nineteenth-Century Literature* appeared on February 7, 1917. There is constant worry over the health of his children and grandchildren, his wife's increasing helplessness, and his own accidents in 1919–20. Upsetting as these accidents were, he saw their humorous side. Struck by an automobile "in a torrent of rain" on Milsom Street hill and tossed onto its hood, when the chauffeur remarked, "You should thank God, sir," Saintsbury retained enough composure to reply, "So I do! But that does not prevent me damning *you*!" He relished the exchange but was less happy when a report appeared in the *Daily Mail*—with a picture (March 13, 1919). He describes the discomfort of rationing and reports "cutting up a hare in twelve parts for next week."

The Russian Revolution suddenly emerges amid this domestic detail as he reminds Hunt (concerning Rasputin and the Empress) that "an hysterical and superstitious woman is the foredoomed prey of a lecherous monk." In 1920, Saintsbury tells Hunt that his *Notes on a Cellar Book* is "coming on" and that Kipling, to whom he dedicates it, is delighted with the project.

In July, 1919, Saintsbury and his wife were taken by automobile for a week's visit to their son, Lewis, and his family at Chiddingford, Surrey. He wrote Helen Waddell twice from there. His grandson recalls the difficulty with which his grandmother was carried up the narrow staircase at the old inn to their room, where she spent the week. Typically Saintsbury writes little regarding the visit or Lewis's illness and his death leaving, three young children.

Letters to Hunt record the inevitable mounting personal losses and Saintsbury's quiet, courageous acceptance of those deaths: his sister Sophie in 1917, Lewis in 1922, his wife on August 16, 1924, his remaining sister, Josephine, in 1925. And during the same years most of his close friends died: Dobson in 1921, Ker in 1923, Frederick Harrison in 1924, Gosse in 1928, Bridges in 1930, Gregory Smith and Hunt in 1932. On Harrison, who had become a Bath neighbor and congenial companion despite their longstanding political differences, Saintsbury wrote a note for the *Fortnightly Review*. He also did one on Gosse for the *London Mercury* at the request of J. C. Squire.[1] With Hunt he discussed the long-rumored Gosse memoirs and expressed his doubt of their existence. On Bridge's death, Saintsbury wrote in warm praise of the man and his poetry, despite their sharp divergence on prosody.

In 1928, Saintsbury reminded Hunt that, in a friendship of forty-four years, they had never quarreled. Having during those years made only one new close friend, W. P. Ker, he comments, "I am not by any means a friend-maker as far as our sex goes."

Saintsbury once said that women write the best letters and get the best ones written to them.[2] Helen Waddell, who received so many of his, said his letters were "quintessential" to knowing him, and in her partiality and Irish flair for exaggeration said he ranked with Walpole and Lamb as a letter writer. He would have disagreed, and his brief letters to Dobson and Hunt do not support her claim. But Dorothy Margaret Stuart, and his niece, Brenda Green,[3] and, more surprisingly, the American poet Marianne Moore, like Helen, found his letters delightful as they too experienced that imaginative flirtatious side of him in his last years.

Through "some strange affinity" that bridged sixty-four years in age, Brenda was the lucky recipient of a "sheaf of letters" from this "'greatly great-uncle'" while she was at Oxford in the late 1920s. She recognized his "courtly attitude" and the warm playful feeling he had for young women. He loved sharing Oxford memories with her; he offered cures for a cold, including "some lovely lines of dactylic doggerel"; he talked shop all too seldom, but once praised the dramatist Webster and suggested that his "magnificent" Vittoria should have married Milton's Satan. He expressed his joy in reading plays but also his intolerance "when anyone he liked showed an inclination for the stage." When no longer up to writing long letters, he sent "the kind . . . that would buy Christmas presents and Easter eggs." And he never lost sight of "the fact that life comes first." He showed an "altogether youthful appreciation of original sin" and said that "there is only one thing in the world better than to be loved, and that is to love."

Dorothy Margaret Stuart recounted her experience in her essay, "The Last Years." "I was a friend who had fun with him," she explained to me.[4] She talked of it all simply and frankly. To him she must have seemed, at twenty-five, the daughter he had always wanted. Even his own son Christopher, a limited, somewhat naive person who was never close to his father, wrote to her after his father's death.

> Though you cannot be said to be one of my father's oldest friends, yet I feel that you were closer in touch and sympathy with him than anyone and your daily letters were the one thing he looked forward to . . . the end was quite peaceful and painless. . . . With regard to flowers, I know he would have accepted yours and they were the only ones save mine which went with him from here and were also buried in the grave.[5]

It began when Miss Stuart sent Saintsbury a pamphlet of her poems. He later reviewed a volume of hers, and he invited her to visit him. On August 12, 1926, she went to Bath for the first of her luncheon visits, made regularly until 1931. She went by train from London, arriving at noon on a Saturday once every two or three months; they talked and lunched, and she took a train back at three or four.[6] For seven years, their correspondence was steady though not daily as his son thought. A long Sunday letter from her, often decorated with sketches, brought a Wednesday reply "equally long," and often there were postcards in the interim. After her mother's death in 1932, for six weeks she received a daily card. On her brief visits, over "a lady's luncheon" of chicken and champagne, and in their letters, they joked. "He was . . . such good company . . . good at cut and thrust," and at times "peppery," she recalled. They discussed "every subject from modern criticism to modern cricket," capped each other's allusions, shared enthusiasms, and she observed that he continued to grieve for his wife. She enjoyed his reminiscences and loved to hear him read poetry in a voice she described as "curiously *young* . . . high, not shrill, with a lilt in it."[7] Both devotees of "the God of Nonsense," they had fun with nicknames and verse making. Begging her pardon lest this be "an impertinence," he gave her a signet ring, bracelet, and locket (from the Army-Navy stores catalog, which he found useful and amusing in these years of confinement). He had Bis (his nickname for her, meaning twice-sainted Dorothy Margaret) and his own, Boj ("Bad old journalist," a quotation from the *Observer*) inscribed on these simple mementos.

For the pleasant companionship of those seven years, Miss Stuart's essay pays handsome tribute as she salutes "his courage, his faith, and the touch of springtime that lingered even in the winter of his days." He wrote, on October 19, 1930, "I *say*, what dear old girls the Fates were when they turned your way me-wards." She had the last word, praising his "boyishness and melancholy, vehemence and gentleness, whimsy and profundity." Both understood their delicate May and January flirtation, "beneficent," innocent, literary—and heart-warmingly natural.

Dorothy Margaret Stuart may well have understood Saintsbury better than others, including Helen Waddell. She was realistic and gives a lively, positive image of him to counteract the legend that had grown up to the effect that Saintsbury was blind, poor, and friendless. She described his tall figure (5'11") with his "curious high-shouldered stance," his beautiful hands (of which he was justifiably vain), his desk and chair overlooking the Royal Crescent fields, his "respectable private fortune sworn for probate," and the strong affection of friends, which he told her kept him from the "grey set life and apathetic end too often the portion of the very old." She also emphasized that he had, to the very end, been able to see, to read, and to write what he wanted to. Like Helen, she was a poet, an editor, and a writer of short fiction. She never married and was living alone in a small flat at Kew when she died of cancer in 1963. Having destroyed his letters and her own as she had promised to do, she had some regrets, but she treasured a few excerpts from him that she had pasted into his books in her tiny library. When she and Helen Waddell met at an English Association dinner soon after his death, she wondered why Saintsbury had never arranged for them to meet. Helen replied, "He never mixed his drinks."

In the very months when his friendship with Dorothy Margaret Stuart began, Saintsbury, now reviewing for the *Dial* (New York), started his transatlantic correspondence with Marianne Moore. The thirty-nine-year-old poet and editor made the distinguished elderly contributor her special responsibility, often transcribing his illegible script in her own longhand. As a file of over 230 letters testifies, the professional exchange soon became personal. They shared opinions and reminiscences and indulged in the playful teasing familiar to Helen Waddell, Dorothy Stuart, and Saintsbury's niece, Brenda. Miss Moore, Anglophile that she was, flattered him, and also perhaps startled him with her enthusiasm for prehistoric animals. She writes him details of her trips to colonial Virginia, Maine, and elsewhere and relates incidents from her childhood. He, in his typical flirtatious style, calls her a Salem Witch "so nice and so clever at once." They plan for her to visit him, as she did in June, 1927, when she and her mother spent a few days in Bath. One wonders, did he offer them a "lady's lunch," but one knows that it was the piles of books tumbling about his parlor floor that prompted her to order him a new set of bookcases before she left Bath. Six months later, she was writing from home about the yellow roses around his entrance door. This is the rose of her poem, "Injudicious Gardening," and of the painting that long hung over her desk. She admired his works; she respected his eminence and enjoyed his attention as she helped brighten his last few years.[8]

Beside these young women, one can place what may be called Saintsbury's "literary loves." Though not a friend maker among men, the gentleman *galant* had an eye for "the eternal feminine." He is hardly objective when he laments, "But few, alas! understand the great, the beneficent, the much abused art of flirtation in all its branches."[9] It had prompted his lecture comment on modern explications of "then come and kiss me, sweet and twenty": "I prefer to think that both sweet and twenty refer to the lady and the number of kisses is quite unlimited."[10]

When he was seventeen, Saintsbury had listed literary heroines he adored: Guinevere, Beatrice Cenci, Princess Ida, and Argemone. At forty-seven he described Miss Notable of Swift's *Polite Conversation* as excelling in "flesh and blood—excellent things in woman . . . this 'Miss' of our heart, this 'Miss' of our soul . . . a picture so delightful, unholy dreams come upon me." She and the dinner, he adds, are "two objects of perennial interest to all men of spirit and taste."[11] Elsewhere, more than half-seriously, he argues that a great heroine is one whom one can fall in love with even if she is not so great that one has to.[12] It was one more game that he liked to play.

Since "flesh and blood" and the spirit of a minx held a high place in Saintsbury's fancy, he disliked both Amelias: Fielding's, who had "too much of the milk of human kindness, unrefreshed and unrelieved of its mawkishness by the rum and whisky of human frailty in her," and her silly, "spiritual granddaughter," Thackeray's "amiable fool." At the same time, he could "*almost* fall in love with Becky Sharp."[13] Laura (in *Pendennis*) shared Amelia's mawkishness and Helen Pendennis was "not only mawkish, but a she-Pharisee." For Blanche Amory, he held "a distinct and open affection," with the sensible qualification that "one would not, I think, marry her."[14]

Who are his other heroines? Conveniently, he named them in his preface to *Pride and Prejudice*, five whom he thinks no man of sense could help falling in love with:

> Elizabeth Bennet, Diane Vernon, Argemone Lavington, Beatrix Esmond, and Barbara Grant. I should have been most in love with Beatrix and Argemone; I should, I think, for occasional companionship, have preferred Diane and Barbara. But to live with and to marry, none can come into competition with Elizabeth.[15]

Argemone is still a favorite, as she was when he was fifteen, but Jane Austen's Elizabeth represents for a "man of taste and spirit . . . what the best modern (not 'new') women have by education and experience, a perfect freedom from the idea that all men may bully her if they choose, and that most will run away with her if they can . . . no mere sensibility, no nasty niceness." She has passion, though Jane Austen allows her little outward show of this. Belonging to "the allegro of allegra division of the band of Venus," she is "a perfectly natural girl" with playfulness, wit, and fearlessness but never "viraginous." She can give as good as she gets but never "scratches," and "she never attacks first." She is affectionate and healthy in her responses. No Janeite could object to his choice, one not exclusively romantic or Victorian. He sometimes voices a conventional Victorian cliche, such as "Who ... expects a lady ... to be accurate? And who deserves it?"[16] But for literary flirtation, he returned most often to Thackeray's Beatrix, "born 'for the destruction of mankind' and fortunately for the delight of some of them as well."[17] He loved any minx: Millamant, "the queen of all her kind,"[18] and Marivaux's Marianne, who is pretty, clever, vain, selfish, "a live girl ... the agreeable ancestress of all the beloved coquettes and piquant minxes in prose fiction since"; Dryden's Doralice, "an accomplished, but not heartless flirt" (in *Marriage à la Mode*), and Swift's Miss Notable.[19]

As for earlier heroines, Delilah is wryly defended: "How many women ... could resist the double temptation of seeing whether the secret *did* lie in the hair, and if so, of possessing complete mistressship of their lovers?"[20] Saintsbury liked Guinevere best in Morris's *Defense* and in the Vulgate Arthurian version. He saw her as an interesting compound: "Beatrix Esmond at a better time, Argemone Lavington raised to a higher power, and the spirit of all that is best and strongest and least paradoxical in Meredith's heroines ... adding the passion of Tennyson's own Fatima and the queenliness of Helen herself."[21] No clinging vine this. Cleopatra? Despite "the splendor and poignancy of the passion" of Shakespeare's play, he thinks her not really romantic but rather "a naughty girl and a rather nasty one."[22] Not young enough for his taste, and certainly not innocent.

Saintsbury enjoyed these literary flirtations all his life and some seem very real, but more seriously he valued the presence in literature of the "intense humanity and infinite passion" he found in *Manon Lescaut*. He praised this "passionate masterpiece" in 1931, for its truth to "the morality of life."[23] Manon he saw as gradually freed of the worst of sins—love for money and love of money—and at last transformed by "the final sword of sorrow and suffering" into a "lady." Inadequate as the term seems to a modern reader, for Saintsbury it spelled integrity. Manon's death he saw as artistic and inevita-

ble in contrast to the false delicacy of a contemporary popular heroine, Virginie of *Paul et Virginie,* in whom he found a disgusting mixture of "sensiblerie and prudery." She refused to be rescued from
drowning by a naked sailor *because* he was naked.[24]

In *Manon,* Saintsbury found the pattern of abstract or Heroic Love
defined in Burton's *Anatomy of Melancholy:* pure, with nothing to gain
but love and early paid for by Des Grieux; flawed but finally exalted
in repentance by Manon. He denied it is a romantic quality and
declared that it made *Manon Lescaut* and Rousseau's *Julie* and Gautier's *La Morte Amoureuse* "the most consummate expression in
fiction . . . of the union of sensual with transcendental enamourment
. . . that requires love of the heart and the head, the soul and the
senses together."[25] This passionate love that he thought filled six-
teenth-, early seventeenth-, and nineteenth-century English literature
he missed in Racine, but not in Shakespeare or Donne. He deplored
an ignorance of it, along with the presence of "mere sensuality" and
"bluntness of taste" in George Sand,[26] and he rejoiced when he felt
that Maupassant, in *Notre Coeur,* created it and thus "sublimed" his
conception of love into very nearly the true form, as it is in the
Canticles and Shakespeare, Donne, Shelley, Heine, Hugo, Musset
and Browning.[27] He put it most eloquently in his response to Swift's
words, "Only a woman's hair," as a final expression of the riddle of
the painful earth, more poignant than anything else outside
Shakespeare.[28] Such responses enrich his criticism with a certain humanity and help answer the charge of superficiality occasionally
lodged against him; they reflect a man who had known passion sometimes in real life, sometimes in the life and loves of fancy and the
literary imagination. He did not substitute literature for life, but he
used it as he did fantasy and dream to escape many aspects of reality.

As a journalist, Saintsbury had little experience of professional
women, but at Edinburgh he taught an increasing number of women.
He respected their intelligence and enjoyed their reactions, and he
believed that women make good teachers. When he opposed the
"Flapper vote" in the 1920s he claimed this did not mean that he
thought women were stupid. Liking intelligence and wit in women,
he wanted these to serve feminine ends as he saw them. He distrusted
the bluestocking and the feminist. Today's feminists would say his
was a patriarchal attitude, but it was consonant with his time.

To return to Helen Waddell in the mid-1920s: as 1920 had set her

free, 1926 to 1928 was also a time of great changes. With her successful publication of *The Wandering Scholars* and her work at Constable's
came her close friendship with Otto Kyllmann and their coming to
love each other. By 1928 they were living together permanently. The
elderly, "very sardonic and engaging" O.K., as she described him, had
had two broken marriages and was depressed over a daughter hospi-
talized for mental illness. He was not free to marry, and their love
was never consummated. When first in his arms, as she later explained to a friend,[29] she had told him she could never take what
belonged to someone else and so she never experienced physical love.
Since he had had two wives, one senses again the fear of marriage
that had led to her rejection of so many suitors. Her passion, limited
and frustrated though it was, was nevertheless real and her sympathies were great. At the same time, she could enjoy Saintsbury as an
epistolary lover, dreamlike as that was. Whether he knew of her love
for Kyllmann or not is never made evident, but if he did, he preferred not to face it as he continued to express his love, assuming
that she loved him. His fantasy passion satisfied him in those last six
years and did not abate while Helen was absorbed by her new relationship with Kyllmann and by increasing success that created a whirl
of London literary and social life.

Not having seen her since 1914, Saintsbury had an image of his
own making that was, perhaps, not very close to reality. It was that
of the girl of twenty-five he had seen *once* in Belfast. She had always
had interests and feelings she had not shared with him, notably her
Liberal Irish loyalties, her deeper spiritual gropings that were fully
shared with Dr. Taylor, and now her love for Otto Kyllmann. But
Saintsbury had what he wanted. He wrote a letter in 1927 thanking
Kyllmann for a gift of Irish whiskey and referred to "our angelic
friend." In 1928, he urged Helen to come to see him and sent train
schedules, but this visit did not materialize. There were two- or three-
month gaps in the flow of his letters in those last years and a longer
one in 1929.

In August, 1931, she asked if he would like to see her; he replied,
"Who wouldn't?" She then made her one visit to him—for "a lady's
lunch" of chicken and champagne like those Miss Stuart had been
enjoying for five years. It is tempting but difficult to picture that
meeting after seventeen years of fantasy and of contact only through
letters. They were linked at the time by his writing the preface for

her *Manon Lescaut* and he was following reviews of it, including a good one by Miss Stuart. The tone of his remaining few letters is unchanged, but there is no reference to the visit. Janet Adam Smith, who heard Helen describe it, said that she seemed quite detached. Helen's own 1933 description of him in her preface to the reprint of his *Cambridge History* chapters on Shakespeare reads like a verbal counterpart of the Nicholson portrait—distanced, like a framed legend.

> ...in the Augustan twilight of the house of his last inhabiting a solitary indomitable figure with straggling grey hair and black skull-cap, gaunt as Merlin and islanded in a fast-encroaching sea of books.... The miseries of old age and the slow coming of death had no dominion over that free spirit...the solitary scholar who was his own best company, Lord not only of Joyous Gard but also of Gard Doloreuse, reading, reading, reading through the small hours in the familiar chair with the two tall candlesticks behind it.[30]

She had come away believing that he now lived most in reminiscence. Was she shocked at seeing him so aged though he had written of his failing health and of the penalties exacted by the years? She was at the peak of her own creative output and riding the waves of literary acclaim. As their letters grew fewer, did she know that correspondence and contact between him and Dorothy Margaret Stuart continued regularly until a week before his death or that Miss Stuart found him much less remote?

When Saintsbury died in January, 1933, Helen was eagerly awaiting the publication of her *Abelard,* which did not come out until May. To her sister she voiced her disappointment over the fact that he would never see it and summed up what he meant to her.

> I suppose you know that dear Saintsbury is gone. I find myself thinking at every turn—"I must tell him this." I hadn't realized how absolutely he was a part of my brain, but just because he was bone of my bone I believe it will make less difference to me, his being dead. We were so extraordinarily alike that his books are just his living voice, as if it were only a prolonged correspondence. But if only he could have seen the novel.[31]

To Enid Starkie, she wrote:

> There won't ever be another Saintsbury. I know it is better for him
> to be dead, even though he lived in most rich memory for these
> last few years.... All the same, if you have been as much enriched
> by a man's mind as I was, you can bear to let him go, for a part of
> him goes on living in your mind.[32]

How consistently her emphasis here is on their minds!

The truth is that she had "let him go" earlier and more fully than
she knew. With immediate, heartfelt loss one is not consoled so
quickly. From 1930 until March, 1932, she had been seeing Gregory
Smith, who had retired to London; he died in 1932 and Saintsbury
had sent her a few lines to be added to his obituary. They both
belonged to her past when they had shaped her mind; now she was
full of plans for new works and had her life with O.K.

Saintsbury expressed no real regrets, and a 1929 letter echoes
Donne, "To have pleased *you* after the way you have pleased me for
fifteen years since that night at Greg's is something. We please each
other mostly and almost wholly soul-wise, but the soul has bodies at
its disposal which don't eat...." When Gregory Smith died, Saintsbury wrote that he could never have thanked him enough for bringing them together. He noted his various ills, the price of aging, and
added, "How good it is to see that fairy hand of yours and to be called
what you call me." That address, most frequently "Excellency" or
"My Lord," epitomized her idea of their relationship, but she regularly signed herself "Your Helen." Saintsbury's last extant letter (September 25, 1932) expressed his dismay that the newly formed Irish
Academy had made her only an associate though she was the equal
of any man they had except Yeats and perhaps Shaw and some specialists he did not know. Thus the story closed.

CHAPTER 18

Finale

> ... it is not by masterpieces alone that the world of litera-
> ture lives."
>
> —G.S., *Fr. Novel*, 2:374

After *The Notes on a Cellar Book* of 1920, Saintsbury kept writing and editing compulsively despite fatigue, illness, and domestic duties. In 1921 he compiled *A Letter Book*, a small anthology, admittedly a potboiler, that earned £100 he then needed. Done with limited spare time and without access to London or Oxford libraries, the volume substantiates his lifelong interest in letters. He is amusing on those he would have liked to read, from Aspasia or Sappho for instance, and he suggests that, like good talk, a letter may be a work of art, but should be natural, not one of artifice. He found no letter writer superior to Walpole, and his enthusiasm here, as in *The Peace of the Augustans* and elsewhere, is contagious.

In 1922, Saintsbury turned to writing the *Scrap Books* so often quoted throughout this study and to assembling his *Collected Essays*—pleasant, nostalgic work that could be fitted into the few hours he had to spare from household tasks and from nursing his wife who, now in constant pain, needed steady attention. To Dobson he reported on March 24, 1921, "Individually my wheels drive rather heavily but they have driven up to this moment." The next year he published his "Trollope Revisited,"[1] for which much rereading was required, and his essay "Dullness" was the opening article in the first issue of *Criterion*.[2] Requested by the young T. S. Eliot, it headed the company that included "The Wasteland," T. Sturge Moore's "Tristram and Isolt," Herman Hesse's "German Poetry Today," and Valéry Larbaud's "Ulysses." Eliot was one of the younger writers who, in an era of revolt, turned to Saintsbury as a grand old man of letters. Saintsbury was delighted by a "praiseful" essay written by J. B. Priestley,[3] somewhat less so by J. C. Squire's efforts to bring others to visit him. Nevertheless, Squire kept Saintsbury's name before the literary public.[4]

In "Dullness," the elderly Saintsbury complained more prophetically than he would live to know of the growing "passivity of the modern mind" and defined "real education" as "first of all gymnastics of the mind which enable it to wrestle with things, to shape them in other forms; to extract from them whatever virtue they have; and secondly, feeding the mind with 'provisions'" so that life should never be dull.

The *Scrap Books* were conceived, Saintsbury confided to Hunt, as serious work "of a high order" that comes from "my head, my memory and my 'nature'" and which, speaking "as a confessed and unabashed fool," may "embody all of the Life that I care to transmit and some of the Opinions that may be worth transmitting."[5] One volume was planned initially, but its popularity brought requests for more, and Saintsbury enjoyed compiling the three small volumes even though he usually distrusted sequels. Opening with his familiar protest of independence for his "homegrown opinions" and the claim that he had not repeated any sentence in all his uncollectable journalism, he promises to give some of the principles on which it was all based. The Little "Necrologies" of his closest friends and the memoir of his Oxford years that had been requested by Merton College are some of the best pages.

He disclaims any great public experiences and admits that old-fashioned tastes would oblige him to leave out the more interesting personal ones because "No gentleman will kiss and tell" or "remember to backbite," but the few personal anecdotes told in his relaxed idiosyncratic manner have charm. This farrago, as he calls it, was suggested by such of his favorite works as Southey's *Omniana*, Locker's *Patchwork*, and Dobson's *Bookman's Budget*. He offers the Greek motto on the title page, translated in his preface, "Lucian wrote this, knowing old things and vain," as a clue to the contents.[6]

A series of "scraps" on education in the first volume gives free expression to Saintsbury's increasing distrust of mass education and the "watering down" of the process. His anti-Labor views (particularly in "The Modern Grendel" and "Casualty," a plea for "casual" or unorganized labor), the series of papers on Conservatism and related political ones are grossly reactionary. His religious feelings find frank expression in "The Oxford Movement" and "The Lost Leaders," in adverse criticisms of the revised Prayer Book and comment on the Thirty-nine Articles. The gourmet and connoisseur are here, too, in bits on food and on soap.

The critic speaks as Saintsbury argues against the demand of moderns (J. Middleton Murray, in particular) for more analysis and less catholicity, declaring "the religion of literature is a sort of Pantheism." He could not resist a last stab at Matthew Arnold: "His power of critical judgment ... seems to me not ... *the* best ... but so unequal and limited as to be sometimes, in his own word of anathema, simply 'capricious.'"[7] For those who know the major Saintsbury, these volumes are pleasant addenda, but they do not stand alone, and the blind social prejudices make one angry.[8]

Meanwhile Saintsbury gathered together his four-volume *Collected Essays*. These include the contents of several earlier volumes and articles from periodicals.[9] Saintsbury ruled out his introductions to novels, though he wanted them brought together, as they were in *A Consideration of Thackeray* (1931) and in three posthumous volumes.

While editing these papers, he found the time to read Proust's *Swann's Way* and to contribute an account of his reactions for *Marcel Proust, an English Tribute*, edited by his former student, C. K. Scott-Moncrieff. He termed the experience "new and satisfactory," seeing in Proust a blend of De Quincey and Stendhal—the dreamlike element of the first combined with "a double measure of the analytical and introspective power" of the second, but without the "aridity" he disliked in Stendhal.[10]

When Saintsbury returned to reviewing soon after retirement, the old pleasure was there though the results were slight and general. He wrote for the *Athenaeum and Nation* (1918–30), the *Dial* (New York) (1926–30), *Country Life* (1926–27), the *London Bookman* (1923–31), and a few others. He wrote some letters to the *Times* and two articles, one in 1923 on modern literature entitled "Twenty-one Years," the other in 1929, "London of the Victorians: How it Struck a Contemporary."[11] Both are vague and disappointing.

The literary prefaces and introductions of Saintsbury's last twelve years read like an index to his wide, lifelong interests, his special enthusiasms, and his knowledge of odd corners of the literary world. They allowed him to evaluate old favorites afresh. These include Heliodorus's *Aetheopian History* (1925), and Longus's *Daphnis and Chloe*

(1923), and Thomas's *Tristan of Brittany* in Dorothy Sayers's translation (1929). Five volumes of *French Tales* in translation allowed him to pay his last attention to writers who had been his first subjects— Flaubert and Gautier, Mérimée, and Balzac, as well as Count de Caylus.

When Saintsbury wrote the preface for Helen Waddell's *Manon* in 1931, he enjoyed being joined with her in a literary project. Though its style is highly involved, packed with allusions and asides, it shows his critical powers unabated as he defines the ill-starred passion of these lovers. He denies that the work had had any appreciable influence, as other critics had claimed. His reference to a PMLA study of Prevost's influence indicates his effort to be au courant. He stresses the work's intense humanity and its completeness, arguing that "fatalité" made any other ending impossible; a few days of joy and mutual "quiet misery and exchange of charities" were all they could expect.

The style of his preface illustrates, in the extreme, Helen Waddell's vivid description of his typical manner, "like a scour of a river in spate, allusion tumbling on allusion, parentheses crammed within parentheses, reckless to reject the straws and faggots that his headlong thought swept up on its course."[12] She also spoke in a letter to him on the style of the *French Novel* as "so turbulent, so distinctive ... sometimes rugged, never barren ... blossoming every so often...." That kind of eloquent flowering is still present in the preface, but, through the years, his style was often careless and unedited; it was involved, often convoluted, full of parentheses, antitheses, inversions, epigrams, unexplained allusions and foreign phrases, not wholly spontaneous or unconscious.[13] The vocabulary was large, often multisyllabic, rich with little-used and strange words and with coinages made for his special, immediate need by an enthusiastic student of Latin, Greek, and French.[14] The style of a nineteenth-century English Mandarin yet not free of slang or journalese, it has been fair game for the hunter of the odd and the esoteric, a joy to some, an annoyance to others.[15]

Many critics speak of Saintsbury's allusiveness but few seem as irritated and impatient as John Gross admits to being. "Does he expect us to identify them all if we are to qualify as fit readers?" he asks. Of course not. Saintsbury enjoyed personally matching wits over them, as he did with Dorothy Margaret Stuart. It is a game you sometimes win, but Saintsbury confessed that, much as he enjoyed an allusion he recognized, he enjoyed even more the one he had to look up. He detested the "explained allusion" because this spoiled the game.[16]

The style is the man embodied, writing as he spoke.[17] Eloquent and moving in his finest moments, immensely varied, with remarkable skill in transitions, flashing the occasional original metaphor but also mixing old ones freely, and never afraid of cliche or catchphrase. These last were his one real indulgence in repetition. He knew his faults and did not apologize. He knew he could not have written so much had he polished more. He remained defiantly himself.

As with other aspects of Saintsbury's work, criticism of his style has run the gamut. At one extreme, the *Nation* (New York) condemned "a style so strained and twisted, and unsimple as to be incredible . . . a menace to good letters and to the peace of English prose."[18] At the other, Edmund Wilson insisted: "His style was excellent: the rhythm . . . never falters. He had, in fact, invented a style of much charm and a certain significance: a modern, conversational prose . . . that however facetious or garrulous it may seem to become, never fails to cover the ground or make the points." Wilson believed that Saintsbury, like Ford Madox Ford, "found out how to manage a fine and flexible English prose on the rhythm of informal speech."[19] Almost fifty years after hearing him, Arthur Mowat, one of Saintsbury's Edinburgh students, described the way to read him.

> You must imagine the gentle stroking of the rather scraggy beard, the light, eager, accentless, unpretentious voice, the whimsical raising of the eyebrows in parentheses, the occasional glint from thick lenses in the sally, the steady oozing of scholarship, the urge-urge-urge to see, hear or feel for yourself, the power to move in words, the words in interplay, the weights and stresses, the overtones, the rhythms, the soul (perhaps in torment) shining through.[20]

Saintsbury had theorized on criticism early and late and some of the ideas he derived from Arnold and Pater, by action and reaction he carried through life, mingled with other company, Classical, Stoic, Epicurean, and Christian. The *Scrap Books* gave him a reason to think about and express further personal views.

Saintsbury thought Pater's doctrine not inconsistent with scripture, thus reminding any reader of *Marius, the Epicurean* that Marius died on the threshold of Christian commitment. He also insisted that "a certain kind of passionate skepticism is compatible with ... orthodoxy."[21] This joining of skepticism and a religious spirit he found in Lucretius's *De Rerum Natura,* in "the extraordinary *religious* character of its apparent atheism; the solemnity of its free-thinking; the mystical intensity of its seemingly materialistic thought," and "its awareness of the irony of life."[22] These and "the passionate pessimism which is in all of us but the basest," he felt were fully shared by Ecclesiastes, later by Swift, also to some degree by Thackeray, Flaubert, and Gautier.[23] He fell in love with Lucretius at fourteen or fifteen, but Ecclesiastes seems an even better key to his basic feelings. "Is there any book greater?" he once asked. He found it significant that the Bible includes such a book and that almost all parts of Holy Writ contain "flashes of confession of the ultimate darkness of the Infinite."[24] There is an echo of Carlyle here, as there is in Saintsbury's belief that the Ideal, the Infinite, and the Eternal, are "the essence of religion,"[25] also in his insistence that all forms of the supernatural and, even more, superstitions are "respectable."[26]

Saintsbury repeatedly spoke of "the accepted hells beneath," the Whitman phrase he adopted early and used often, "the sad pageant of men's miseries,"[27] and the pain of mortality caught up in the ironic Leconte de Lisle lines he often quoted:

Mais le plus sage en rit,
sachant qu'il doit mourir.[28]

He rarely goes beyond these generalities. Along with skeptical irony and what Elton described well as "a conditional pessimism,"[29] the strain of melancholy preserved in the Nicholson portrait is a trait many friends noted in Saintsbury, as they often noted his wit. He wrote of Molière, "If God has given you brains, and courage, and the upward countenance, if you have loved, if you have had your day and lived your life, what more do you want? Molière had had and done all this. ... "[30]

Though in his last years Saintsbury thought a good deal about these matters, he seems not to have felt any relation of this spirit in himself to the undermining of faith by science that had so agonized some of his contemporaries. Nor did he approve it in the naturalists. Discontent he regarded as a "corruption of melancholy," the sin of sloth, though he saw it as sometimes inevitable. Mere sulky spleen he thought "a little contemptible—pessimism and water, mere peevishness . . . mere whining"—not justified or pardonable as is the *saeva indignatio*, "the great ironic despair" of Swift or the *arduus furor Lucretii*.[31] He accepted the carpe diem of Fielding because behind it was "that vast ironic consciousness of the before and after."[32]

He knew the force and persistence of melancholy and its dangers. No man born her servant, he says, can wholly escape. But he had faith in two means of partial escape—"Humor and Study." He needed both routes as the best means to protect him "lest her sway become tyranny."[33] He also feared continued exaltation as a temptation to nemesis and he saw Balzac's *Peau de Chagrin* as a small masterpiece embodying that law. Explaining its profound importance, he linked the secular and Biblical versions of this "eternal and immutable" truth, "that every extraordinary expansion or satisfaction of heart or brain or will is paid for."[34] This mood, romantic as it is in some measure, is no mere mal de siècle or weltschmerz. Shored up by classical awareness, by strong religious faith and a dose of saving irony, it helped to relieve Saintsbury of many neurotic complications other Victorians suffered. He expressed it at many levels, even the facetious.

> Whether this world is the best of all possible worlds is a complicated religious and philosophical question . . . it has in it toothache, gout, bad wine, bad weather, bad poets, puffery, political charlatans, American cheese, advanced thinkers, spelling reformers, and many other evil beasts and evil things.

But, he concludes, it is not as bad as the Zolaists make out.[35] This list of evils might better have included some of the world's more profound wrongs—slavery, war's miseries, and man's ageless inhumanity to man—but it has a wry wisdom.

Saintsbury's formal religious allegiance and practice is an orthodoxy not incompatible with skepticism, but he rarely discussed it. He described his family as "practicingly religious with no controversial element about it and nothing to make me, either by attraction or repulsion, High Church or Evangelical."[36] As an Anglo-Catholic, his sympathy was with the Oxford Movement as he saw it epitomized in Pusey and in Newman before his conversion.[37] In "Lost Leaders," his tribute to Newman is eloquent though he was temperamentally closer to Pusey as Newman saw him, "haunted by no intellectual perplexities."[38] His unwillingness to probe doubts made him want to ask the modernist, "Is Christianity something like a catalogue or restaurant bill of fare, from which you take what you like and leave the rest?"[39]

Saintsbury, always a regular communicant of the Church even when kneeling became painful and then impossible, only wrote about his views in his last years. In letters to Hunt he could express their shared concerns: some anti-Romanism, including sorrowful anger over his sister's conversion; a firm rejection of biblical criticism and evolutionary science; distrust of ecumenical reform, of prayer book revision, and of "pseudo-Anglo-Catholics" with their excessive concern for vestments and "frippery" and "babble about masses." He found the Thirty-nine Articles orthodox where they should be and "ingeniously noncommittal" where desirable.[40] He and Hunt, who wrote a *History of the English Church*, were at one in their "high" orthodoxy—even in not opposing that old chestnut, the prohibiting of marriage to a deceased wife's sister.[41]

The mask of irony is frequent when Saintsbury voices personal feelings, especially about profound matters. But the import is serious and unequivocal in the facetious note he wrote when he heard that Rome claimed W. H. Mallock (1849–1923) as a "*submortem* convert": If friends hear any such claim after his death, "they may rest assured either that the report is false, or that I was non compos mentis at the time of the alleged conversion." Born an Englishman and member of the Church of England, he thought it wise not to interfere with acts of God.[42]

"Priggishness . . . pedantry . . . dullness . . . absolute vulgarity" Saintsbury once named as "four things from which literature ought to keep men."[43] All four he wished to avoid. And he saw humor as one means. He once cited Charles S. Calverley, Lewis Carroll, and W. S. Gilbert (he omitted Edward Lear and added Traill) as the expression of the spirit of their age, "one that aspired to and rejoiced in humor."[44] And he always fought the humorlessness of the more earnest Victorians. He looked upon nonsense and people's love of it as a strength not a failing, and with Hazlitt he claimed that the English "are almost alone in enjoying and recognizing it." He thought Shakespeare wise in daring often simply to be foolish,[45] and he confessed to Hunt, "If I didn't make foolish jokes, I should be bored to death." He once wished that he could read Donne on the coincidence of Ash Wednesday and St. Valentine's Day, St. Paul on Prohibition in the United States, and Swinburne on Gosse's biography of him.[46] Like Dr. Johnson, he once described his own "sides aching with laughter." He believed "life would be absolutely worthless without jest, without quip, without punning," and rejoiced that Englishmen have been given "a pretty general ability to giggle and make giggle."[47]

He had no theories of humor, but thought the central clue was irony and twice at least he offered "thinking in jest while feeling in earnest" as a satisfactory definition of humor.[48] He explains "pure irony" as "the reflex sense of the other side, of the drawback, of the end, which is required to save passion from fatuity and rapture from cloying."[49] He thought that few poeple can enjoy this view of life because it requires "a certain mystical faith," "a readiness to laugh at oneself," tolerance and pessimism.[50] He was quick to note a lack of humor—notably in Milton and Wordsworth. Unlike the great humorists—Aristophanes, Horace, Lucian, Saint-Evrémond, Rabelais, Montaigne, and the five great Englishmen, Shakespeare, Fielding, Swift, Thackeray, and Carlyle—they never learned "to escape from the labyrinth of life's riddle" by "the humor gate," or to use "this sovereign preservative for self and more sovereign charm for others."[51] All great humorists, he felt, hate stupidity, vulgarity, cant, mere progress as progress, and enjoy "the simpler and more humane pleasures, above all good fellowship."

These are all general literary pronouncements, but he did make jokes and he shared nonsense with Helen and Dorothy Margaret. His friends and his students all recalled his wit, but the distinctive character of it is hard to gauge. It was sometimes a put-down and prompted by antipathy, as with Gladstone and Parnell. Largely literary, it seems not wholly spontaneous. Helen once referred to his "Big Bow Wow manner." Like the early Thackeray and Hood that he loved, it now dates and sometimes seems heavy-handed. Needless to say, it lacked the sophisticated brilliance of Wilde and Shaw.

Saintsbury's range of enjoyment of humor was pretty wide. He preferred Thackeray to Dickens; he loved Fielding, Jane Austen, and the *Ingoldsby Legends*. He did not enjoy Mark Twain at all, but fantastic humor and pure cap and bells, yes, as he found it in Southey's *The Doctor*, which he reread all his life.[52] He could enjoy the dirty joke or indecency if it was frank, not underhand, and robust with laughter as in Rabelais or Aristophanes or saved by frank passion as in Catullus, or in Swift because it was rooted in despair, but not when cold as in Ben Jonson or "sniggering" in Voltaire and Sterne.

Of the practical joke, he was an enemy, but he could be amusing about an accidental one. For the *Cambridge History Of English Literature* he inadvertently wrote up Samuel Waddington, a living minor poet, as dead. The victim protested and remained unreconciled even when, with apologies, Saintsbury tried to persuade him "how much nicer it is to be alive and called dead" than the reverse. More amused than annoyed and hardly penitent, Saintsbury remarked, "He is worse than Partridge, for Swift did persist in killing him."[53]

Saintsbury's letters record the consolation of honors bestowed and genuinely appreciated. He speaks of seven gowns, all honorary. The degree from Edinburgh came late (1919), and he could not make the long journey to receive it. But that October he read a paper, "Eighteenth-Century Poetry," at the Pump Room in Bath, and he journeyed to Oxford in 1920 to cast his vote for the retention of Greek. There had been a "presentation" before he left Edinburgh from the hands of colleagues, students, and friends: a commemorative plaque depicting the University Quadrangle with its Adam buildings in silver.

A more elaborate testimonial came in 1922, on Saintsbury's seventy-seventh birthday. A handsome manuscript scroll signed by three hundred friends, students, and literary men was presented to him at his home in Bath, accompanied by a generous purse made up by the signers and, by his choice, used to commission the portrait by Sir William Nicholson. He enjoyed the sittings, the two men liked each other, and Saintsbury liked the portrait. He spent a good bit of his time that year pleasantly acknowledging each participant's share in the tribute as well as the flood of letters that followed, but when the formal testimonial (what he termed "a purely personal circular") appeared in the *Times*, he feared that he might seem to have been "putting himself forward unpleasantly" and that the "good fellows who started the idea" might be hurt.[54]

Saintsbury tells Hunt he was again "snowed under" with letters and telegrams on his eightieth birthday, in 1925, and was visited by the Mayor and Mayoress of Bath, who presented him with a beautifully bound copy of *The Book of Bath*, to which he had contributed a piece on "Bath and Literature." Being offered the Freedom of Bath, he had had to refuse because his infirmities forbade his attending the long ceremony.

Occasional academic tasks still gave Saintsbury some contact with the university world. Examining continued at Liverpool after 1915, and in the early 1920s he was again reading examinations for Belfast, though he was unable to attend examiners' meetings. In 1928, Cambridge asked him and Nichol Smith to examine a doctoral candidate. Nichol Smith, recalling the viva they conducted at Bath, tells of Saintsbury's characteristic hospitality and its ironic outcome. At the end, the host offered a glass of port to the candidate who, learning later that he had failed, angrily misinterpreted the kindly gesture.[55]

The letters to Hunt frequently convey a sense of Saintsbury's failing strength. On May 8, 1928, he wrote, "I am rather breaking up I think." And, on July 16, "... my 'vital spirits fail' but ... there are many small enjoyments." He then described a pony in the field outside his window "who rolled about like a puppy and apparently made the sun glint on the bottom of his shoes." Reading is curtailed as his eyes weaken, but in 1926 he was reading proofs not his own (probably Helen Waddell's *Wandering Scholars*). On June 14, 1928, he says, "I have a general crumbling sensation about me but *vixi*." In May, 1932, after Hunt's death, he wrote Mrs. Hunt that he sees no visitors.

Saintsbury died at the Royal Crescent, Bath, on January 28, 1933. As he so much hoped, he was not totally bedridden for long, but he had battled increasing ailments and disabilities for three decades. Even the reading he had found "as natural as breathing" at last was limited. His son, Christopher, who had come from Scotland to care for him in the late 1920s, arranged for burial in the family plot in Southampton, and Nichol Smith was present to represent Oxford. He recalled just six mourners, local relatives chiefly. By Saintsbury's will, his Lucretius went to Merton, which received the Nicholson portrait in 1924, and later his handsome silver inkwell and pen, a gift from Miss Stuart in his memory.

But the major legacy of this long, busy, vastly productive life was the publication of so many volumes. One of the last of the Victorians and a prototype of that age with his drive to literary omniscience, his compulsion to read everything, to share it and to place it in its historical frame, Saintsbury was his own man, a feisty social reactionary cherishing his prejudices but grateful for long, richly enjoyed literary experience. Belletrist and formalist he was, yet a journalist's strenuous life in the last days of anonymity and the powerful editorial chair conditioned and toughened him. His authority as a critic and historian has faded, but his initiative in several areas stands as his monument: one of the first to develop the concept of comparative literature, pioneer in urging French literature upon English readers and providing them with its history, historian of European criticism and of English prosody and prose rhythm, and, always, the uniquely enthusiastic interpreter of minor writers.

As Lafcadio Hearn remarked, Saintsbury "is never so simple as he appears."[56] The sheer bulk of his work reinforces the impression of simplicity, even of superficiality, but the man who early embraced the art-for-art's-sake creed was also, one remembers, something of a melancholy pessimist, a lover of Lucretius, Donne, Swift, and Ecclesiastes, but also of Rabelais, Shelley, *Manon Lescaut,* and many other diverse writers and works.

Behind the public image and the huge printed output stood the personal escapist who found in fantasy, dream, and make-believe, in the pleasant euphoria of wine and the table, in compulsive work patterns and constant reading, and in a wall of protective social prejudices the means of evading direct personal intimacy and family feeling. Like most people, he embodied great contradictions that he never explicitly faced.

Where, finally, does Saintsbury stand in the long line of English critics? James R. Sutherland described his criticism as "a sort of controlled impressionism" when, in 1952, he set out to define the main tradition of English criticism.[57] Three of the four critics he selected to represent that tradition would have been Saintsbury's choice: Dryden, who gave it "urbanity...sedate cheerfulness and lively discursiveness"; Dr. Johnson with his life-and-letters approach and his freedom from pedantry; Hazlitt, marked by liveliness, a great critical energy, and a personal love for literature. For Sutherland, this was "the essential condition of all good criticism." As the fourth representative of the tradition, though not one of the greatest, Sutherland named Saintsbury. In him he found the distinctive characteristics of the other three and the same kind of literary response, "well-informed rather than learned; open-minded...the considered and disciplined response of one who had read widely and intelligently...who has kept and cultivated a sense of proportion" and who, finally, offers a value judgment. Sutherland defends his omission of other great English critics, of Coleridge in particular, "the greatest...but a critical phoenix," and Arnold, "the greatest of our

Puritans in criticism." Neither of them he thought truly as representative as his chosen four.

Though the view is British and may exaggerate some points, Sutherland grasped Saintsbury's centrality and something of his lasting import for English criticism. As for the literary historian, in his variety and range he will survive as an important innovator during forty years (1879–1919) of the development of that genre. He would have liked to be enjoyed as a real combination of the two, critic and historian, but will rather live on not as "king of critics" but as a rare cultivator of literary enthusiasm, "the great adulator," as someone called him, in a long history of appreciative criticism, one who sends us back to read and to share his joy in books—"the only friends who never change."

Abbreviations

Acad.	*Academy*
Arnold	*Matthew Arnold*
Athen.	*Athenaeum*
CHEL	*The Cambridge History of English Literature*
Cellar Bk.	*Notes on a Cellar Book*
Coll. Essays	*The Collected Essays and Papers*, 4 vols.
Consid. of Thack.	*A Consideration of Thackeray*
Corr. Impr.	*Corrected Impressions*
Derby	*Earl of Derby*
DNB	*Dictionary of National Biography*
Dryden	*John Dryden*
Earlier Renaiss.	*Earlier Renaissance*, Periods of European Literature Series
Eliz. Lit.	*A History of Elizabethan Literature*
EMLS	English Men of Letters Series
Ency. Brit.	*Encyclopedia Britannica*
Eng. Crit.	*A History of English Criticism*
Eng. Novel	*English Novel*
Essays in Eng. Lit.	*Essays in English Literature, 1780—1860* (1st and 2d ser.)
First Bk. of Eng. Lit.	*A First Book of English Literature*
Flour. of Romance	*Flourishing of Romance*, Periods of European Literature Series
Fort. Rev.	*Fortnightly Review*
Fr. Novel	*A History of the French Novel*, 2 vols.
Fr. Novelists	*Essays on French Novelists*
G.S.	George Saintsbury
G.S. Mem. Vol.	*George Saintsbury: Memorial Volume: A New Collection of His Essays and Papers*
Hist. of Crit.	*A History of Criticism and Literary Taste in Europe from the Earliest Texts to the Present Day*, 3 vols.
Hist. of Prose Rhythm	*A History of English Prose Rhythm*
Hist. of Prosody	*A History of English Prosody from the Twelfth Century to the Present Day*, 3 vols.

Last Scrap Bk.	*A Last Scrap Book*
Last Vintage	*A Last Vintage: Essays and Papers*
Later 19th Cent.	*Later Nineteenth Century,* Periods of European Literature Series
Macmillan's Mag.	*Macmillan's Magazine*
Manual of Eng. Prosody	*A Historical Manual of English Prosody*
Minor Caroline Poets	*Minor Poets of the Caroline Period,* 3 vols.
Miscell. Essays	*Miscellaneous Essays*
19th-Cent. Lit.	*A History of Nineteenth-Century English Literature*
OED	*Oxford English Dictionary* (Unabridged)
Peace of the Augs.	*The Peace of the Augustans: A Survey of Eighteenth-Century English Literature*
Prefs. and Essays	*Prefaces and Essays*
Primer of Fr. Lit.	*A Primer of French Literature*
Procs. of Brit. Acad.	*Proceedings of the British Academy*
Quart. Rev.	*Quarterly Review*
Sat. Rev.	*Saturday Review* (London)
Scott	*Sir Walter Scott*
Scrap Bk.	*A Scrap Book*
Second Scrap Bk.	*A Second Scrap Book*
Short Hist. of Eng. Lit.	*A Short History of English Literature*
Short Hist. of Fr. Lit.	*A Short History of French Literature*
TLS	*Times Literary Supplement* (London)

Notes

Chapter 1

1. Manuscript: given to the author by George Saintsbury's grandson, George. "The Land o' Leal," a Jacobite song written anonymously by Carolina Baroness Nairne (1766–1845), was published in 1846.

2. According to county borough records, George Saintsbury, senior, was living at Oak Lodge, Bitterne, in 1845 and by 1847 had moved to 9 Portland Terrace, Southampton. The register of births gives Lottery Hall, St. Mary's, as the birthplace of his son, George.

3. Quoted in Oliver Elton, "George Saintsbury," *Procs. of the Brit. Acad.* 19 (1933): 325.

4. G. S., *Consid. of Thack.*, 14.

5. In 1945, Christopher Saintsbury gave a quaint, miniature three-volume set of bound calligraphic shorthand manuscripts done in 1795–98 by his great uncle, John Saintsbury, to the British Museum.

6. I acknowledge my appreciation for this information to Brigit Williams, the archivist of Sainsbury's. She insisted that there was no relationship between the families, that, in fact, the Sainsburys had few relations. She mentioned some of the more distinguished ones, adding that many people call to ask whether they are related and none ever is.

7. G.S., *Last Scrap Book*, 342–43.

8. With a lapse of memory, in 1921, G.S. called his dedication of *Notes on a Cellar Book* to Kipling his "first and last" dedication.

9. In the *Short Hist. of Fr. Lit.* (4th ed.), G.S. describes Chasles as "a lively writer" whose judgment on English literature did not equal his affection for it (565). All later references to the *Short History* are to this edition unless otherwise noted.

10. G.S., *Last Vintage*, 90.

11. G.S., letter to William Hunt, 1923, Merton College Library collection. Later references will be to this unpublished collection of the letters of Hunt and G.S. given to Merton by Mrs. Hunt and put into typescript at her expense.

12. For G.S.'s reactions to Kensington and Notting Hill, see G.S., *Consid. of Thack.*, 14; *Last Vintage*, 104–7; "Municipal London," *Quart. Rev.* 158 (July,

1884): 1–39; "London of the Victorians: How it Struck a Right Timer—Lost Charms," *The Times* (London), January 25, 1929; *Scrap Bks.*

13. G.S., letter to Austin Dobson, June 11, 1908, Dobson Collection, University of London Library. All later references to the Dobson-Saintsbury letters will be to this unpublished collection.

14. G.S., letter to his great-niece, Brenda Green Insley, October 25, 1927. Mrs. Insley kindly let me read some of these letters, which form the basis of her article, "Behind the Legend of George Saintsbury," *London Mercury*, March, 1933, 442–44.

15. G.S., *Fr. Novel*, 2:76n.

16. G.S., *Scrap Bk.*, 214. G.S., *Second Scrap Bk.* and *Corr. Imprs.* are the chief sources for knowledge of this early reading.

17. G.S., *Last Scrap Bk.*, 88–91; *Last Vintage*, 116–23 (an address given in 1905 to the Classical Association of Scotland) are supplemented by information kindly supplied in 1963 by D. G. Dalziel, Hon. Secretary of Old King's College School, from records. *The Centenary History of King's College London* by F. J. C. Hearnshaw (London, 1929, 91, 154, 263) records that Dr. Major was appointed Headmaster of the King's College Junior Department November 26, 1830. The Department became known as King's College School. In 1866, the College Council called for the resignation of Dr. Major as "a gentleman who took his degree forty-seven years ago."

18. G.S., *Prose Rhythm*, 41n. Cockayne edited *Anglo-Saxon Leechdoms, etc.* in the Rolls series in 1864–66.

19. G.S., *Last Vintage*, 116; *Last Scrap Bk.*, 88–91.

20. G.S., *Second Scrap Bk.*, 3–6. "Postmaster" was Merton's name for the status on the Foundation more generally called "Scholar."

21. A copy of the poem, in the boy's hand, was given to me by G.S.'s grandson, George. His account of the occasion is in G.S., *Scrap Bk.*, 232–35.

22. G.S.'s reply to the Address presented to him on his seventy-seventh birthday (G.S., *G. S. Mem. Vol.*, 215–18).

23. G.S., "Pisgah Looking Both Ways," *Dial* (New York) 86 (March, 1929): 248. In *Last Scrap Bk.*, Saintsbury says, "How many people have read *The Library of Useless Knowledge* by Athanasius Gasker, Esq., F.R.S., etc., etc., London, William Pickering, MDCXXXVI?" (10). This pamphlet of fifty-two pages was written by E. W. Clarke, a contemporary at Cambridge of Thackeray, Fitzgerald, and Sir Frederick Pollock. G.S. gave his copy to W. P. Ker with the understanding it would go to the Codrington Library at All Souls College, Oxford.

Chapter 2

1. G.S., *Scrap Bk.*, 1–103. Also see G.S., *Prefs. and Essays*, 345–60; Creighton 1904; Green 1957.

2. Given to the author by G.S.'s grandson.

3. Mark Pattison, quoted in Green 1957, 240–48.

4. G.S., *Prefs. and Essays*, 350.

5. Quoted in Green 1957, 246.

6. G.S., letter to Hunt, January 10, 1915, comments on Compton Mac-Kenzie's *Sinister Street:* "I have made bonfires and drawn a 'bun cordon' and wandered about quads at midnight in a state of dubious sobriety . . . too often to object to the 'rowdy side.'"

7. "George Saintsbury," *Manchester Guardian,* January 30, 1933.

8. G.S., *Derby,* 1.

9. Ibid.; see also G.S., *Prose Rhythm,* 416, 469.

10. Creighton 1904 I: 17.

11. See G.S., *Scrap Bk.,* 107–112.

12. On Creighton, in addition to Creighton 1904, see Gosse 1913, vol. 5 (*Collected Essays*); Strachey (n.d.) presents a typically ironic and biased account.

13. G.S., *G. S. Mem. Vol.,* 131.

14. Reference to the Bridges-G.S. correspondence by courtesy of Lord Bridges, who preferred not to have full, direct quotation.

15. G.S., quoted in Creighton 1904 1:23.

16. Ibid., 24.

17. Ibid., 29–30.

18. G.S., *Prefs. and Essays,* 353.

19. G.S. *Scrap Bk.,* 188–189; *Second Scrap Bk.,* 41. G.S. says Creighton's version of the story reflects the "inalienable right of storytellers to decorate the stories they tell" and adds, "I was *very* like Habbakuk at the time." The less pleasant and somewhat resented encounter with Mark Pattison over G.S.'s application for a Lincoln Fellowship (G.S., *Second Scrap Bk.,* 47–49) led to a finally sympathetic judgment on "Mark's Way."

20. G.S., *G.S. Mem. Vol.,* 134.

21. G.S., *Prefs. and Essays,* 352–53; he tells of a similar abortive society at Oxford in his time called the "Eclectics."

22. Thackeray 1960, chaps. 18–21.

23. G.S., *Second Scrap Bk.,* 40; see also G.S., *Fr. Novel,* 2:xi.

24. G.S., *Second Scrap Bk.,* 57–58. Cf. G.S., *Last Scrap Bk.,* 257–58: " . . . the Third . . . lacks the peculiar 'sting of the miss' which a Second inflicts . . . it is the 'just-not-having-got-a-first' feeling that is the devil. . . ."

25. See Wilson 1950, 369.

26. G.S., *Last Scrap Bk.,* 250–59.

27. Gosse 1917, 134.

28. Swinburne 1926, xvi, 369.

29. G.S., *Last Vintage,* 77–83.

30. G.S., *Second Scrap Bk.,* 59n. He reports recurrent dreams of going up to Oxford again to try for Firsts and Fellowships, dreams that vanished when the College made him an Honorary Fellow.

31. G.S., *Arnold,* 118–19, 165.

32. G.S., *Coll. Essays,* 2:342.

33. G.S., *Cellar Bk.,* 153.

34. G.S., letter to Hunt, 1916; *Second Scrap Bk.,* 165.

35. G.S., Oxford account book.

36. Creighton 1904, 1:21.

37. See Moers 1960, chaps. 3,7.

38. G.S., *Scrap Bk.*, 38n.

39. Purves, in *G.S. Mem. Vol.*, says the drawing purchased at "the Chelsea sale" was never printed (15).

40. G.S., *Prefs. and Essays*, 354, 359–60.

41. "A Sure Foundation," an unpublished lecture quoted in Elton, *Proc.*, 1933, 335.

42. G.S., *Fr. Novelists*, 194–95.

Chapter 3

1. G.S., *Last Scrap Bk.*, 198.

2. G.S., *Second Scrap Bk.*, 160n.

3. G.S., *Manchester*, preface and note. G.S. and Freeman disagreed, possibly over Saintsbury's coming close to condoning the Peterloo massacre (1819).

4. Axon 1887, 114–15.

5. G.S., *Manchester*, 95–96, 163, 166.

6. G.S., *Fr. Novel*, 2:316.

7. G.S., *Last Vintage*, 78.

8. G.S., *Cellar Bk.*, 9.

9. G.S., *Fr. Novel*, 2:118.

10. G.S., *Second Scrap Bk.*, 72.

11. Stapfer 1905, 12–14. Stapfer (1846–1917) took his *docteur-ès-lettres* diploma in 1870, at Paris. Saintsbury acknowledged his aid in *Primer of Fr. Lit.*, and in a brief anonymous review (*Athen.*, June 8, 1895), praised his *Montaigne*. See Dartique 1918.

12. G.S., *Second Scrap Bk.*, 273–74. G.S. had had a week's hospitality in barracks in Devon while at Oxford. His account of his "only ghost," one seen on a moonlit midnight walk from Fort George to his home at Cambridge Park, Guernsey (G.S., *Scrap Bk.*, 99–103) concludes: "She did me no harm, and I was the real intruder on what may have been merely a rest in a journey from El Dorado to Samarcand. . . ."

13. G.S., *Coll. Essays*, 2:266.

14. G.S., *Minster*, February 1895, 103.

15. G.S., *Fr. Novel*, 2:205; letter to Hunt, December 8, 1918.

16. G.S., *Second Scrap Bk.*, 72n.

17. Durand 1898.

18. G.S., *Prose Rhythm*, 168–69. In the *Second Scrap Bk.*, G.S. calls Pattison "a morbid and rather bad-blooded creature" (307).

19. Stapfer 1905, 8.

20. Ibid., 8–9.

21. G.S., *Second Scrap Bk.*, 163.

22. G.S., *Last Vintage*, 115.

23. Ibid., 120.

24. Ibid. Cf. 120–21; G.S., *Peace of the Augs.*, 78–80; *First Bk. of Eng. Lit.*, preface.

25. G.S., *Last Vintage*, 115.

26. G.S., *Scrap Bk.*, 139–40. Another, "Pastiche Ampoulé," from the 1880s, is dismissed with a similar verdict. Webster 1933, 13–14, cites all the creative pieces that have survived in print as well as the verses addressed to G.S. by Dobson and Lang.

27. See Creighton 1904, vol. 1, on these years.

28. G.S., *Fr. Novel*, 2:230n. "A" is surely Saintsbury; "B," Creighton.

29. *The Savile Club* 1923, 30.

30. G.S., *Second Scrap Bk.*, 331.

31. Besant 1902, 176; also Kipling 1937, 92–93.

32. Information from *Elgin Schools and Schoolmasters*, a local publication supplied to me in 1962 by the Director of Education for Moray and Nairn, Wm. F. Lindsay.

33. "George Saintsbury," *Student* (University of Edinburgh), January 26, 1916, 46.

34. G.S., *Cellar Bk.*, 115.

35. Printed fifty years later as "Edgar Allen Poe," *Dial* (New York) 83:451–63.

36. G.S., letters to the Secretary, Clarendon Press, Bodleian Ms. Autograph d. 24, fol. 144–45, fol. 146.

37. See Mills 1921; Hammond 1934.

38. G.S., letter, undated, in the Gosse Collection, Brotherton Library, Leeds. Further references to Gosse-G.S. letters will be to the Gosse Collection (largely unpublished).

39. G.S., *Cellar Bk.*, 153.

40. G.S.'s *Athenaeum* reviews done before 1896 are identified in the official file now held by the *New Statesman and Nation* and kindly made available to me. His account book makes unnecessary speculation about what and for what organs he wrote, anonymously or otherwise, from 1877 on. The book was lent to me by Saintsbury's grandson, George.

41. Dorothy Margaret Stuart, interview, 1962. G.S. would have called a daughter Voluptas.

42. Wilson 1950, 368.

43. An oral report to me by George Kitchen, one of Saintsbury's Edinburgh assistants, in 1962. His judgment that she was "a cabbage" seemed a cruel, youthful one.

44. G.S. felt a great affinity with Scott. One suspects that he was identifying with him when he wrote of Sir Walter's wife: "She does not seem to have been extremely wise, and was entirely unliterary; but neither of these defects is a *causa redihibitionis* in marriage; and she was certainly a faithful and affectionate wife" (G.S., *Scott*, 16).

45. Waddell, in *Last Vintage*, 27.

46. G.S., *Cellar Book*, xxix.

47. Gross 1969, 135.

48. G.S., *Acad,* July 1, 1873, 241–43. Cf. G.S., *Later 19th Cent.,* 50–51.

49. G.S., in *Acad.,* August 1, 1873, 281–83. G.S. reviewed *Garvarni,* a biography, welcoming it because it exhibits "the life and manners of that generation of 1830, which no student of literature and art can ever weary of contemplating" (*Acad.,* October 15, 1873, 385).

50. *Acad.,* January 24, 1874, 84. G.S.'s preoccupation with Baudelaire is evident in references in his review of Whitman and in an early novel review (*Acad.,* July 4, 1874, 7–8).

51. *Acad.,* October 10, 1874, 398–99. He analyzes the vers libre and praises Whitman as original and universal.

52. G.S., *Last Scrap Bk.,* 62–63; *Scrap Bk.,* 278; *Hist. of Prosody,* 3:191. The *Nation* ([New York] 21 [December 2, 1875]: 355), being asked by a correspondent whether he should follow Edmond Scherer or G.S. on Baudelaire, while "bludgeoning . . . the neo-pagan school at large," recommended Scherer on the ground that G.S. had praised "the most spurious-sounding passages in Whitman." For G.S.'s, reply to this unjust charge, see *Nation* (New York) 22 (January 13, 1876):27.

53. *Nation* (New York) 19 (December 5, 1874):559. The "heresy of instruction" concept descended from Poe's "Poetic Principle" through Baudelaire and Gautier to Swinburne.

54. Flaubert 1889–93, 2:70–71; Swinburne 1926, xvi, 138.

55. G.S., *Acad.,* June 13, 1874, 651–53.

56. *Acad.,.* July 2, 1875, 4–6. See Rosenblatt 1931, 164n. The *Quarterly Rev.* (April, 1876, 507–26) was still condemning Swinburne.

57. G.S., *Acad.,* July 3, 1875, 5.

58. Bradley 1909, 17.

59. G.S., *Coll. Essays,* 4:1–29. Additions of 1892 and 1924 are clearly indicated. Quotations are from the 1875 text only.

60. Cf. Starkie 1960, 36; Robinson 1953; Temple 1953, 88–89, 225.

61. G.S., *Coll. Essays,* 4:28.

62. G.S., *Prefs. and Essays,* 287.

63. G.S., *Later 19th Cent.,* 51.

64. G.S., *Scrap Bk.,* 115.

65. G.S., *Coll. Essays,* 3:62–87.

66. G.S., *Acad.,* September 9, 1876, 254; *Last Scrap Bk.,* 270–71. C. A. B. Appleton, the editor, had asked Saintsbury not to be too severe because the *Academy* was one of the few periodicals Lewes still let his wife read and "it would be a pity if she were quite choked off."

67. G.S., *Miscell. Essays,* vii. He notes that examples of "deliberately elaborate style" have been numerous since 1876.

Chapter 4

1. Robinson 1953, 733. Robinson (1953) and Temple (1953) give a slightly different selection of details. G.S. would have agreed with Robinson that Swinburne was "less 'aesthetic' than anti–philistine."

2.Temple 1953, pt. 4, "Edmund Gosse." Since she is concerned solely with the efforts of English critics to understand and interpret contemporary French literature to English readers in the latter part of the century, she is severe on those whose sympathies stop short of Mallarmé, Verlaine, and the later symbolists. G.S. is merely glanced at.

3. G.S., *Acad.*, January 31, 1874, 108.

4. G.S. included the poem, "L'Art," in his *French Lyrics* (1883, 220–22) and cited it in *Fr. Novel* 2:206, as applicable to any art.

5. See Dobson 1928, 9, 98.

6. Edited by W. Davenport Adams (London), 331–49. See Temple 1953, 190–228.

7. G.S., *Acad.*, June 23, 1878, 548–49. A Gosse review of *Le Livre des Ballades, Acad.* (April 21, 1877, 336), surveys the history of this form.

8. G.S. letter, 1877, Gosse Collection.

9. Letters, Dobson Collection; Dobson letter dated June 29, 1878; G.S. letter undated. Dobson seems to have sent a copy of the second edition of his *Proverbs in Porcelain*. G.S. comments on several "novelties" but laments the omission of a "charming" verse on "the man who plants cabbages."

10. G.S., *Hist. of Prosody*, 3:388–90; he refers also to Dobson's *Note*.

11. G.S., "Some Memories of Edmund Gosse," *London Mercury* 18 (July, 1928): 264.

12. Charteris 1931, 101.

13. Undated Lang letter, Dobson Collection. Cf. another letter, undated (but probably from the 1880s), "The rondeau has been sat on by Saintsbury and Pollock . . . " (presumably as *Sat. Rev.* editors).

14. G.S., *Scrap Bk.*, 240.

15. "The Gosse Guest Book," Cambridge University Library, in Gosse's hand; see also A. Waugh, "The Book of Gosse," *Fort. Rev.* 137, o.s. (September 1, 1932): 284–302. The Dobsons and Langs were among the regular visitors several times a year until 1912. G.S. was present on May 19 and December 1, 1878 (Robert Louis Stevenson was also there) and at three luncheons at the National Club given by Gosse in the 1890s: June 3, 1892; January 23, 1894 (when Henry James and Arthur Symons were present); and July 28, 1894 (when Aubrey Beardsley, E. F. Benson, and John Davidson were present). Gross 1969, 139–49, gives thumbnail portraits of "the Saintsbury–Lang Savile Club circle." He found these bellettrists "wistful, enervated, Alexandrian," adjectives inappropriate to Saintsbury.

16. G.S., *Scrap Bk.*, 241, 249.

17. G.S. letter, January 27, 1879, Dobson Collection. Dobson was a teetotaler.

18. G.S., letter, January 15, 1892, Dobson Collection. The *Chanson* was from the *St. James Magazine* of June, 1763.

19. See Dobson 1928, 191, 244 for the "Fable." The lines "Dobson kind and Dobson just" expressed gratitude when Dobson proposed him to edit the Oxford Thackeray.

20. G.S., *Lond. Merc.* 18:264–68.

21. Ibid.

22. G.S.'s letter to Gosse, n.d. Gosse Collection.

23. Gosse, letter to Dobson, December 6, 1880, Gosse Collection. See Charteris 1931, 136, on another, earlier misunderstanding with the *Sat. Rev.*

24. G.S., *Scrap Bk.*, 60.

25. Ibid., 65, 67; *Last Vintage*, 93.

26. Green 1946, 197. Lang said that Dobson taught him to "*think* in ballades" (Green, 1946, 62; see G.S., *Scrap Bk.*, 63–64).

27. See Buckley 1945; Henley's verse of the 1870s is chiefly in *Bric–a–Brac* (1879), which became a section of *A Book of Verse* (1888). See also Robinson 1953, 747, 752.

28. G.S., *Scrap Bk.*, 155; *Minister* May, 1895, 212. See George Meredith's letter to Robert Louis Stevenson, March 17, 1883, (Cline 1971, 2:692).

29. G.S., *Short Hist. of Fr. Lit.*, 4th ed., 581. Unless otherwise noted, all references are to this edition.

30. Cf. Temple 1953, 15.

31. G.S., *Coll. Essays*, 4:221–49.

32. Ibid., 221–22, 248–49.

33. G.S., *Coll. Essays*, 4:4.

34. G.S., *Fr. Novelists*, vi.

35. Ibid., 223.

36. Richard Garnett, "A Bookish Gossip Around George Saintsbury," *Blackwood's Magazine* 230 (December, 1931): 822–34. Cf. Chrystal 1933.

37. G.S., *Fr. Novelists* 414–15, 418. Webster says rightly that any anthology of Saintsbury's best should include this attractive essay (1933, 18).

38. G.S., *Fr. Novelists*, 328–29.

39. Ibid., 291.

40. Ibid., 197–224. The next decade produced a strong reaction in Dumas's favor. Lang, Stevenson, Walter Pollock, and Henley all did "him reason and justice," though the *Quarterly Review* revived the old "misapprehension and misrepresentation" in 1890.

41. G.S., *Fr. Novelists*, 229.

42. Ibid., 235. Cf. G.S., *Short Hist. of Fr. Lit.*, 537–39. The preface is not mentioned, but the novel is said to have "the most remarkable qualities of style and artistic conception," plus "a willful disregard of the proprieties." In the ninth edition of the *Ency. Brit.*, G.S. stressed the same virtues of artistry. Cf. G.S. "Two Men of Letters" (on Gautier and Charles Lever), *Fort. Rev.* 32 (September 1, 1879): 385–400; *Primer of Fr. Lit.*, 4th ed., 122, 126, 131.

43. Ibid., 242, 259.

44. Anon. [G.S.], *Cornhill*, 27(1873): 151–69. As for external evidence on the authorship of the *Cornhill* essay, G.S. accounts for 1873 do not survive. He never refers to it, just as he never mentioned all the anonymous writing he did for the *Athenaeum*. Robinson (1953, 745), assigns the essay to G.S., but gives no reasons. *The Index to Victorian Periodicals*, 1, #1241, cites Sidney Colvin as the author because of "a list drawn up by Leonard Huxley about 1917."

45. Simcox, Obituary, *Acad.*, February 1, 1873, 41–43. He deplored the

lack of morality and decorum in Gautier while praising his style but gave no attention to his role in the aesthetic movement.

46. G.S., *Coll. Essays*, 4:281–307, Cf. G.S., *Hist. of Crit.*, 3:339–42, where he deplores a rumor that France has forgotten Gautier and rates him as "one of the greatest" literary men of his century.

47. G.S., *Coll. Essays*, 4:31–65; including the note added in 1891 in *Fr. Novelists*, 377–80.

48. G.S., *Coll. Essays*, 4:63–65.

49. G.S., *Coll. Essays*, 4:preface, mentions this fact. Webster (1933, 47) quotes Flaubert's enthusiastic letter of September 1, 1878.

50. G.S., *Fr. Novel*, 2:vi–vii.

51. G.S., *Athen.*, March 27, 1880, 401–2; February 4, 1882, 151–52; March 8, 1884, 305–6; January 9, 1886, 64.

52. G.S., *Acad.*, April 20, 1878, 337–38.

53. G.S., *Acad.*, May 11, 1878, 405. In *Sat. Rev.* (April 5, 1884, 459, and November 14, 1885, 657), it is probably G.S. who is condemning Brunetière's one-sided cramping theory of literature as he does in *Athen.* (July 19, 1884, 79–80) and elsewhere.

54. G.S., *Acad.*, January 12, 1884, 24.

55. G.S., *Coll. Essays*, 4:114, 191.

56. G.S., on Renan, *Athen.*, June 24, 1884, 757; August 27, 1887, 273–74; June 25, 1892, 821; obituary, October 8, 1892; and G.S., *Coll. Essays*, 4:163–99.

57. Scherer 1891, Preface.

58. Review (anon.) of *Miscell. Essays* by G.S., *Spectator*, 69 (July 16, 1892):98–99.

59. The thirty-four articles for the ninth edition were retained, slightly revised, and some were extended in the eleventh edition, where three new ones—on Balzac, Thomas Corneille, and Mérimée—were added.

60. Cairns (1946, vi–vii) says G.S.'s essays are comparable in quality to those of Arnold, Gosse, Dowden, Symons, and Havelock Ellis.

61. This last phrase G.S. used early in *Academy* reviews. The *Ency. Brit.*, 11th ed. adds " . . . who thus miss his extraordinary command of the poetical appeal in sounds, in imagery, and in suggestion generally."

62. These examples are in G.S., "French Literature," *Ency. Brit*, 9th ed.

63. Ibid., 641.

64. G.S., *Acad.*, March 24, 1877, 241–42; *Acad.*, January 12, 1878, 26.

65. J. D. Demogeot, *Histoire de la littérature française depuis ses origines jusqu'à nos jours* (1870), and Nicholas E. Geruzez, *Essais d'histoire littéraire* (1853) and *Littérature pendant la révolution, 1789–1800* (1850). See G.S., "A History of French Literature," *Bookman* (London), 33 (November, 1907):92.

66. The sale of G.S.'s library (Catalogue #183, James Thin, Edinburgh, 1916) listed 1,901 items, of which 186 are French literature.

67. G.S., *Primer of Fr. Lit.*, 4th ed., 140.

68. The last edition (1926) carried a supplementary chapter on modern literature by Charles Rudmore Brown, who said the *Primer* had been his "first teacher of French literature."

69. Illustrative extracts supplied only for the medieval period were dropped in the 5th edition. The *Specimens* ran from Villon to Hugo.

70. G.S., *Short Hist. of Fr. Lit.*, 586. The last pages of the *Ency. Brit.* survey became a part of the conclusion of the *Short History* at the suggestion of some authoritative critics.

71. Bourget, *Acad.*, February 10, 1883, 98–99. Gaston Paris agreed that no Frenchman could accept such an estimate (*Romania* 12 [1883]:602–605).

72. Arnold, "Introduction," in Ward 1880, 1:xxxvii–xl.

73. G.S., *Short Hist. of Eng. Lit.*, 113.

74. G.S. *Primer of Fr. Lit.*, 120; *Hist. of Crit.*, 1:137, and 3:334; *Coll. Essays*, 4:292; *Short Hist. of Fr. Lit.*, 394, 462, 528–29; Hugo 1879, 3.

75. Anon. Review, *Sat. Rev.*, October 14, 1882, 507–9.

76. Bourget on G.S. *Primer, Acad.*, November 6, 1880, 324; on G.S. *Short History, Acad.*, February 10, 1883, 98–99; Paris, on the *Short History, Romania* 12 (1883):602–5, limited himself to the medieval section and gave two columns of errors and omissions. Saintsbury acknowledged the usefulness of the corrections and expressed his gratitude for the praise of both Paris and Bourget in G.S., *Hist. of Crit.*, 3:464, and the preface to his *Fr. Novel*. Webster, (1933, 22), cites Elton, Scherer, and Nichol Smith, who agree that G.S.'s taste was distinctly English.

77. Henley on G.S. *Primer, Athen.*, February 19, 1881, 262–63; on G.S. *Short Hist., Athen.*, October 21, 1882, 522–23; also on G.S. *French Lyrics, Athen.*, February 24, 1883, 242–43.

78. The 4th ed., 564, contains G.S.'s answer to Scherer and states that he had "not known a critic more acute within his range, or more honest according to what he saw."

79. G.S., *Fr. Novelists*, 92, 103–4.

80. Webster (1933, 18), claims these volumes set a new standard in English editing of foreign classics. He also wrote the introductions for Corneille's *Horace*, Racine's *Esther* and Voltaire's *Mérope*.

81. Symons, *Athen.*, March 26, 1892, 399.

82. Anon. review, *Manchester Guardian*, November 5, 1889, 12.

83. G.S., on Dante, *New Review* 6 (April, 1892):501.

84. G.S., *Last Vintage*, 128–35.

85. Anon. [G.S.], *Athen.*, August 19, 1893, 256–57. In discussing Lord Derby's translation of the *Iliad*, G.S. (*Prefs. and Essays*, 303–13) compared seven English translations, one from each half–century from Chapman to Derby, and concluded that, though Chapman's is the best, Derby's is the only *true* translation: ". . . nothing that is not Homer, and . . . everything of Homer's that is not ornament."

86. G.S., *French Lyrics*, xviii. A tenth edition appeared in 1910.

87. See Temple 1953, 44, 277 nn. 53, 56.

88. G.S., *Prefs. and Essays*, 361–73.

89. G.S. *Prefs. and Essays*, 374–407. He revised an older translation of Marmontel, "a little brushed up and set straight."

90. G.S., *Fr. Novelists,* 112–63. Revised to serve as chap. 12, in G.S., *Fr. Novel,* vol. 1, the essay lost some of the merit of the original.

91. With this choice there can be little quarrel: *Le Père Goriot, Eugènie Grandet, La Cousine Bette, Le Peau de Chagrin,* or even *La Recherche de l'Absolu;* the sixth, *Seraphita,* he included for its personal mystical interest as well as for the "mere writing."

92. G.S., "Preface to *The Peasantry,*" in Balzac 1895–1900, ix–x. G.S., the Tory journalist, tips his hand when he says Balzac's vision could have come right out of a "novel on the Irish Land League."

93. Lukacs 1950; G.S., "Preface to *The Peasantry,*" x–xi.

94. Symons 1904, 5–21.

95. G.S., "Honoré de Balzac and M. Brunetière," *Quart. Rev.,* 206 (January, 1907): 124–47. The chief quarrel was with Brunetière.

96. G.S., *Acad.,* February 7, 1880, 104. O'Shaughnessy was the English correspondent of the bibliographical journal, *Le Livre,* G.S. protests in the name of the *Academy.*

97. G.S., "Guy de Maupassant," *National Review* 21 (August, 1893):817; also see *Short Hist. of Fr. Lit.,* 552.

Chapter 5

1. G.S., *Coll. Essays,* 4:248.

2. G.S., *Scrap Bk.,* 153–58, tells the story; see also Green 1946, 55, 75; Connell 1949.

3. G.S., *Hist. of Crit.,* 3:561.

4. G.S., *Scrap Bk.,* 54–69; *Last Vintage,* 84–94.

5. G.S., *Scrap Bk.,* 155, 65n.

6. A letter from G.S. to Gosse (April 23, 1878 or 1879, Gosse Collection) says, "Lang has gone into the meadows to see the young lambs and . . . I have undertaken to do more than usual this week."

7. G.S., *Last Scrap Bk.,* 270–79; see also Green 1946, 56.

8. Cf. G.S., *Second Scrap Bk.,* 359; *Coll. Essays,* 1:123; *Hist. of Crit.,* 3:267.

9. G.S., *Last Scrap Bk.,* 279.

10. "An Independent Weekly Review of Politics, Literature, Science and Art." He wrote for it from December, 1878, until April, 1880.

11. May 1–August 25, 1877, G.S. received £110.18.6; he lists £127 as a "bad debt."

12. Escott 1911, 244; Bevington 1941, 320.

13. See Bevington 1941; Arnold was referring to *The World* and *Truth.*

14. G.S., *Last Scrap Bk.,* 64–65.

15. W. Earl Hodgson, *Unrest or the Newer Republic,* a satire on the *Sat. Rev.* as the "Slashaway," was reviewed by G.S. in *Athen.,* August 20, 1887, 243. John Bright used the term *The Reviler.*

16. Law and Law 1925, 217.

17. Bevington 1941, 322, quoting Fox Bourne 1887, 2:291.

18. Matthews 1917, 298.

19. Bevington 1941, ix; from the story, "A Fascinating Friend."

20. The *Saturday Review* met its first threat of real competition in the *Spectator* and the *Guardian*.

21. Besant 1902, 94.

22. Escott 1911, 239.

23. Pollock 1933, 93.

24. G.S., *Scrap Bk.*, 130. This view G.S. developed in "Journalism Fifty Years Ago," *G.S. Mem. Vol.*, 94.

25. G.S., *Derby*, 3.

26. See G.S., *Scrap Bk.*, 127. Venables, a friend of Thackeray from Charterhouse School days, was purportedly the original of Warrington in *Pendennis*. G.S. characterizes him in *19th-Cent. Lit.*, 207.

27. G.S., *Fr. Novel*, 2:437.

28. G.S., letter, Ms. 4622, #157, National Library of Scotland.

29. G.S., *Hist. of Crit.*, 3:555.

30. G.S., *Scrap Bk.*, 6–8.

31. G.S., letter to Wm. Hunt.

32. G.S., *Sat. Rev.*, December 8, 1883, 724–25; *Sat. Rev.*, January 19, 1884, 75–76. See G.S., *Second Scrap Bk.*, 186–91.

33. G.S., *Sat. Rev.*, September 28, 1889, 532.

34. *Sat. Rev.*, September 17, 1887, 384–85.

35. *Sat. Rev.*, November 14, 1885, 637–38, *Sat. Rev.* August 21, 1886, 242.

36. H. Warner Allen, a member of the staff of the paper in its days of brief revival in the 1930s under the Pollocks' aegis, provided this information. He assumed that Frank Harris had destroyed the files.

37. G.S. letter (Dobson Collection), quoted in Dobson 1928, 122, asking Dobson to review Courthope's *Addison*.

38. Bevington agrees (1941, 323–24).

39. G.S., letter to Gosse, January 18, 1910, Gosse Collection.

40. G.S., *Last Scrap Bk.*, 279.

41. Escott 1911, 24.

42. G.S., *Last Scrap Bk.*, 270–79; see also *Coll. Essays*, 3:305.

43. G.S. (letter to Hunt) says Walter Pollock was never a man to stand total solitude. G.S. was friendly with all the Pollock brothers. Walter wrote some novels and poetry and gave lectures on French writers at the Royal Institution (1879).

44. G.S., letter to Gosse, 1879, Gosse Collection (quoted in Charteris, 1931, 114). Green (1946, 65) tells of Pollock's forcing Lang to admit his authorship of the parody *Much Darker Days* by asking him to review it.

45. Obituary, *Sat. Rev.*, October 22, 1887, 539; Memoir, *Sat. Rev.*, October 29, 1887, 585–86. See also G.S., *Last Scrap Bk.*, 276n.

46. Pollock (1933, 90), says inquiry at one office for those of the other could be met by a "stare of blank ignorance." See also Wells 1934, 2:521; Matthews 1917, 295–301. G.S. (*Consid. of Thack.*, 141) says "Write your reply

as stingingly as you possibly can; keep it a night, and put it in the fire next day."

47. G.S., *Second Scrap Bk.*, 227.

48. G.S., *Scrap Bk.*, 238.

49. G.S., *Last Vintage*, 153.

50. G.S., *Last Scrap Bk.*, 200.

51. G.S., *19th-Cent. Lit.*, 380–81.

52. G.S., *Consid. of Thack.*, 50. His account book shows that Saintsbury ended 1877 (his first year on the press) "in the red": his income, £708, from journalism, was short of expenses by £222. Once he became Assistant Editor of the *Sat. Rev.* in 1883, his annual salary ranged from £1000 to £1400. His Edinburgh University income (Crown salary plus fees) was £900 a year, which gave him a pension of £450 in 1916.

53. G.S., "The Newspaper Press," *Quart. Rev.*, 150 (October, 1880):500.

54. G.S., *Consid. of Thack*, 70.

55. G.S., *Coll. Essays*, 1:166.

56. Ibid., 4:298.

57. G.S., *Hist of Crit.*, 3:455n; *Later 19th-Cent.*, 364; G.S., *19th Cent. Lit.*, 448.

58. G.S., letter to Gosse, October 13, 1882, Gosse Collection.

59. Gosse 1913, 206.

60. Marcus 1969, 46.

61. C. H. Herford, review, *Acad.*, December 3, 1887, 363.

62. G.S., letter to Gosse, October 13, 1882, Gosse Collection.

63. G.S., *19th-Cent. Lit.*, 448.

64. G.S., *Coll. Essays*, 1:110.

65. G.S., *Hist. of Crit.*, 3:555.

66. G.S., *Coll. Essays*, 2:20.

67. G.S., letter to Matthews, December 19 (sometime between 1885 and 1894), Columbia University Library.

68. Marcus 1969, 46.

69. Gross 1969, 131.

Chapter 6

1. G.S., *Hist of Crit.*, 3:555.

2. G.S., *Scrap Bk.*, 10–11; Orwell 1937.

3. G.S., *Coll. Essays*, 2:383–408.

4. G.S., *Last Scrap Bk.*, 288–302; *Coll. Essays*, 1:267–301, and 2:1–30.

5. G.S., *Dryden*, 74, 76–90.

6. G.S., *Coll. Essays*, 1:269, 301.

7. Ibid., 2:2, 20, 26–27.

8. Ibid., 2:5, 30.

9. Traill, "The Anonymous Critic," *Nineteenth Century* 34 (December, 1893): 932–43.

10. G.S., *Scrap Bk.*, 10–11.

11. Gross 1969, 145, 148–49.

12. G.S.'s phrase (*Coll. Essays*, 1:274) and Henley's also.

13. "George Saintsbury," *Times* (London), June 26, 1931.

14. Grierson, in *G.S. Mem. Vol.*, 9.

15. Webster 1933, 8.

16. G.S., *Derby*, 172; *Scrap Bk.*, 92–93.

17. G.S., *Scrap Bk.*, 45, see also, *Second Scrap Bk.*, 319–21.

18. G.S., *Scott*, 114.

19. G.S., *Cellar Book*, 115.

20. G.S., *Second Scrap Bk.*, 239–40; *Last Scrap Bk.*, 143–73.

21. G.S., *Coll. Essays*, 1:299–300.

22. G.S., *Coll. Essays*, 1:254–69.

23. G.S., *Arnold*, 198.

24. G.S., *Coll. Essays*, 3:270–84.

25. Arnold, "The Zenith of Conservatism," *Nineteenth Century* 21 (January, 155–56).

26. Trevelyan 1930, 392–93. Other sources are Ensor 1936; Hammond 1938; Magnus 1956; Petrie 1960; Jenkins 1965.

27. G.S. states that Parnell's denial was received not with jeers, but in silence, if not "of incredulity, yet of the profoundest uncertainty and doubt" ("The Privilege Debate," *Sat. Rev.*, February 15, 1890, 189). G.S., *Scrap Bk.*, 133, refers to "walking home with A [Lang] from the House late at night."

28. M. R. D. Foot, *TLS* (London), September 4, 1969, 978.

29. The *Times*'s use of them was arranged by their Dublin correspondent E. C. Houston, after Pigott had tried to sell the letters to Harwood, Greenwood, Frank Harris, and goodness knows whom else. See G.S., *Last Scrap Bk.*, 273–76. G.S. (*Scrap Bk.*, 238–39), describes a meeting at Bognor between G.S. and "the *Times* man" which, if they had discussed Pigott, might have saved the *Times*, too. See *History of "The Times" 1884–1912* (London, 1947), 43–89; see also Trevelyan 1930; Hammond 1934; Ensor 1936. It cost the *Times* about £250,000 and much of its prestige.

30. *Pall Mall Gazette*, October 28, 1886, 3, reports a judgment of £350 for libel collected from the *Sat. Rev.* for an attack upon Sir Charles Wilson. The *PMG* editor (Stead?) moralizes: "The *Saturday Review*'s policy of 'no corrections' and habit of not admitting errors thus cost them £300 though they purport to be 'written by gentlemen for gentlemen.'"

31. Hammond 1934, 580–94.

32. G.S., *Second Scrap Bk.*, 220.

33. In 1889, the editors of the *Sat. Rev.* celebrated in satiric verse with "Pigott and I" in five stanzas by "A Humble Friend of Truth" and "A Parnellite Hymn" with the refrain, "Hark the Herald Angels sing, 'Murder, Theft and Boycotting'"—a kind of humor G.S. enjoyed.

34. Twenty-four hours after the Pigott letters appeared, in a speech Salisbury indicated his acceptance of them as authentic. The *Sat. Rev.*, with good reasons for thinking otherwise, held its fire.

35. Godkin, "Home Rule and English Journalism," *Nation* (New York), 44 (May 26, 1887): 444–45. Godkin was the founder and editor of the *Nation*.

36. G.S., *Second Scrap Bk.*, 344.

Chapter 7

1. G.S., *Cellar Book,* 112.

2. Ibid.

3. G.S., *Scrap Bk.,* 31; *Cellar Bk.,* 158–73.

4. Kipling 1937, 85–86.

5. Dent 1938, 94.

6. G.S., *Second Scrap Bk.,* 346.

7. See Ker 1955, introduction.

8. "George Saintsbury," *Student,* January 21, 1916, 45.

9. *G.S. Mem. Vol.,* 85.

10. Besant 1902, 240. *The Rabelais Club* was in three vols., privately printed for the members (100 copies).

11. Matthews 1917, 282–83. Cf. G.S., *Last Scrap Bk.,* 203–6. Matthews omits the French version by Walter Pollock.

12. *The Critic,* February 13, 1888, 53.

13. G.S., *Hist. of Eliz. Lit.,* 461.

14. *Acad.,* December 15, 1873, 462; at this time, the *Acad.* became a weekly.

15. G.S., *Last Vintage,* 189; *Consid. of Thack.,* 245. Richards, (1934, 290–91), says much *Academy* work under James Cotton was done by distinguished writers for nothing. G.S. earned £86 for fifty-seven reviews (1887–1895).

16. G.S., *Eng. Novel,* 309.

17. G.S., *Coll. Essays,* 1:413; *G.S. Mem. Vol.,* 87–97; *Second Scrap Bk.,* 306.

18. G.S., *Essays on Eng. Lit.,* 1st ser., xxii–xxiii.

19. G.S., *Coll. Essays,* 3:285–313.

20. Ibid.

21. G.S., *Essays on Eng. Lit.,* 1st ser., xxiv.

22. G.S., *Coll. Essays,* 3:285–313.

23. The *Guardian* ledger records the number of reviews done for each payment and eight of the reviews are fully identified.

24. *Sat. Rev.,* March 24, 1888, 356–57.

25. *Sat. Rev.,* November 27, 1886, 728.

26. E. K. Chambers (*Acad.,* June 1, 1895, 459) thought the essays sane and sensible, learned but "never pedantic . . . quite intelligible"—and "absolutely safe."

27. G.S., *Scribner's Monthly* 22 (May, 1881): 92–106.

28. Henley 1883.

29. G.S., *Coll. Essays,* 1:409, 422, 433; anon. [G.S.] review of *Steele* by Aitken, *Manchester Guardian,* October 15, 1889. Cf. G.S., *Coll. Essays,* 1:261; G.S., *Hist. of Crit.,* 3:555–56.

30. G.S., *Coll. Essays,* 2:11, 16. Gosse lent him editions of seventeenth-century works and he read the proofs. The Dryden articles were rejected by

George Grove of *Macmillan's Magazine,* one of only three rejections G.S. recalls.

31. G.S., *Dryden,* 184–85, 187, 62.

32. Ibid., 92, 102.

33. Ibid., 189–92. Webster says that G.S. was the first to demand full justice for *All for Love* (1933, 26).

34. Arnold, "Introduction," in Ward 1880.

35. G.S., *Dryden,* 129–31, 189–90.

36. G.S., ed., *Dryden Works* (1882–93).

37. Ibid., 1:x, 56; 2: 6–7.

38. Sargeaunt, 1910, introduction. Sargeaunt condemned G.S.'s spelling changes as "corrupting the text" and charged that he "resorts to misplaced and impossible conjecture." For Summers, G.S.'s is the worst edition " . . . with blunders no scholar can make. . . . " (Summers 1931–32, preface).

39. See Nichol Smith in G.S., *Last Vintage,* 16–17; G.S. (*Minor Caroline Poets,* vol. 3) offered some explanation of his problem of poor eyesight and lack of training. Cf. G.S., *Last Scrap Bk.,* 126.

40. See Van Doren 1960, 240.

41. Ker 1900.

42. G.S., *Hist. of Crit.,* 2:374n. He notes here that, unlike Ker, he is not willing to father Dryden's critical style on Chapelain or any Frenchman before Evrémond.

43. G.S., "Introduction," in Shadwell 1907, xiii.

44. G.S., *Coll. Essays,* 2:17–18.

45. The year 1972 saw the definitive two-volume Edgar Johnson *Life of Scott,* and four studies of Scott were reviewed in 1970 under the title, "The Slow Resuscitation of Sir Walter Scott" (*TLS,* January 15, 1972, 51–52).

46. G.S., letter to Wm. Blackwood, April 1, 1898.

47. *Spectator,* July 29, 1899, 156.

48. *Nation* (New York), November 23, 1899, 396–97. Cf. Richard Garnett, Review of *Matthew Arnold* by G.S., *Bookman* (London), July 1899, 102; anon., review of *Matthew Arnold* by G.S., *Literature,* June, 1899, 648–49.

49. G.S., letter to Charles Sarolea, August 11, 1914, University of Edinburgh Library.

50. Webster 1933, 25. The late Kathleen Campbell, author of *Sarah, Duchess of Marlborough* (1934), gave me a similar judgment.

Chapter 8

1. Wilson 1956, 362. Wilson says these men are "unique and fully developed . . . and G.S. explored and appraised them as nobody else has done." J. Ellis Roberts said, "Mr. Saintsbury can make us enjoy not only good books but bad ones" (*Bookman* [London], 69 [October, 1925]: 20).

2. G.S., *Coll. Essays,* 1:57, 67, 168, 289, 397.

3. Ibid, 233–34, 99. Cf. Ibid., 227.

4. G.S., *Arnold,* 183–84.

5. G.S., *Prefs. and Essays*, 212.

6. Elton, "Introduction," in G.S., *Prefs. and Essays*, xii.

7. G.S., *Prefs. and Essays*, 283, 291. See Grierson 1912, 1:248; 2:cxliii, cli. Gosse wrote an essay on Donne in 1893 and was at work on his biography of Donne, not published until 1899. G.S. confesses (*Fr. Novel*, 2:26) he would exchange "the mystical melancholy of certain passages of Donne's for half a hundred of the liveliest love songs of the time."

8. G.S., *Prefs. and Essays*, 257–59.

9. Ibid., 8. G.S. used the 1738 edition of *Polite Conversation* that Dobson had given him.

10. G.S., *Hist. of Crit.*, 3:80. Cf. 1:75–76, on the Alexandrian scholars.

11. Ibid., 3:196.

12. Traill 1903, 3:462.

13. G.S., *Prefs. and Essays*, 393.

14. Wellek and Warren 1949, 167.

15. Nichol Smith, interview with the author, Oxford, August, 1961.

16. G.S., *Hist. of Prosody*, 3:506.

17. Wellek and Warren 1949, 167.

18. G.S., *Hist. of Prosody*, 1:4, 6.

19. G.S., *Hist. of the Fr. Novel*, 2:266; *Hist. of Prosody*, 1:7n.; *Short Hist. of Fr. Lit.*, 264; *Hist. of Crit.*, 3:330; *Later 19th Cent.*, 144–45, 173–74, 185, 463.

20. Wellek and Warren 1949, 264. O'Leary describes G.S. as a major contributor to the early stages of English literary–history writing, and one who "bridged the gulf between history and criticism" (1924, 84).

21. J. Morley, *Fort. Rev.* 21 (April, 1874): 434–35.

22. Pater 1928, 106.

23. Symonds 1907, 1–52.

24. Courthope 1895–1910. Wellek and Warren (1949, 263–65) find it not a history of *art* and weak in the necessary "balance of history and criticism"; G.S. and O'Leary both regarded it as too exlusively concerned with subject matter and with the fluctuations of taste.

25. Gosse 1898, 390–91.

26. G.S., *Coll. Essays*, 4:224–26.

27. On Taine's theory, see G.S., *Acad.*, January 17, 1880, 41; *Short Hist. of Fr. Lit.*, 564–78; *Later 19th Cent.*, 143–45.

28. G.S., in *Dryden* 1893, 18:287–88. See G.S., *Essays in Eng. Lit.*, 1st ser., x, xvii.

29. G.S., *Later 19th Cent.*, 442; *Hist. of Prosody*, 2:4

30. G.S., *Later 19th Cent.*, 392n; *Short Hist. of Eng. Lit.*, 636.

31. G.S., *Later 19th Cent.*, 463–64.

32. G.S., *Short Hist. of Eng. Lit.*, 467; *Hist. of Crit.*, 3:609–10; *Fr. Novel*, 2:558.

33. Symonds, 1907, 37, 49.

34. G.S., "Dickens," in *CHEL*, 13: 341.

35. G.S., *Later 19th Cent.*, 463; italics added.

36. G.S., *Hist. of Crit.*, 1:170–71; 3:398.

37. G.S., *Short Hist. of Eng. Lit.*, 650; see *English Novel* (on *Pamela*), 82; also see *Dryden*, 135–36.

38. G.S., *Later 19th Cent.*, 132.

39. Lindenberger 1984.

40. Wellek and Warren 1949, 264, 271–72, 277–78. G.S. rarely uses the term *convention*. See also Wellek 1965, 4:423.

41. Watson 1962, 164–65.

42. Wimsatt and Brooks 1957, 541.

43. Stopford Brooke and Gosse did the first and third volumes. The last volume, announced as by Edward Dowden, was taken over by Saintsbury. See "George Saintsbury," *DNB*, 776.

44. G.S., *Eliz. Lit.*, ix.

45. Herford, Review of *Eliz. Lit.* by *G.S.*, *Acad.*, December 3, 1887, 363–65.

46. Anon. review in *Athen.*, November 26, 1887, 704–5. The phrase "nothing if not critical" is G.S.'s.

47. G.S., *Short Hist. of Eng. Lit.*, vi.

48. Wilson says in defense, "If you feel, say, that Shakespeare seems slighted in his *History of Elizabethan Literature*, you will find [Saintsbury] has done him magnificently in the *Cambridge History of English Literature*" (1950, 362).

49. G.S., *Short Hist. of Eng. Lit.*, 365–68, 418–19; *Eliz. Lit.*, 146–51, 354–59.

50. G.S., *19th-Cent. Lit.*, 56–59, 115. Such poets as Beddoes, he says, "When they do shine, illumine the whole of their world."

51. G.S., *19th-Cent. Lit.*, 462–66.

52. Ibid., 468–69.

52. G.S., *Short Hist. of Eng. Lit.*, probably his best known work, had run to seven editions, twenty–one printings, and 60,000 copies by 1963 (Macmillan report, by 1962 letter); for *Eliz. Lit.*, the total number of copies was 16,000; for *19th-Cent. Lit.*, 17,500.

53. Nichol Smith, interview with author, 1961.

54. G.S., *Short Hist. of Eng. Lit.*, 1.

55. Herford, Review of *19th Cent. Lit.* by G.S., *Bookman* (London) 9 (March, 1896):185–86; Review of *A Short Hist. of Eng. Lit.* by G.S., *Bookman* (London) 15 (November, 1898):45–46.

56. Symons, Review, *Athen.*, December 5, 1896, 790–91.

57. Anon., "G.S.," *Life and Letters Today* 9 (June 1933):186.

Chapter 9

1. Mills 1921, 48. Cook records this in his diary (1892), quoted in Whyte 1925, 1:80.

2. Morley (1917, 2:154–55) added, "I like the dull men best." He also judged that these stunts and Stead's reforming zeal during 1883–85 had made him "the most powerful journalist in the island."

3. Quoted in Fyfe 1949, 36.

4. Whyte 1925, 1:102, 104.

5. Fyfe, 1949, 36.

6. Ibid.; also see Ensor 1936, which emphasizes commercialism as the "key feature of the New Journalism" (310).

7. Whyte 1925, 1:104.

8. Herd 1973, 229–30.

9. Charteris 1931, 187.

10. Ibid., 184.

11. G.S., letter to Gosse, Gosse Collection. G.S. quotes the same lines in a review of Browning verse in the *Manchester Guardian*, July 2, 1889, 59.

12. Collins 1912, 108–10.

13. Hart-Davis 1962.

14. This is pt. 2*a* of the full definition: "U.S. slang—combination for political or other cooperation, (suggested by the phrase 'you roll my log and I'll roll yours.' 1823)."

15. G.S., letter to Gosse, January 2, 1886, Gosse Collection: "I believe you are quite right about answering though I have sometimes thought otherwise in moments of spleen. Indeed I have told Garnett as much in reply to his exceedingly generous offer to take up the cudgels."

16. Anon. Review, *Pall Mall Gazette*, December 11, 1885. The biography is called "a wire–drawn production" with "involved sophistries and wearisome abortive hair–splitting," which gives too little space to the warrior and assumes wrongly that readers have knowledge of the historical surroundings.

17. Creighton 1907, 1:222 (quoted letter).

18. G.S., letter to Gosse, December 15, 1886, Gosse Collection.

19. Collins, *Quarterly Rev.*, October, 1885.

20. G.S., letter to Dobson, Dobson Collection. He adds that he did mention A. H. Bullen because he was not "as far as I know obnoxious to the P.M.G. reviewers."

21. G.S., *Eliz. Lit.*, viii–ix.

22. Charteris 1931, 201.

23. G.S., letter to Gosse, October 20, 1886, Gosse Collection. G.S. added two typical parentheses: "(I did not please Lang this afternoon by calling it blackguardism)" and, regarding Collins, "(I think that my knowledge of English literature is, to say the least, equal to our friend's.)"

24. "The Ethics of Reviewing," *Sat. Rev.*, October 30, 1886, 579–80; "The Teaching of English Literaure," *Sat. Rev.*, November 6, 1886, 611–12.

25. "As some unkind persons have said, the first part is a scream of rage because Mr. Gosse is a lecturer at Cambridge, and the second a scream of rage because Mr. Collins is not a professor at Oxford." Lang and Pollock were at work on *He*, a parody of Rider Haggard's *She*. Stead is gently satirized as "Pellmelli," and the work is signed "Two of the Ama-Logrolla." Students at Oxford were speaking of anyone who had committed a boner as making "a Gosse of himself."

26. G.S., *Sat. Rev.*, October 30, 1886, 579–80.

27. G.S., letter to Wm. Hunt, August 5, 1915. Other references to Collins show a lack of resentment and a sense of irony as well. On December 27,

1922, he wrote to Hunt, "Poor Churton Collins was envious: I don't think Henley was exactly so."

28. Purves, in *G.S. Mem. Vol.*, 15.

29. Sidney Lee, "John Churton Collins," *DNB*.

30. Collins 1895 and 1901.

31. Collins, "Mr. Saintsbury as a Critic," *Sat. Rev.*, February 23, 1895, 257–58.

32. Collins, "A Professor of English Literature on His Own Subject," *Sat. Rev.*, November 30, 1895, 725–26.

33. Collins, *Sat. Rev.*, April 25, 1896, 423–25.

34. E. K. Chambers, "Living Critics VII," *Bookman* (London) 10 (August, 1896):136.

35. Waugh 1896, 134.

36. G.S., *Minster* 1 (April, 1895):315–18.

37. Traill, "The Anonymous Critic," *Nineteenth Century* 34 (December, 1893):938.

38. Connell 1949, 98.

39. G.S., *Coll. Essays*, 3:285–313. In a letter to Wm. Blackwood, December 26, 1896, he anticipated some abuse but claimed the article was "at least as full of experience and reason as anything that has been written about the subject."

40. Anon. review, *Sat. Rev.*, January 2, 1886, 23–24. The *Pall Mall* praised the preface but later used it to quarrel with the style of his Borrow essay. Praise of friends was not limited to the anonymous, as Saintsbury's signed reviews of Dobson for the *Academy* in 1877 and 1879 prove.

41. Wells 1934, 2:521.

42. G.S., *G.S. Mem. Vol.*, 90.

43. G.S., *Coll. Essays*, 3:305.

44. Lang, "At the Sign of the Ship," *Longman's Magazine* 34 (July, 1899):287–88. Cf., Traill, "The Anonymous Critic," *Nineteenth Century*, 34 (December, 1893):938. See Donald Carsell and Catherine Carsell, *Nineteenth Century*, 113 (January, 1933):111–12, where multiple reviewing is discussed.

45. Green 1946, 157.

46. Arnold is dealt with in nine G.S. volumes, 1895–1912. We do not know how often he reviewed Arnold anonymously.

Chapter 10

1. Symons (anon. but identified in *Athen.* files), Review of *Essays on Fr. Novelists* and *Miscell. Essays* by G.S., *Athen.*, August 27, 1892, 277–78.

2. Symons, signed review, *Acad.*, July 11, 1891, 30; the other anon. reviews are: *Athen.*, June 27, 1891, 819; *Athen.*, March 23, 1895, 369–70; *Athen.*, December 5, 1896, 790–91.

3. Symons, *Athen.*, June 27, 1891, 819. Symons labeled G.S. second rate as compared to Pater and Bourget. In *Athen.*, March 26, 1892, 399–400, he says G.S.'s preface to Scherer's essays is a "model" because G.S. here was

dealing with a critic who is safe and not clever, and he could therefore be sympathetic. G.S., in his epigraph to the "Baudelaire," in *Miscell. Essays,* admits that Baudelaire is now admired "even by *les imbéciles.*"

4. Temple treats his criticism of French poetry (1953, 121–81).

5. G.S., "The Present State of the French Novel," pt. 2, (*Fort. Rev.* 49, o.s. [January 1, 1888]:112–23) became the opening one in *Fr. Novelists.* Further refs. are to this volume.

6. G.S., *Coll. Essays,* 4:63–65.

7. G.S., *Fr. Novelists,* 5–7.

8. Decker records Swinburne's attack on Zola in 1878, Lang's favorable article in the *Fort. Rev.* in 1882, and many successive attacks (1934, 1140–1153). G.S. made almost no references to Vizetelly, who was fined £100 in 1888 and £200 in 1889 when he was sent to prison for three months.

9. G.S., *Coll. Essays,* 4:273, 279–80.

10. *Daily Graphic,* December 27, 1890, 11.

11. Temple 1953, 210–13. Verlaine was sponsored by Rothstein, Symons, and York Powell. Mallarmé was invited to give the Taylorian Lecture at Oxford, and gave the same lecture, "La Musique et Les Lettres," at Cambridge. Mallarmé lunched with Gosse, Whibley, and Henley, and Gosse wrote three essays on Mallarmé. There is no evidence that G.S. met either poet.

12. Nerval is mentioned in G.S., *Short History of Fr. Lit.;* Maeterlinck, in *Later 19th Cent.;* Huysmans and Nerval in *Fr. Novel.*

13. G.S., anon. review, *Bookman* (New York) 1 (April, 1895):178–80.

14. G.S., anon. review, *Sat. Rev.,* November 1, 1890, 515.

15. G.S., anon. review, *Sat. Rev.,* August 2, 1890, 132–33.

16. G.S., *Coll. Essays,* 3:127. He continues even more alarmingly: "Its material must always be either the abiding qualities or the floating appearances of social existence, *quicquid agunt homines* not *quicquid cogitant.*"

17. Houghton 1957, 420, citing an 1896 critique that was not G.S.'s.

18. Ibid., 424.

19. G.S., *Second Scrap Bk.,* 145.

20. Ibid., 254. He adds that you would be ashamed to kick him for fear he would tell his mother.

21. G.S., *Fr. Novel,* 1:93–94. His point here is that Scott condemned the obscenity of *les Nouvelles Nouvelles,* as he himself does.

22. G.S., review of Hall Caine, *Fort. Rev.* 63 (February, 1895):192.

23. G.S., *Prefs. and Essays,* 98.

24. G.S., *Eliz. Lit.,* 162–64.

25. G.S., letters to Hunt, January 10, 1915, June 17, 1923, November 10, 1914.

26. G.S., anon. review, *Athen.,* March 15, 1890, 339.

27. G.S., *Short Hist. of Eng. Lit.,* 786.

28. G.S., letter to Hunt, January 29, 1926.

29. G.S., *Earlier Renaiss.,* 185.

30. G.S., *Prefs. and Essays,* 149.

31. Symons 1989, 35, 81.

32. Gross 1969, 145.

33. G.S., *Hist of Crit.*, 3:340.

34. G.S., *Yellow Book* I (April, 1894):119–24.

35. G.S., *Earlier Renaiss.*

36. Corrigan 1986, 149.

37. G.S., *Essays on Eng. Lit.*, 1st ser., xi–xv.

38. Ibid., xv–xvi; cf. Gosse, Lang, and James, in symposium, "The Science of Criticism," *New Review* 5 (1891):398–411.

39. G.S., *Essays on Eng. Lit.*, 1st ser.

40. G.S., "Introduction," in Scherer 1891, xxiv–xxv.

41. G.S., *Essays on Eng. Lit.*, 1st ser., xxvi.

42. Ibid., xliii.

43. G.S., *Coll. Essays*, 1:99.

44. G.S., *Hist. of Crit.*, 2:276.

45. G.S., *Arnold*, vii.

46. Eliot 1932, 115.

47. G.S., *Coll. Essays*, 2:268–69.

48. Ibid., 226, 229.

49. G.S., *Last Scrap Bk.*, 195.

50. G.S., *Later 19th Cent.*, 163.

51. G.S., *Short Hist. of Eng. Lit*, 764.

52. G.S., *Arnold*, 213–14.

53. G.S., *New Review*, 11 (October, 1894):420.

54. G.S., *Arnold*, 213.

55. Ibid., 200.

56. G.S., *Hist. of Crit.*, 3:517. Cf. G.S., *Arnold*, 36–37, on Arnold's preface to his poems of 1853.

57. G.S., *Arnold*, 190–91.

58. G.S., *Acad.*, February 26, 1881, 148–49.

59. G.S., *Eliz. Lit.*, 162–63.

60. G.S., *Arnold*, 26, 191; *19th-Cent. Lit.*, 61–62; *Short Hist. of Eng. Lit.*, 8; *Last Scrap Bk.*, 198; *A Calendar of Verse*, xiv.

61. G.S., *Eliz. Lit.*, 162–63.

62. G.S., *Dryden*, 190–92.

63. G.S., *Hist. of Crit.*, 3:611–12; italics added.

64. Ibid., 369, 375–76, 534. Cf. *Eng. Crit.*, 12, 328.

65. G.S., "Introduction," in Scherer 1891, xxxvi.

66. G.S., *Coll. Essays*, 4:260; see also G.S., *Arnold*, 88–90; Arnold's *Notebooks*, ed. H. F. Lowry, et al. (*OUP*, 1952), 344–45, quoted passages from G.S.'s *Primer of Fr. Lit.* on the importance of French literature.

67. G.S., *Arnold*, 71–72; *Hist. of Prosody*, 3:134.

68. G.S., anon. review, *Sat. Rev.*, April 21, 1888, 449–50; November 17, 1888, 589–90.

69. G.S., anon. review, *Sat. Rev.*, April 21, 1888, 459.

70. G.S., *Prefs. and Essays*, 354–55, 358.

71. Pater 1873, 1st ed., xxvii.

72. G.S., *Hist. of Crit.*, 3:546. Cf. T. S. Eliot's description of "the Impressionistic critic at his best" (1948, 3). Arthur Symons is his choice in "the Perfect Critic." Steinberg cites a passage in Gerard's *Essay on Taste* (1780) as much closer to G.S.'s phrasing than to Pater's, but he decided that G.S.'s paraphrasing of Pater is just (1926, 536).

73. G.S., *Coll. Essays*, 1:115.

74. G.S., in Craik 1893–96, 5:167.

75. G.S., *Hist. of Crit.*, 3:264–65.

76. Daiches 1956, 285–86.

Chapter 11

1. Henley letter, Feburary 18, 1889, quoted in Connell 1949, 153. Henley, editing the *Scots Observer*, was hardly impartial since he aimed initially to rival the *Sat. Rev.* and looked forward "to having a share of its inheritance."

2. Bevington 1941, 324.

3. Root 1947, 135–37; Wells, 1934, 2:520–21.

4. Fyfe 1949, 41. G.S. said little of Frank Harris, but in a letter to Professor Sarolea declining to do an article for *Everyman* on Harris (August 16, 1912), he says, "I'd rather you ask someone else. But he is admirably clever and (I admit) rather popular."

5. Bevington 1941, 325; Root's version of Harris's advice agrees: "He told them to avoid being ferociously negative and bloodily critical like the *Quarterly Review*-ers . . . and to find and defend genius" (1947, 136).

6. Fyfe 1949, 41.

7. Henley, letter to Whibley, November 5, 1894; Connell 1949, 290.

8. Charteris 1931, 241 (a letter to Mr. G. B. Foote). Gosse's accounts show that he was paid £70 each in 1895 by the *Saturday* and the *Realm*.

9. G.S. (letter to Gosse, September 7, 1894, Gosse Collection) thanks Gosse for this warning.

10. Ibid. refers to the *Athenaeum* item.

11. G.S., *Scrap Bk.* speaks of G.S.'s last day on the *Sat. Rev.* staff spent at Greenwich alone (89). Before dining, he passed an old lady on the quay who muttered, "You've caught a line."

12. G.S., letter to Gosse, Gosse Collection.

13. Wilde 1962, 720. Lady Pollock was Juliet Creed and Walter was her second son. Pollock invited Wilde to contribute to his "wicked and Philistine" paper.

14. Of numerous references, see G.S., *Arnold*, 169: ". . . the fixed halting place to which we can always resort for fresh starts, fresh calculations"—from Samuel Johnson's *Lives*.

15. G.S.'s phrase quoted by Elton (*Proc.*, 1933, 329).

16. To regular reviewing for the *Acad.* and *Manchester Guardian* and articles for *Macmillan's Mag.*, he added the *New Review*, the *Critic* (New York), *National Observer, Illustrated London News, Indian Daily News,* and the *Bookman* (New York).

17. The start of a good and profitable relationship that lasted over thirty years. The letters are in the National Library and are unpublished.

18. G.S., letter to Blackwood, November 28, 1894, January 25, 1895.

19. G.S., letter to Hunt, September 15 and October 8, 1923.

20. For this photograph, see Webster 1933, frontispiece. The *Student* (November 11, 1911, 116) also had an oval pen sketch of G.S.

21. Elton, in *G.S. Mem. Vol.*, 1.

22. "George Saintsbury," *London Mercury* 27 (March, 1933), 436. Of those hands, Dorothy Stuart (G.S., *Last Vintage*, 19) says: "One little vanity alone he had—his hands, which were and remained really beautiful." From the 1920s, she recalls his "trick of sitting with them clasped around a flexed left knee while the right leg was stuck straight out, a youthful attitude."

23. Oliver, in *G.S., Mem. Vol.*, 22, and Elton in *G.S., Mem. Vol.*, 1. Oliver also gave the account of G.S.'s Edinburgh servitor who, during World War I, homesick for Edinburgh, took from the library a G.S. volume and reported, "'I didna understand much of it, but, man, I could just hear him speaking'"(22).

24. Grierson, in *G.S. Mem. Vol.*, 9–10.

25. Webster 1933, 9–10, 42. Dr. Middleton is supposedly a portrait of Peacock.

26. Ibid., 7–9, 42–43.

27. Elton, in *G.S. Mem. Vol.*, 4.

28. G.S., *Fr. Novelists*, 260–61.

29. G.S., letter to Hunt, August 14, 1922.

30. *Student*, January 14, 1904, 203.

31. G.S., *Fr. Novelists*, 30.

32. Houghton 1957, 264.

33. G.S., letter to Hunt, November 7, 1911.

34. G.S., *Last Scrap Bk.*, 70; *Cellar Bk.*, 148; *Peace of the Augs.*, 288.

35. G.S., *Cellar Bk.*, 157, 153–54; G.S., *Second Scrap Bk.*, 90–94.

36. "G.S.," *London Mercury* 27 (March, 1933):438; "A Great Reader at Eighty," *Living Age*, December 5, 1925, 547–48; the latter quotes R. E. Roberts in the *Bookman*.

37. G.S., *Coll. Essays*, vol. 4. *The End of the Chapter*.

38. G.S., *Fr. Novel*, 2:185.

39. G.S., *Coll. Essays*, 1:77; 4:244, 247–49.

40. G.S., *Fr. Novel*, 1:389.

41. G.S., *Coll. Essays*, 2:228–29.

42. G.S., *Arnold*, 40.

43. G.S., *Last Vintage*, 124–27.

44. Ibid., 248.

45. Grierson, in *G.S. Mem. Vol.*, 11.

46. G.S., *Peace of the Augs.*, 119.

47. Redman, "Saintsbury the Connoisseur," *Saturday Review of Literature*, February 11, 1933, 421–22.

48. G.S., *Coll. Essays*, 2:46.

49. G.S., *Fr. Novel,* 217–18.

50. G.S., *Coll. Essays,* 3:38.

51. G.S., *Fr. Novelists,* 221–22, 223–24.

52. G.S., *Coll. Essays,* 1:425, 2:93.

53. G.S., *Peace of the Augs.,* 166.

54. G.S., *Eng. Novel,* 303–4.

55. G.S., *Fr. Novel,* 1:355.

56. Ibid., 211–18.

57. G.S., *Peace of the Augs.,* 152, 161. He often makes a distinction between his "countless dippings" and "reading straight through"; see G.S. *Coll. Essays,* 1:413. Boswell is for "dipping," as are Fanny Burney's diaries (ibid., 1: 376).

58. G.S., *Fr. Novel,* 1:287.

59. G.S., Preface to Balzac's "César Birotteux," in Balzac 1895–1900.

60. G.S., *Eng. Novel,* 45.

61. G.S., Balzac memoir, in Balzac 1895–1900, 1:xxiii.

62. G.S., *Prefs. and Essays,* 174.

63. G.S., *Scrap Bk.,* 29–30.

64. Grierson, in *G.S. Mem. Vol.,* 11.

65. G.S., *Last Scrap Bk.,* 311–13. G.S. cherished the belief that Lang's script was almost as bad as his; Bereford-Hope's, worse.

66. G.S., letter to a Mr. Sproul (regarding an introduction to *Old Curiosity Shop* for an Autograph edition of Dickens), January 4, 1902, #104, University of Edingburgh Library. He refused to sign copies, never having done it, finding it repellent.

67. "Specialization," ms. labeled, in G.S.'s scraggly script, "This is d——d good" (ca. 1900), given to me by his grandson.

68. G.S., letter to Professor Sarolea, August 11, 1914, University of Edinburgh Library.

69. G.S., letter to D. Nichol Smith (November, 1895, University of Edinburgh Library); Smith was hired to check *19th-Cent. Lit.* Elsewhere G.S. did the job himself.

70. G.S., *Coll. Essays,* 1:65, 122, 336–37.

71. G.S., *Hist. of Crit.,* 3:256.

72. Cf. G.S., *Hist. of Prosody,* 3:227, 239, on Browning.

73. G.S., letter to Sproul, #104, University of Edinburgh Library.

Chapter 12

1. Courthope, 1893, 486–99. See Firth 1909 for developments at Oxford from 1893 to 1909; Potter 1957 and Tillyard 1958 tell the later story, but not impartially.

2. See Kerr 1910; Meikle 1945; Logan Turner 1933; Davie 1961.

3. Webster 1933, 38; Meikle 1945.

4. G.S., letter to Blackwood, June 25, 1894.

5. His personal copies, tied together with green ribbon, were given to me by his grandson.

6. Some of these are listed in *Acad.*, July 20, 1895, 70; *Acad.*, August 3, 1895, 90.

7. Smith 1926, 184–85.

8. Ibid., 186–87.

9. Connell 1949, 304–5.

10. Ibid., 307.

11. G.S. gave the series of Dryden lectures in 1880; he also lectured to young women at Cambridge and read the Tripos there.

12. G.S., *Last Scrap Bk.*, 271n.

13. Grierson, in *G.S. Mem. Vol.*, 11.

14. Turner 1933, 9.

15. *Scotsman*, September 28 and October 16, 1895. In the latter issue, the editors state that G.S.'s Inaugural and that of W. R. Hardie, delivered the same day, justified "the confident faith of those who knew them best" and that the appointments would "shed lustre upon the University." They liked G.S.'s recognition of Scottish contributions to revivifying English literature.

16. Chrystal 1933, 435; Purves, in *G.S. Mem. Vol.*, 13.

17. Purves, in *G.S. Mem. Vol.*, 13.

18. J. L. Geddie ('01) recalled this fact in a 1962 interview. He and his brother, William Geddie ('99), ran Chambers Publishing House.

19. Chrystal 1933, 435.

20. The G.S. Inaugural Lecture, in *G.S. Mem. Vol.*, 172–83. His reply to a presentation made on his retirement (*Scotsman*, October 1, 1915, 8) states that he had tried always for originality, had never given a written lecture, had tried never to press opinions of his own upon classes but rather had tried "to make them read and think and enjoy themselves."

21. *Student*, October 24, 1895, the main editorial, 65–66.

22. G.S., *Scrap Bk.*, vii.

23. G.S., *Coll. Essays*, 1:208.

24. G.S., letter to the Senate, Senate Proceedings 1915–16, Minutes, November 4, 1915, University of Edinburgh.

25. *Student*, February 7, 1933, 179.

26. Kitchen recalled that when one of them occasionally substituted for G.S. they found his notecards illegible.

27. G.S., letter to Hunt, January 23, 1916. G.S. describes Masson as "no posture-monger or man of megrims, but one of genial temper and sturdy sense," (*Consid. of Thack.*, 195), and as "a really excellent replica of Victor Hugo in person and Carlyle on his more amiable side in manner" (letter to Hunt, Christmas Eve, 1895).

28. G.S., *G.S. Mem. Vol.*, 203–4.

29. Author's interviews with students, 1962.

30. G.S., "Chairs Made Famous," *Student*, June 29, 1909, 273. The first Ordinary lecture each year was devoted to Blair's *Lectures on Rhetoric* "as an act of piety," and three lectures a year were on Scottish literature.

31. Webster 1933, 38n.

32. *Student,* February 7, 1933, 178–79.

33. The first-hand observations by the twenty-five students, most of them Edinburgh people, add to the impressions offered in 1962 by his assistant, George Kitchin (Webster and Gregory Smith were already dead, as was Grierson, his successor).

34. *Student,* Feburary 20, 1896, 251; *Student,*October 22, 1896, 4; *Student,* November 27, 1896, 38; *Student,* Feburary 25, 1897, 252; *Student,* March 4, 1897, 274.

35. *Student,* October 19, 1897, 10. A review of G.S.'s *Short Hist. of Eng. Lit.* (November 17, 1898, 102) laments, "We are beginning to think Professor Saintsbury has read too much" yet welcomes it as a substitute "for those lectures we can't get down."

36. *Student,* October 20, 1899, 9.

37. *Student,* October 22, 1903, 3–4.

38. Professor Butt experienced it as late as 1960.

39. "An Eminent Bookworm," *Bookman's Journal* 7 (November, 1922):63, quoting Herbert Brook. A *TSL* letter, November 17, 1945, 547, signed "Septuagenarian," described G.S. as "imposing and aristocratic but not prepossessing."

40. "The Professor of Rhetoric and English Literature," *Student,* February 1, 1900, 245–47. Forty years later, Purves (in *G.S. Mem. Vol.,* 13–17) recalled best G.S.'s negative judgments and remembered the Ordinary class lectures better than the more intimate *causeries* of the Honors course, though he regarded G.S.'s exposition of Longinus and of Dante's *De Vulgaria* to the Honors group as "inspired."

41. B. H. W. (probably Bertha Wright), "An Impression," *Student,* January 11, 1907, 378.

42. "University Cartoons," #1, *Student,* January 14, 1904, 202–3; rpt., January 11, 1907, 378–79.

43. *Student,* December 4, 1912, 147.

44. C. W. Ingliss Wardrop, *Times* (London), October 10, 1944.

45. Oliver, in *G.S. Mem. Vol.,* 18–22.

46. Mary Martin, letter to author, November, 1962.

47. Ibid.

48. In letters to the author (November, 1962), R. K. M. Simpson (a 1914 Second) notes that by 1910, though other classes were often thoroughly rowdy, G.S. had none of this, and Alexander Campbell (a 1914 First) said that G.S. came "to enjoy the scraping feet" even when the Young Fabians were objecting to his opinions.

49. These include an L.L.D. from Aberdeen, 1898; from Durham, 1906; a Litt. D. from Edinburgh, 1919; Fellow of the British Academy, 1911; Warton lecture, 1912; the Taylorian at Oxford, 1904; president of the English Association, 1909; The Royal Society, with three lectures, 1908, 1910, 1912.

50. G.S., *Coll. Essays,* 3:341–64.

51. Statement by Professors Baldwin Brown and T. H. Millar, Minutes, University of Edinburgh Senate Proceedings, October 7, 1915, 294.

52. G.S., *Last Scrap Bk.*, 256–66; a prophetic reaction to a proposal in the 1920s to do away with Third Class degrees.

53. Memorial Tribute, University of Edinburgh Senate, Proceedings, March 9, 1933.

54. G.S., review of *Letters of Sir Walter Raleigh, Country Life* (British), December 4, 1926, 890.

55. G.S., letter to Brander Matthews, no date, Columbia University Library.

56. G.S., letter to Hunt, November 28, 1912.

57. G.S., letter to Wm. Blackwood, December 28, 1899. On March 25, 1899, G.S. invited Blackwood to Murrayfield to meet Elton—and as almost "a last chance" to visit there. Elton was External Examiner during 1898–1902 and 1914–15.

58. Chrystal 1933, 436–37.

59. G.S. (letter to Hunt, December 26, 1912) describes the walkout as precipitated by one girl's having been "mildly remonstrated with on having too many gentlemen (as she called it)." G.S.'s threat that if they left it was "without wages, without characters, and with the probability of police court summons for breach of contracts" was unavailing. He adds, "... since then ... chaos ... 'characters' and 'temporaries' appear and disappear generally with plunder."

60. G.S., *Second Scrap Bk.*, 222–24.

61. G.S., letter to Hunt, February 9, 1896.

62. G.S., *Second Scrap Bk.*, 343.

63. Grierson, in *G.S. Mem. Vol.*, 10.

64. G.S., letters to Hunt, Christmas Eve, 1895, and New Year's Day, 1911 (after Butcher's death). He came to know Gilbert Murray through Butcher.

65. G.S., *Coll. Essays*, 2:172n.

66. *Student*, January 26, 1916, 25, 27.

67. Elton 1932, prefaces.

68. G.S., letter to Dobson, March 30, 1904.

69. G.S., letter to Hunt, October 16, 1916; letter to George Blackwood, July 16, 1907.

70. A lecturer at Edinburgh until 1920, Webster was professor of English at St. Andrews, 1920–55, and died in 1956. There persisted at St. Andrews into the 1960s an odd and false legend that he had married G.S.'s daughter (the daughter G.S. always wished for and never had?).

71. George Kitchin preserved several famous anecdotes in *Student*, February 7, 1933, 178–79. He retired from Edinburgh only in 1961; in his eighties he was lecturing part-time and was still a great golfer.

72. Alexander Campbell (letter to author, November 12, 1962) recalled that Mrs. Saintsbury's "small talk was very small."

73. G.S., letter to Dobson, October 3, 1896. It was Dobson's third series of vignettes.

74. G.S., letters to Dobson, July 14 and 18, 1907; March 29, 31, and April 2, 1911; March 2, 27, and Palm Sunday, 1913.

75. Dobson, letter to G.S., April 30, 1913; G.S., letters to Dobson, January 12 and 29, 1910.

76. G.S., letter to Dobson, March 30, 1904.

77. Blackett (1973), 27. There is no record of his having visited Paris alone, but G.S. told Helen that he had vowed on his last visit never to visit it again alone.

78. G.S., *Peace of the Augs.*, 38.

79. G.S., letter to Waller, May 12, 1917 (from Bath), British Museum #84, Add'l Mss. 43681.

80. G.S., letter to Dobson, April, 1913 (between Easter and Dobson's letter of April 30).

81. G.S., letters to Hunt, January 11, 1911, March 20, 1912.

82. G.S., letter to Hunt, March 24, 1907. On Whitsunday, 1915, he writes of a bad throat and says that, with two lectures on one afternoon, he "gets through" by taking a small bottle of sherry in the hour between.

83. G.S., letter to Sarolea, September 26, 1912, University of Edinburgh Library.

84. G.S., letters to Hunt, St. John's Day, June 24, 1904, October 6 and August 28, 1917.

85. G.S., letter to Hunt, Whitsunday, 1915; letter to Dobson, August 29, 1915; to A. R. Waller, June 22, 1915; letter to George Blackwood, August 9, 1915.

86. G.S., letters to Hunt, August 5, 1915, December 5, 1915.

87. G.S., letter to Hunt, August 28, 1915.

88. Personal interviews by the author with Kitchin and Geddie, 1962.

89. G.S., letters to Dobson, November 8, 1915, April 12, 1916.

90. G.S., letters to Hunt, September 2, 1916, December 19, 1916.

Chapter 13

1. G.S., letter to Wm. Blackwood, March 17, 1895; letter to George Blackwood, January 5, 1903.

2. Lang, Raleigh, and Platt of Trinity, Traill, Dobson, Craik, Pollock, Gosse, and one illegible were in G.S.'s original list. The later refusals were Quiller-Couch, Firth, and E. K. Chambers.

3. G.S., letter to Wm. Blackwood, July 22, 1898. Other matter from Blackwood's 1897 correspondence file.

4. G.S., letter to Wm. Blackwood, February 12, 1900.

5. G.S., letter to Wm. Blackwood, January 2, 1901; this was the last addressed to William and was the last in the file at George Street rather than in the National Library.

6. G.S., letter to George Blackwood, September 17, 1902.

7. G.S., letter to Hunt, October 6, 1905.

8. Elton memoir (*Procs. of the Brit. Acad.* [1933]), 337. G.S. (letter to

George Blackwood, March 2, 1903) requests that a copy of the *History of Crit.* be sent to Croce because Croce had sent him useful books of his own and said he would be "beatissimo" to have it. The ironic outcome was Croce's review with the condemning charge, "digiuno di filosofia."

9. G.S., letter to Hunt, November 7, 1911: "I have never got anything but the £100 a volume which I received in advance royalty. I must have been at least half as much out of pocket for books and journeyings. . . ." A letter to Wm. Blackwood (March 17, 1895) shows that the first terms for the *Hist. of Crit.* were for 600 to 700 pages, £200 down for 750 copies and 2d royalty on the shilling thereafter. G.S. finally received £150 each for vols. 1 & 2 and royalties thereafter.

10. G.S., *Flour. of Romance*, 413. See Richardson [Jones] 1946, 32–35.

11. G.S., *Flour. of Romance*, vi.

12. Ibid., xi. He cites Ticknor's ignorance of the chanson de geste, which distorted his view of Berceo's prosody, but rates his *Spanish Literature* (3 vols., 1849) as "one of the very best literary histories." He admits having relied heavily upon it.

13. G.S., *Flour. of Romance*, 397.

14. G.S., *Earlier Renaiss.*, preface.

15. *Comparative Literature* 54:76. See Weisstein 1973, 222–23, Appendix I.

16. Baldensperger 1921, 25–29; G.S. (*Later 19th Cent.*, 46n) calls the term *Comparative Literature* ugly, and not English, but "Comparative Study of Literature" though proper seemed too long.

17. Weisstein 1973, 174–75.

18. Baldensperger 1921, 24–25. See Weisstein 1973, 177–79, 226–27, on two articles by G. Gregory Smith: "The Foible of Comparative Literature," *Blackwood's Edinburgh Magazine* 169 (January, 1901):34–48; "Some Notes on the Comparative Study of Literature," *Modern Language Review* 1 (October, 1905):1–8. Smith, G.S.'s assistant at Edinburgh until 1904, wrote vol. 4 of the *Periods of European Literature*.

19. G.S., *Hist. of Crit.*, 3:294.

20. Ibid., 462, 609.

21. G.S., *Flour. of Romance*, vi.

22. Ibid., 9–10, 124 ff., 289ff.

23. Ibid., 116–19, 245–46, 257.

24. Ibid., preface, 369–70; the "Saracen theory of literature" is consigned to some future critic.

25. G.S., *Earlier Renaiss.*, vi, viii. Spanish developments were postponed to *The Later Renaissance*.

26. G.S., *Earlier Renaiss.*, 89–98.

27. G.S., *Hist. of Crit.*, 2:569; 3:265.

28. Babbitt 1906 and 1912 .

29. G.S., *Hist of Crit.*, 2:440–41.

30. Ibid., 2:545.

31. Ibid., 1:3–5, 8; 3:142–44, 610–11, define his limits.

32. G.S., *Hist. of Crit.* 3:168–69.

33. The translations are his own and biographical and lexicographical data are relegated to the index. W. P. Ker, S. H. Butcher, and W. R. Hardie are warmly acknowledged as readers of vol. 1; Elton, Gregory Smith, and Ker of vols. 2 and 3.

34. Atkins 1943, vi. He gives a chapter to John of Salisbury.

35. Spingarn, "Origins," 1904, 1–7.

36. Babbitt letter (*Nation*, May 16, 1912, 493) an answer to a Homer E. Woodbridge letter defending Saintsbury.

37. Elder Olson 1942 and 1953.

38. G.S., *Hist. of Crit.* 3:485, 492–93, 496.

39. Ibid., 91, 96–97, 194–95. In similar fashion, G.S. celebrates single critical statements by critics of no great stature (such as Joubert) as "germinal truth" of great critical importance.

40. G.S., *Prosody* 3:426.

41. G.S., "An Encyclopedia of Literary Taste," Review, *Bookman* (London) 27 (November, 1904):84.

42. Ker 1901, 125–27; H. O. Taylor 1901, 294–98; Greenslet 1904, 104–9; Spingarn 1903, 50–58; 1904, 1–7.

43. "An Atlas of Criticism," anon. review of *Hist. of Crit.*, *Acad.*, December 29, 1900, 639–40. Anon. review of *Hist. of Crit.*, *Independent*, 55 (January, 1903):268–70.

44. Babbitt, review, 1912, 282, 311; anon. review, of *Hist. of Crit.*, *Bookman* (London), November 24, 1904.

45. Croce, review of *Hist. of Crit.* (1924), 281, my translation. Croce listed eight pages of errors on Italian critics.

46. Raleigh 1926, 215–16.

47. Wellek 1965, 416–28.

48. Eliot 1933, 61.

49. G.S., *Loci Critici*, 241n. Ginn and Company did an American edition.

50. Blackwood inadvertently announced *Eng. Crit.* as new, not revised. See G.S. letter to Blackwood, March 1, 1911. The fee was £20.

Chapter 14

1. Elton, *Life and Letters Today*, 1933, 14; G.S., *Hist. of Prosody*, 2:138: "Our business is not so much with poetry as with the form of it."

2. Fraser 1970, 82.

3. G.S., *Coll. Essays*, 2:46.

4. G.S., *Hist. of Prosody*, 3:575.

5. Omond noted that this was true of G.S. and of Bayfield as well (1921, 264).

6. G.S., *Hist. of Prosody*, 2:337.

7. Ibid., 1:ixn.

8. The conclusion of preface to vol. 1, *Hist. of Prosody*, 1st ed., is reprinted in 2d ed. (1923), 1:x.

9. Ibid., 2:106; 3:381.

10. Ibid., 2:56. Italics added.

11. Ibid., 1:404–5; 3:362–63.

12. Ker 1907, 214–16. "Mothers" is G.S.'s term.

13. G.S., Review, *Athen.*, June 15, 1878, 757.

14. G.S., *Manual of Eng. Prosody*, 1966 ed., 287.

15. G.S., *Hist. of Prosody*, 1:6. Problems of text are dismissed as beyond the scope of the work. On the Chaucer canon, see p. 144, on classical scholarship: " . . . things are sometimes done at which a tolerably lachrymose angel would shed floods of tears."

16. G.S., *Hist. of Prosody*, 3:506, 513–14.

17. Ibid., 2d ed., 1:viin.

18. See G.S., *Hist. of Prosody*, 1:39n., on the difference between sound "length" and quantity "length."

19. See McKerrow 1906, 65–70; anon. review of *Hist. of Prosody*, *Sat. Rev.* 1908, 670–71; Macaulay 1910, 521–27.

20. G.S., *Hist. of Prosody*, 1:370; also 7n, and 3:475.

21. Ibid., 1:110 n. 1, 182 n. 1; 299.

22. G.S., *Manual of Eng. Prosody*, (1966 ed.), 130.

23. Ibid., 133–34.

24. Harvey Gross, "Introduction," in G.S., *Manual of Eng. Prosody*, 1979 ed., xxi.

25. G.S., *Hist. of Prosody*, 1:346: " . . . that peculiarly *biological* character, that quality of life and growth, where the very sports and monstrosities have their connection and explanation."

26. G.S., *Later 19th Cent.*, 377.

27. G.S., *Hist. of Prosody*, 2:128.

28. Ibid., 3:92, 94; 2:127; *Manual of Eng. Prosody*, (1966 ed.), 203.

29. G.S., *History of Prosody*, 2:168, 170–78, 140n.

30. Ibid., 3:73, 96, 99, 109.

31. Harvey Gross, "Introduction," xx.

32. Sampson 1970, 611.

33. Fraser 1970, 82. This view echoes Omond 1921.

34. Wellek and Warren 1949, 167, 264, 271; Wellek 1965, 4:423–24.

35. Harvey Gross 1979, 9. Gross includes Saintsbury's chapter, "The Mothers," from *Hist. of Prosody*, vol. 1, in this anthology.

36. Gross, "Introduction," xxiii. See Wimsatt and Beardsley 1965, 108–45, especially 118.

37. Gross, "Introduction," xxiv–xxv. Modern prosodists concerned with linguistic science and more particularly those who accept the Trager-Smith system of scansion with its assumption that four degrees of stress are natural to the English language and those who like Sidney Lanier resort to musical analogy or even to musical notation could never be satisfied by G.S.'s system. Their dissatisfaction, like that of the stress or accentual school best represented by Robert Bridges, is matched by G.S.'s rejection of all the efforts of their kinds that he knew.

38. Eliot, quoted in Gross 1966, 218.

39. G.S., "Twenty–One Years," *TLS,* January 4, 1923, 1–2.

40. G.S., *Hist. of Prosody,* 2nd ed., 1:vi.

41. G.S., "The Historical Character of the English Lyric," Warton Lecture on English Poetry (read October 30, 1912), *Procs. of the Brit. Acad.* 5 (1912):476–90; "Some Recent Studies in English Prosody," *Procs. of the Brit. Acad.* 9 (1919–20):78–79.

42. G.S., *Hist. of Eng. Prosody,* 3:29. For Ossian, see Ibid., 3:43–46.

43. G.S., *Hist. of Eng. Prosody,* 3:4, 90–92, 492–93; *Prose Rhythm,* Appendix 1.

44. G.S., *Prose Rhythm,* 469–70.

45. Ibid., 464.

46. A. C. Clark and the German scholar, E. Nordau (*Die Antike Kunstprosa,* Leipzig, 1898), had dealt with Latin clausulae, and Elton had begun and dropped a study similar to that of G.S.

47. Read 1928, 63. Quiller-Couch (1926, 67–68) welcomes the work as a "capital anthology . . . a genuine effort of learning" offering "speculations that may lead to much in time." As for less favorable responses: "Mr. Saintsbury's system is, indeed, no system, and hides more than it reveals," said the *Contemporary Review* 102 (November, 1912):752.

48. G.S., review, *Acad.,* March 26, 1881, 217.

49. G.S., *Prose Rhythm,* 415–20.

50. Ibid., 341–42, 344, 465.

51. *G.S. Mem. Vol.,* 109–15.

52. G.S., *Prose Rhythm,* 157.

53. Ibid., 9n.

54. Ibid., ix.

55. Pater 1910, 15; Bradley 1901.

56. Bradley 1901, 17–18; Chapman 1929, 101–14.

57. G.S., *Hist. of Eng. Prosody,* 3:75.

58. Ibid., 333n.

59. Swinburne 1925–27, 16:134.

60. G.S., *Scrap Book,* 88.

61. G.S., *Hist. of Prosody,* 3:514.

62. G.S., *Scrap Book,* 85–86.

63. Flaubert 1889–93, 3:116; cf.1:157.

64. Pater 1914, 139.

65. G.S., *Hist. of Crit.,* 3:548. See Pater 1911, 38.

66. G.S., *Eliz. Lit.,* 163.

67. G.S., *Arnold,* 29.

68. G.S., *Hist. of Crit.,* 1:19.

69. G.S., *Coll. Essays,* 4:293; *Later 19th Cent.,* 72–73.

70. G.S., *Scrap Bk.,* 116–17.

71. G.S., *Coll. Essays,* 3:343.

72. G.S. praises Gautier for naturalness (*Coll. Essays,* 4: 289) and condemns Flaubert's followers (*Later 19th Cent.,* 74) for "lack of freshness, spontaneity, clear air and open sky." Similarly, in Ruskin's followers, he found "something too much of the lamp" (*Coll. Essays,* 2:309).

73. G.S., *Fr. Novel*, 2:464. At least once, G.S. admitted the reverse (on Samuel Butler) in *Specimens of English Prose Style*, 177: "The thought is always noble and sometimes it forces the rebellious style into harmony."

74. G.S., *Hist. of Crit.*, 3:334–35.

75. G.S., "Shakespeare and the Grand Style" was done for *Essays and Studies*, vol.1 (English Association, 1910); "Milton and the Grand Style" for the Royal Society of Literature (1908, for the Tercentenary). "Dante and the Grand Style" was delivered at the Dante Society in 1912. All are in *Coll. Essays*.

76. G.S., *Coll. Essays*, 3:197–98; Super 1960 1:188. In *Hist. of Crit.*, G.S. asked, "Why the unnecessary asceticism and grudging in the connotation of grandeur?" (3:525).

77. G.S., *Coll. Essays*, 3:216, 219.

78. G.S., *Coll. Essays*, 2:152.

79. Wellek 1965, 4:419.

80. Ibid., 427.

81. G.S., *Minor Caroline Poets*, 1:10n, 2:67–68, 235, 3:7–12, 163.

82. Ibid., 3:iii. Having made rather a mess of Godolphin's verse, which existed only in manuscript, G.S. offered some emendation in the last volume.

83. Morris and Withington (1967, lxxii) quote one "perceptive comment" by G.S.

84. G.S., *Minor Caroline Poets*, 2:266, on Philip Ayres. In another context (*Fr. Novel*, 2:374), G.S. wrote what might have been the epigraph to these volumes: " . . . it is not by masterpieces alone that the world of literature lives."

85. G.S., *Hist. of Prosody*, 3:367.

Chapter 15

1. Chambers 1895, 459.

2. Waugh 1896, 134–36.

3. G.S., letter to Dobson, April 12, 1916, recalls this.

4. Anon. review of *Hist. of Crit.*, vol.1, *Acad.*, December 29, 1900, 639–40.

5. Anon. review, *Sat. Rev.*, October 8, 1904, 462.

6. Lynd 1921, 178.

7. Gross 1969, 141–42.

8. G.S., letter to Brander Matthews, December 18, 1902, Columbia University Library.

9. Edited by Charles Sarolea, Professor of French at Edinburgh; see Dent 1938, 158.

10. G.S., *Eng. Novel*, v–vi.

11. Booth 1964, 2.

12. G.S., *Eng. Novel*, 271–72, 285–86; cf. *Coll. Essays*, 3:143–50.

13. G.S., *Coll. Essays*, 3:47; 2, 190; *Last Vintage*, 159; "The Novels of Hall Caine," *Fort. Rev.* 63 (February, 1895):193.

14. G.S., *First Bk. of Eng. Lit.*, 236.

15. Ibid., 139.

16. Corrigan 1986, 151.

17. Wellek 1965, 416, 424–26.

18. Temple 1953, 225.

19. "George Saintsbury," *Mercure de France*, April 1, 1933. Specific reference is to *Hist. of the Fr. Novel*.

Cet ouvrage manifeste une connaissance incroyable de la littérature française et témoigné d'une sympathie pénétrante et d'une comprehension subtile de son sujet. . . . Toute sa vie, journaliste et professeur, Saintsbury se partage entre la France et l'Angleterre. . . . Il est un des rares critiques qui, pendant le dernier tiers du dix-neuvième siècle, se firent les champions de la pensée française. Il persista par une conviction que rien découragea, malgré l'indifférence que les Français lui témoignerent. . . .

20. John Gross 1969, 139–40, citing Arnold, "Sainte-Beuve," *Ency. Brit.*, 9th ed.

21. Hunt's letter to Saintsbury, December 8, 1918.

22. G.S., *Hist. of Crit.*, 3:412.

23. Meredith, letter to Robert Louis Stevenson, March 17, 1883; Cline 1970, 2:692.

24. Dobson, letter to G.S., July 8, 1920. In the 1933 American edition of the *Cellar Book*, a preface by Owen Wister expresses the hope that the book may "help to cure [America's] present perversion."

25. G.S.'s undated, one-page plan in his own hand, labeled "The Unwritten History of Wine," is in my possession. It projects two volumes. G.S.'s personal cellar book, sold at Sotheby's in the fall of 1963, included a plan of his London cellar in 1884 and lists of the contents entered as bought, with amusing annotations.

26. G.S., *Cellar*, xvii–xxi, 174n, and a note added to the third edition (xxiii–xxix, October 20, 1920).

27. Ibid., 124, gives his recipe: "Instead of soda water . . . sparkling Moselle, in the proportion of a pint of this to a bottle of claret, with thick slices of pineapple instead of lemon, and one lump of ice as big as a baby's head."

28. G.S., *Peace of the Augs.*, 143–44.

29. André Simon in his autobiography, *By Request* (1957). He repeated this to me in an interview in 1963.

30. These include *Literature of Wine* (1945) by Augustus Muir, a former student of G.S.; the centenary tribute in 1945 by Nichol Smith (*Last Vintage*, 11–17); *Saintsbury, the Rhetorician* (1947), by Thomas Bodkin; and others by Laver 1949; Meynell 1943; Charles Morgan; Potter 1936, etc.

31. Simon 1957, 81n; 1963 interview with author; Stuart, in *Last Vintage*, 18–22. There was also a letter from Christopher Saintsbury to Simon on the subject, another in *English*, one in the Wine and Food Society Bulletin, and one by Mary Lodge in the *Times*.

32. Stuart, in *Last Vintage*, 22.

33. G.S., *Last Vintage*, 205–9.

Chapter 16

1. Corrigan 1986, 138.

2. The book was picked up on a Marchmont Street bookstall by the University of London Librarian.

3. Blackett 1973, 34. Dr. Taylor had died in India before this letter reached him.

4. I examined this odd volume in London in 1974, at the time I read the G.S. letters in the files of Harold Rubenstein at Gray's Inn.

5. Corrigan 1986, 147.

6. She held a year's lectureship at Bedford College, but a failure to achieve permanent academic appointment there (or later at King's College or Westfield) as she had failed at Queen's University, Belfast, sent her to the publishing world.

7. Corrigan 1986, 205.

8. Blackett 1973, 59.

9. A recollection of G.S.'s landlord's daughter in Bath.

Chapter 17

1. G.S.'s close relations with Gosse ended about 1905, with some abrupt break. Hunt urged him several times to forget the cause and renew contact with their mutual friend. This he did formally in the 1920s, but he told Hunt cryptically that one learns not to be burned twice by a man who would play you a "monkey trick" (G.S., letter to Hunt, February 16, 1916). See *Fr. Novel*, 1:378, for this allusion to Voltaire and Frederick the Great. It may also be the real subject of G.S.'s "Fable for Dobson."

2. G.S., *A Letter Book*, 12.

3. Green 1933, 442–44.

4. In the visit I had with her at Kew in 1961.

5. Text given me by Miss Stuart. Christopher left his father's silver inkwell and pen to Miss Stuart, who gave them to Merton College in 1961. This letter she had pasted into her copy of *Last Vintage*, which she lent me. She wrote of her entrance to his apartments in the Royal Crescent (there was a main door and a garden wicket):

Unto which door shall I repair?

At either I'd rejoice

Apollo's face would greet me there

And here, Apollo's voice.

6. Stuart, in *Last Vintage*, 20, 22.

7. Ibid.

8. Molesworth 1990, 225–26. The G.S.-Marianne Moore correspondence (1926–30) in the Rosenbach Museum and Library in Philadelphia includes about 230 letters, both drafts of Miss Moore's letters and those by G.S. Some of the latter are replies on the bottom of her letters to him.

9. G.S., *Peace of the Augs.*, 36–37n.

10. Oliver, in *G.S. Mem. Vol.*, 20.

11. G.S., *Prefs. and Essays*, 5–6.

12. G.S., *Peace of the Augs.*, 149, on Charlotte Lennox's Arabella as such a heroine.

13. G.S., *Consid. of Thack.*, 69. As for Joe Sedley's death, he argued that Becky Sharp is too clever to have done it, because she "knew tricks a good deal better than that and less dangerous."

14. Ibid., 182, 184.

15. G.S., *Prefs. and Essays*, 208–9. Diana Vernon is in Scott's *The Heart of Midlothian;* Argemone, in *Yeast;* Barbara, in Stevenson's *Catriona.*

16. G.S., *Peace of the Augs.*, 234.

17. G.S., *Consid. of Thack.*, 195.

18. G.S., *Short Hist. of Eng. Lit.*, 493.

19. G.S., *Fr. Novel*, 1:348, 352 on Marianne; on Doralice, *G.S. Mem. Vol.*, 76.

20. G.S., *Fr. Novel*, 2:416n.

21. Ibid., 1:49.

22. G.S., letter to Hunt, December 12, 1927, expressing his disagreement with "Gosse among the Asps," a Gosse essay on Cleopatra that Hunt had just read and so labeled.

23. G.S., *Fr. Novel*, 1:364; 2:225; *Last Vintage*, 156–70.

24. G.S., *Fr. Novel*, 1:425–26n. The author is Bernardin de Saint-Pierre.

25. Ibid., 2: 226. On Julie, ibid., 1:397–98.

26. Ibid., 2:178n.

27. Ibid., 2:497. A long note analyzes the "eternal feminine" in Homer—in Circe, Hera, Aphrodite, Calypso, Helen, and Nausicaa (496).

28. G.S., *Peace of the Augs.*, 31–32.

29. Corrigan 1986, 263.

30. G.S., *Last Vintage*, 23.

31. Corrigan 1986, 268.

32. Ibid.

Chapter 18

1. G.S., *Coll. Essays*, 2:312–92.

2. G.S., *Last Vintage*, 124–27.

3. Priestley 1922.

4. See J.C. Squire 1937.

5. G.S., letter to Hunt, November 25, 1923.

6. G.S., *Scrap Bk.*, xin. On the title page, G.S. substituted his own name in Greek transliteration for that of Lucian. The rest of the epigram (not quoted) reads:

For vain is also that which men think wise:

No human thought is wholly clear and plain,

What thou adorest is scorn in others' eyes.

G.S. translated these lines from the *Greek Anthology* (*Hist. of Crit.*, 1:147n) and gave the original Greek as "too perfect not to be quoted."

7. G.S., *Last Scrap Bk.*, 187–98.

8. See Webster 1933, 42. Nichol Smith (in *Last Vintage*, 15) said there was "no surer way to learn what sort of man he was in his later years than to read" them. Elton generously saw them as "the mirror of the real, the ultimate Saintsbury" (*G.S. Mem. Vol.*, 1) and described their "released . . . easy, odd, defiant and bright apparel . . . quips and twirls and sallies and parentheses" (G.S., *Prefs. and Essays*, xii).

9. Recent pieces included "Anatole France," the lecture G.S. delivered at the Taylorian Institute in 1923.

10. G.S., *Last Vintage*, 222–23.

11. Ibid., 36–37. He wrote letters to the *Times* on the deaths of Sir Sidney Lee (1926), Hardy (1928), Thistleton Dyer (1928), Scott-Moncrieff (1930), and Gregory Smith (1932).

12. Waddell, in G.S., *Last Vintage*, 23.

13. G.S., *Hist. of Crit.*, 1:178n: "The harmless and necessary parenthesis, the delight of all full minds and quick wits, and the terror of the ignorant and the slow." *Prose Rhythm* contains an extensive defense of some characteristics of his style, notably neologisms, slang, and parentheses, as not slovenly because they are deliberate (350–51).

14. For example, "disrealize," used so often, or "disreason" (see G.S., *Coll. Essays*, 1:274, on the need for this term).

15. Webster (1933, 43n) lists a baker's dozen of G.S.'s neologisms, as did Seccombe in a review of the *Hist. of Crit. OED* acknowledges G.S.'s use of "ephectic" and "stramineous."

16. G.S., *Prose Rhythm*, 402n; *Fr. Novel* 2:380n.

17. Elton says it is the "native idiom of the speaker in his talk and letters and his thoughts" (*G.S. Mem. Vol.*, 1).

18. Anon. review, *Nation* (New York), November 23, 1889, 396–97.

19. Wilson 1950, 74; Leuba devoted a chapter to G.S.'s style (1967, 63–77). He quoted many writers, added his own praise, and gave fifteen examples of G.S.'s epigrammatic tendency.

20. Arthur Mowat, letter to the author, November 11, 1962.

21. G.S., *Scrap Bk.*, 181.

22. G.S., *Last Scrap Bk.*, 128.

23. G.S., *Fr. Novel*, 2:492.

24. G.S., *Last Scrap Bk.*, 342–43; *Second Scrap Bk.*, 182.

25. G.S., *Prefs. and Essays*, 91.

26. G.S., *Second Scrap Bk.*, 131.

27. Words from what he thought one of the finest lines in Spenser. Purves (in *G.S. Mem. Vol.*, 17) saw the choice as a key to G.S.'s thinking. G.S. chose Shelley's "O World! O Life! O Time!" as the greatest English lyric because it expresses the "passionate experience of life" (*Last Vintage*, 240).

28. From "Requies."

29. Elton in *G.S. Mem. Vol.*, 3.

30. Molière 1907, 1:xlviii; also in *Oxford Book of English Prose*, 1924.

31. G.S., *Arnold*, 28; *Second Scrap Bk.*, 181. The phrase is from Statius.

32. G.S., *Prefs. and Essays*, 26–27.

33. G.S., *Hist. of Crit.*, 3:597.

34. G.S., "Preface to *Peau de Chagrin*," in Balzac 1895–1900.

35. G.S., *Fr. Novelists*, 25–26.

36. G.S., *Scrap Bk.*, ix.

37. G.S., *Coll. Essays*, 2:165.

38. G.S., *Second Scrap Bk.*, 301–4; Webster (1933, 10–11) lists other relevant sections of the *Scrap Books*.

39. G.S., review of *Assessments and Anticipations* by W. R. Inge, *Country Life* (Britain), February 3, 1929, 147.

40. G.S., *Last Scrap Bk.*, 231–40.

41. Note by Mrs. Hunt on a G.S. letter to Hunt on David Hannay's 1911 then-quite-legal marriage to his deceased wife's sister.

42. G.S., *Second Scrap Bk.*, 176n.

43. *G.S. Mem. Vol.*, 202.

44. G.S., *Scrap Bk.*, xii.

45. G.S., *Coll. Essays*, 2:127; *Eliz. Lit.*, 168.

46. G.S., letters to Hunt, March 5, 1911 and April 13, 1917; *Second Scrap Bk.*, 197.

47. G.S., *Coll. Essays*, 2:148.

48. G.S., *Short Hist. of Fr. Lit.*, 583; *Consid. of Thack.*, 269.

49. G.S., *Prefs. and Essays*, 56.

50. Ibid., 222, 226.

51. G.S., *Coll. Essays*, 2:102; G.S., *Fr. Novel*, 1:509.

52. G.S., *Coll. Essays*, 1:264.

53. G.S., letter to A. R. Waller, May 12, 1917, British Museum Add'l Mss. 43681, no. 224; letter to Hunt, May 21, 1917.

54. G.S., letter to Hunt, August 15, 1922.

55. Author's interview with Nichol Smith; Smith in G.S., *Last Vintage*, 15.

56. Hearn 1929, 94.

57. Sutherland 1952, 18.

Bibliography

Arnold, Matthew. *Essays in Criticism,* 1st ser. London: Macmillan, 1865.
———. *Notebooks.* Ed. H. F. Lowry, et al. Oxford: Oxford University Press, 1952.
Atkins, J. W. H. *English Literary Criticism: The Medieval Phase.* Cambridge: Cambridge University Press, 1943.
Axon, W. E. A., Review of *Manchester* by George Saintsbury. *Academy,* August 20, 1887, 114–15.
Babbitt, Irving. "Impressionist versus Judicial Criticism." *PMLA* 21, 1906, 687–705.
———. "Are the English Critical?" *Nation,* March 21 and 28, 1912, 282–84, 309–11.
———. "In re Babbitt vs. Saintsbury" [letter]. *Nation,* May 16, 1912, 492–93.
Baldensperger, F. "Littérature Comparée le mot et la chose." *Revue de la littérature comparée* 1 (January-March, 1921):5–29.
Balzac, Honoré. *Comédie Humaine* [The Human Comedy]. 40 vols. Ed. with introduction by George Saintsbury, London: J. M. Dent and Sons, 1895–1900.
Beckson, Karl, and John M. Munro, eds. *Arthur Symons: Collected Letters.* Iowa City: University of Iowa Press, 1989.
Bennett, Arnold. "The Professor" and "English Criticism." In *Books and Persons.* London: Chatto and Windus, 1917, 41–46, 267–70.
Besant, Walter. *Autobiography.* New York: Dodd, Mead 1902.
Bevington, Merle M. *The Saturday Review, 1855–1868.* New York: Columbia University Press, 1941.
Blackett, Mona. *The Mark of the Maker: A Portrait of Helen Waddell.* London: Constable, 1973.
Bodkin, Thomas. *The Saintsbury Oration: Saintsbury the Rhetorician.* London: Privately printed for the Saintsbury Club, 1947.
Booth, Bradford. "General Materials." In *Victorian Fiction: A Guide to Research,* ed. Lionel Stevenson, 1–20. Cambridge, Mass.: Harvard University Press, 1964.
Bosanquet, Bernard. *A History of Aesthetics.* New York: Macmillan, 1892.
Bourget, Paul. Review of *Primer of French Literature* by George Saintsbury. *Academy* 18 (November 6, 1880):324.
Bradley, A. C. *Poetry for Poetry's Sake.* An inaugural lecture delivered on June 5, 1901. Oxford: Clarendon Press, 1901.

Buckley, Jerome. *W. E. Henley: A Study in the "Counter-Decadence" of the Nineties*. Princeton: Princeton University Press, 1945.

Cairns, Huntington, ed. *French Literature and Its Masters*. Twelve articles from the eleventh edition of *Encyclopedia Britannica* by George Saintsbury. New York: Knopf, 1946.

Cambridge History of English Literature. 14 vols. Ed. A. W. Ward and A. R. Waller. New York: G. P. Putnam's Sons, 1907–18.

Carsell, Catherine, and Donald Carsell. "The Crisis in Criticism." *20th Century* 113 (January 1933): 111–12.

Chambers, Edmund K. "Saintsbury as a Critic." *Academy*, June 1, 1895, 459.

Chapman, John A. "Dr. Saintsbury's Heresy." In *Papers on Shelley, Wordsworth, and Others*. London: Oxford University Press, 1929, 103–14.

Charteris, Evan. *Life and Letters of Edmund Gosse*, London: Heinemann, 1931.

Chew, Samuel C. Review of *Cambridge History of English Literature* vol. 13, *Modern Language Notes* (1916):483.

———. Review of *English Novel* by George Saintsbury. *Modern Language Notes* 29 (1914):89–90.

Chrystal, Sir George. "George Saintsbury, 1845–1933." *London Mercury*, March, 1933, 434–41.

Clark, G. Kitson. *The Making of Victorian England*. London: Methuen, 1962.

Cline, C. L. ed. *George Meredith: Letters*. 3 vols. Oxford: Oxford University Press, 1970.

Collins, John Churton. *Ephemera Critica*. London: Constable, 1901.

———. *Essays and Studies*. London: Constable, 1895.

———. Review of *John Dryden* by George Saintsbury. *Academy*, April 9, 1881, 254–55.

Collins, L. C. *The Life and Memoirs of Churton Collins by His Son*. New York: John Lane, 1912.

Connell, John [pseud. for John Henry Robertson]. *W. E. Henley*, London: Macmillan, 1949.

Corrigan, D. Felicitas. *Helen Waddell*. London: Gollancz, 1986.

Courthope, W. J. *English Poetry from Chaucer to Scott*. London: Macmillan, 1895–1910.

———. "The Study of English Language and Literature as Part of a Liberal Education." *National Review*, June, 1893, 486–99.

Craik, Sir Henry. "Sir Henry Craik, K.C.B., and Professor Saintsbury" [letter by Craik]. *Blackwood's Edinburgh Magazine*, September, 1897, 853–57.

———, ed. *English Prose*. 5 vols. London: Macmillan, 1893–96.

Creighton, Louise. *Life and Letters of Mandell Creighton*. 2 vols. London: Longmans, Green, 1904.

Croce, Benedetto. *Conversazione Critiche*. Bari, Italy: Laterza Figli, 1924.

Daiches, David, ed. *Critical Approaches to Literature*. Englewood Cliffs, N.J.: Prentice-Hall, 1956.

Dartique, Henry. *Paul Stapher: A Memoir*. Paris: Librairie Fischbacker, 1918.

Davie, George Elder. *The Democratic Intellect: Scotland and Her Universities in the Nineteenth Century*. Edinburgh: University of Edinburgh Press, 1961.

Decker, C. R. "Zola's Literary Reputation in England," *PMLA* 49 (1934): 1140–53.

Dent, J. M. *The House of Dent.* London: Dent and Sons, 1938.

Dobson, Alban. *Austin Dobson: Some Notes.* London: Oxford University Press, 1928.

Dryden, John. *Works.* 18 vols. Illustrated with historical, criticial and explanatory notes and a life of the author by Sir Walter Scott; revised and corrected by George Saintsbury. Edinburgh: W. Paterson, 1882–93.

Durand, C. J., K. Brock, and E. C. Ozanne. *Elizabeth College Register 1824–1873: A Chapter of Island History,* Guernsey: Frederick Clarke, 1898.

Eliot, T. S. *The Sacred Wood.* London: Methuen, 1948.

———. *The Uses of Poetry and the Uses of Criticism.* London: Faber and Faber, 1933.

Elton, Oliver. "English Prose Numbers." In *A Sheaf of Papers.* London: Hodder and Stoughton, 1922, 78–79, 130–63.

———. "George Edward Bateman Saintsbury: 1845–1933." *Proceedings of the British Academy* 19 (1933): 325–44.

———. "George Saintsbury." *Life and Letters Today.* No. 49 (June-August, 1933):181–90.

———. "George Saintsbury." In *Essays and Addresses.* London: Edward Arnold, 1939, 239–49.

———. *Survey of English Literature.* 6 vols. New York: AMS, 1932.

———, ed. "Introductory Note." In George Saintsbury, *Prefaces and Essays.* London: Macmillan, 1933, ix–xiii.

Encyclopedia Britannica. 9th ed., 24 vols. Eds. Spencer Baynes and William Robertson Smith. London: 1875–89.

Encyclopedia Britannica. 11th ed., 29 vols. Ed. Horace A. Hooper. London: 1911.

Ensor, R. C. K. *History of England, 1870–1914.* Oxford: Clarendon Press, 1936.

Escott, T. H. S. *Masters of Journalism.* London: T. Fisher Unwin, 1911.

Firth, Charles Harding. *The Faculties and Their Power.* Oxford: B. H. Blackwell, 1909.

Flaubert, Gustave. *Correspondence.* 4 vols. Paris: G. Charpentier, 1891–94.

Fox Bourne, H. R. *English Newspapers.* 2 vols. London: Chatto and Windus, 1887.

Fraser, George. *Metre, Rhyme, and Free Verse.* London: Methuen, 1970.

Fyfe, Hamilton. *Sixty Years of Fleet Street,* London: W. H. Allen, 1949.

"George Saintsbury." *Dictionary of National Biography,* 5th suppl. London: Oxford University Press, 1949, 775–77.

"George Saintsbury." *Manchester Guardian,* January 30, 1933.

"George Saintsbury." *Mercure de France,* April 1, 1933, 212–15.

"George Saintsbury." *Nation* (New York), Feburary 8, 1933, 135.

Godkin, E. L. "Home Rule and English Journalism," *Nation* (New York) 44 (May 26, 1887):444–45.

Gosse, Edmund. *Collected Essays.* 3 vols. London: Heinemann, 1913.

————. *Life of Swinburne.* New York: Macmillan, 1917.

————. *Short History of Modern English Literature.* London: Heinemann, 1898.

————. *Silhouettes.* London: Heinemann, 1925.

Green, Brenda. "Behind the Legend of George Saintsbury." *London Mercury,* March, 1933, 442–44.

Green, Roger Lancelyn. *Andrew Lang.* Leicester: University Press, 1946.

Green, V. H. H. *Oxford Common Room: A Study of Lincoln College and Mark Pattison.* London: Edward Arnold, 1957.

Greenslet, Ferris. "Criticism and Mr. Saintsbury." Review of *History of Criticism* by George Saintsbury. *Atlantic Monthly,* July, 1905, 104–9.

Grierson, H. J. C. *The Backgrounds of English Literature.* Edinburgh: James Thin, 1916.

————. ed. *John Donne: Poetical Works.* Oxford: Oxford University Press, 1912.

Gross, Harvey, ed. *The Structure of Verse: Modern Essays on Prosody.* Greenwich, Conn.: Fawcett Publications, 1979.

————. *George Saintsbury, Historical Manual of English Prosody.* New York: Schocken Books, 1966.

Gross, John. *The Rise and Fall of the Man of Letters: Aspects of English Literary Life since 1800.* London: Weidenfeld and Nicholson, 1969.

Grosskerth, Phyllis. *John Addington Symonds, A Biography.* London: Longmans, Green, 1964.

Hammond, J. L. *C. P. Scott.* London: G. Bell, 1934.

Hart-Davis, Rupert, ed. *Oscar Wilde: Collected Letters.* New York: Harcourt, Brace, 1962.

Hearn, Lafcadio. "On Modern English Criticism and the Contemporary Relations of French to English Literature." In *Life and Literature,* ed. John Erskine, 80–107. New York: Dodd, Mead, 1929.

Herd, Harold. *The March of Journalism.* London: Allen and Unwin, 1952.

Herford, C. H. "Dante's Theory of Poetry." *Quarterly Review,* October, 1910, 402.

————. Review of *A History of Elizabethan Literature* by George Saintsbury. *Academy,* December 3, 1887, 363–65.

————. Review of *A History of Nineteenth Century Literature* by George Saintsbury, *Bookman* (London), March, 1896, 185–86.

————. Review of *Short Hist. of Eng. Lit.* by George Saintsbury. *Bookman* (London), November, 1898, 45–46.

Houghton, Walter E. *The Victorian Frame of Mind 1830–1870.* New Haven: Yale University Press, 1957.

Hugo, Victor. *Les Orientales.* Paris: Libraire Hatchette, 1829.

James, Henry. "The Art of Fiction." In *Partial Portraits.* London: Macmillan, 1888, 375–408.

————. *Letters.* Ed. Leon Edel. Cambridge, Mass.: Belknap, 1980.

————. *Letters.* Ed. Percy Lubbock. 2 vols. New York: Scribner's, 1920.

Jenkins, Roy. *Sir Charles Dilke.* Rev. ed. New York: Chilmark Press, 1965.

Jones, Dorothy R. See Richardson, Dorothy.

Ker, W. P. *Essays on Medieval Literature*. London: Macmillan, 1900.

————. *Form and Style in Poetry*. Ed. E. K. Chambers. London: Macmillan, 1929.

————. *On Modern Literature*. Introduction by Terence Spencer and John Sutherland. Oxford: Clarendon Press, 1955.

————. Review of *A History of Criticism and Literary Taste in Europe from the Earliest Texts to the Present Day*, vol. 1, by George Saintsbury. *Bookman* (London) January, 1901, 125–27.

————. Review of *A History of English Prosody from the Twelfth Century to the Present Day*, vol. 1, by George Saintsbury. *Scottish Historical Review* 4 (March, 1907):214–16.

Kerr, J. *Scottish Education*. Cambridge: Cambridge University Press, 1910.

Kipling, Rudyard. *Something of Myself*. New York: Doubleday Doran, 1937.

Koeppel, Emile. Reviews of *A History of Criticism and Literary Taste in Europe from the Earliest Texts to the Present Day*, 3 vols. by George Saintsbury. *Anglia B*. 12 (August, 1901):225–33; 15 (January, 1904):1–6; 18 (May, 1907): 129–34.

Law, Henry William, and Irene Law. *The Book of the Beresford Hopes*. London: Heath Cranton, 1925.

Lesage, Alain René. *Adventures of Gil Blas*. Introduction by George Saintsbury. London: Nimmo and Bain, 1881.

Leuba, Walter. *George Saintsbury*. New York: Twayne Publishers, 1967.

Lewisohn, Ludwig. "Saintsbury." In *Cities and Men*. New York: Harper and Bros., 1927, 43–49.

Lindenberger, H. S. "Historian and Critic." *Profession* (1984), 16–29.

Lukacs, Georg. *Studies in European Realism*. Trans. Edith Bone. London: Hillway Publishing, 1950.

Lynd, Robert. "Two English Critics." Review of *Peace of the Augustans*, by George Saintsbury. In *Art of Letters*. New York: Charles Scribner's Sons, 1921, 172–78.

Macaulay, G. C. Review of *History of English Prosody from the Twelfth Century to the Present Day*, by George Saintsbury. *Modern Language Review* 5 (1910):227–33, 521–27.

Magnus, Philip. *Gladstone*. London: John Murray, 1954.

Matthews, Brander. *These Many Years*. New York: Charles Scribner's Sons, 1917.

Meikle, Henry W. "The Chair of Rhetoric and Belles Lettres in the University of Edinburgh." Paper presented to the Edinburgh Branch of the English Association. *University of Edinburgh Journal*. Autumn, 1945, 90–101.

Mills, Willliam Haslam. *The Manchester Guardian*. London: Chatto and Windus, 1921.

Moers, Ellen. *The Dandy: Brummel to Beerbohm*. New York: Viking, 1960.

Molière, Jean Baptiste. *The Plays*. 8 vols., ed. A. R. Waller. Introduction by George Saintsbury. Edinburgh: John Grant, 1907.

Morley, John. "On Compromise." *Fortnightly Review* 21 (April, 1874):434–35.

————. *Recollections*. London: Macmillan, 1917.

Morris, Brian, and Eleanor Withington. *The Poems of John Cleveland.* Oxford: Clarendon Press, 1967.

O'Leary, John Gerard. "Saintsbury." In *English Literary History.* London: Grafton, 1928, 76–85.

Olson, Elder. "The Argument of Longinus's 'On the Sublime.'" *Modern Philology* 39 (February, 1942):225–58.

————"Longinus and the 'New Criticism.'" In *The Forlorn Demon,* Chicago: Regnery, 1953, 131–56.

Omond, Thomas. *English Metrists.* London: Oxford University Press, 1921.

————. *A Study of Metre.* London: Grant Richards, 1903.

Orel, Harold. *Victorian Literary Critics: George Henry Lewes, Walter Bagehot, Richard Holt Hutton, Leslie Stephen, Andrew Lang, George Saintsbury, and Edmund Gosse.* London: Macmillan, 1984.

Orwell, George. *The Road to Wigan Pier.* London: Gollancz, 1937.

Paris, Gaston. Review of *Short History of French Literature,* by George Saintsbury. *Romania* 12 (1883):602–5.

Pater, Walter. *Appreciations.* London: Macmillan, 1911

————. *Essays From the* Guardian. London: Macmillan, 1910.

————. *Greek Studies.* London: Macmillan, 1928.

————. *Studies in the History of the Renaissance.* London: Macmillan, 1873; library ed., 1910.

Petrie, Sir Charles. *The Victorians.* London: Eyre and Spottiswood, 1960.

Pollock, Sir Frederick. *For My Grandson.* London: John Murray, 1933.

————. "George Saintsbury, an Appreciation." *Saturday Review,* February 4, 1933, 113.

Posnett, H. M. *Comparative Literature.* International Scientific Series, New York: Appleton and Co., 1886.

Potter, Stephen. "King Saintsbury." In *The Muse in Chains: A Study in Education.* London: Jonathan Cape, 1937.

Priestley, J. B. "Mr. George Saintsbury." *London Mercury* 6 (September 1922):502–12.

Quiller-Couch, Arthur. "On the Differences between Verse and Prose." In *On the Art of Writing.* Cambridge: Cambridge University Press, 1929, 52–75.

Raleigh, Sir Walter. *The Letters of Sir Walter Raleigh: 1879–1922,* 2 vols. Ed. Lady Raleigh; enlarged ed. by D. Nichol Smith. London: Methuen, 1926.

————. *On Writing and Writers.* Ed. George Gordon. London: Edward Arnold, 1926.

Read, Herbert. *English Prose Style.* London: G. Bell, 1928.

————. "George Saintsbury." In *A Coat of Many Colours.* New York: Horizon Press, 1956.

Redman, B. R. "George Saintsbury, the Connoisseur." In *Saturday Review of Literature,* May 27, 1933, 619.

Richards, Grant. *Author Hunting by an Old Literary Sportsman: Memories of Years Spent Mainly in Publishing, 1897–1925.* New York: Coward, McCann and Geoghagan, 1934.

Richardson [Jones], Dorothy. "Saintsbury and Art for Art's Sake in England." *PMLA* 5 (March 1944):243–60.

―――. "Saintsbury—Early Advocate of Comparative Literature." *Comparative Literature Newsletter* (NCTE) 4 (February, 1946).

Robinson, James K. "A Neglected Phase of the Aesthetic Movement." *PMLA* 68 (September 1953):733–54.

Root, E. Merrill. *Frank Harris*. New York: Odyssey Press, 1947.

Rosenblatt, Louise. *L'Idée de l'art pour l'art en Angleterre*. Bibliothèque de la revue de la littérature comparée, vol. 70. Paris: Libraire Ancienne Honoré Champion, 1931.

Saintsbury, George. *The Collected Essays and Papers, 1875–1920*. 4 vols. London: J. M. Dent, 1923–24.

―――. *A Consideration of Thackeray*. London: Oxford University Press, 1931.

―――. *The Earl of Derby*. Prime Ministers of Victoria Series. London: J. M. Dent, 1890.

―――. *The Earlier Renaissance*. Vol. 5 of Periods of European Literature Series. Edinburgh: W. Blackwood, 1901.

―――. *The English Novel*. Channels of English Literature Series. London: J. M. Dent, 1913.

―――. *Essays on English Literature, 1780–1860*. 1st ser., London: Percival, 1890. Reprinted (except preface) in *Collected Essays*.

―――. *Essays on French Novelists*. London: Rivington, Percival, 1891.

―――. *A First Book of English Literature*. London: Macmillan, 1914.

―――. *The Flourishing of Romance and the Rise of Allegory*. Vol. 2 of Periods of European Literature Series. Edinburgh: W. Blackwood, 1897.

―――."The Frost of Poetry in France." *Daily Graphic*, December 27, 1890, 4.

―――. *George Saintsbury: The Memorial Volume*. Ed. Augustus Muir and John W. Oliver. Personal portraits by Oliver Elton, Sir Herbert Grierson, John W. Oliver, John Purves. Biographical memoir by Adam Blyth Webster. London: Methuen, 1945.

―――. *A Historical Manual of English Prosody*. Ed. Harvey Gross. New York: Schocken Books, 1966.

―――. *A History of Criticism and Literary Taste in Europe from the Earliest Texts to the Present Day*. 3 vols, Edinburgh: W. Blackwood, 1900–1904.

―――. *A History of Elizabethan Literature*. London: Macmillan, 1887.

―――. *A History of English Criticism*. Selected and adapted from *A History of Criticism and Literary Taste in Europe*. Edinburgh: W. Blackwood, 1911.

―――. *A History of English Prose Rhythm*. London: Macmillan, 1912.

―――. *A History of English Prosody from the Twelfth Centruy to the Present Day*. 3 vols. London: Macmillan, 1906–10. 2d ed. 1923.

―――. *A History of the French Novel to the Close of the Nineteenth Century*. 2 vols. London: Macmillan, 1917–19.

―――. *A History of Nineteenth-Century Literature: 1780–1895*. New York: Macmillan, 1896.

―――. *Inaugural Address*. Edinburgh: W. Blackwood, 1895.

―――. *John Dryden*. English Men of Letters Series. London: Macmillan, 1881.

———. *A Last Scrap Book.* London: Macmillan, 1924.

———. *A Last Vintage: Essays and Papers.* Ed. John W. Oliver, Arthur Melville Clark, and Augustus Muir. Personal Portraits by David Nichol Smith, Dorothy Margaret Stuart, Helen Waddell; bibliography by William Parker. London: Methuen, 1950.

———. *The Later Nineteenth Century.* Vol.12 of Periods of European Literature Series. Edinburgh: W. Blackwood, 1907.

———. *Manchester: A History of the Town.* Historic Towns Series. London: Longmans, Green, 1887.

———. *Marlborough.* English Worthies Series. London: Longmans, Green, 1885.

———. *Matthew Arnold.* Modern English Writers Series. Edinburgh: W. Blackwood, 1899.

———. *Miscellaneous Essays.* London: Percival, 1892. Reprinted (except preface) in *Collected Essays.*

———. *Notes on a Cellar Book.* London: Macmillan, 1920. Reprinted with preface by Owen Wister, New York: Macmillan, 1933.

———. *The Peace of the Augustans: A Survey of Eighteenth-Century Literature as a Place of Rest and Refreshment.* London: G. Bell, 1916.

———. *Prefaces and Essays.* Ed. Oliver Elton. London: Macmillan, 1933.

———. *A Primer of French Literature.* Oxford: Clarendon Press, 1880. Sixth ed., with chapter on modern literature by Charles Rudmore Brown, 1926.

———. *A Scrap Book.* London: Macmillan, 1922.

———. *A Second Scrap Book.* London: Macmillan, 1923.

———. *Shakespeare.* Ed. with an appreciation by Helen Waddell. London: Macmillan , 1934.

———. *A Short History of English Literature.* London: Macmillan, 1898.

———. *A Short History of French Literature.* Oxford: Clarendon Press, 1882.

———. *Sir Walter Scott: A Biographical Sketch,* Famous Scots Series. Edinburgh: Oliphant, Anderson and Ferrier, 1897.

———. [attributed]. "Théophile Gautier." *Cornhill Magazine* 27 (February 1873):157–69.

Saintsbury, George, ed. *Calendar of Verse.* London: Percival, 1892.

———. *French Lyrics.* London: Kegan Paul, 1882.

———. *A Letter Book.* London: G. Bell, 1922.

———. *Loci Critici: Passages Illustrative of Critical Theory and Practice from Aristotle Downwards.* London: Ginn, 1903.

———. *The Minor Poets of the Caroline Period.* 3 vols. Oxford: Clarendon Press, 1905–21.

———. *Periods of European Literature.* 12 vols. Edinburgh: W. Blackwood, 1897–1907.

———. *Specimens of English Prose Style from Malory to Macaulay.* Selected and annotated, with introductory essay. London: Kegan, Paul Trench, 1884. Introduction reprinted in *Collected Essays.*

Sampson, George. *Concise Cambridge History of English Literature.* 3d ed. Cambridge: Cambridge University Press, 1970.

Sargent, John, ed. *The Poems of John Dryden*. London: Oxford Univerity Press, 1910.

Savile Club, *The Savile Club 1868–1923*. London: Privately printed for the Committee of the Club, 1923.

Saxon Mills, S. J. *Life of Sir Edward Cook*. New York: E. P. Dutton, 1921.

Scherer, Edmond. *Essays on English Literature*. Trans. with intro. by George Saintsbury. London: Sampson, Low, Marston, 1891.

Scott-Moncrieff, C. K., ed. *Marcel Proust: An English Tribute*. London: Chatto and Windus, 1923.

Shadwell, Thomas. *Best Plays*. Mermaid Series. Ed. with introduction and notes by George Saintsbury. London: T. F. Unwin, 1907.

Simcox, G. A. Obituary, Théophile Gautier. *Academy*, February 1, 1873, 41–46.

Simon, André. *By Request*. London: Wine and Food Society, 1957.

Smith, D. Nichol, ed. *Letters of Sir Walter Raleigh*. 2d enl. ed. London: Methuen, 1926.

———. *Saintsbury: A Centenary Tribute*. London: Privately printed for the Saintsbury Club, 1945.

Spingarn, Joel E. "Origins of Modern Criticism." *Modern Philology* 1 (April 1904):1–7.

———. Review of *History of Criticism and Literary Taste in Europe from the Earliest Texts to the Present Day*, vol. 2, by George Saintsbury. *Modern Philology* 1 (1904)477– 96.

———. Review of *History of Criticism and Literary Taste in Europe from the Earliest Texts to the Present Day*, vol. 2, by George Saintsbury. *Nation* (New York) 76, January 15, 1903, 56–58.

Squire, J. C. Review of *History of English Prose Rhythm* by George Saintsbury. *Poetry Review* 1 (November, 1912):517–18.

———. "Saintsbury." In *The Honey and the Bee*. London: Heinemann, 1937, 139–43.

———. "Saintsbury." *London Mercury*, March, 1933, 385–87.

Stapfer, Paul. *Victor Hugo à Guernsey: Souvenirs Personnels*. Paris: Société Française, 1905.

Starkie, Enid. *From Gautier to Eliot: The Influence of France on English Literature, 1851–1939*. London: Hutchinson, 1960.

Steinberg, Theodore. "The Pater-Saintsbury Definition of Criticism." *Modern Language Notes* 41 (December, 1912):536.

Stephen, Leslie. *Some Early Impressions*. London: Hogarth Press, 1924.

Strachey, Lytton. *Biographical Essays*. New York: Harcourt, Brace and World, n.d.

Summers, Montague, ed. *John Dryden: The Dramatic Works*. 6 vols., London: Nonesuch Press, 1931–32.

Super, R. H., ed. *The Complete Works of Matthew Arnold*. Ann Arbor: University of Michigan Press, 1960.

Sutherland, James R. *The English Critic*. London: H. K. Lewis, 1952.

Swift, Jonathan. *Polite Conversation*. Introduction and notes by George Saintsbury. London: Chiswick Press, 1892. Introduction reprinted in G.S., *Prefaces and Essays.*

Swinburne, Algernon C. *Complete Works.* 20 vols. Bonchurch edition. Ed. Edmund Gosse and Thomas J. Wise. London: William Heinemann, 1925–27.

Swinnerton, Frank. "George Saintsbury." In *A London Bookman.* London: Secker, 1928.

Symonds, John Addington. *Essays Speculative and Suggestive.* London: Chapman, Hall and Co., 1890.

Symons, Arthur. *Selected Letters, 1880–1935.* Ed. Karl Beckson and John M. Munro. Iowa City: University of Iowa Press, 1989.

———. Review of *Essays in English Literature* by George Saintsbury. First series. *Academy,* July 11, 1891, 30–31.

———. Anonymous reviews of Saintsbury's works identified in files of *Athenaeum: Essays in English Literature,* January 27, 1891, 819; *Miscellaneous Essays,* August 27, 1892, 277–78; Edmond Scherer, *Essays on English Literature,* March 26, 1892, 399–400; *Corrected Impressions,* March 23, 1895, 369–70; *History of Nineteenth Century Literature* and *Essays in English Literature,* December 5, 1896.

———. *Studies in Prose and Verse.* New York: Dutton, 1904.

Taylor, H. O. Review of *History of Criticism and Literary Taste in Europe from the Earliest Texts to the Present Day* vol.1, by George Saintsbury. *International Monthly* 4 (1901):294–98.

Temple, Ruth Z. *The Critic's Alchemy.* New York: Twayne, 1953.

Thackeray, William Makepeace. *The History of Pendennis.* New York: Dutton, 1960.

Thwaite, Ann. *Edmund Gosse: A Literary Landscape, 1849--1928,* Oxford: Oxford University Press, 1985.

Tillyard, E. H. W. *The Muse Unchained.* Cambridge: Bowes and Bowes, 1958.

Traill, H. D., and J. S. Mann. *Social England.* 6 vols. London: Cassell Publishing, 1894–97.

Turner, A. Logan, ed. *A History of the University of Edinburgh.* Edinburgh: Oliver and Boyd, 1933.

Van Doren, Mark. "A First Glance." *Nation* (New York) March 4, 1925, 243.

Ward, Thomas H., ed. *English Poets.* 6 vols. London: Macmillan, 1880–1918.

Watson, George. *The Literary Critics.* Middlesex: Pelican Books, 1962.

Watson, William. "Critics and Their Craft." Review of *Essays in English Literature,* 1st ser., by George Saintsbury. In *Excursions in Criticism,* New York: Macmillan, 1893, 81–88.

Waugh, Arthur. "Living Critics VIII: George Saintsbury." *Bookman* (London), August, 1896, 134–36.

Webster, Adam Blyth. *George Saintsbury.* Edinburgh: Oliver and Boyd, 1933.

Weisstein, Ulrich. *Comparative Literature and Literary Theory.* Trans. William Regger. Bloomington: Indiana University Press, 1973.

Wellek, René. *A History of Modern Criticism: 1750–1950.* Vol. 4, *The Later Nineteenth Century.* New Haven: Yale University Press, 1965.

Wellek, René, and Austin Warren. *A Theory of Literature.* New York: Harcourt, Brace, 1949.

Wells, H. G. *Experiment in Autobiography.* 2 vols. London: Gollancz Cresset Press, 1934.

Whittaker, T. *Sights and Scenes in Oxford City and University.* Introduction by George Saintsbury. London: Cassell Publishing Co., 1896.

Whyte, Frederick. *The Life of W. T. Stead.* London: Jonathan Cape, 1925.

Williams, Orlo. "Practical Critics—George Saintsbury," In *Contemporary Criticism of Literature,* London: Leonard Parsons, 1924, 166–200.

Wilson, Edmund. "George Saintsbury, Gourmet and Glutton." In *Classics and Commercials.* New York: Farrar Straus, 1950.

———. "George Saintsbury's Centenary." In *A Literary Chronicle.* New York: Anchor Books, 1956, 359–63.

Wimsatt, W. K., and Monroe C. Beardsley. *Hateful Contraries.* Lexington, Ky.: University of Kentucky Press, 1965.

Wimsatt, W. K., and Cleanth Brooks. *Literary Critic.m: A Short History.* New York: Knopf, 1957.

Index

**Personal and Professional Life of
  George Saintsbury**